The Campaign Manager

FIFTH EDITION

The Campaign
Manager

Running and Winning Local Elections

CATHERINE SHAW

**WESTVIEW
PRESS**

A Member of the Perseus Books Group

Westview Press was founded in 1975 in Boulder, Colorado, by notable publisher and intellectual Fred Praeger. Westview Press continues to publish scholarly titles and high-quality undergraduate-and graduate-level textbooks in core social science disciplines. With books developed, written, and edited with the needs of serious nonfiction readers, professors, and students in mind, Westview Press honors its long history of publishing books that matter.

Westview Press books are available at special discounts for bulk purchases in the United States by corporations, institutions, and other organizations. For more information, please contact the Special Markets Department at the Perseus Books Group, 2300 Chestnut Street, Suite 200, Philadelphia, PA 19103, or call (800) 810-4145, ext. 5000, or email special.markets@perseusbooks.com.

Designed by Linda Mark

Library of Congress Cataloging-in-Publication Data
  Shaw, Catherine M. (Catherine Marie), 1953–
  The campaign manager : running and winning local elections /
Catherine Shaw.—Fifth edition.
    p. cm.
  ISBN 978-0-8133-4863-6 (pbk.)—ISBN 978-0-8133-4864-3 (e-book)
1. Local elections—United States—Handbooks, manuals, etc. 2. Campaign management—United States—Handbooks, manuals, etc. I. Title.
  JS395.S43 2014
  324.70973—dc23
                                                         2013035605

10 9 8 7 6 5 4 3

To Rick

Contents

Preface

RUNNING FOR LOCAL OFFICE CAN BE ONE OF THE MOST DEMANDING and yet exhilarating experiences of your life. Your house will be a wreck, your children ignored, and your partner, whether involved in the campaign or not, will be stressed. And yet seeking office or pushing through an issue-based campaign gives you an opportunity to be a leader, to effect change in your community, and to repay something to the city, county, state, or country you love. The campaign experience also offers you an opportunity to grow personally. You will be challenged and stretched as never before. When it's all over, win or lose, you will be a different person, with a different outlook on our political process and a new respect for those who run and serve.

When I first ran for mayor of Ashland, Oregon, in 1988, I had little prior government or management experience. Many felt I should start at the council level and work my way up before taking on the position of CEO of a multimillion-dollar municipality. However, having so little experience allowed me to view things with a fresh eye. During my three terms and twelve years at that post, the council, the city staff, the community, and I implemented dozens of programs, including open space,

> "Politics—good politics—is public service. There is no life or occupation in which a man can find a greater opportunity to serve his community or his country."
> **HARRY TRUMAN**

water conservation, community composting and recycling, voter-approved air-quality standards, wetland and floodplain preservation, wastewater treatment plant upgrades, forest management, and restoration and expansion of the library, fire station, and city offices. We also worked closely with our public school system to find ways to ease its budget shortfalls in the wake of state education cutbacks. We divested our hospital, helped save a ski resort, and acquired an ambulance service. We installed a dark fiber ring in our city, providing direct-connect, high-speed internet access and cable TV services.

By having community and government work in partnership, we were able to create and act on opportunities normally available only to large metropolitan areas.

There are over a half million elective offices in the United States. If you have an inclination to serve and a desire to be a leader in your community, do it. Being in a position where you can have a positive impact on your community and bring about change is more rewarding and fun than you can imagine. Ultimately the only real credentials you need are integrity, a caring heart, and a strong work ethic.

> "You have to be smart enough to understand the game and dumb enough to think it's important."
>
> **GENE MCCARTHY** on how politics is like coaching football

Since 1985 I have worked on or run many campaigns in my region. Through years of experimentation and collaboration with other seasoned campaigners, I found organizational techniques that work in political campaigns. This book is the culmination of campaign trial and error and will give you the tools you need to organize the efforts of others on your behalf. Whether you are a novice or a seasoned campaigner, you will find information here to make your efforts more organized and effective.

Good luck, and enjoy the process.

How to Use This Handbook

RUNNING AN EFFECTIVE LOCAL ELECTION IS MORE WORK THAN YOU can possibly imagine. It involves recruiting volunteers, raising money (lots of it), running phone banks, creating media presentations, canvassing, fully engaging in social media, and getting out the vote. The candidate or issue must be "packaged" in a believable and compelling way, and resources must be effectively allocated.

This handbook breaks down a campaign into manageable units for easy implementation. If you are the candidate, you will find the necessary tools to coordinate your efforts with those of your campaign manager and committee. If you're the campaign manager, either for a candidate or for an issue-based campaign, this handbook will organize and guide you and your team through the campaign process.

Because implementing each of the components of a winning campaign is easier if you understand the complexity of the whole process, take time to read this entire handbook before drafting your campaign plan. But for those who came to this book late in the process, each chapter is designed to stand alone. If you have lawn sign installation in a week, you can go straight to that chapter and, following the instructions, implement that portion of the campaign.

> "Behind all political success is attention to detail."
>
> **LARRY O'BRIEN,**
> adviser to John F. Kennedy

The Framework

In local politics, there are generally three types of political campaigns:

- Partisan candidate
- Nonpartisan candidate
- Issue-based

Although some states allow a primary winner who receives more than 50 percent of the vote to take office with no runoff, a partisan race typically has a primary, with party winners squaring off in a general election.

A nonpartisan race usually has only one election, the general election, in which the winner takes all. However, some nonpartisan races with more than two candidates, including judicial elections, require one candidate to receive 50 percent of the votes cast or face a general election runoff; this book includes strategies for winning 50 percent of the vote to avoid a runoff.

An issue-based campaign, like a nonpartisan race, takes place in one election cycle, but unlike candidate races, depending on the state and locality, the campaign can occur in any election. Issue-based campaigns may be brought to the voters either by the governing body (referral) or, in some states, through the citizen initiative process. For the down-ballot, nonpartisan, or issue-based campaign, Appendix B, "Campaigning on a Shoestring," is a quick overview of what needs to be done to run an effective three-month campaign on less than $3,000. All of the pertinent material from the chapter on developing brochures is repeated in that section for those who do not want to slog through the entire manual.

Within these pages are field-tested systems designed to establish an organizational framework for campaign activities such as phone banks, clerical teams, brochure development, media, fundraising, lawn sign dispersal and maintenance, canvassing, social media, and the get-out-the-vote (GOTV) effort. Underlying each is the framework for systematically organizing other people's efforts on your behalf through the campaign committee, the campaign team, and extended volunteer organization in the field.

Also included are branding your campaign on social media, tips for building theme and message, as well as disciplines to stay on your message whether you are in debates, facing the media, or creating campaign literature or media production.

By breaking down a campaign into manageable units and organizing the activities within each component, you will never overload your workforce. Once you have decided what you can or want to do in organizing your cam-

paign, you will need to plot these activities on a campaign flowchart, calendar,
or plan. Campaign plans are probably
the most widely accepted blueprint for a
campaign. However, some prefer a more

"Play for more than you can afford to
lose and you will learn the game."
WINSTON CHURCHILL

visual campaign flowchart because it presents a campaign timeline that can
be understood at a glance. Both options, as well as the campaign calendar,
are included.

The Layout

Chapter 1, "Precinct Analysis," looks at voter behavior based on social context. Although the actual process for conducting a precinct analysis is located
in Appendix A, Chapter 1 explains the importance of and reasoning behind
the many aspects of a precinct analysis. Conducting a precinct analysis will
focus campaign time and resources for the biggest return. Further, it will
reveal whether a candidate or an issue has a fighting chance.

A precinct analysis is the foundation for finding support, swing voters,
persuadable voters, and the votes needed to win, all while avoiding voters
who are opposed to your efforts. Precinct analysis can and should be done
well before the campaign kickoff.

After conducting your precinct analysis and determining your chances,
the remainder of the book targets organizational systems.

Chapter 2, "The Campaign Team and Volunteer Organization," covers
both the small, select group that will develop campaign strategies (the campaign committee) and the greater force behind activity implementation:
volunteers.

Chapter 3, "The Campaign Brochure," details the single most important
thing the committee will do in the campaign: develop a theme and message.
Within this chapter, you will also find detailed information on benchmark
polling, slogans, logo design, and the voters' pamphlet as well as tips on drafting an effective brochure.

Chapter 4, "Digital and Social Media," touches on all aspects of social media communication and how best to employ them in campaigning. Although
the focus is primarily those most effectively used in down-ballot races, it also
covers systems used successfully on well-funded up-ballot campaigns in the
advent they may soon be within reach of all campaigning.

Chapter 5, "Fundraising," outlines the many ways a campaign can raise
money through events, direct mail, and candidate and volunteer solicitation calls and includes sample budgets as well as a budget form to assist

campaigns in creating their own. Raising money on the internet is also covered in this chapter.

Chapter 6, "Lawn Signs," covers designing a logo, finding locations, establishing structure for volunteer systems for placement, and maintaining and removing both lawn and field signs. Also included are examples of signs that work.

Targeting voters, the topic of Chapter 7, builds on the precinct analysis to help you find likely voters. The chapter also outlines how to communicate with such voters.

Chapter 8, "Media," provides examples of how to get the most out of your media dollars while effectively communicating with voters. Through the media, candidates and issue-based campaigns gain credibility. Given the expense and the power of this campaign line item, the more you know, the more effective you will be in getting the most out of each media dollar.

Chapter 9, "The Candidate," outlines how best to package the candidate to project as positive an image as possible. It also covers negative campaigning, attacks, debates, and dealing with the press in detail.

Chapter 10, "The Issue-Based Campaign," covers initiative, referendum, recall, and school and library money issues, along with a couple of "monsters in the night": the double majority and the super majority.

Chapter 11, "Getting Out the Vote," encompasses the all-important voter activation effort that is critical to a winning campaign. This chapter offers tips for last-minute voter persuasion, dealing with the hybrid campaign—that is, the election with both absentee mail voting and poll voting—and tried-and-true methods for elections conducted partly or entirely through vote by mail. With nearly three decades of vote-by-mail experience, Oregon has this system down. GOTV, as with other aspects of campaigning, is influenced by the evolution of voter contact systems; this chapter examines both old and new approaches to activate voters.

Chapter 12, "The Campaign Plan," puts in chronological order everything you will need to do to win. Although creating a campaign plan or flowchart is one of the first things you will do to organize your campaign, without the baseline knowledge of the first eleven chapters, drafting either would be more difficult. Also included in this chapter is a campaign calendar, yet another alternative to the campaign plan, which works equally well for organizing campaign efforts.

Chapter 13, "After the Ball," is simply about winning and losing gracefully, putting your campaign to bed, election night, and retiring a campaign debt (should you have one).

Appendix A: "Conducting a Precinct Analysis" outlines the necessary steps to successfully execute a precinct analysis. *Why* you should conduct one is covered in Chapter 1.

Appendix B: "Campaigning on a Shoestring," is designed for running a short, three-month campaign on less than $3,000 for either nonpartisan races, partisan primaries, noncontroversial issue-based campaigns, or those conducted in homogeneous populations where one party dominates in registration. As noted above, it stands alone for those unwilling to read this entire manual.

Know the Law

First things first: Visit the county clerk, election office, or city recorder to become familiar with state and local election laws. For example, in my city, you are not allowed to place lawn signs more than six weeks before an election. You are also not allowed to place them on the strip between the sidewalk and the street. Although the homeowner may plant, mow, water, and care for this area, it is in fact part of the public right-of-way. Placing a lawn sign here could be interpreted in one of two ways: Either you feel you're above the law, or you don't know the law. Either interpretation is a problem if you hope to be in government.

It is against federal law to place campaign literature in and around mailboxes. Even though you bought and installed your mailbox, the federal government dictates how it can be used. The same goes for the little boxes on the side of your home. Also, publicly owned buildings are maintained, lit, and owned by the taxpayers and so should not be used for campaign purposes either. And on and on. Throughout this book you will find alerts to potential legal missteps noted by: "Know the law."

The county clerk or city recorder will also draw attention to filing dates that you and your treasurer must know. Missing a campaign expenditure filing deadline will almost always get you media coverage, but not the kind you need or want. Also missing the voters' pamphlet deadline can unnecessarily hobble your efforts. These deadlines should be noted in the campaign plan.

Other than the legal materials from the county clerk, the city recorder, or the secretary of state, everything you need to run a successful campaign is included in this handbook.

"One thing I know: The only ones among you who will be really happy are those who will have sought and found how to serve."

ALBERT SCHWEITZER

THE TEN COMMANDMENTS OF CAMPAIGNING

Honor thy base

Stay on message

Money is thy savior

Never tell a lie

Aim at the souls that can be saved

Never waste donors' money

Do not commit adultery

Start early

Be prepared in all things

Know who you are

THE CARDINAL SINS OF CAMPAIGNING

Being caught in a provable lie

Committing a crime

Having a relationship with a member of your staff

Committing adultery

Declaring bankruptcy

1

Precinct Analysis: The Sinners, the Saints, and the Savables

IN THIS CHAPTER
- Context of Neighborhood
- Independents
- The Undervote
- Finding Swing Voters

THERE'S VIRTUALLY NOTHING YOU CAN DO IN A CAMPAIGN THAT WILL give you a better cost/benefit ratio than a comprehensive precinct analysis. Precinct analysis looks at past voting patterns and the dynamic of party affiliation within the context of neighborhood. It is based on the premise that people who share similar values, politically and otherwise, live near one another. It looks for voting trends, precinct by precinct, to provide a geographic location of your core supporters. And using data from past elections, it will reveal where to find support, swing, and undervote for similar candidates or causes. Using this information, you may direct your efforts to activate and engage likely support. This is fundamental to a win: You want to invest effort and resources where they will do the most good.

The ease of locating potential-candidate and issue-based supporters through data mining of social media and internet activity has moved many consultants to declare precinct-level modeling to be dead. However, for the down-ballot campaign, targeting voters based on geographic location and combining that information with targeting voters through data mining, canvassing, lawn signs, and advertising is extraordinarily effective. Precinct analysis reveals geographic areas of voter behavior. It is no different than when presidential campaigns identify which states will be battleground territory and which ones will be an automatic win or loss for the nominee. And just as presidential campaigns will not spend precious resources in states whose outcome is certain, the down-ballot campaign must also know where to effectively direct campaign resources for the best outcome. Indeed, once you have determined the cities, communities, and precincts where voters can be persuaded to support your efforts, you can implement resources to influence those voters. Precinct analysis is about identifying battleground precincts.

Unlike some campaign activities, a precinct analysis may be conducted months or even years before the campaign, because it is based on voting history. Take advantage of this fact and get it out of the way. It's also cheap. Using this handbook and a few dollars,

> "Aim at the souls that can be saved."
>
> — **BILL MEULEMANS**

anyone can conduct a precinct analysis. Although election offices charge a nominal fee for past election records, the information you need is public, relatively easy to obtain, and inexpensive. The only exception would be in counties that do not keep records broken down by party, turnout, or precinct. For such counties, you may have to go elsewhere to get your data, such as a voter contact service, your party, or a political action committee (PAC) that has endorsed you and tracks voting history. If it is a voter contact service, be prepared to pay, but your party or an endorsing PAC will usually provide some voter contact information as an in-kind donation to your campaign. If your campaign is too local for PAC or party support, go to a candidate who has such support and offer to include him or her in a precinct analysis if the person's campaign can get you what you need.

In addition to voting history from election offices, you may also use US Census data (www.uscensus.gov) to further profile your voters with demographic and economic data. The census database will give you demographic information by state, county, and city. This information is a fabulous resource, because data are presented separately for each incorporated city, irrespective of size, by neighborhood for larger cities, and by geographic area for rural communities. If your area of concern includes one or more small cities, you're in luck.

Whereas polling data will tell you who supports your cause by gender, race, age, income, education, and party affiliation, a precinct analysis will give you an idea of how neighborhoods (precincts) vote on issues and candidates that parallel your campaign. For example, if you are working on a countywide election and your polling data show that 60 percent of women support your cause, you do not know whether that is 60 percent across the board or 70 percent in one city and 30 percent in another. To make your polling work better for your purposes, ask the polling firm to break down your data by region—or better yet, by zone. While a poll may tell you where you are on an issue at a given moment, a precinct analysis will give you more of a continuum of voter tendencies.

There will be times, however, when a precinct analysis is of minimal help: for example, if you are running a partisan race in an area with a huge registration disadvantage and no voter history of a win from anyone in your party. In this example, a precinct analysis will tell you where your voters are lazy—that is, those in your party who tend to be nonvoters—and it may provide some information on swing voters, depending on the quality of the candidates in the previous elections, but that's about it for candidate history information. Nevertheless, knowing where your lazy support lives can improve your odds come Election Day. These potential voters can be activated through lawn sign placement, social media, direct mail, canvassing, and phone-bank calling. Still, unless your opposition is running his or her campaign from prison, if the voter registration difference is more than 15 percent, you are about to launch into an unwinnable race. Indeed, with voters sticking so keenly to party in recent elections, if your voter registration disadvantage is greater than 5 percent, you could be in an unwinnable race.

Basically, there are two kinds of voters: those with their minds made up and those who are undecided. Voters with their minds made up are either for you ("saints") or against you ("sinners"). Those who are undecided or persuadable are the "savables." For precinct analysis purposes, we have to understand the first two groups—the sinners and the saints—but we focus on the third group, the savables.

I used to believe saints and sinners would cross the aisle if their candidate was profoundly compromised. Now I know better: A few years ago, a Republican candidate for the Oregon House maintained a five-point registration advantage win even after court documents surfaced alleging he force-fed his unwilling child to the point of vomiting, locked the child in a dark closet to help him get over his fear of the dark, squeezed him so tight that bruising resulted, and pleaded guilty to a misdemeanor assault charge after beating the child over the head with a screwdriver. The candidate was running against a mother of three, and a school budget committee member who had lots of political experience as a legislative assistant.

> "If you would persuade, you must appeal to interest, rather than intellect."
> **BEN FRANKLIN**

The Sinners. Sinners will not cast a vote your way, no matter what you say or do. You never want to give sinners a reason to vote: Don't canvass them, call them, or send direct mail to them. Nothing you say or do will convince these voters to support your candidate or issue. Sinners will vote against you if they vote in your election; they will never cross the aisle. If they do not stay home altogether on Election Day, the best you can hope for is an undervote. Remember, when it comes to sinners, apathy is your friend.

The Saints. Saints will vote for you, no matter what. They will not cross the aisle, but they can, and do, undervote. That means you do not want to completely ignore these voters, but you also do not want to waste valuable campaign resources on them.

The Savables. Savables are registered voters who are neither saints nor sinners, as they do not adhere to party lines. These are the voters you're looking for in a precinct analysis. They tend to be undecided, may be moved by hot-button issues, and often pay little or no attention to politics. Sometimes they are partisans of one party, hiding from their neighbors by registering in another party. And sometimes they are simply lazy voters who need more prodding.

With precinct analysis, you can determine where the savables live and then, by further analysis of education, age, and voting history, determine the likely numbers of those who will actually get out and vote. A precinct analysis will give you important information for canvassing and for where to send direct mail, and even provide a profile for media, social networking, and phoning.

Election offices, political parties, and PACs often track voters by turnout. Voting frequency typically will be listed next to the registered voter's name as 4/4, 3/4, 2/4, 1/4—that is, people voting in four out of four of the last elections, three out of four, and so on. They're referred to as fours, threes, twos, and ones. Fours will take very little prodding to get to the polls. The others can be a little trickier to pin down, because some of the occasional voters vote only in presidential elections, some only in general elections, and others in their own individual pattern. However, with a little push, threes and often twos can be activated to get to the polls. This is where your precinct analysis is so critical: You never want to activate voters who are in your low-priority precincts, or you will turn out votes for the opposition. Your goal is to activate likely voters in high-priority and persuadable precincts who will support your candidate or issue-based campaign.

> "Democracy is the worst form of government except for all the others that have been tried."
>
> — WINSTON CHURCHILL

People who went to the polls only once in the past four elections are pretty tough, and courting those who have never voted is a waste of time and money.

Context of Neighborhood

Social Context, Individual Traits, and Microtargeting

Pollsters and political consultants dismiss social context as old school, but after thirty years of tracking registration trends both by precinct and zone in my county and state, I find social context is more reliable today than ever for identifying pockets of support. Further, its patterning dates back to the very founding of the nation. In *1776,* David McCullough highlights the adversity the British troops suffered during the siege of Boston, a city sympathetic to the revolution, and how anxious the British were to move on to New York, where they would enjoy a warmer welcome. Even then, Americans segregated themselves by political ideology.

But it goes back even further. The genesis of our nation was the coupling of religious devotees with those seeking financial opportunity untethered to bloodlines. Not much has changed.

The fracturing within each of the voting blocs on a continuum of time is the essence of a precinct analysis. Indeed, not all whites vote the same, not all Chinese, not all women, not all men, not all eighteen- to twenty-five-year-olds, not all white women between eighteen and twenty-five. What we do today, and have done since getting on ships to cross the Atlantic, is pack up and move next door to people who share core values

> "The more things seem to change, the more they stay the same."
> **CORINNE BAILEY RAE**

and think and vote like we do. As Bruce Oppenheimer of Vanderbilt University said, "A lot of this has to do with self-selection. Democrats tend to live next to Democrats. Republicans tend to live next to Republicans."[1]

Microtargeting

Microtargeting, which determines voter patterns according to lifestyle and consumptive behavior, absolutely works. Stores with member or discount cards capture information each time the card is swiped at the checkout counter; every time you charge on your credit card, information is captured. Information about the community in which you live, the car you drive, the cell phone you use, the movies you rent, the books you buy, and the television you watch is captured through sales, your internet searches, Facebook posts, and even polling data. And all that captured information is worth something, and that something gets sold to campaigns and other marketers, who can accurately determine whether you will vote and, if so, whom you will vote for. Further, the data can profile people just like you all over the nation and come up with a precise picture of voting behavior based on age, residency, and buying patterns. It works. And for a price, you can buy this information.

Practitioners of microtargeting suggest that the failing of precinct analysis is that "geography, party registration and electoral turnout alone leaves some of your best voters stranded and untouched."[2] This is absolutely accurate; precinct analysis is about mining for gold in the veins rather than spending time going after the dust, and does so using data that are relatively easy to find and cheap to acquire. And because precinct analysis places the voter in a social context, it is indispensable to a winning strategy.

> "The larger the mob, the harder the test."
>
> — H. L. MENCKEN

Precinct analysis shows which neighborhoods and communities are trending where, and more important, it will tell you where the greatest numbers of swing voters live. Once you're in the gold veins, precinct analysis behaves and looks very much like microtargeting because neighborhoods get profiled; that's why it has worked for two hundred years in some form or another.

Social Context

Knowing the social context of cities within a county is just as important as knowing the social context of neighborhoods within a city. This fine-grained knowledge allows the down-ballot campaign to profile voters within a context of historic voting and registration trends.

For example, when I first began tracking voter registration in 1984, my county was fairly evenly mixed in registration, with a 2 percent countywide Republican registration advantage. Over the course of twenty-five years, this advantage moved from 2 percent to 11 percent and back to 2 percent in 2008. In 1986, the registration difference between Democrats and Republicans in my city was 16 percent; now it's 60 percent. Some communities completely flipped in registration, moving from a 20-point Democratic advantage to a 20-point Republican advantage. During the period between 2002 and 2006, one boom city in my region had one Democrat move in for every 30 Republicans; between 2002 and 2012 this same town had 400 Republicans move in for every 18 Democrats who moved *out*.

And the same profile that is flipping here is also flipping in small communities in other parts of the state that I've tracked. Although this profile may not hold where you live, in my corner of the world the new Republicans are landed poor, Roosevelt Democrats, blue-collar workers, undereducated people, truck owners, the religious right, survivalist militia, and people deeply suspicious of government. They also have a real resentment for public education and the educated, and endorsements from newspapers are the kiss of death. Where the Democrats are gaining ground is with the educated, the wealthy, small-business owners, Reagan Democrats, McCall Republicans (http://en.wikipedia.org/wiki/Tom_McCall), secular people, youths, minorities, and unmarried women.

Nearly every sector of my county has become extreme in registration and voting pattern. When areas become extreme in registration, attitudes and voting will also be extreme. For example, a Republican living in a heavily registered Democratic area will be left of (more liberal than) Democrats living in heavily registered Republican areas. A Democrat in a very Democratic area may have trouble getting blue enough, just as a Republican in a heavily registered Republican city may have trouble getting red enough.

> "No self-respecting woman should wish or work for the success of a party who ignores her sex."
> **SUSAN B. ANTHONY**

In a recent election, the wife of a Democratic county commission candidate was chased out of the yard of a registered Democrat in a heavily registered Republican precinct. As she left, the home owner yelled, "We don't want your kind up here." Tolerance is low out there right now, very low.

Individual Traits

Polling uses individual traits in conjunction with issue questions to target direct mail and media. For our purposes, individual traits include gender, ethnicity, education, economic standing, age, and other similar demographics. Although individual traits are important and will be thoroughly covered in Chapter 7, exclusively targeting voters using individual traits, without social context, can lead to missteps. Counties with many small cities, a mix of urban and rural voters, and multiple school districts are the stuff of down-ballot races. In these races, a strategy that treats all female, nonaffiliated voters—or all those within a certain gender, age, education, or income—as though they were one and the same, irrespective of where they live, is deeply flawed. On the other hand, a strategy based on individual traits among homogeneous populations is very effective.

Precinct analysis accepts the premise that a campaign should expend the bulk of time and resources in areas of the most persuadable voters, moderately acknowledge the party faithful, and virtually ignore areas of overwhelming opposition; the analysis puts this premise to work with the tools available within the public domain. This approach provides a campaign with the best outcome-to-money ratio of any other political strategy. However, should your campaign have the resources to run a poll or purchase information about voters' lifestyle and consumer habits, the book covers how to incorporate these data in your precinct analysis. For example, the shortcoming of a poll centered on individual traits can be mitigated by assigning precincts to geographic zones and then looking at similarities of voters within those zones.

Independents

So-called independent voters are registered voters who are not affiliated with a political party. In the twenty-seven states and District of Columbia where voters register by party, the ranks of independents have swelled in the past few decades and now occupy a third of the voter rolls. In the twenty-three states whose voters do not register by party, polls report similar numbers.[3]

Traditionally, a *swing vote* comes from a Democrat who votes Republican or a Republican who votes Democrat. However, political pundits, the media, and polling firms have elevated the status of independents (nonaffiliated voters, or NAVs) by heralding them as the swing vote and often credit them in postelection analysis for a particular win or loss. Further, in the face of substantive and credible research to the contrary, in news and television dramas independents are presented side by side with Democrats and Republicans, as though they were a political party with a shared ideology.

A Misnomer

Polling conducted by the *Washington Post* and ABC in July 2002 and other polling by the *Washington Post*, Harvard University, and the Kaiser Family Foundation in 2007 indicate that independents are anything but. In the 2007 study, independents were assigned to one of five categories, with the "disguised partisans" and the "disengaged" composing 48 percent of the polled independents. The "dislocated" (the socially liberal/fiscally conservative) were 16 percent of these voters, with the "disillusioned" (angry voters) and "deliberators" (true swing voters) evenly divided among the remaining 36 percent. Much of this study mirrors the conclusions drawn in the 1992 book *The Myth of the Independent*, by Bruce E. Keith. When the disengaged are combined with the disillusioned, who are less inclined to vote, the study highlights that 42 percent are unlikely to participate in elections. Indeed, in the states that keep election returns by party and turnout, nonaffiliated voters consistently underperform registered Democrats and Republicans by twenty points.

Nevertheless, with nonaffiliated voters occupying one-third of the registration, a campaign must know who these voters are, where they live, and how to effectively predict their voting behavior.

Closet Partisans

A few years back, I was stuffing envelopes with a volunteer who lived in an area with a Republican-registration advantage of eighteen points. I told him that two years before, I had worked a campaign in his area and, during the get-out-the-vote (GOTV) effort, discovered that many registered Democrats believed they were registered Republicans. He said, "I have a confession to make: I'm a registered Republican—always have been—but I've never voted for a Republican in my life."

I began to wonder: Within swing precincts, how many Republicans or Democrats *never* vote party? Finding the answer to that question was the genesis of the survey outlined below.

In partisan races, voters generally must choose between a Democrat and a Republican when casting a vote, and each party maintains a baseline of guaranteed votes, reflected by registration percentages—usually about 33 percent. But what about the remaining voters? Can an equally predictable percentage of nonaffiliated and third-party registrants be ascribed to partisan candidates? In 2004, after ten years of observing that NAVs appeared to consistently track party registration, precinct by precinct, I tested this assertion. To do so, I removed all third-party and nonaffiliated voters from registration totals and determined percentages of party registrants according to the new total.

Let me explain by way of example: Two actual precincts are listed in table 1.1. Precinct 2 has a total registration of 3,613 voters, of which 2,383 are Democrats (66 percent), 407 are Republicans (11 percent), and 823 are nonaffiliated voters and third-party registrants (23 percent). To determine whether registered voters outside the major parties track their partisan neighbors in party performance, I generated a new percentage for each of the parties by omitting NAVs plus third-party registrants from the total registration. Calculating the percentage of the combined total that Republicans and Democrats each hold generates a new percentage amazingly close to actual percentages of votes cast for each of the parties. So, in Precinct 2, the Democratic registration of 2,383 is added to the Republican registration of 407, totaling 2,790 voters. The new registration percentage for either Democrats or Republicans is calculated by dividing each party registration by the combined Democratic and Republican registration numbers.

That means if all those registered outside the two parties tracked their partisan neighbors, a Democratic candidate in Precinct 2 would receive 85 percent of the votes cast (Barack Obama received 86 percent), and a Republican would receive 15 percent (John McCain received 12 percent).

Precinct	Reg	TO	Dem Reg	% D Reg	Rep Reg	% R Reg	others	% otr Reg	D+R	% owed Ds	% owed R's
Pct 2	3613	3325	2383	0.66	407	0.11	823	0.23	2790	0.85	0.15
Pct 27	4366	3637	1139	0.26	2156	0.49	1071	0.25	3295	0.35	0.65

TABLE 1.1 Tale of Two Precincts. Collapsing other registrants (third-party registrants and nonaffiliated voters) into Democratic (D) and Republican (R) yields a predictable percentage of votes owed candidates according to party affiliation.

Similarly, in Precinct 27, out of the 4,366 registered voters, 1,139 are Democrats (26 percent), 2,156 are Republicans (49 percent), and 1,071 are NAVs plus others (25 percent) (table 1.1). Exercising the same computation as done for Precinct 2, if NAVs and all others were to track the parties by the same percentages, the votes owed Democrats in Precinct 27 would be 35 percent (Obama received 34 percent), and the votes owed Republicans would be 65 percent (McCain received 62 percent).

So, within a percentage point or two, each precinct does exactly what it is predicted to do, revealing that NAVs and third-party registrants track the behavior of their neighbors when it comes to voting. In fact in eight out of ten precincts, party registrants get the votes they are owed within a percentage point or two. The remaining precincts that deviate from "votes owed" percentages are where the swing voters live.

Once you have calculated a percentage of votes owed, that number is multiplied by the turnout to get a votes-owed number. By subtracting the number of votes owed from the actual votes received by candidates, swing vote is revealed. Some precincts come in within 1 percent of votes owed; others consistently depart and do so always in the same direction, giving hundreds of votes to the other party's candidate. Those that consistently differ, or swing, are the focus of winning campaigns.

Expanding the Test

To determine whether this model worked outside my county, I compared election outcomes of two very different counties in Oregon: Jackson and Lane. I examined both issue-based and partisan elections from 2002 to 2006 to determine whether nonaffiliated voters performed predictably in concert with their partisan neighbors.

Jackson County, located in southern Oregon, with a 2006 Republican-registration advantage of eleven points, and Lane County, home of the University of Oregon, with a 2006 Democratic-registration advantage of eighteen points, offered a wide array of voters and voting history for comparison. I began by assigning each precinct in each county with a new percentage owed partisan candidates based solely on the registration of Republicans and Democrats. I then multiplied these percentages by the voter turnout to determine the votes owed to each of the partisan candidates. In this way, NAVs and third-party registrants collapsed into the Republican and Democratic registration in the same percentages as party registrants.

Votes owed the partisan candidates, determined by the new registration percentage, were repeated for each election year and for all partisan candidates from 2002 through 2006. Issue-based campaigns were also charted to determine whether they too tracked predictably, precinct by

"There is no knowledge that is not power."
RALPH WALDO EMERSON

precinct. I also looked back at returns between 1986 and 2000 in Jackson County, where data were more easily accessed than in Lane County.

In both counties, the outcome was the same. Partisan candidates received the votes they were owed in better than 80 percent of the precincts. In precincts where voters did not follow the new party-registration percentages, some gave more votes to the Democratic candidates than were owed (left-leaning), and some gave more votes to the Republican candidates than were owed (right-leaning).

To determine which voters, partisans or independents, moved, a massive three-month volunteer effort was launched in Jackson County to systematically call through and identify all precincts where candidates were not getting the votes they were owed. Where precincts leaned right, all Democrats and independents were called, and where precincts leaned left, all Republicans and independents were called. In all, 23,356 voters were called, and 5,206 participated in the survey.

We asked only three questions in the survey:

1. In general, do you think the state is headed in the right or wrong direction?
2. In general, do you think the county is headed in the right or wrong direction?
3. In general, do you vote Republican or Democrat?

While it was our hope to force the voter to answer "Republican" or "Democrat" in the last question, many simply offered up "both," and that information was recorded.

The Outcome

Irrespective of whether a precinct moved left or right, a similar percentage of partisan voters confessed to never voting for a candidate in his or her party and a similar percentage of nonaffiliated voters, evenly divided among Republicans and Democrats, confessed to always voting for one party or the other.

However, what distinguished the precincts that deviated from votes owed was the percentage of partisans and nonaffiliated voters who confessed to mixing their ballots—that is, voting for candidates in both parties on the same ballot, or split-ticket voting. Of all surveyed voters in the selected precincts—whether their precinct leaned left or right, and whether they were nonaffiliated, Republican, or Democrat—16 percent to 18 percent offered that they split their ticket. In short, in precincts where Republicans moved left and others where Democrats moved right, the independents directly mirrored the partisan registrants in the percentage of split-ticket voting. In other words, the swing vote among independents mirrored party swing in exactly the same percentages, precinct by precinct.

> "Spend the time to make the foundation right or you will pay in time and money all the way to the roof."
>
> TONY NUNES, BUILDER

Knowing where nonaffiliated voter support predictably falls provides a roadmap for campaign targeting, saving money in mail and time in canvassing, and offers an opportunity to alter registration disparity through the GOTV effort. A campaign does this by avoiding nonaffiliated voters along with the registrants of the opposing party in precincts that are leaning away from their efforts.

Polarized Populations, Skewed Registration, and Independents

If independents mirror partisan voters, then they should continue to do so even as registration percentages shift. Voter-registration shifts often occur as economies change, churches arrive, or development reshapes an area. Indeed, voters relocate to a neighborhood near their place of worship and move to find work, better schools, or less congestion. For example, in one city in southern Oregon, the Republican-registration advantage increased 38 percent between 1986 and 2006. In another city thirty miles away, the Democratic registration advantage increased 44 percent in the same period. Clearly, voters are choosing to locate near like-minded neighbors, selecting a state, a region within a state, a community within a region, and a neighborhood within a city. It's a self-selecting process: Voters identify who they are and how they will vote by where they choose to live. That's true with Democrats and Republicans and no less so with nonaffiliated voters or independents.

In the above study, independents in both Lane and Jackson Counties continued to track party affiliation as registration shifted. This is good news for political campaigns: As voters segregate themselves with like-minded people, targeting becomes easier, and campaigns become more efficient and economical. If independents mirror the voting behavior of their neighbors, then within any given voting region with a large Republican voter-registration advantage, independents will actually be Republicans, just as independents living in areas with skewed Democratic-registration advantage will actually be Democrats.

> "The art of being wise is the art of knowing what to overlook."
> **WILLIAM JAMES**

Implications for a Campaign

Because vendors (those who provide mail, television, radio, and other communications services for a campaign) are often the same people who provide targeting strategies, it is not in their best economic interest to determine how communication can be fine-tuned to avoid activating voters for the opposition. Furthermore, because vendors tend to live and work in large metropolitan areas, they're often unaware of the unique voting patterns of small cities in a given region and apply a one-size-fits-all approach. Campaigns that cover both rural and urban areas, as well as small and large cities, and that treat all nonaffiliated voters as the same, ignoring the registration of their neighbors, do so at their own peril.

> "It gets late early out there."
> **YOGI BERRA**

Polling firms will typically contact Republicans, Democrats, and NAVs to test message and issues that may resonate with voters. They then present findings within each of these categories. But when a nonaffiliated voter is polled, the campaign cannot be certain whether that voter is actually a Democrat or a Republican. This can result in unreliable information for the campaign.

After the Jackson-Lane study, I reviewed four polls for state and county races where preelection polls predicted a very different outcome than what eventually materialized. In each, once the nonaffiliated voters were removed, the preelection poll results fell within the margin of error. Granted, this is a small sample of the thousands of polls that are conducted each campaign season, but is still food for thought.

Indeed, in one race in 2004, a tracking poll showed the Democratic candidate winning by twenty points. Given that the district enjoyed a Republican registration advantage of six points and that it had been held by a Republican for twenty-eight years, the projection was suspect. After the election, which the Democrat won by two points, I removed the NAVs from the tracking poll and again found the poll fell within the margin of error, showing the Democrat winning by only a projected five points.

Important to campaigning is the understanding that when news teams, pollsters, or strategists report where so-called independents fall within a targeted question, they are sharing meaningless information. Independents should be omitted from polling and targeted with campaign efforts only in precincts where partisan registrants support the candidate or cause.

The Undervote

Undervotes occur when voters skip a particular candidate or issue on their ballot. Generally this happens for one of three reasons: Don't know. Don't like. Don't care. Voters who have not been paying attention to a particular race will "leave it up to those who do know" and typically skip a race.

In a primary in which candidates are running unopposed, much of the undervote can be attributed to "don't care." A high undervote in a primary is a potential problem in the general election, and your campaign should work to understand the undervote and avoid it.

Unopposed candidates or campaign teams who think they will save money for the general election by not running a primary are misguided. The primary is your opportunity to curry your base, amass volunteers, establish an organization, build name recognition, and test your campaign and volunteer team. If you are running for a state legislative office, it is an opportunity to show the lobby that your campaign is organized and means business. It is also an opportunity to lock your base while getting your message out—all without attacks from the opposition that could cause damage in the general.

Running a campaign in an unopposed primary may entail no more than securing locations for lawn and field signs, printing them, and organizing volunteers to put them up, maintain them, and pull them down after the election. Given that your campaign must do all these things for the general anyway, there is simply no reason not to conduct a primary. Ideally, if a campaign can see a killer general in the offing, canvassing neighborhoods of overwhelming support to lock your base provides more time for canvassing swing precincts for the general. If you do not run a primary and your undervote comes in over 50 percent, you have a lot of work to do on your base that could have been managed with a modest primary campaign. If your undervote is over 60 percent, you're in trouble. Save yourself the heartache: Run a primary.

Your undervote and that of your opposition provide important information for your campaign.

Your Undervote

Hotly contested general elections usually have undervotes in the 3 percent to 5 percent range, depending on the type of ballot. (Punch-card ballots have an undervote about three points higher than do scanned ballots.) However, unopposed primaries are very different from hotly contested general elections.

Coming out of an unopposed primary, you want as low an undervote as possible, but even if you run a primary campaign, be prepared for undervotes in the 20 percent to 30 percent range. Should high-priority precincts come in with significant undervotes (40 percent or more), you must determine why, so that the problem can be fixed in time for the general election. If a high undervote comes in where your saints live, don't worry, but in precincts with potentially high percentages of swing voters, it should be dealt with. Consider sending a persuasion piece to your party. Look for opportunities within those precincts for coffees and other social gatherings. At the very least, send the candidate in for the canvass. A high undervote in a primary means additional work for you in the general, so put your team on notice.

I once worked for a candidate who ran uncontested in the primary and, to save money, did no campaigning for it. When I came onboard for the general, I conducted a precinct analysis on the primary for each candidate and found that the opposition, which had run a modest primary campaign, had a relatively small undervote compared with my candidate, who had undervotes that went as high as 60 percent. The high undervote may have been the result of the voters' perception that the candidate was aloof and somehow thought he was too good to campaign. His invisibility during the primary only fed this belief.

The Opposition's Undervote

If both you and your opponent ran unopposed primaries, you now have some great information on your opposition for the general.

After a primary, spend some time with the results published by the elections office. Abstracts often do not list undervotes, but these can be easily calculated by adding votes received by a candidate and subtracting that number from the total turnout for the party. When it comes to the opposition's undervote, you are looking for high undervotes in areas where there is a high swing voter potential.

After completing your precinct analysis (see Appendix A), look for any precincts previously considered off limits and that have both a modest swing voter potential and a high primary undervote in the opposing party, and put them back on the table. Your job is to determine whether some of the under-votes in these precincts resulted from voters who didn't like the candidate of their party. It is these voters the campaign should identify. Too often, campaigns take time conducting voter identification on members of their own party in precincts that historically vote for their party. Assume you have this support, and instead go behind enemy lines and pull votes from your opposition's base. Identify them, communicate with them, and canvass them. With a little effort, you may move these voters.

Undervotes and Negative Campaigning

Your precinct analysis will tell you where a party is consistently undervoted in past elections. Abdicating registration strength by undervoting is helpful in close elections. Indeed, I consistently win issue-based and candidate races by the undervote. But sometimes a campaign can add to their problems.

Because the undervote can help win races, I study them. In the beginning of this chapter, I referenced a race in which a Democrat lost a legislative race to a Republican who pleaded guilty to misdemeanor assault charges on his child. The Democrat had out-raised and outspent the Republican by more than two to one. In my research, I looked at the television spots of the Democratic candidate. In these ads, all the abuses were reviewed for the voter. It was off-putting to me, and I'm in the business. So, I looked at the undervote to see if perhaps voters were also disturbed by what they saw. I found that in this race—where nearly a half million dollars was spent—the undervote was 14 percent. Given that the Democrat lost by six points (the spread plus 1 percent), one might wonder whether watching this horse getting flogged on television repeatedly, night after night, contributed to the undervote and the loss.

"Our goal is progress, not perfection."

_____ WILLIAMS & WILLIAMS

Assigning the Undervote

In 2004 a Democratic state representative ran against a local Republican businessman for the state senate. In one precinct with 3,400 registered voters, the Democrat was owed 80 percent of the ballots cast, and the Republican was owed 20 percent based on the formula previously outlined. However, after the ballots were cast, the Democrat received only 79 percent of the ballots

cast and the Republican only 17 percent. So where wer
of the votes? If there is no third-party candidate—and th
find the missing votes in the undervote, that is, those w
candidate but still participated in the election.

By determining a percentage of votes owed to eac
and then calculating the percentage received versus th
you can assign both a percentage and an actual count of the undervote to
each of the party candidates. In other words, you now know the undervote each candidate receives. So, again using our example—the above precinct with 3,400 registered voters—the Democrat who received only 79
percent of the votes cast instead of 80 percent is attributed 1 percent of
the undervote, or 34 votes, and the Republican is attributed 3 percent of the
undervote, or 102 votes.

Being able to assign the undervote helps diagnose potential problem areas
so they may be remedied. For example, if the undervote is coming primarily
from your party, your efforts must focus on waking up and energizing your
voters so they care enough to fill in the bubbles on their voter card. Typically
voters are not activated with vacuous mail that simply talks about what a
wonderful person the candidate is. Similarly, negative mail may depress participation even more. Therefore, a consistent and large undervote for your
party's candidates may dictate a more aggressive mail and media campaign of
comparison pieces delivered with a knock at the door.

After you have completed your precinct analysis and charted your results, if some precincts consistently give more votes than are owed to your
candidate's party while others con-
sistently give more votes to the opposing party, you know where to
concentrate money, voter identification, and campaign efforts as well as
which areas to avoid.

> "What should be done to give power into the hands of capable and well-meaning persons has so far resisted all efforts."
> **ALBERT EINSTEIN**

Once you know neighborhoods that are swinging in your direction, use
them to profile other voters outside that area. What do their homes look
like? Do they have porches? What are people watching on television when a
canvasser knocks on the door? Do they have children? Pets? Do they keep up
their homes and property? Are they rural? Urban?

Finding Swing Voters

Although I typically determine swing based on the votes-owed model, which
is covered in depth in Appendix A, there are other ways to do it as well. One
remarkably easy way is outlined below that can be done only if you happen to

wo candidates very similar to yours and your opponent who previously
in different races on the same ballot. Stick with me—this is pretty cool.

In 2004 I was working for Democrat Alan Bates, a local physician who
was running against a moderate Republican from Medford—the largest
city in the county. Two years before, a local physician, Dave Gilmour, also a
Democrat, ran for county commissioner, and in a judicial race on the same
ballot was a moderate Republican from the same neighborhood as our opponent. Although the judicial race was nonpartisan, voters knew who was the
Democrat and who was the Republican.

To determine swing, I matched the doctor from 2002 with the moderate Republican of 2002 as though they were running against each other.
But because voters could legitimately vote for both the moderate Republican and the doctor (remember, they were two different races on
the same ballot), putting together these two candidates from different
races as though they were running against each other created an overvote.
Typically an overvote occurs when a person votes for two candidates *in
the same race on the same ballot.* However, in this instance, the overvote
was artificially created by lining up two candidates from two races on the
same ballot as though they opposed each other. To figure the artificial
overvote, I simply added the totals of the two candidates that mirrored
those in my race and subtracted their total from the total voter turnout,
precinct by precinct.

The results were quite revealing. Out of the thirty precincts in the senate district, eight of them had a combined overvote of 2,253 votes; the remaining twenty-two precincts had a combined overvote of only 54 votes.

> "An elected official is one who
> gets 51 percent of the vote cast
> by 40 percent of the 60 percent of
> voters who registered."
>
> —————————— **DAN BENNETT**

The majority of the swing lived in eight
precincts. Of those eight, however, four
were precincts of solid saints—that is,
voters who never leave their Democratic
candidate. The other four precincts were
the same ones that popped off the charts
in the precinct analysis as left-leaning. All
this meant our entire campaign needed to focus only on four precincts,
which is exactly what we did: The candidate and volunteers repeatedly
canvassed targeted neighborhoods with targeted literature. We flipped a
twenty-eight-year Republican hold on the senate seat while being outspent
nearly two to one. It was magic.

Microtargeting is about getting those 54 votes in the remaining twenty-
two precincts. Precinct analysis is about getting the 2,253 votes in eight
precincts.

Work Smart

I once worked for a candidate who did not fully believe in precinct analysis. I had conducted an in-depth analysis of a number of elections in which candidates who embraced a similar political ideology to my candidate's ran for office. I also reviewed initiatives that covered issues similar to ones with which my candidate was closely aligned. This candidate had also faced a recall attempt while in office, so I conducted an analysis of a successful recall of an elected official who had similar political leanings. All pointed to the same precincts for sinners, saints, and savables. No exceptions. It was clear from the analysis that a handful of precincts would never support the candidate, and given that they typically turned out in lower numbers, there was a real concern that if activated they would vote for the opposition.

Notwithstanding the warning, toward the end of the campaign, after all the high- and medium-priority precincts were done, the candidate decided to burn up some restless energy by covering these low-priority precincts. His feeling was that if he personally went to the door, people would be swayed.

Not surprisingly, the low-support precincts turned out to be difficult canvasses. People were rude, and mishaps occurred. The candidate came back demoralized but decided to press on. Ultimately, he lost the election by a few hundred votes out of 30,000 cast. After the election, a postmortem analysis showed that the low-priority precincts had turned out in record numbers and voted two to one against the candidate.

Precinct analysis tells you not only where your support lives so that it can be activated, but also where the opposition's support lives so that it can be avoided. You never want to activate voters for the opposition.

Campaigns are often so strapped for money that they must be highly focused. Under these circumstances, no matter your party, if certain areas represent solid support and solid turnout (your saints), you need to assume that they will vote for you. If they don't, you'll lose anyway, and that will be that. You must feel that you can count on them without spending too much money or time on getting their vote.

Conversely, there will also be areas that support candidates in the opposing party, election after election. With the exception of the swing or undervote alignment outlined above, these areas should be avoided so that votes for the opposition are not activated; it will save volunteer time and

> "If you are not part of the solution, you are part of the problem."
> **ELDRIDGE CLEAVER**

campaign money. After all, if you spend time, money, or energy in areas where you will lose, that means you are not spending time, money, and energy in areas where you need to win. Work smart: Write off the sinners, trust the saints, and persuade the savables.

Finally

I have received candidate calls from all over the nation, and at some point in the conversation, each person says, "I'm just going to go out and start canvassing." The single biggest challenge campaigns face is the tendency to confuse motion with progress. Unless some study of historic voting patterns and behavior is conducted, no matter how modest the study, candidates risk contacting voters who, once activated, will support the opposition.

In Appendix A, you will find the step-by-step process for conducting a precinct analysis. Do as much as you're capable of doing, but know that the more comprehensively you look at historic voting patterns and incorporate that information in decisions of message and activities, the more likely you are to win.

A precinct analysis is the first step to a winning effort.

2

The Campaign Team and Volunteer Organization

IN THIS CHAPTER
- The Campaign Committee
- The Treasurer
- The Campaign Manager
- The Campaign Chair or Co-Chairs
- Volunteer Organization
- Applying the Methodology
- Phone Banks
- Clerical Workers
- Time Allotments for Volunteer Tasks

THE CAMPAIGN TEAM REFERS TO ALL THOSE WHO HELP ORGANIZE YOUR efforts: the committee, the treasurer, your volunteers, and each of the individual teams that oversees a portion of the campaign. Your media team, for example, may have a liaison to the campaign committee, but the media team should be viewed as part of your overall campaign team rather than part of the committee itself (figure 2.1). Aspects of the campaign team will be covered in this chapter. Campaign efforts that involve large numbers of people and independent efforts, such as lawn sign activities, media projects, brochure development, social media, and fundraising, will be covered in separate chapters.

The Campaign Committee

The relatively small campaign committee serves two functions: First, it is a support group, both for itself and for the candidate or issue-based campaign;

The Campaign Team

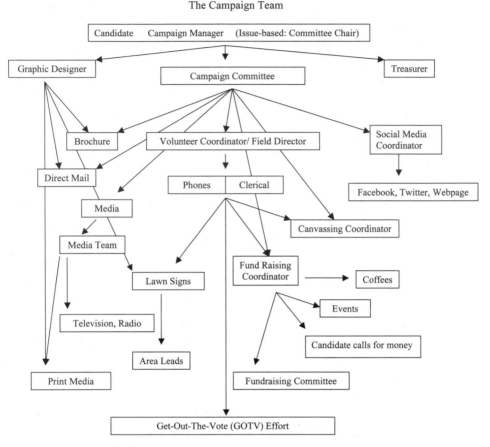

FIGURE 2.1 Campaign Organization Chart

second, it is the primary source of expertise for the campaign. This small, select group will maneuver and steer a campaign while drawing on the resources of the community. The committee should consist of individuals who have different personal strengths and areas of ability.

Your campaign committee is an insiders' group. The candidate, the manager, and each of the members must feel safe in speaking candidly without fear of recrimination. Treat them like insiders and keep them informed of any campaign development. You would never want a committee member to first learn about a problem with the campaign in the newspaper or through the rumor mill. Call or email your committee members often. Welcome their criticism. Encourage them and support their individual efforts in the campaign. Listen carefully to determine when they might need additional help. Be clear about their tasks, expectations, and time commitment.

Take time in choosing the right number of people for a campaign committee. I have worked on countywide campaigns with four committee members (including the candidate), which was too few, and citywide campaigns with twelve members, which was too many. I have found that six or seven committee members is perfect. In countywide campaigns a successful

> "The impersonal hand of government can never replace the helping hand of a neighbor."
> **HUBERT HUMPHREY**

committee might also include members who come from each targeted region or city and who oversee teams within their respective areas.

You want only enough committee members to cover the campaign activities that you have decided to do. Keep in mind that not all campaign activities occur at the same time, so it is often possible to have more than one task assigned to a single committee member. For example, the campaign brochure is written and printed at the beginning of the campaign, whereas the demands on the canvassing coordinator are greatest toward the end of the campaign. On the other hand, activities such as fundraising responsibilities and volunteer coordination (field operations) are ongoing tasks and should *not* be combined with any other campaign responsibilities.

Once the campaign starts, meet with the committee each week for one hour unless it is the first meeting and you're setting up the campaign. For this first meeting, allow additional time by starting the meeting earlier, or have the meeting at a different time—for example, set up a morning retreat followed by a lunch at which the campaign becomes official. For countywide campaigns, it works well for the committee to meet in a central location at the end of the workday before dinner.

Campaign Committee Packets

Your committee may quickly break down into specialized campaign functions. Once specialized groups are formed, keep track of their progress through weekly reports. When the committee gathers, meetings should be productive. Always have an agenda. It is important that all meetings begin and end on time.

A campaign committee packet is a great organizational tool for committee members (figure 2.2). Each pocket folder contains tiered sheets of alternating colors organized by category for the tasks the committee will undertake in the course of the campaign, such as lawn signs, canvassing, phone banks, letters to the editor, and so on. Although one sheet should be dedicated to listing committee members and all contact information for each person, the remaining sheets clearly outline job descriptions for each campaign duty and

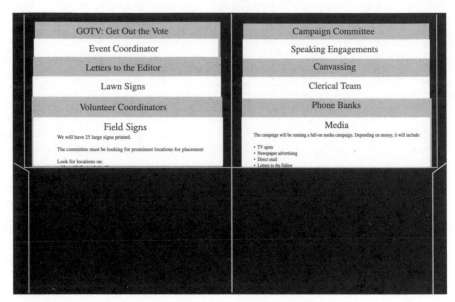

FIGURE 2.2 Example of a Campaign Committee Packet

indicate who will oversee that particular job. The folders travel with committee members to committee meetings and contain information that may be distributed there. Helping volunteers with this kind of organizational framework keeps members happy and makes your campaign a little more volunteer friendly.

In addition to the weekly meeting for the full committee, you should occasionally get together with the individuals who are responsible for specific campaign tasks, and bring this information back to the committee. For example, you may meet with the ad person to hammer out two or three ads and then bring these to the regular committee meeting to have them critiqued.

The makeup of the campaign committee is discretionary, based on how many people will be needed to plan and supervise the campaign. You will depend on the people you invite to join your campaign committee, so they should be capable of organizing and directing some particular aspect of the campaign. In addition to a campaign manager, your committee must include one or more people to oversee letters to the editor, canvassing, clerical work, brochures, the media, lawn signs, phone banks, fundraising, getting out the vote, direct mail, social media, and volunteer workers.

> "The time to win a fight is before it starts."
>
> _____ **FREDERICK W. LEWIS**

The Treasurer

A capable volunteer who has attention to detail can serve as the campaign treasurer. Look for someone who is well respected in the community and who will lend credibility to an issue-based campaign or balance a candidate campaign. Selecting the right person for this position is important. Depending upon the laws of your state, the name of your treasurer may appear on every campaign publication. He or she may be called from time to time by the press, or even the opposition, and asked questions. Like a vice president in a presidential election, the treasurer should balance the ticket. For example, if you are a retired senior, then select a prominent, involved young person of the opposite sex. If you are a young progressive man and relatively new to your community, consider an older conservative woman who has been in town a number of years. Find a person who complements rather than merely repeats your strengths. If you're a Democrat, find a respected Republican. If you are working for more taxes for schools, get someone who may have sometimes spoken out against tax increases.

> "Loyalty is more important than experience."
> **BILL MEULEMANS**

If possible, find someone willing to represent the campaign, discharge the official duties of treasurer, and help in other ways. For example, a treasurer may take on all thank-you notes and keep donor files up-to-date in a database. In one campaign I managed, the treasurer sat in on war room meetings, canvassed, helped with lawn signs, and oversaw data input on campaign donations, but this level of involvement by the treasurer is the exception and not the rule.

The treasurer, campaign manager, and candidate are responsible for obtaining and completing the registration forms required for participation in an election. The necessary forms can be obtained from the city recorder's office for city races, from the county clerk's office for county races, and from the election division under the secretary of state for elections to state offices. Don't be afraid to use these offices. The people who staff government offices are extremely helpful and accommodating.

Not all the forms and information in the election packet are necessary or applicable to every race or election. Ask exactly what you need to read, what is required, and when it is required. Typically all campaign deadlines are available online but if not, ask the local elections office for a schedule of the pertinent dates for filing your campaign contributions and expenditures. While the filing of these reports is the principal job of the treasurer, it is a good idea for both the candidate and the campaign manager to be aware of them. As a reminder, these tasks should be placed in your campaign plan, on the flowchart, or on the calendar as outlined in Chapter 12.

Because campaign finance laws have become very complex in some states, with a plethora of filing deadlines and fines for those who miss them, I now employ a hybrid system where a banker or retired certified public accountant (CPA) actually does all the work for the treasurer named on campaign literature. If I can't find one who will volunteer to oversee the reports, I use campaign funds to hire someone. Having a professional on board is actually a great comfort to the volunteer treasurer and helps reduce the overall stress of a demanding campaign cycle. The hired and volunteer treasurers should work together closely.

Note: I've found that practicing CPAs who volunteer for the treasurer position can ramp up the stress of a primary-election campaign simply because paying customers whose taxes are due at the same time as filing periods will get priority over a volunteer campaign position. Late filings can be a public and financial disaster for a down-ballot race.

"Making the simple complicated is commonplace; making the complicated simple, awesomely simple, that's creativity."

———————— CHARLES MINGUS

Finally, if the "perfect" treasurer cannot be found, simply press on. Look for someone who is thorough, honest, easy to work with, trustworthy, and committed to your cause or candidate. If that fails, hire a professional to cover the task. There are now companies that specialize in campaign finances; they know the law because they do nothing but campaigns and often will generate thank-you notes and receipts for an additional fee.

Contributions and Expenditures

Your treasurer and the CPA or banker should be sticklers for detail. The opposition will be examining your contributions and expenditures (C&Es) filings for any mistakes to report to the state elections office. If a mistake is found, it is bound to make the local papers. That sort of damage is completely preventable.

After the C&E forms have been filed, local newspapers may do a story on who spent how much on what. If you are running a modest campaign and your opposition is funded by outside money, make sure that this information makes it to the media. Running a visibly hardworking campaign with modest funds gives people the sense that you are fiscally responsible. That trait is desirable in office, and voters will make the connection.

Although it is difficult to work on a campaign whose opposition has unlimited funds, it can also work in your favor. In a small community election that involves no TV ads, there is just so much ad space to buy in the newspaper and just so much direct mail that can be sent to homes without it becoming pretty clear that the election is being bought. In one campaign I ran, we were outspent five to one by the opposition, and we publicized this spending discrepancy to our advantage. When the newspapers ran the usual C&E article, many in the community were stunned by the amount of money coming in from outside interests. Since we had a good idea of how much the opposition was spending, we were ready when the press called for our reaction. Supporters wrote and sent letters to the editor for those who missed the newspaper articles when they first appeared.

In that particular race, the opposition was convinced that the accounting in our campaign was wrong and regularly sent people to the recorder's office to check our C&Es. (This is where having a meticulous treasurer pays off.) Finally, convinced of foul play, the opposition called the paper and suggested there must be something wrong. When the press called me, I explained that we were in fact spending a normal amount for a small-town race and it was the opposition whose expenditures were excessive. We got another great newspaper story.

Committee to Support

Given the importance of a good treasurer, what do you do if you can't find the right one for you? Not to worry. You have two options: First, you can place a short list of carefully selected supporters (six to nine) at the bottom of all your literature and ads. This "committee to support" should represent a good cross-section of the community. Although some of these people might be working on your campaign, this is not your campaign committee. The primary job of this group is to give your cause credibility by lending their names. Depending on the issue, the committee to support may include people in business, environmental groups, real estate, labor, and so on.

Using a committee to support works well if you have broad-based support up front, but it does not work at all if your support is marginal. I once worked on a campaign that was so controversial that I could get only three people to sign their names to the committee-to-support list. Rather than have such a short list that didn't cover the political spectrum of the city, I dropped the notion of listing the committee. In fact, it helped the campaign to discover the level of controversy so early in the campaign. Information of this sort should not discourage, but rather help set the course.

> "Putting a bunch of people to work on the same problem doesn't make them a team."
> **GERALD M. WEINBERG** (The Psychology of Computer Programming)

Let me caution you here: When you are working on a very controversial campaign and have a listed committee to support at the bottom of all your literature, you run the risk that opponents to the campaign will get to one or more of those listed and will undermine your public support. The newspapers also may call these people and grill them on the cause. This can get a little dicey. I find it best to use a committee to support for relatively unknown candidates or difficult yet uncontroversial initiatives, propositions, or measures, such as school or public library funding.

The Campaign Manager

The campaign manager is the single most important position in a campaign. Where other jobs have finite responsibilities and time commitments, the job of campaign manager is open-ended. It is a lot to ask of anyone, especially on a volunteer basis. For this reason it is usually the first and sometimes the only paid position.

A campaign manager will interact with your volunteers more than any other person in the campaign, so good communication skills, especially phone and computer skills, are a must. The duties of the campaign manager vary greatly, depending on the number of individuals working in the inner circle. In general, he or she will do such things as attend coffees, debates, and events with the candidate and set up sign-in sheets while lending moral support. The campaign manager also *must* give candid feedback to the candidate without being indelicate.

> "Even the highest towers begin from the ground."
> CHINESE SAYING

If you are running a countywide partisan election campaign, having a manager is critical. You need someone to oversee it all and to be a source of support for the candidate. Although I believe it is a mistake to run for office without a campaign manager, if you are running for office in a small city, you can probably get away with it. Whether you're serving as your own campaign manager or have hired one, you still need capable people to head up various campaign tasks such as lawn signs, canvassing, field work, the internet, and letters to the editor. The most effective campaign teams are those with volunteer team members supervised by a strong manager.

Potential Sources for a Campaign Manager

I highly recommend teachers as campaign managers. They are generally smart, organized, articulate, and personable. They are able to speak to large groups of people and ask for things in simple, understandable ways. They tend to know computers, have a nice collection of presentable clothes, work hard, and are generally politically savvy. They are also likely to be available all summer. If you choose wisely, a teacher who is a campaign manager will force you to get everything ready during the summer so that your fall campaign will go much easier. The drawback of using a teacher is that he or she may be overwhelmed with school responsibilities in the fall and less available to the campaign.

Other potential sources for campaign managers are development directors for local charities, private schools, or nonprofit organizations. These people might consider short-term work for a candidate, and they will have a proven track record. Other leads: people who have worked on other political campaigns, for a United Way campaign, or for a Heart and Lung fund drive, and those who have organized local parades, 4-H fair shows, concerts, or county fairs. Also check with colleges nearby for political science graduates looking for field experience. Each summer the Oregon Bus Project (OBP) runs a ten-week course (Policorps) to train future campaign managers and field operatives. Although Policorps is held in Portland, Oregon, the students are from all over the nation. For information on the graduates and the Oregon Bus Project, go to busproject.org.

In general, a good campaign manager is hardworking, organized, intelligent, self-confident, reliable, and loyal. And because appearance is important, this person should reflect the values and style of the candidate or campaign.

Maintaining Control

Recently I was an adviser to a campaign whose manager became problematic; he was parking illegally on city-owned land and then hassling the police with a "do-you-know-who-I'm-working-for?" attitude. To make matters worse, volunteers were complaining to the candidate about the campaign manager's unnecessary rudeness. The candidate was at the end of his rope and called me to help find a way to let this volunteer go.

Although a candidate does not need this kind of stress, firing a volunteer manager can bring more headaches than it cures. So, short of firing the manager, what can the candidate do?

First, the candidate always has the option of reorganizing the campaign so that the manager has less involvement and responsibility. Second, the candidate could deal with the

> "We've run into a couple of problems, but nothing minor."
> **BRENDA COLLIER** _____

campaign manager and the situation in a clear and straightforward manner. He or she could kindly explain how others were interpreting the manager's actions and how they were reflecting negatively on the campaign and the candidate. Because campaign managers are so closely affiliated with the candidate, there is an assumption that the candidate condones their activities. A problematic situation like this must get immediate attention. Campaigns not only allow the community to see how a candidate will perform both publicly and under pressure, but also allow the candidate to get some experience in dealing with awkward situations and people. Once a candidate is in office, difficult people materialize all the time. If none of this works, the volunteer must be fired.

When running for state legislative office, be prepared to pay the campaign manager handsomely. A good manager speaks truth to power, brings many skills to the table, and can mean big money to your campaign. Individuals, organizations, political action committees (PACs), and lobbyists want to contribute to a winning campaign, and your manager is a big indicator. A strong, experienced, well-organized, hardworking manager will bring an air of confidence to a candidate and campaign team. A candidate should listen to the campaign manager and follow his or her advice.

The Campaign Chair or Co-Chairs

When working on an issue-based campaign, the messenger is the message. Who heads it up is therefore directly linked to the campaign's success. Here you have the choice of using either one person serving as a campaign chair or two people serving as co-chairs. Campaign chairs should be noncontroversial leaders in your community and may serve either in name only as figureheads or as the actual campaign co-coordinators. Mostly they are the face of the campaign. They meet the media, they are part of the war room, and they work the endorsement circles of the community—the Rotary Club, the Chamber of Commerce, business leaders, and more. They gain power and stature when they seemingly have nothing personally to gain by the passage of the measure. Avoid using as a campaign chair someone who has a vested interest in the outcome of a campaign, such as a county commissioner for a county tax base or a teacher for a school levy.

> "If you want something done, ask a busy person."
>
> —————— BENJAMIN FRANKLIN

Choose your co-chairs carefully. Well-respected community leaders with a strong community network are best. Their community relationships are part of the network the campaign will lean on to raise money and activate volunteers. The co-chairs should balance each other, in gender and in interests. For a county measure, one chair may be from the rural area with ranching or farming ties, and the other from the city with business ties. Selection of your chair or co-chairs depends completely on the ballot measure.

If the right chair or co-chairs cannot be found, don't use a campaign chair, but be sure to have top people able to respond to the press and willing to debate the opposition.

Volunteer Organization

Finding Volunteers

Those involved in grassroots campaigning must find people willing to help. Finding volunteers can initially seem daunting, but remember, the only people you can be certain will not help you are those you do not ask. The following is a list of places to look for potential volunteers:

- Your family, friends, and business associates
- Women's rights groups
- Former candidates, office holders, and their volunteers
- Local service groups, churches, and clubs
- Labor unions
- Teachers or school associations
- Any special-interest groups dealing, for example, with the environment, human services, hunting, fishing, and farming

In nearly every election, there is an issue so controversial that voters will act solely on the basis of the opposing positions held by the two candidates. These issues create "ticket splitters," voters who allow an issue to influence what would otherwise be a straight-line party vote. Issues that lead to ticket splitting can motivate a voter to work or vote *against* a candidate rather than *for* a candidate.

In general, issues that create ticket splitters can translate into both volunteers and money for your campaign. Here is a list of some groups and issues that are more inclined than most to let a single issue influence their votes:

> "Nonpolitical issues are the most political."
> **BILL MEULEMANS**

- Veterans
- Sportsmen, fly fishermen, and hunters
- Environmentalists
- Timber and logging advocates
- Prochoice and prolife groups
- Land-use advocates
- Seniors
- Tax and antitax groups
- Gay-rights and anti-gay-rights activists
- Public union employees
- Identifiable work groups such as teachers and firefighters
- Advocates for and against gun restrictions

VOLUNTEER SIGN-UP SHEET

Name (please print)	Home Phone	I would like to volunteer for the following (please check all that apply):							
		Canvass Neighborhoods	Phone Banks	Clerical	Lawn Sign Location Address	Donation	Letter-to-the-Editor	Endor. ad?	E-mail

FIGURE 2.3 Example of a Volunteer Sign-Up Sheet

Volunteer Sign-Up Sheet

In addition to finding volunteers in the groups listed above, you can create a form for sign-ups at coffees, debates, and other gatherings once the campaign is under way (figure 2.3).

Basic Rules for the Volunteer Workforce

Directing volunteers is almost the same for each campaign task. Although the tasks vary considerably, only a small modification is necessary to organize your volunteer force for each specialized campaign activity.

Regardless of the activity, there are seven important things to remember about using volunteers:

1. Don't waste the volunteers' time. Have everything laid out and ready to go the moment they walk in the door. Begin and end on time. Do not encourage late arrivals by delaying the start of meetings.

2. Be prepared with anything they might need. If the task is to stuff envelopes, make sure there are enough stamps, sponges, pens, staples, and other necessities.

3. Eliminate no-shows: Call them ahead of time, and let them know what they need to bring, such as extra staple guns, clipboards, good walking shoes, a truck, or a hammer.

4. Be clear about their tasks, expectations, and time commitments. Give clear written instructions and deadlines. This is especially important for those on phone banks.

5. Pick the right people for the job. Don't ask out-of-shape people to canvass steep hills; don't place counterculture people as canvassers in conservative areas.

6. Keep volunteers informed, and support them. When you call, let them know how the campaign is going. Be sensitive to their schedules.

7. Treat your volunteers as you would highly paid employees.

It is a serious mistake to undervalue volunteer time simply because it is free. Disorganized campaigns lead to irritated and frustrated workers who may not return if things seem poorly run more than once. Some of the very best volunteers will not come back after even one bad encounter. Worse yet: In small towns people gossip about poor organization. To avoid such problems, the manager should assemble clerical teams to help set up other tasks, such as assembling lawn signs in preparation for the lawn sign team, cutting turf for canvassers, or preparing phone lists for phone bankers. This preplanning is vital to creating a volunteer-friendly campaign, helps ensure the success of campaign activities, and allows the campaign to place people in jobs where they will excel.

> "In life, as in any game whose outcome depends on both skill and luck, the rational response to bad odds is to try harder."
> **MARVIN HARRIS**

Build a Database

No matter where you find your volunteers, a campaign must have a system to organize, direct, and assign responsibilities.

Using a spreadsheet program, list all of your contacts from your initial cold calls, family, friends, work, remittance envelopes, and sign-up sheets generated by your or other campaigns. First, create a master list of activities from which you can break out specific duties that volunteers have indicated they will perform. Here are examples of column labels that could run along the top of your master list: last name, first name, spouse/partner name, house number, street, city, zip code, phone numbers (cell, home, and work). Volunteer work and services categories (which can be filled in with yes or no), include canvass, clerical, lawn sign, lawn sign install, LTEs (letters to the editor), data input, Web page design/upkeep, Facebook upkeep, and endorsement ad. Finally, a column labeled "$" indicates whether a volunteer has also contributed funds, and a column labeled "notes" may contain brief comments (figure 2.4).

Although you usually include a column for donations ($), remember, this sheet is for *volunteer* activities. The $ column simply tracks which of your volunteers have also contributed money. Since states have specific filing requirements for campaign donors, it is important to keep track of donor information apart from your volunteer spreadsheet. Check with the elections office or secretary of state to determine the required information on each of your contributors. For example, in Oregon a campaign must list the person who signed the check, the contributor's occupation, the address of the contributor, and the name and address of the contributor's workplace. Specific ways to keep track of your donors and an example of a donation spreadsheet are presented in Chapter 5.

The "notes" section of your spreadsheet is where you note such information as "Won't canvass hills"; "Don't call early a.m."; "Don't call after 8:00 p.m.";

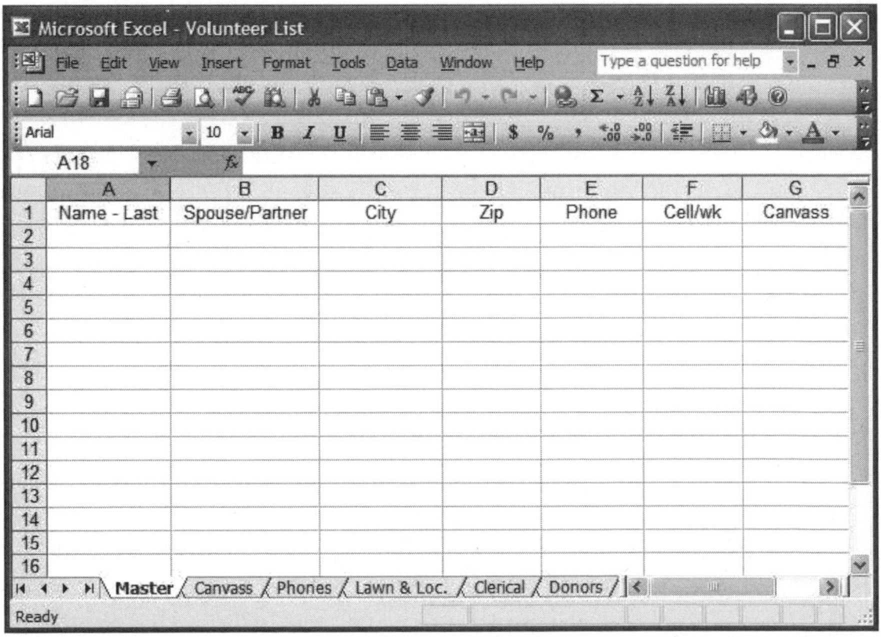

FIGURE 2.4 Example of an Excel Spreadsheet for Keeping Track of Volunteer Workers

"No phones"; and "Has three staple guns." Also use this section to make a note when someone has been rude ("Do not contact again"), so that other campaign volunteers needn't be subjected to verbal abuse. After hundreds of phone calls, it is impossible to remember such details if a record is not kept somewhere.

Organize Volunteer Activities

Once information is in your spreadsheet, create different pages from your master according to activity: phones, canvassing, clerical, lawn sign installation, events, and so on (figure 2.4). Always keep on a coded master sheet.

No matter the activity, when contacting a volunteer, be sure to have a number of dates lined up for it so that each volunteer is called only once for scheduling. When calling for an ongoing activity such as canvassing, have four or five dates and times, so if one date doesn't work, another may. If a volunteer can do none of the times offered, it is important to determine why and to note this on the spreadsheet. If it is a temporary scheduling conflict, note when the conflict will be resolved. However, if it sounds as though the

> "It is one of the beautiful compensations of life that no one can sincerely try to help another without helping himself."
> **RALPH WALDO EMERSON**

volunteer will *never* do the activity, offer another campaign job. Keep this person on the phone until it can be determined what is going on. If it is clear that he or she will never volunteer, that person's name should be removed from the volunteer list. For now, however, the name remains on your working list with a line through it so that you will remember that you called. If you do not do this, you will forget and call again. If you are working directly from a list on a computer rather than a printout, you can distinguish those who have been called and who will never volunteer by highlighting the cell or changing the color of the font.

A couple days before the activity, call back every volunteer who agreed to work and place a check (✓) in the "CB?" column. It is best to actually talk to the worker on the callback, so leave a message or send an email only as a last resort. On the callback, do not ask workers if they still intend to help. Do not even call to remind them directly of the upcoming volunteer activity. They said they would do it, and the tone of your conversation should reflect that verbal contract. Plus, if they are very organized, they will resent the call. Instead, think of this call as a small rattling of the cage and make it about something else: Remind them to bring a clipboard, or ask if they mind doing hills, or check to make sure that they were given the correct meeting place or the correct time. Whatever it is, it's your fault or it's about a small detail that

> "You can't have divided authority around a campaign headquarters."
>
> **JAMES FARLEY,** campaign manager for Franklin D. Roosevelt

wasn't addressed in the first conversation. You're just checking to make sure the information given previously was correct. If the volunteer has forgotten, the call serves as a reminder. If the person inadvertently made other plans, this is your opportunity to reschedule. Potential no-shows, discovered in a call-back reminder, are incredibly easy to reschedule.

Applying the Methodology

Every campaign consists of basic campaign activities, such as:

- Running phone banks
- Canvassing the voters
- Developing campaign events
- Designing ads or other media
- Organizing clerical support (including thank-you notes)
- Preparing, installing, and maintaining lawn signs
- Raising money: events
- Data input
- Web page and Facebook upkeep

Matching Volunteers to Skills

Although a small campaign can be run without volunteers, it would be a mistake to do so. When people work for a campaign, they become invested and want to see the investment pay off. Also, involving people in the process brings more interest to government and the political system. There is, however, one caution: If potential workers indicate an unwillingness to do a particular activity, don't make the mistake of begging and pleading to get help in that task.

> "It's not very difficult to persuade people to do what they already long to do."
>
> **ALDOUS HUXLEY**

I once placed on the phones a woman who told me she didn't like to phone. I found it hard to believe that in this day and age anyone would have trouble talking on the phone—plus I was desperate. What a mistake. She was painfully uncomfortable calling people she didn't know and projected a poor image of the campaign. I couldn't take her off once I saw my error, because that would have called further attention to the problem, making her more uncomfortable. I left her on the phone for about a half hour and then told her that I had finished my work and asked if she would mind if we shared her phone. She gratefully gave it up. Similarly, if a volunteer reports that he doesn't like to canvass, believe him. It is better for the campaign to have people doing tasks they enjoy.

Here is a tip for placing people who say they would rather not call or canvass: Some who do not like to work phones actually do not like to make cold calls—that is, they do not like to call people who may be opposed to the candidate or measure. Quite often, these same people may be willing to make calls to activate identified supporters, such as in a get-out-the-vote effort. Similarly with canvassers, some do not like to canvass, because they dislike knocking on doors and talking to the residents. However, these same people may be willing to do a literature drop, a door hanger, install lawn signs, or other tasks where knocking and talking are not involved.

Supervise volunteers so that workers who have difficulty with a task are not called a second time to help in the same task. For instance, if a volunteer is struggling at a phone bank because age has made hearing more difficult, simply note it in the spreadsheet you use to keep track of volunteers. In this way, campaign workers will not mistakenly call the person again for that task.

> "Many [candidates] lose due to their failure to organize large numbers of people in their campaigns."
> **MORTON BLACKWELL**, The Leadership Institute newsletter, May-June 1998

Similarly, if an individual is great at a task like phoning, keep him or her away from other campaign activities to avoid campaign burnout. Use volunteers where they excel. For example, I've found older men who are hard of hearing make great drivers for lawn-sign installation teams.

The same kind of supervision is necessary for each volunteer activity. For example, if a canvasser returns without notes for lawn signs, has no impressions of voter attitudes, and only partially covered the assigned area, perhaps canvassing is not the best job for that individual. Note this in the volunteer data system. Be sure to make a note as to why, and move that person over to something like lawn sign placement and maintenance. If it can be avoided, do not place volunteers in jobs where they will have a bad time or may reflect poorly on the campaign. Attention to these kinds of details helps volunteers be more successful and keeps them returning to help.

Phone Banks

Phone banks can be used throughout a campaign and are the most efficient way to retrieve information in a short time. They can be used to get a head count for a fundraiser, to get lawn sign locations, to raise money, and to get the campaign more volunteers. If you plan to do a get-out-the-vote (GOTV) effort on Election Day, you will have to identify voters who intend to vote for your candidate or cause. This can be done while canvassing, by phone, or both. Although conducting a GOTV by canvassing activates the greatest number of voters, few campaigns have the volunteer resources to do so and rely on phone banks to do the heavy lifting. When signing up volunteers, assure them that they will receive training before actually working on the phones.

I used to schedule a phone banker to work for one hour and fifteen minutes (fifteen minutes for training and then one hour on the phone), as almost anyone will give up an hour or so for a campaign they believe in, and if it turns out that the volunteer is bad on the phone, an hour is plenty. However, I now use people for two-hour shifts and pile on more callers for the shift using their personal cell phones. Callers will let the campaign know if two hours is too long; if it is, have others scheduled to replace a caller coming off the phones early.

If callers are working a one-hour shift, have two or three shifts per evening and ask them to arrive fifteen minutes before their shift for training. No one likes to go on the phone cold, so people rarely miss training when it's offered and expected.

Each phone bank should have a "lead." This is the person responsible for unlocking the doors of the phone bank location, training volunteers, calling the next evening's callers, answering questions for phone bankers, and finally, picking up after the volunteers leave and closing up the phone bank. Training begins by handing a phone banker a brochure and an instruction sheet, which should include prepared scripts. If the campaign is using volunteers to conduct a poll, a prepared script must be followed to the letter; in all other phone bank activities, however, a caller who ad-libs will generally do best.

"It does not require a majority to prevail, but rather an irate, tireless minority keen to set brush fires in people's minds."

— SAMUEL ADAMS

Once the volunteers have read the instructions, do a walk-through of what is expected on the phones, and explain any peculiarities the phone system may have (such as dialing 9 first). Tell volunteers where the bathroom is, and let them know that you will provide water. For the lead person, have a list of all the details that need to be shared with a new volunteer before he or she starts working the phone.

After a fifteen-minute training session, volunteers begin calling. The first twenty to thirty minutes that volunteers are on the phone, the lead should circulate, answer questions, and take water to people rather than making calls. The lead will have only ten or fifteen minutes between shifts, as the second crew will arrive for training fifteen minutes early, or forty-five minutes into the hour of the previous shift's calls. This way, exactly one hour after the first shift starts, volunteers get a tap on the shoulder from someone on the next shift, and they are off the phones.

Avoid job creep by telling people that you want them for a specific amount of time, then pushing them to stay longer. This is how a campaign can lose volunteers. When you ask someone to work for you, you have made a verbal contract with him or her for a specific job and a specific amount of time.

Once the second shift is in place, happily making calls and supplied with water, and all campaign questions asked and answered, the lead must then call all those listed to volunteer on phone banks for the following evening. Giving a quick reminder of place and scheduled time for work avoids no-shows.

Note: Do not expect your phone bank people to look up phone numbers; all calling lists must include phone numbers.

Phone Bank Training

The following is an example of what you might prepare for your volunteers who are phoning for the campaign:

> Thank you for your help. Tonight we are calling people who live on arterial streets in hopes of beefing up our lawn sign list. While the lists you're calling have the same party registration as our candidate, they have not been previously identified as a supporter. Just so you know, that may make some of the calls a little harder. Please make a note on your list next to the name of the voter whether he or she will take a lawn sign, and if not, whether that person will be supporting our candidate.

Boxes 2.1 and 2.2 are examples of materials given to phone bankers.

What you ask for will vary according to the phone bank. You could be calling for lawn sign locations, money, volunteer workers, a head count for an event, or voter ID (that is, finding out whether a voter supports your campaign). Think about your mission, and prepare a short introduction for the caller.

Phone Bank Locations

The introduction of cell phones with unlimited minutes and prepaid cell phones has all but eliminated the nightmare of finding friendly commercial offices with enough lines to accommodate phone banks. Still, you need a

"Hello, this is (your name). Tonight I am volunteering to help the Ada Kay campaign. As you may know, Ada is running for reelection to the House, and I was hoping you would consider having one of her lawn signs in front of your home."

If no, thank the caller and ask if Ada can count on his or her support in the upcoming election.

If yes, verify address and ask if there are any special instructions for where and how the homeowner would like the sign placed. Then say:

"Someone will be coming by to place the sign about six weeks before the election. We will also have some maintenance crews checking signs from time to time. However, if you would occasionally check the sign and set it up if it falls over, that would be very helpful. When the sign is placed, there will be a note left on your door so you can contact the campaign should it disappear or be vandalized. Thanks for helping us out."

BOX 2.1 Example of Phone Instructions and Script for Lawn Sign Locations

Before You Pick Up the Phone—

1. *Be proud of what you are doing.* You are working for a cause you believe in. You are on the front line of a campaign.

2. *Think about what has motivated you to give up your time to work for the candidate (or ballot measure).* People will ask how a candidate stands on a particular issue. While you cannot speak directly to that, you can share why *you* are working for this individual (or cause).

3. *Identify yourself only as a volunteer working for the campaign.* In general, you want the candidate's name to make it into the consciousness of the voter, not yours, unless, of course, you know the person.

4. *No matter what else happens, get something from the individual before you get off the phone.* "You can't canvass, ever? How about a lawn sign?" "You have a bad lawn-sign location? Do you have a friend who might want one?" "Can we use your name on the endorsement ad?" "Would you make a contribution?" Whatever. You want them in on the campaign with that single call, or to know how they will be voting. (This is helpful information for the campaign.)

5. And thank you for taking the time to help in this important cause.

BOX 2.2 Example of Phone Bank Instructions

comfortable and professional location where people are calling in close proximity to each other and where supervision is easily conducted.

The best locations have plenty of rooms and desks, such as offices for lawyers, realtors, or physicians; you can also use party headquarters but caller ID will reduce the number of pick-ups on the receiving end. Wherever you end up, the location must be equipped with four or five land lines for volunteers without access to a cell phone or whose calling plan limits their minutes. The remaining ten to fifteen volunteers at the phone banks use personal cell phones.

What makes this approach so ideal is that voters are more apt to pick up a phone call if their caller ID indicates a real person, a friend or neighbor, is on the other end of the call rather than "party headquarters." This hybrid phone-bank approach allows the phone banks to be as large as necessary to get through the required calls for the task in front of you.

One note of caution: Remind the cell phone users to bring their chargers.

Scripts

Wherever your phone bank is located, the important part of campaign phoning is to have an effective message. You should have scripts made up in advance for each campaign activity. While it is preferable to have callers ad-lib, they generally need a prepared script for the first few calls. It gets much easier after that. Also don't have the volunteers ask the person, "How are you doing tonight?" The reality is that the volunteer doesn't care, and the person on the other end knows it. When calling for money, the calls will be a bit longer and more in-

> "There is as much greatness of mind in acknowledging a good turn, as in doing it."
>
> **SENECA**

volved, so I usually start by asking the person who answers if they have a moment to talk. However, with volunteer recruitment, the calls are so short that you can just cut to the chase. The following paragraphs suggest some sample scripts for typical campaign phone sessions.

Lawn Sign Location. "Hello, I'm a volunteer working for the Kate Newhall campaign for state senate. Tonight we're looking for locations for lawn signs. Will you be supporting Kate in the general election? Great, could we place a lawn sign? Let me verify your address. Someone will be coming by about six weeks before the election to place it. We also have a crew who will be maintaining these signs; however, if it needs some attention, maybe you could help with it. Great. Thanks."

Special Activity. "Hello, I'm a volunteer working for the Daniel Golden campaign for state senate. Did you receive the invitation for the campaign dinner this Saturday? The restaurant needs a pretty accurate head count, so we're trying to get an idea of the number of supporters who will be attending the dinner for Daniel. Will you be joining us?"

Canvassing. "Hello, I'm a volunteer helping in the Peter Buckley campaign. We are hoping to canvass the city this Saturday with a last-minute door hanger and need about eighty-five volunteers. There will be no door-knocking, just great exercise. Can you help?"

Another. "Hello, I'm a volunteer working for the 'JoAnne Verger for Senate' campaign. Our notes indicate that you might be willing to canvass. Is that correct?" [Answer] "Great. I have a number of dates for some upcoming canvasses. Do you have your calendar handy?"

GOTV for Absentee and Mail-in Ballots. "Hello, I'm a volunteer from the Jeff Barker campaign. We're down here working on phone banks tonight to turn out as many of Jeff's supporters as possible. As of a couple of days ago, your ballot had not yet been received at county elections; is it possible you still have it at home?"

Voter ID. "Hello, I'm a volunteer working for the Amy Amrhein campaign. As you may know, Amy is a candidate for school board. Do you know if you'll be supporting her this November?" [Yes, No, Need more info]

Undecided: With any of these scripts, if I call and discover that someone is undecided or leaning, I ask whether the person would like more information from the candidate or campaign committee. Finally, whatever a potential supporter might say, ask volunteers to make a note so that the campaign can follow up if need be.

Negative Response: Get off the phone as quickly as possible, and make a note for the campaign.

Clerical Workers

The clerical team is an extremely important part of your campaign. Normally you think of people sitting around, addressing, stamping, and stuffing envelopes. While these tasks might make up some of your clerical team's work, you should think of this group in broader terms.

> "Nothing is particularly hard, if you divide it into small jobs."
>
> **HENRY FORD**

Wherever I can break down activities into more manageable units, I do so. For example, on the day that lawn signs go up, you *cannot* expect your lawn sign team to arrive early in the morning, staple lawn signs, organize lists, and then head out for two hours of stake pounding. Each of these functions is very different and should be treated differently.

A clerical team can come in days ahead of time to staple lawn signs or bolt them to the stakes, depending on the type of sign you use, and then another clerical team can organize the map packets and lawn sign lists for either printed lists or hand-held devices.

Your clerical team is crucial in keeping your campaign tight and organized. Use them creatively wherever they can help with your workload or with organizing an upcoming activity. Here are some examples of how the clerical team can be used:

- Lawn sign assembly
- Assemble maps for a canvass (cutting turf)
- Attach inserts in the brochures for a canvass
- Write thank-you notes for money, lawn sign locations, or volunteers' time
- Stuff, stamp, and address a mailing
- Prepare items for a fundraiser, such as a yard sale or an auction
- Set up for a campaign gathering—decorate, print name tags, etc.

To set up a campaign activity requiring clerical workers, contact people who have indicated they will help with clerical work. If you need additional volunteers, try the League of Women Voters, your friends and neighbors, and senior groups that support you. Given how much fun a clerical work party can be, it is usually pretty easy to turn out a crowd.

A clerical work party is a social time in campaigns; it's a time to chat with friends while helping with a cause everyone supports. It's a time to share war stories about canvassing, to talk news, to gossip, or to do whatever else while having coffee and cookies and doing a mindless task. These meetings are enjoyable and highly productive for the small effort involved.

It is important for people to be comfortable while working and sitting for two or more hours, so be sure to have enough table space for each volunteer. Do not do clerical work in an already cluttered house. Because no one's back is getting younger—and many of the clerical volunteers are older—I take the time to put together a comfortable work area. Avoid having people work on their laps in soft, overstuffed couches and chairs; they will not be as productive. This is akin to cleaning house or doing yard work in flip-flops—you can do it, just not as efficiently.

Have some snacks around—coffee, tea, cookies, and the like—but not on the table where work is being conducted.

Have everything set up. Do not waste your volunteers' time.

Do one activity at a time. If the task is to get out a mailing or to staple lawn signs, do just that. When the task is done—and usually they're done ahead of schedule—don't bring out one more thing for people to do. Remember, as with any other task in a campaign, you have made a verbal contract with your workers. Once they are captive workers in your home, to ask them to work past the designated time or beyond the designated task creates hard feelings. Workers who complete a task early and then go home feel good about their participation and feel that they are helping in a well-organized effort.

> "We are here to add to what we can to life, not to get what we can from it."
>
> **WILLIAM OSLER**

Make sure that you have all the necessary materials at each station, so that people are not idle. Have extras of everything you need—staplers, sponges, stamps, envelopes, rubber bands, electric screwdrivers, drywall screws, washers, or whatever else the task might require.

Time Allotments for Volunteer Tasks

Below are some general guidelines for what volunteers can do in a designated amount of time. From here, you can calculate how many people you'll need to accomplish a task in the time available. For the task to be completed by a certain date, work your way backward from that date so that you have enough time to complete the task, given your resources and task goal—number of calls to make, signs to put up, homes to canvass, and so on.

> "Luck is the crossroads where preparation and opportunity meet."
>
> **ANONYMOUS**

Phone Banks

In general, each volunteer can complete twenty to thirty calls per hour, depending on the nature of the calls. In a GOTV effort, people can make fifty calls during a ninety-minute shift. So, for example, if you want to make 4,000 calls by Election Day and have only one phone bank location with six phones, you will need people on all six phones, for two ninety-minute shifts, for seven nights. Naturally, if you have callers bring cell phones, the number of calling nights goes down, and the number of volunteers per shift goes up.

Canvassing

Some precincts are huge, by either population or geography, and can have anywhere from 300 to 3,000 voters per precinct, or 200 to 1,800 homes. You can use voter lists to get an accurate number of houses in each precinct.

Two types of canvassing are used for our purposes here: a knock, and a simple lit drop without talking.

Knock. Depending on how hilly, rural, or compact a neighborhood is, canvassers can cover ten to fifteen houses per hour. That means that a precinct with 120 to 200 houses would require six canvassers working two to three hours each to cover the distance.

Drop. A literature drop can be done quite a bit faster than a knock canvass. With a drop, again depending on street grade and the density of homes, a canvasser can cover twenty-five to thirty homes in an hour.

Clerical (Direct Mail)

A five hundred–count mailing requires a fifteen-person clerical team working one hour to stuff, stamp, seal, and address envelopes.

> "To get the most from the people you manage, you must put them in the right spot at the right time."
> **JOE TORRE**

Lawn Signs

One lawn sign team—a driver and a pounder—can put up about twelve lawn signs an hour. So, for example, if you have two hundred lawn signs to place, you will need sixteen people (eight teams) working two hours each.

Your campaign committee and volunteer teams are central to a winning campaign effort. A thoroughly organized and properly executed volunteer structure minimizes wasted time and reflects well on the campaign manager and candidate.

3

The Campaign Brochure

IN THIS CHAPTER
- Campaign Theme and Message Development
- Polling
- Brochure Development
- Campaign Slogans
- Logo
- Layout
- Voters' Pamphlet

THE CAMPAIGN BROCHURE IS FUNDAMENTAL TO A CAMPAIGN. IT SERVES as an introductory piece for candidates and should include photos, a biography, and information that identifies why the candidate would be ideal in public office. If the candidate has previously held office, the brochure underscores past accomplishments and activities and brings them to the attention of the electorate. Unless the campaign plan calls for developing different brochures for the primary and the general election, the brochure should be free of partisan politics, because it travels with the candidate to all public functions.

In an issue-based campaign, the brochure may give a sense of time and history reflecting on past community goals and ideals. An issue-based brochure should clearly explain what is before the voters, delineate the potential impacts of yes and no votes, and include testimonials from important community leaders advocating the passage or defeat of the ballot item.

In either a candidate or an issue-based campaign, it is important to develop a theme and a message before writing and printing a brochure, because it is from this framework that campaign activities will develop and flow.

Campaign Theme and Message Development

Before you sit down to write a brochure, you must develop a campaign theme and message. Although political strategists use the words *theme* and *message* in different ways and sometimes interchangeably, for our purposes a theme covers the overarching issues that capture the spirit of what voters want, whereas a message is a single idea used to bring that theme to the voters.

> "Reining in government and all of that other stuff."
>
> **BOB DOLE, 1995,** outlining his presidential campaign platform

For example, if you're working on a campaign to fund cocurricular activities that were eliminated from your school district because of budget cuts, your *theme* will probably include the idea of reinstating these programs. However, your *message* will center on the idea that it is no longer enough for students to have a 4.0 GPA if they want to get into a good college or land a better job—they must also be involved in cocurricular and extracurricular school activities. Briefly, your message is "opportunity."

A theme embraces what the voters want and defines the candidate or issue-based campaign in that context, whereas a message is a believable application of the theme to the voters that cuts through to the emotional level. The voters want great schools, which must have a combination of challenging coursework and cocurricular activities. You sell these programs for what they are: opportunity for our children. They help students get into competitive universities or land great jobs, they are the reason some kids stay in school, and they represent another layer of preparation that enriches the next generation's future. It all comes back to providing opportunities for

> "Democracy is the theory that the common people know what they want . . . and deserve to get it good and hard."
>
> **H. L. MENCKEN**

youths to excel. It isn't about money; it isn't about how little your property taxes will go up. If you're justifying money, you're on their message.

When you're selling a bond measure to maintain money for operation and maintenance (O&M) of a community asset, such as a library, you are not selling what a great deal the voters are getting or how this generation owes it to the next; you're selling much more. You know what the voters want: They want a community resource that is properly managed and protected from cuts. That's your theme, and you're going to give them what they want.

Your message, however, is about community. It's about a place where old and young can gather, as they have for a hundred years, to read a book, study, and connect with others.

However, if you're selling a *capital improvement* project, the campaign actually does sell money; you're selling "a stitch in time saves nine": It is cheaper to repair roads now rather than later, to fix leaky roofs to protect books from mildew, to avoid federal fines for dumping wastewater into streams, to upgrade wiring to make classrooms safer. What a campaign should *not* do is mix operation and maintenance arguments with capital improvement (CI) arguments. O&M is about keeping the library open; CI is about protecting the asset. O&M is about more teachers per student; CI is about boilers exploding. O&M is about hope and opportunity; CI is about being responsible. There's a difference.

In the 1992 presidential campaign, Bill Clinton had a theme of environmental protection, lower crime rates, education, and universal health care, among other things—things that voters wanted. Each of the issues of the overall campaign theme was then conveyed to the American people through the message "It's the economy." Let me underscore that the message is never stated, but is the tool used for framing. For example, we need to protect our environment to ensure better *jobs* in the future; we need to provide our children with better education if we want a *workforce* that can compete on the world market; providing opportunities for everyone to get a college education means *keeping America competitive*; affordable health care allows a family *to get ahead*; high crime rates are destroying our communities and marginalizing *businesses*; and so on. Everything comes back to the message "It's the economy": Addressing the issues that people want will lead to a better economy. This message had added strength in that it suggested the incumbent was unaware that the electorate was concerned about the economy.

A campaign message is how a theme is communicated to the public. It's a story you tell over and over, a story you can tell in a few seconds: "It's the economy"; "This is about opportunity"; "It's the small issues"; "It's hope"; "It's about community." A well-crafted message moves the debate away from which candidate can be trusted to whom the voters trust to do the job. A theme and a message articulate the point that the candidate knows *what* job needs to be done. Voters will naturally make the connection that the candidate who knows what needs to be done will be the one more likely to do it.

> "It is dangerous for a national candidate to say things that people might remember."
>
> —————— EUGENE McCARTHY

Stay On Message

To create a theme and a message, your campaign committee must assess the strengths and weaknesses of your candidate or ballot measure.

By taking a critical look at your candidate or issue and listing the strengths and weaknesses, your campaign team is better able to shape and communicate the theme of a campaign through the message. For example, a woman who is energetic, feisty, and steadfast translates into pluses and minuses. The pluses are that she's a fighter, has integrity, is honest, and will fight for the community. The minuses may be that she is pushy, shrill, dogmatic, or overbearing (a word reserved in American society almost exclusively for women).

The charge of the campaign committee is to frame the negative into a positive: Pushy becomes persistent or steadfast; dogmatic becomes directness, which goes with honesty and integrity. All this is communicated through the message that flows from what the candidate represents. For instance, if a community is being overrun by developers and the quality of life is compromised by the inherent impacts of growth, couple a message of thoughtful, planned growth with a candidate's strengths of honesty, integrity, persistence, and willingness to fight for the community. Again, the message is planned, thoughtful growth, and every question answered comes back to this message—all under the umbrella of the theme "quality of life."

Through this process, campaigns identify issues that create relationships with the voters and that translates into money, volunteers, and votes. For example, people in a particular neighborhood are concerned about development, so the campaign underscores the creation of a park near the neighborhood. It is not about stopping growth but rather about mitigating the negative effects of growth. The

> "Leaders can conceive and articulate goals that lift people out of their petty preoccupations and carry them above the conflicts that tear a society apart."
> **JOHN W. GARDNER**

campaign looks at the impacts growth has on the community and presents approaches that allow growth without compromising quality of life. This in turn will create relationships within the community. For parents and teachers, growth affects class size; for others, it's about traffic, open space, or availability of resources, such as water. If you present yourself as antigrowth, you risk being tagged as a single-issue candidate. Instead, lead people to where two worlds can coexist or even enhance one another rather than prophesying what will happen if these two worlds are allowed to collide. In short, planning for growth is good for business, education, resources, neighborhood integrity, and so on.

This concept is important in campaign communications and it will be given further attention in later sections and chapters. Establishing a strong, succinct, and believable theme and message creates relationships, which in turn creates voters interested in helping and giving.

Very simply, you want a majority to see your side as a better choice than the other side. This is the time to assess the strengths and weakness of your opponent. If your opponent has not defined himself or herself, you can work this process in reverse and define that person for the voters: "My opponent is pro-growth."

The brochure is basic to your campaign. You will walk it door-to-door, mail it to households, and hand it out at debates. The message must resonate with voters who receive the brochure, which will state in subtle and not-so-subtle ways why people should vote as you want them to. It should also imply why they should *not* vote for your opponent.

Polling

Polling provides a campaign with a snapshot of public opinion. While a benchmark poll looks at where the candidate or a ballot issue is ranked among voters before any campaigning or distribution of information has been done, tracking polls provide ongoing feedback on the impact a campaign has in swaying public opinion.

Benchmark Polls

Conducting a benchmark poll may be the most efficient and accurate way to determine voter concerns before you develop your message. As First Lady Rosalynn Carter remarked, "It is difficult to lead people where they do not want to go." While it is important to have elected officials with strong core values, it is even more important that officials listen to and embrace "where people want to go." Having a clear reading of voter concerns will help your campaign develop and direct a message that will be heard. It can also inform you about when to keep quiet and which issues to avoid where. Generally, a benchmark poll is done before a campaign, and it can be invaluable in developing a campaign strategy, theme, and message.

> "Public sentiment is everything. With public sentiment, nothing can fail. Without it, nothing can succeed."
>
> — **ABRAHAM LINCOLN**

A good benchmark poll can take as long as thirty minutes per call. It will include questions that lead to information about the following:

- The name recognition of the major candidates
- The favorability of that name recognition
- The voter's knowledge of state and local politics
- The degree of the voter's partisanship

- The issues most important to the voter, by gender, age, and party affiliation
- The education, age, and gender of those who support you and of those who support your opposition
- The income level of those who support you and your opponent
- Whom the voter will support if the election were held tomorrow (or which direction the voter is leaning)
- Whether the voter intends to vote, is likely to vote, or is unlikely to vote
- What form of message works best, both for your candidate and for the opposition
- What attacks will hurt the most, for both you and your opposition

Although benchmark polls are long and questions are at a premium, try to include some that help determine radio listening habits and cable networks watched; getting this sort of information will allow the campaign to zero in on where best to communicate with those you're trying to lock or persuade.

A good benchmark poll can be expensive but will provide specifics that influence where you communicate what message. For example, a persuadable voter between the ages of forty and forty-nine, female, without a college education, and who is not married, watches *The View,* HGTV, and CNN, and cares about cuts to local schools. You can use this information to work on this very small slice of the electorate with mail, canvassing, and targeted media.

"I've got to follow them; I am their leader."

ALEXANDRE LEDRU-ROLLIN

Polling Message with Push Questions

Push questions, not to be mistaken with push polling, "are recognized by all the major associations and leading political consultants as a valid and legitimate research tool for the purposes of testing ad messages and examining the collective viewpoints of electorate subgroups."[1]

Push *questioning* will ask whether a statement is very, somewhat, or not at all convincing and will do so for both the candidate (or issue) paying for the poll and the opposition. The questions will test both positives and negatives on each of side of the debate—and will do so equally.

In one section of a benchmark poll for a state legislative race between our candidate, Democrat Alan Bates, and his opponent, Republican Jane Hunts, we were looking for what the opposition might use against our candidate as well as how negatives might play against his opponent. Of the questions testing the negatives of Alan Bates, this question came out on top:

Is this a very convincing, somewhat convincing, not very convincing, or not at all convincing reason to vote *against* Alan Bates?

"Alan Bates is opposed to every antitax measure on the ballot this fall. He opposes cutting the state income tax, opposes increasing the deductibility of federal tax, opposes allowing voters the right to decide on all new or increased taxes, and opposes amending the state constitution to require government to return the tax kicker."

This question had a "very convincing" rating of sixteen points and a total "convincing" score (the total of "very" and "somewhat convincing") of fifty-two points. The "not convincing" side weighed in at thirty-seven points. This information put the committee on notice that our candidate needed a good response to any attack regarding taxes. It also gave us some comfort because our candidate, up until that election, had only been a school board member. He had no track record that would lead to these accusations.

Of the six anti-Hunts push questions, this one came out at the bottom:

Is this a very convincing, somewhat convincing, not very convincing, or not at all convincing reason to vote *against* Jane Hunts?

"Jane Hunts has absolutely no government experience. She has never been elected or appointed to any office. In order to effectively represent southern Oregon in Salem, our representative needs the experience Jane Hunts just doesn't have."

This question came in with a total "convincing" score of forty-one (of which only nineteen points were for "very convincing") and with forty-eight points for "not convincing." Hmmm. Better think twice about going after Hunts on experience, or even running our candidate *on* experience.

Our benchmark poll gave us information about what would or would not work for both candidates as positive messaging as well as what would and would not work on attacks.

Getting Data Without a Poll

If your campaign has no money or, more to the point, does not want to spend thousands on a benchmark poll, you can get much of the information a benchmark would give you, for free. Using recent voting history of issue-based campaigns can provide candidates with a clear road map of voter opinion—precinct by precinct. For example, in one general election, Oregon had twenty-five ballot measures before the voters. Among other things, the measures covered issues involving school funding, gay and lesbian rights, mandatory sentencing, campaign finance reform, drug-related property forfeiture, land use, taxes, powers of the state legislature, tobacco settlement funds, baiting traps, background checks for firearm purchases, and linking teacher pay to student performance. Although some of these measures passed (or failed) in every county, that does not mean they passed or failed equally in every precinct within the county.

If you're running a campaign in a state that is not as measure-happy as Oregon, potential campaign issues in your voting area can be ferreted out in other ways: letters to the editor, minutes of city council or county commission meetings, editorials, general news stories, blogs following local articles, and county and city elections. Given that issues pop up in candidate elections, reviewing which issues were at the center of those campaigns can be very helpful.

Recently I worked on a county commissioner campaign in which the candidate had been elected to his conservative city council post on a no-growth platform. Knowing that growth was an issue in my city as well and that the two cities represent opposite ends of the political spectrum, we knew we had an issue that would transcend the county's political

> "When two people agree all the time, one of them is unnecessary."
> **WILLIAM WRIGLEY**

schism: growth and the effects it has on our region. Using a tone of "keeping a little of what makes this area special" in our candidate's last television ad before the election, we took an issue that everyone cared about and coupled it with a pro-environment undertone. This allowed us to go back and lock his drifting base without losing swing voters. The approach proved to be an important move in his close election (figure 8.15).

Be Creative

Many small communities conduct citizen surveys to track residents' concerns and to assess city employees' job performance. This is part of the public record and is available for the asking. You can get similar information, minus the job performance of the governing body, at the local chamber of commerce. The census also has a wealth of information broken down by city, county, region, and state.

Special-interest groups that support your candidate or issue may have recently conducted a poll to track voter support of a particular issue, especially if that issue has been or soon will be placed before the voters. Such polls typically assess support according to voter profile within a region, county, or city.

Benchmark Polls on a Shoestring

If you have no money and are determined to run a benchmark poll, you can do so using volunteers and a professional pollster or a college professor who knows or teaches polling. Depending on the length of the questionnaire, each caller can complete three to five calls per hour.

To pull this off, you must have three things in order. First, draft the questions for the professional who is overseeing the project. I don't care how impartial you think your questions are—they're biased. If you do not have a seasoned pollster reviewing the questions, you will spend a lot of volunteer hours on a poll that may or may not give you accurate results and, in a worst-case scenario, could lead your campaign in the wrong direction.

Second, have plenty of volunteers who excel on the phone. Let's say you want to conduct a benchmark poll with three hundred randomly selected voters. If each caller can poll three people per hour, you need a hundred volunteer hours; that means you need two one-hour shifts of ten phone bankers (twenty volunteers) per night for five nights. That's a lot of volunteers.

Third, obtain (or generate) a random voter list from your county clerk or election office of likely voters; if you do not know how to create a random list, Google it.

A Hybrid Approach

In 2010 I hired the Campaign Solutions Group in Los Angeles to conduct tracking polls; they created a random call list using criteria I specified, and rather than campaign volunteers, the Solutions Group made the calls. Also, for a few cents more per voter contact, they retained each contact's name and correlating response, data we used to augment our voter ID efforts. The bill for these services came in at $590, with a margin of error between 3 percent and 4 percent for each of the two tracking polls; the polling showed our candidate was in a dead heat winning the election with 50.2 percent of the vote, compared to his opponent, with 49.7 percent. After the final vote was counted, the opponent actually had 49.8 percent to our 50.2 percent (we won by 281 votes out of nearly 50,000 cast). This polling approach gave us an exact and accurate percentage of the final vote for a very affordable price.

We mapped the captured IDs, which gave us a quick glimpse of where our support was strong and where it was weak so we could adjust campaign activities accordingly.

Polling for Dollars

If you're working on a state legislative race, a professionally conducted poll can mean money for your campaign. Lobbyists and PACs are reluctant to give money to campaigns that "think" they will win. However, show that you're close to your opponent in a legitimate poll, and checkbooks will open. To spend thousands on a poll in hopes of attracting PAC money is risky and works against common sense. Still, it happens, and if the numbers are good, it can pay off. Polls run by volunteers don't count here.

Professionally conducted polling tends to be expensive. To cut costs, you might consider offering to include other candidates in the poll if their campaigns will contribute to the cost or ask a PAC or state party to help financially by paying the polling firm directly.

Polls can also cost a campaign support and money. Although this will be covered in subsequent chapters on targeting, a professional poll indicating a losing effort will shut all sorts of doors. So if your registration is wildly skewed, resist doing a poll; save your money.

Push Polling

Push polling is a form of negative campaigning and comes to the voter through telemarketing disguised as a legitimate poll. The objective of push polling is to *persuade* voters, *not* to gain information. And since they are only about persuasion, push polls typically do not collect data.

Because many confuse push questions with push polling, it is important to again underscore the difference: As indicated above, benchmark polls ask push questions that reveal the dark side of *both* candidates. Campaigns do this so they know the effectiveness of hitting an opponent or receiving hits from the

> "[Push polls] breed cynicism about politics, and we believe they contribute to declining response rates for polls."
> **MICHAEL TRAUGOTT**, AAPOR

opposition with little-known but truthful information. All campaigns want to know what will work for and against both their campaign and the opposition.

Benchmarks take twenty to thirty minutes, whereas tracking polls are relatively quick, grabbing a snapshot of a moment. Only a very specific voter will invest twenty or thirty minutes in a benchmark; many more will jump in on a tracking poll.

Push polls use the goodwill of tracking polls, which are based on brevity ("If the election were held tomorrow, would you vote for Candidate A or Candidate B?") to persuade unwitting voters. Push polls typically take under five minutes, but unlike their tracking-poll sister, they add a little "something, something" at the end to close the deal.

Here is how Rachel, a blogger on the *Huffington Post*, described a push poll regarding the Obama and McCain 2008 presidential campaign in Ohio:

> When I said that I was voting for Obama, they asked if I would be more or less likely to vote for Obama if I knew that he voted to let convicted child sex offenders out early, voted to allow convicted child sex offenders to live near schools, is for sex education in Kindergarten, voted for some offensive and incredibly graphic abortion procedure, and so on and so on for 5 minutes. This was a really offensive push-poll. They also brought up the statements of Rev. Wright and Michelle Obama.[2]

That is a push poll: It typically shares with the voter something inflammatory and typically skewed about the opposition. The polls call as many voters as humanly possible before getting busted by the media. Because there must be some tangential thread between the question and truth, push polls can tip leaning voters. Both ways.

Push polling is condemned by everyone and yet seemingly is done all the time—or so some think.

In one campaign on which I worked, a Democratic state representative and doctor ran against a local Republican businessman and beloved philanthropist. The Republican was fiscally conservative and socially liberal. Both candidates were identical on every single issue, from sales tax to education. However, the Republican enjoyed a 6 percent registration advantage and was so well known and well liked that he could routinely turn out four hundred people for a 6 a.m. breakfast or three hundred for a Tuesday lunch. Yikes.

Then a friend called and read me the riot act.

Apparently her husband had received (ostensibly) from our campaign a call that was obviously "push polling," she said. After assuring her that it was not us, I asked her on what she had based her allegation. She said her husband was asked whether he would be more or less likely to vote for the Republican if he knew he was blind.

The truth is, our opponent, who had suffered from macular degeneration for most of his life, *was* legally blind. However, I do not believe you can poll for prejudice, because when you try, voters lie. Indeed, there are many examples of campaigns in which polling for prejudice resulted in unreliable data. The so-called Bradley effect in the 1982 California gubernatorial race is one such example, and the appeal to people's prejudice through their love of the Confederate flag in Georgia and South Carolina in the 2000 gubernatorial races is another.[3] Similarly, there was a reason FDR kept his wheelchair from public view.

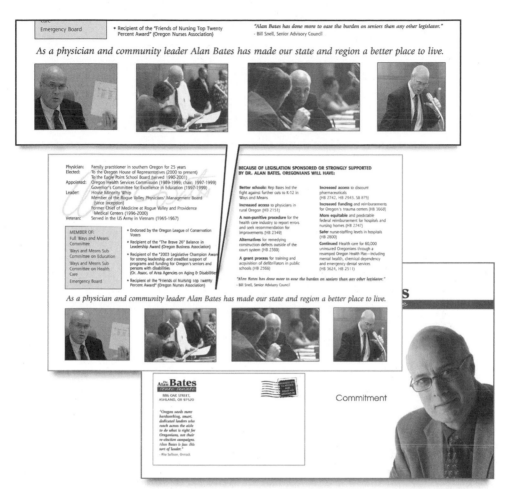

FIGURE 3.1 Example of a Full-Color Brochure That Subtly Addresses Voters' Concerns with the Opponent

In 2004, Democrat Alan Bates ran for a state senate seat recently vacated by a twenty-eight-year Republican veteran; the seat had a six-point Republican registration advantage. His opponent, a highly respected, fabulously wealthy, and generous philanthropist, was legally blind. Once we discovered that the opposing campaign polled for, and was concerned about, his disability, the challenge became how to subtly remind voters of the importance of sight in dealing with the sheer volume of material coming across a legislator's desk. (Design by Brian Freeman, Crystal Castle Graphics)

Indeed, before our benchmark poll, I argued against a question regarding our opponent's vision problems. Besides being shallow, it seemed disingenuous if we allowed a doctor to attack an opponent on a disability; some might even see it as cruel. So, I contended that if we would *never* use it, why ask? Indeed, polling this question could actually inflame the narrow swing vote needed to win.

Some on our team argued that "to ask" was not "to use."

Don't be fooled: If you have a handgun in your pocket while committing a robbery, the jury doesn't care if you never intended to use it. Voters are no different. In small communities, friends share information about telephone polls.

Clearly our opponent was asking this push question on his benchmark poll, and knowing that offered important information to our campaign: They wondered about their candidate's disability. Knowing the opposition was worried or at least curious about voter response to our opponent's macular degeneration was gold. Indeed, service in government is largely about being able to move quickly through unbelievable volumes of material and grasp information for effective communication. How to convey and indirectly remind voters of this without being heavy-handed became the goal (figure 3.1).

Brochure Development

Though the campaign committee will help develop the campaign message and theme, you should have only one or two people work with you or the candidate in writing the brochure. Obviously you want a good writer who has some free time. The initial writing takes only a few hours, but it is almost always followed by many rewrites. These rewrites should return to the committee for approval. Allow enough time: If the committee does not like what it sees, you need time to make the necessary corrections before delivering the material to the printer.

If you write your own campaign brochure, have someone read it critically when you've finished. The emphasis here is on *critically*. We all love our own words, and our friends are often loath to condemn them. You need someone you can trust, someone who has the political savvy to read your work, correct any errors, and make appropriate suggestions.

Brochure Copy

The brochure, walking piece, or voters' pamphlet should be no more than 325 words and should include the following:

Occupational background. Include names of companies or jobs held and actual years worked at each—not "27" but rather 1983–2010, that sort of thing. If the candidate has a laundry list, then forgo the years to save on word count.

Prior government experience. This is where the planning commission and such gets listed—not Little League coach or pink lady at the hospital.

Educational background. Include degrees and the universities or schools and years the candidate attended. If he or she did not get a degree, just list the school with no actual dates and hopefully voters will think a degree was involved.

Military service. If the candidate served in the military, this is important; indicate years and rank. If he or she never served, omit this category.

> "The aim of marketing is to make selling superfluous."
> **PETER DRUCKER**

Community service. This is where the Little League and chamber of commerce stuff goes; if the candidate received special awards or recognition, bullet-point those here as well.

Proven Leadership

Next is a short list of candidate accomplishments that relate to the office sought. For a reelection campaign, list what the candidate and the body on which he or she served accomplished while in office. Bullet-point this stuff. People are going to look at the brochure or walking piece for ten seconds, so be brief and articulate.

Together We Can Do More

The next section will offer bullet points regarding issues that your town or community could be doing to make its corner of the world a better place. For example, dealing with the homeless, upgrading the wastewater treatment plant, placing electric lines underground to prevent future outages, safeguarding the water system by removing dead and dying timber from the watershed, getting sidewalks installed near schools—that sort of thing.

Values We Respect

Depending on word count, the final section will consist of two to four *short* quotes from prominent community leaders. They and not you will say just how great the candidate is. They and not the committee will describe the crumbling school or closed library or dilapidated park system that increased taxes will fix. This is where the voter is reassured. For example, if the candidate is a businessperson, the brochure copy will balance that strength with a quote from a credible person who may be considered anti-business. If the candidate is on the left, get a quote from someone on the right. One caution:

Do not choose people who are extreme; you want to balance a weakness with someone just slightly over the line in the other camp. Think about the candidate's strengths versus the opponent's, and enhance your candidate's strengths at your opponent's expense.

When I ask people for a quote, I also ask if I can edit it down for space. No one says no to that. Most will ask that the campaign generate the quote and run it by the endorser. Make the individual sound believably smart.

Also important to note here is that your endorsements can actually say what you highlighted under "proven leadership" above. So if you want to say the candidate worked the floor of a cannery and everyone went to him for advice, have a former coworker say, "He was always there for us with great advice and he set an example by working hard. He's a born leader" (Sally Smith, Borden Foods supervisor).

And Now a Word from Our Sponsor

When you complete all the above sections and find you still have space for a few words, the candidate can make a special appeal: "It would be an honor to serve our city. I hope I can count on your vote." Then have the candidate's printed signature appear on the brochure or walking piece under this appeal.

Pictures

Before the brochure is laid out, the candidate should visit a professional photographer and search personal files for great family photos. Just remember: Amateurish photos will hurt your campaign. If a professional will not volunteer his or her time, this is a good place to spend

> "Genius is 1 percent inspiration and 99 percent perspiration."
>
> ———————— THOMAS ALVA EDISON

money. If the first sitting does not produce the right photo, ask for a second sitting. Also provide the local papers with a photo (usually different shots but from the same sitting) so they will use your photo rather than one generated by their news team. If you email a good-quality photo, it will be particularly easy for the newspapers to use. After your candidate is elected, continue this practice.

When you are campaigning for an issue-based campaign, photos are often easier to come by, although more time-consuming to gather. For example, if you're working on a school tax base measure, visit the yearbook class at the middle and high school. They save photographs of all age groups and in many activities. For a park program, try the YMCA or the parks department; even city and county offices may have photos, so check there as well. For historic photos of your city or county, try a local historian or historical society. Show through pictures as well as text what passing your measure will accomplish. Many photographers will let you use their photos in issue-based campaigns as long as their name appears with the photo in a credit line. Don't forget to look online for stock photos to purchase.

Use pictures as a way to break up the text and give the brochure a substantive feel. Most candidate brochures contain at least one picture of the candidate. This is important to increase name and face recognition. With that recognition comes familiarity, which is psychologically important for the voter. The candidate begins to feel like a friend and a celebrity all at once. You may also carefully select other photos to create an image of who this person is. There may be pictures of the candidate at work, with the family, at play (e.g., batting in a softball game or fly-fishing), with seniors, or at a preschool, a public school, a hospital, or a park. Include whatever might both positively connect the candidate with his or her lifestyle and characterize what is important in the community.

Depending on your budget and the size of your brochure, you may just stop with the picture of the candidate. But if you have more resources, be sure the pictures add to or underscore the story the campaign wants to tell. Put thought into selecting pictures. Try to show the diversity of your community in the photos: people of all ages and ethnic groups, working class and professionals, men and women. Whether the campaign is doing a studio shot or one of the candidate on the stump, be sure to bring extra clothes for different settings. Brochures that show a candidate at a school, at a senior center, in a park, with family, or whatever ostensibly intend to show the individual in his or her everyday life over a period of time; but if the candidate is wearing the same clothes in each shot, the result appears contrived and the opportunity to evoke specific emotions is lost.

Avoid photos that picture the candidate standing or sitting coincidentally near a celebrity. Novice campaigners are eager to show they hobnob with the elite and will select pictures that show themselves in the general proximity of a celebrity—elected or otherwise. If you want to use a photo of your candidate with the governor, be sure it is a photo of your candidate with the governor. One brochure I saw had the candidate looking around a plant that was situated behind the governor, who was being photographed with other people. This is interpreted by the voters for just what it is.

Some candidates when being photographed with a "name" lean toward or tilt their head toward the celebrity ("I'm with him"). This pose suggests weakness on the part of your candidate and may have a subtle but negative influence on the voters.

Photo by Christopher Briscoe

Photo by Cathy Shaw

Photo by Christopher Briscoe

Photo by Christopher Briscoe

FIGURE 3.2A
Examples of Candidate
Photos That Work Well
in Brochures

Photo by Marietta Gilmour

FIGURE 3.2B
Examples of Photos
That Work Well in an
Issue-Based Brochure

When selecting photos for
issue-based campaigns, look
for ones with movement and
that elicit emotion. The photos
to the right were used for
funding youth sports programs,
water conservation, and state
funding for seniors and public
schools. The bottom right had
the caption, "What future do
we offer them?"

Photo by Cathy Shaw

Photo by Marla Cates

Photo by Cathy Shaw

Urge the photographer to take some pictures of the candidate outside. Change the background, walk toward the camera, sit on a bike and lean on the handlebars. (This particular pose, with or without the bike in it, makes a great shot.) Arrange for people to meet you and the photographer for a few shots that can be taken outside, in front of businesses, with the backdrop of trees or historic buildings (figures 3.2A and 3.2B).

Eager to show a candidate with all the typical campaign requisites, campaigns will typically use pictures of their candidate at a senior center, in front of a police car, shaking hands with a business leader in front of a factory, reading to children, and on the front lawn with the family. But when a majority of campaign brochures include the same array, your literature will fade into the background. Make an effort to use the medium effectively, and bring spontaneity and motion into your brochure photos. Capture your candidate in a quiet moment reading over papers, through a window at night burning the midnight oil, conferring with a colleague while leaning over a desk, and playing with the family from last summer's vacation.

When selecting pictures for either a candidate or issue-based campaign, be sure to look at the whole picture, not just the subject of the picture. In the Campaign for the Carnegie, a local library campaign for capital improvements, I selected an interior library photo with a young patron reading in a crowded, cluttered

"Out of intense complexities, intense simplicities emerge."
WINSTON CHURCHILL

room to demonstrate the dismal state of our library. However, I did not notice that directly behind the subject was a display rack with *Mad* magazines. Luckily, the librarians on the committee caught my error.

Campaign Slogans

Years ago, slogans were printed next to a candidate's name on the ballot. At that time, with media playing a lesser role in politics, having a catchy slogan was critical for a win on Election Day. Slogans can still be very effective if given proper thought by the campaign committee. Do not invent a slogan just to have one. Use your campaign message and design a slogan that underscores and reinforces it. Sit with your committee, list the strengths of your candidate or measure, and brainstorm possibilities. Once you think you have one, brainstorm on all the ways it could be used against you or hurt your cause. Work through this process until you come up with the right combination.

The slogan is a simple statement about why you should be elected or why the voters should vote for your issue. It should also imply why *not* to vote for your opponent or what a no vote may lead to in an issue-based campaign. Your slogan must not depart from your campaign message, and it should evoke a gut emotion. One very effective slogan used in an issue-based campaign in California simply said, "Share the Water." Who can argue with the idea of sharing? It is a friendly thought that is encouraged throughout our lives. It also implies that the water is not being shared.

I was on a campaign that used the slogan "Now Let's Choose Leadership." I was concerned that this slogan would sound patronizing. I was also concerned that those who previously voted for the incumbent, who enjoyed a six-point registration advantage, would feel they were being scolded. Furthermore, this slogan tended to reinforce the perception that our candidate was arrogant and that the campaign was about the candidate, not the community.

A Democrat running against an incumbent for the Second Congressional District in Oregon used another problematic slogan. Here's the backstory: For nearly four decades Republicans have been elected to Oregon's Second Congressional District, by at least a thirty-point margin. However, in this particular election, the incumbent, Wes Cooley, had committed so many campaign violations and was misbehaving both in public and in Congress in such a way that it looked as though this Democrat might have a chance.

The Democrat invited me and some other local people to talk strategy in our part of the district, and he also took that opportunity to show us his brochure. Although it was a handsome brochure, it featured a poorly conceived slogan: "It's time we had a Congressman we can be proud of." Although I understood that the brochure referred to the incumbent, who was in core meltdown, it overlooked the fact that for more than ten years, Second District Oregonians had voted in huge numbers for a congressman they were proud of. You can't hope to attract voters to your side of the street by insulting them.

Most important, the slogans in both of these examples imply that the campaign is about the candidate. Effective slogans stem from messages that are about the voters and their communities, not the candidate or, as in these two examples, the incumbent.

In 2008 a police officer of a neighboring community living in Ashland, Oregon, wanted to run for city council. He had run and narrowly lost in 2006 after the Green Party attacked his occupation and Republican registration. (In Ashland, there's a pronounced anti-law-enforcement sentiment, and better than eight in ten voters cast a Democratic ballot.)

With the previous loss under his belt, he tried again in the 2008 election cycle. To remove party bias, he changed his registration to nonaffiliated. His opponent in the nonpartisan race was both a green Democrat and an incumbent with loyal supporters. However, she also had detractors. She was publicly accused of micromanaging city departments and grinding council action to a crawl. Some believed she was responsible for elevating the dysfunctional city government to national attention when a therapist was hired and received $37,000 in tax dollars to help the council work together more productively.[4] With nearly every Ashland voter supporting Barack Obama, we looked for a way to piggyback on those coattails without being obvious. To do so, we used the same font as Obama (Gothic), took an Obama lawn sign to the graphic designer to match the colors exactly, and used the slogan "Change Starts Here." Our council candidate won by eighteen points.

For a local restaurant tax to fund wastewater treatment plant upgrades and open-space land acquisition, our opposition used the slogan "Don't Swallow the Meals Tax." This is a clever slogan because it works on different levels: People who swallow something are duped, and then, of course, the tax was on food.

In one open-space campaign, we used the slogan "Parks: Now and Forever." People who opposed the measure saw our slogan and used their own modification: "Parks: *Pay* Now and Forever." A very clever counter-slogan. We should have chosen ours more carefully.

In 1997 a group of Oregonians put together an initiative to overturn a previously voter-approved ballot measure allowing physician-assisted suicide. The new initiative was well financed, with billboards and lawn signs everywhere. In the upper right-hand corner of the signs, they had the previous measure's number (16) in a circle with a line through it. Next to that was the slogan "Fatally Flawed" and below the slogan was "Yes on 51." While this was clearly a professional campaign, they mistakenly used a very ambiguous approach. Basically they meant to state that the previously passed ballot initiative (Measure 16, for physician-assisted suicide) was "fatally flawed" and that a yes vote on *this* measure (51) would overturn that one. However, the way the sign was laid out, it appeared that Measure 51, not 16, was "fatally flawed."

During the campaign, a campaign organizer called me to help defeat the referendum. I suggested that the campaign did not need any help; it needed only to adopt the same slogan that the opposition had used: "Fatally Flawed." Because voters naturally associate a negative slogan with a negative vote, every "Yes on 51" lawn sign, billboard, and commercial would become a "No on 51" pitch. Whether the team members took my advice or came to it themselves, the "No on 51" campaign co-opted the same slogan of the "Yes on 51" campaign, and with very little money, the referendum was defeated at the polls—only this time instead of losing by one point, the referendum lost by twenty. Further, because the "no" campaign co-opted the slogan of the "yes" campaign, those supporting the referendum had to create a new slogan, reprint field and lawn signs, and replace all installed billboards and field signs with the new look. Changing the look of a campaign in the middle of a cycle is a death knell.

DON'T SWALLOW THE MEALS TAX

[VOTE NO ON 15-1]

Measure 15-1, Ashland's proposed meals tax, is a regressive tax because:

15-1 IS NOT A TOURIST TAX. THE BURDEN OF THE TAX WILL BE PAID BY YOU, THE ASHLAND CONSUMER.

FOOD IS A BASIC NECESSITY. THIS TAX WILL SEVERELY IMPACT STUDENTS, THE ELDERLY, THE POOR, AND OTHERS ON A FIXED INCOME.

IT IS NOT A LUXURY TAX. BECAUSE OF TODAY'S BUSY SCHEDULES, AN AVERAGE OF 48¢ OF EVERY FOOD DOLLAR IS SPENT ON PREPARED MEALS OUTSIDE THE HOME.

IT WILL AUTHORIZE INCREASES UP TO 5% WITHOUT FURTHER VOTE FROM THE PUBLIC.

IT IS CONFUSING, DIFFICULT TO MANAGE, AND COSTLY TO IMPLEMENT.

IT IS SHORTSIGHTED. IF THE STATE LEGISLATURE IMPOSES A STATEWIDE SALES TAX IT COULD NEGATE ANY LOCAL SALES TAXES.

IT WILL PUT ASHLAND ON THE MAP AS THE ONLY CITY IN AMERICA TO IMPOSE A MEALS TAX WITHOUT FIRST HAVING AN OVERALL SALES TAX IN PLACE.

BROCHURE DESIGN BY ERIC BRADFORD WARREN

ADD a 5% TAX TO YOUR CHECK

[Ashland Meaure 15-1]

Back   *Front*

FIGURE 3.3 "Don't Swallow the Meals Tax" Brochure

Brochure layout: two-panel, front and back, pictured above. Note that the front and top back of the brochure are visually striking, but the lower, dense, reversed type is hard to read. Also note that this brochure went to press with a typo on the front panel. This is not the responsibility of the graphic designer but rather the campaign team. Avoid errors like this by having a number of people proofread the text. (Design by Eric Bradford Warren)

As a general rule, you don't want a negative slogan or idea associated with a yes vote ("Fatally Flawed"). It's preferable to have a negative slogan, such as in the meals tax example given above, associated with a no vote and a positive slogan ("Share the Water") associated with a yes vote on a ballot measure or proposition. In the campaign to overturn the measure allowing physician-assisted suicide, the slogan "Yes on 51" campaign expected too much of the voter.

During my first run for mayor, I used the slogan "Building a Better Community." I chose this slogan because of citywide concerns about growth and development. I wanted a positive slogan that suggested to the voters that more was not necessarily better and that it was "community" that needed to be built, not indiscriminate construction.

People love to throw exclamation points into campaign literature and especially slogans. Avoid this. In 2008 a candidate committee and I came to the slogan "It's about integrity." We landed on this because her opponent, a local realtor, was using his position in the legislature to pass legislation to protect his industry and because of reversals of his votes once industries got to him. For example, he changed his mind on a vote to impose a cigarette tax to fund children's health insurance, after which his campaign was rewarded with contributions from the tobacco industry. At some point, the period in the slogan turned into an exclamation point: "It's about integrity!" The first version implies, in a matter-of-fact way, that the opponent is bought and sold, that our candidate had integrity, and that the community should expect nothing less than integrity from elected officials. Once the exclamation point was added, the slogan lost all meaning.

And while we're here, if you love to use exclamation points, remove them from every single little thing you do in a campaign, especially the use of multiple exclamation points, which make the writer appear goofy at best and illiterate at worse. Once the campaign is over, you can go back to using them as you please. The following slogans are examples I have pulled from brochures in my files:

"It's about people, not politics."
"Experience * Leadership * Commitment"
"The best . . . for the best"
"A voice that will be heard"
"A Strong Voice for [Place]"
"With his experience . . . It makes sense."
"Unbought and unbossed"
"Because nothing counts like results"
"Straightforward, Fair, Effective"

"Tough, committed, fighting for us"
"It's time to rotate the crops."
"A leader who makes a difference"
"At a time when experience and dedication are needed most"
"Taking care of [Place]"
"Experience money can't buy"
"This is about governing . . . and I've done it."
"People over politics"
"The Change Will Do Us Good."
"It's Time for a Change."
"Change We Can Believe In."
"Change starts here."

For more ideas, go to www.presidentsusa.net/campaignslogans.html or http://en.wikipedia.org/wiki/Political_slogan.

Logo

I regularly use the lawn sign image as the logo on my brochures, Web banner, Facebook page, and ads. I think it adds continuity to a campaign, conveying a subtle message that it is well organized and connected. If your race is a difficult one, such as a write-in, a logo can be more important. Write-ins for candidates are covered in Chapter 9.

A logo is like a trademark. It can simply be how the candidate's name is written, or for an issue-based campaign, it can be an image. Figures 3.4, 3.5, and 3.6 present some very effective logos. Obviously, if you have a name like that of Shayne Maxwell, a candidate for the Oregon legislature, you want to take advantage of it in your logo: "Maxwell for the House." In the Maxwell for the House race, we continually had people say "good to the last drop" after hearing her name. It did not hurt that she ran in an area whose residents were predominantly seniors—and undoubtedly still bought their coffee in a Maxwell House can with the slogan "good to the last drop" across the top. Spend some time thinking about the name of the candidate, and come up with creative ways to link the name with the office being sought, like Audie Bock, who used a play on her name in a reelection campaign: "Bock By Popular Demand."

Layout

The layout of a brochure depends on its size, how much you want to say, and the quality and quantity of photos. Unless you know the business professionally, you will need the help of a layout artist or graphic designer. Do not

FIGURE 3.4 "Maxwell for the House" Walking Piece

Example of a logo using the candidate's name to piggyback onto a positive corporate slogan. We used this walking piece to get newspaper endorsements to homes in the district; the back had photos, a bio, and individual endorsements. (Design by Crystal Castle Graphics)

make the mistake of trying to save a hundred bucks by doing this yourself or by using someone just because he or she has a desktop publishing program.

A good way to get ideas on layout is to go over past political campaign brochures. Often you can find the look you want and then emulate that look. Some examples of different types of brochures are presented later in this section, but your best resource will be the politically experienced graphic designer or layout artist.

COMMITTEE FOR THE CARNEGIE

FIGURE 3.5 Example of a Logo for a Campaign to Restore and Expand Ashland's Carnegie Library

The logo builds one idea on top of another. (Design by Crystal Castle Graphics)

FIGURE 3.6 Example of a Logo Using Lettering That Appeals to the American Love of Baseball

(Design by Eric Bradford Warren)

Although many experienced campaigners believe that brochure copy should be kept to a minimum, there is the possibility of offending the astute voter with an empty brochure. The challenge is to arrange your 325 words without overwhelming the voter. As stated above: Minimize the impact of the text by placing it in boxes and using bullet points for a candidate's qualifications and experience.

Avoid long narratives. In an effort to establish credibility, candidates will drag out every accomplishment since high school and argue vociferously that it's all essential. In my first run for mayor, my opponent had his picture taken in front of the local high school with the caption "When he graduated, he never dreamed he would one day be mayor of Ashland." Candidates love to underscore their longevity in a city, county, state, or region: "born and raised." Voters put very little into presumptive entitlement to an office based on birthright. Similarly, voters care less about experience than you'd imagine. At some point, a candidate and the team must decide between including everything, with nothing read by the voter, and including a partial list of accomplishments—a list that is read by most. Remember, if George Donner had left either the organ or wood cookstove behind, his family might have made it over the Sierra Nevada.

If you want people to read your literature, don't waste their time. A good rule of thumb is that your pictures and graphics should consume as much space as, or slightly more than, the text. No one, not even the most sophisticated voter, will read unappealing brochures. Brochures are advertisements, so they must catch the eye and create a feeling or positive reaction in seconds.

> "We cannot insure success, but we can deserve it."
> **JOHN ADAMS**

Brochures can easily be created on a tight budget. A brochure may be laid out three up on a single sheet of paper so that each sheet yields three brochures. Although each sheet of paper must be cut into thirds, the cost of cutting is less than the cost of folding. Consider using a light card stock for a three-up brochure. By using card stock, you have the advantage of being able to shove the brochure into doorjambs. Go to a print shop, and check out colors and sizes. Clearly, in this small format, text will dominate. However, pictures add nothing to the cost and provide an effective visual relief, so they remain important, no matter the final brochure size.

Consider using 8½-by-14-inch paper for a bifold or single-fold brochure. This size lends itself to easy layout and visual impact, and it breathes. As paper size increases, layout becomes easier, but paper costs increase. Obviously, the size of paper you use determines the number of pictures you can include in your brochure, but your word count should not exceed 325. Once settled

FIGURE 3.7 "The County Has Changed" Brochure

Example of a bifold brochure on 8½-by-14-inch paper. Larger pictures with less text would make a better presentation. Also, the front images work against each other here.

on pictures and content, create a mock-up of the brochure and run it by your campaign committee for final approval.

Figures 3.7 and 3.8 are examples of bifold brochures that were used for local money measures: one for a new county tax base and the other for extracurricular programs for Ashland schools; both are also examples of what to avoid in a brochure. The county tax base brochure had a couple of fundamental problems that should have been corrected (figure 3.7). First,

Questions & Answers

WHAT IS THE CHILDREN'S CULTURAL & RECREATIONAL TAX LEVY ~15-3?
The city charter allows the Parks & Recreation Department to propose a two-year serial levy that would fund recreational and cultural activities usually provided by the school district. If approved by the voters, the city would collect the money and contract with the school district to provide the activities. The two year levy will restore funds to the Ashland School District budget to accomplish the return of some of the programs now designated for cuts. This is designed to provide interim financing only.

IF THE LEVY PASSES, WILL MY PROPERTY TAXES GO UP?
No. They will still continue downward, as mandated by Measure 5, but just not as much. Each of the next two years, they will drop by $1.53 per thousand, instead of $2.50 per thousand.

WHY HASN'T THE SCHOOL DISTRICT PLANNED AHEAD AND SET ASIDE FUNDS IN ANTICIPATION OF THESE CUTS?
The school district made the decision to use all monies available to continue the very programs we are now wanting to fund with the tax levy.

WILL THE LEVY SOLVE ALL OF OUR FUNDING PROBLEMS FOR THE SCHOOLS?
No. With a 2.9 million dollar shortfall this $800,000 is truly a temporary measure to bring back or keep in place a portion of the essentials, until the state comes up with replacement revenue that would make up the lost funding for the school district.

WHY ARE WE DOING THIS? ISN'T THE STATE SUPPOSED TO HANDLE IT?
The state failed to resolve the school funding crisis brought on by Measure 5. Ashlanders said, "Let's raise our own money and keep it in Ashland so we can save these programs and also regain some local control."

FUNNELING MONEY FOR EDUCATION THROUGH CITY GOVERNMENT SOUNDS UNUSUAL — IS THIS LEGAL?
Yes. Legislative Counsel has researched and confirmed it.

Questions & Answers

HOW WERE THE PROGRAMS TO BE REINSTATED SELECTED?
The list represents the best ideas of the whole community. It was developed by parents of Ashland students, the school board, the city Parks and Recreation Commission, the Booster Club, Ashland Community Coalition, city government officials and the Ashland Schools Foundation. The list was endorsed by school principals.

YOU HEAR A LOT ABOUT "GETTING BACK TO BASICS" AND "CUTTING FRILLS" IN EDUCATION — ISN'T THIS FUNDING DROP A GOOD STEP IN THAT DIRECTION?
No. We are trying to keep the basics: this levy directly protects co-curricular activities that public schools throughout the United States have offered for most of the 20th century: just check your own high school yearbook.

WILL CITY RESIDENTS END UP FOOTING THE BILL FOR THE 20% OF ASHLAND STUDENTS WHO LIVE IN THE COUNTY?
County students will have to pay to participate in these "co-curricular" programs.

WHY DOES IT SEEM LIKE SO MUCH IS GOING TO THE HIGH SCHOOL AND NOT MIDDLE OR ELEMENTARY SCHOOLS?
Remember this is a stop gap measure. If the students now attending high school do not have these programs, we jeopardize their opportunities for college entrance or securing skilled labor jobs. Hopefully, as funding becomes available, many of our excellent elementary and middle school programs will be reinstated.

WHAT HAPPENS IF THE PROPOSED STATE SALES TAX FOR SCHOOLS DOES PASS THIS FALL?
It will not be in time to save the cut programs for the 1993/94, 1994/95 school years. If broader funding sources become adequate again to fund the programs, this levy can be eliminated.

Authorized by United Ashland Committee, Linda and Chuck Butler, Treasurers, P.O. Box 1145, Ashland, OR 97520.

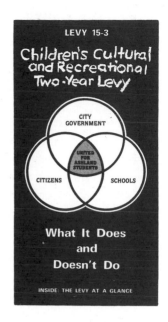

LEVY 15-3

Children's Cultural and Recreational Two-Year Levy

CITY GOVERNMENT — UNITED FOR ASHLAND STUDENTS — CITIZENS — SCHOOLS

What It Does and Doesn't Do

INSIDE: THE LEVY AT A GLANCE

RECREATIONAL AND CULTURAL PROGRAMS AFFECTED BY LEVY	WHAT LEVY DIRECTLY PAYS FOR	PROGRAMS BROUGHT BACK BECAUSE OF MONEY FREED UP BY LEVY	PROGRAMS CUT IF LEVY FAILS	PROGRAMS PARTIALLY FUNDED IF LEVY FAILS	NON SCHOOL RELATED PROGRAMS NEEDED TO COMPLY WITH STATE LAW	AFFECTS HIGH SCHOOL	AFFECTS MIDDLE SCHOOL	AFFECTS ELEMENTARY SCHOOLS	NUMBER OF STUDENTS AFFECTED
RESIDENT OUTDOOR SCHOOL (ROS)	•		•			•	•		280
LIBRARIES (½ of Budgeted Amount)	•			•		•	•	•	3,431
CO-CURRICULUM:									
SPEECH & DEBATE	•		•			•			
DECA (Marketing)	•		•			•			
FBLA (Business)	•		•			•			
VICA (Industrial)	•		•			•			400
YEARBOOK	•		•			•	•		
NEWSPAPER	•		•			•	•		
DRAMA	•		•			•	•		
K-12 MUSIC PERFORMANCES	•		•						
ORCHESTRA						•	•	•	
BANDS						•	•	•	700
CHOIR						•		•	
ATHLETICS:									
SOCCER	•		•			•			
CROSS-COUNTRY	•		•			•			
FOOTBALL	•			•		•	•		
VOLLEYBALL	•			•		•	•		
SWIMMING	•			•		•			
WRESTLING	•			•		•	•		
BASKETBALL	•			•		•	•		650
GOLF	•		•			•			
TRACK	•			•		•	•		
SOFTBALL	•			•		•			
BASEBALL	•			•		•			
TENNIS	•			•		•			
INTRAMURALS	•		•			•		•	
STUDENT AT RISK PROGRAMS:									
SUBSTANCE ABUSE COUNSELOR		•	•			•	•	•	
CHILD DEVELOPMENT SPECIALIST		•	•					•	860
YOUTH AT RISK SERVICES		•	•			•	•		
FOREIGN LANGUAGE		•		•		•			670
TEEN CENTER	N/A	N/A	N/A	N/A	•				
COMMUNITY CENTER ACTIVITIES	N/A	N/A	N/A	N/A	•				

FIGURE 3.8 "Youth Activities Levy" Brochure

Example of a bifold brochure. Although this was a very complicated serial levy presented to the Ashland voters, we made matters worse with this brochure. The levy was intended to bring back extracurricular and co-curricular activities that had been cut by a statewide property tax limitation measure. Our idea was to let people know exactly what it would bring back. It was too much information, presented too sterilely. (Design by Brian Freeman, Crystal Castle Graphics) the pictures were too small in relation to the text inside the brochure. A greater effort to reduce the amount of text and tell the story more through pictures would have strengthened the piece. Second, the front of the brochure features two photos (also too small) that should have been selected more carefully. While they were intended to show that government has dramatically changed since the approval of the last tax base, they actually tell another story. The historical photo evokes more emotion and reflects back to a simpler, less chaotic time. The current photo, of an ugly, new building, suggests that we would be better off not encouraging that kind of architecture with our tax dollars.

The other example of a bifold 8½-by-14-inch brochure was one we used for the Children's Cultural and Recreational Two-Year Levy (figure 3.8). This may be the worst brochure I have ever been associated with and breaks just about every rule I outline in this chapter. In our defense, it was a complicated proposal that I had thought up just weeks before it was placed in front of the voters. It didn't help that only two members of the campaign committee had any campaign experience or that the group had a fundamental breakdown about which voters the campaign should talk to and which ones should be ignored. The measure failed by just a few hundred votes.

> "It's about the right message to the right people at the right time."
>
> — **ELAINE FRANKLIN**

Less than a year later, we came back to the voters with the Youth Activity Levy, but used a single-fold 8½-by-14-inch brochure (figure 3.9). In both brochures, we asked for the same amount of money and sold the same thing: opportunity. But the way the message was delivered in the single-fold brochure is more compelling. Ironically, the second brochure is less clear about *where* the money would be spent. This is great information to have: Most voters don't want to be a curriculum committee for a school district at the ballot box. Their preference is to know where the money would be spent (bricks versus programs), with technical decisions made through the elected school board, school administration, and a citizens budget committee.

Brochures designed for mailing can be reconfigured for a walking piece. One will reinforce the other, and the two can be done at the same time by your graphic designer (figures 3.10 and 3.11).

Voters' Pamphlet

See the above "Brochure Copy" section for detail on what to include in a voters' pamphlet.

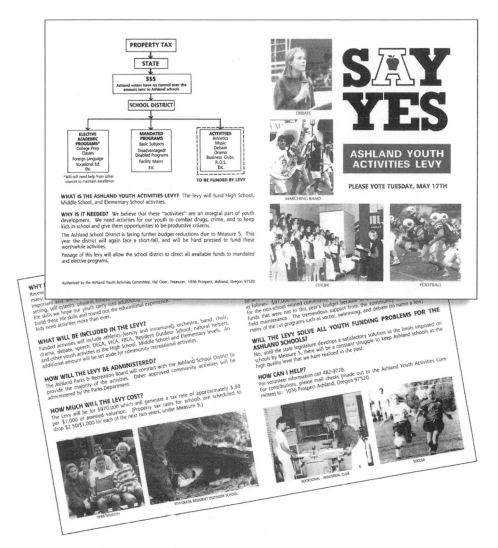

FIGURE 3.9 "Youth Activities Levy" Brochure, Take 2

Example of a single-fold brochure on 8½-by-14-inch paper. After the failure of the first Youth Activities Levy, this brochure was designed to speak more to emotion and less to nuts and bolts. It makes great use of pictures and clearly relays the message: opportunity. (Design by Brian Freeman, Crystal Castle Graphics)

Although much of the voters' pamphlet statement may be dictated by election offices, portions that are not dictated allow for highlighting, italicizing, underlining, and such. Here are ten dos and don'ts to consider when accenting your portion of the voters' pamphlet.

FIGURE 3.10 Front of Full-Color Brochure to Elect Dr. Alan Bates, State Representative

Because the candidate was an unkown, we wanted to push people to open the brochure, so the front is intentionally ambiguous. People did just as we hoped. Voters tested on the layout said, "Who's the candidate?" while flipping it open. (Design by Crystal Castle Graphics)

1. Use a professional photo of the candidate and face it toward his or her written submission to the pamphlet. In Oregon, the criteria are the same for a primary and a general election voters' pamphlet. Candidates have the option of including a photo, which has to be a certain size, cannot be more than four years old, and cannot have any identifying props, such as a stethoscope around a physician's neck or Rotary pin on the lapel. This is where you will use your candidate's best "mug shot."

FIGURE 3.11 Full-Color Walking Piece for Alan Bates

We wanted this piece to reinforce the brochure (figure 3.10) which was mailed during the primary campaign. (Design by Crystal Castle Graphics)

Photos of poor quality get worse when put in the voters' pamphlet, so pay attention to this detail.

2. Let others do your bidding through testimonials, and put their **names** in boldface, not the testimonial. A common practice is to boldface what someone says about a candidate rather than the endorser's name.

Do not make this mistake. When entire lines are boldface in a small area, they will make anything in between the boldface area seemingly disappear into the page. You do not want endorsers' names to disappear. If voters do not know a candidate, they will look for prominent names; make these names easy to find.

3. Boldface headings. Voters will often skim a pamphlet, so boldface what you want them to see. The ten-second rule of direct mail applies here as well. Do not randomly make words boldface in the **middle** of a sentence or a bullet point.

4. Avoid using all caps. An exception may be headings; otherwise it looks FRANTIC and unsophisticated when words are capped in the middle of sentences. Similarly, do not use exclamation points.

5. Do not use narratives. No one cares where you were born and raised or what you were thinking when you moved to your community. Keep the pamphlet crisp with bullet points and breathing space between lines. Break things up.

6. Cite accomplishments. If your candidate has held office and the community is a better place because of legislation he or she designed, highlight those accomplishments. When listing legislation, be sure to place bill numbers next to the claim; this gives it authenticity.

7. Place your website address at the bottom, and place your voters' pamphlet statement on your Web page.

8. Use the available space wisely. Do not bunch everything at the top, leaving white space at the bottom. Lay out your submission so it fits comfortably in the available space. Rather than creating distance between lines using the return key on your keyboard, instead go to the "Format" tab in Word and then insert spacing between lines using "Paragraph."

9. Do not use the voters' pamphlet to attack your opponent. Stay on the sunny side.

10. Don't exaggerate; don't lie. Candidates like to beef up their résumé when running for office and although he or she might get away with that in direct mail or in advertising, listing false information in a voters' pamphlet is a felony. Nevertheless, there are ways to get the most out of what you have. For example, you attended Harvard as an undergraduate but dropped out before receiving a degree. Later you were accepted into graduate school at Stanford University, solely on the basis of your Graduate Record Examination scores, and there you received a master's degree in communications. Under "education," you would list "Harvard, undergraduate; Stanford, master's in communication." While

voters may assume you received an undergraduate degree at Harvard, you never actually say one way or another. If you completed only a couple of years of undergraduate work at a college or university before heading out into the real world, you would simply list the institution without referring to any degree or year of graduation. If you list more than one without a degree notation after any of them, voters will know you attended but never graduated.

Primary Voters' Pamphlet

Remember, your objective in the primary is to lock your base. Given that the voters' pamphlet goes to every registered voter and is referred to by most, you need to be in it, whether you have an opponent or not. While your text should keep partisan material to a minimum, those whose names are included in testimonials may be closely aligned with your party. Each testimonial should bring voters on board, from both the name and the text. Here, less is more. On one issue-based cam-

> "Little things can make as much difference as big things."
> **MALCOLM GLADWELL**

paign in 2006, there was a vote to change the Ashland city charter to a weak-mayor form of government. Initially I thought about filling every square inch of the voters' pamphlet just with names in opposition, but ultimately decided that six names were stronger than a long list of hundreds, especially since the six were a former congressman; a sitting state senator; a sitting state representative; a current county commissioner; a former well-known and well-liked radio personality who was also a former county commissioner; and finally, a former mayor of Ashland. The voters' pamphlet was the entirety of the campaign opposing this shift of power. We turned it away by 28 percent.

General Election Voters' Pamphlet

A statement for the general election voters' pamphlet will look a lot like the one for the primary, except for the candidate statement or testimonial section. For the general election, you are looking for names and statements that will give voters in the other party permission to jump ship on party and split their ticket. However, you must also speak to those within your party, so look for balance in the big names you use.

Figure 3.12 is an example of a candidate statement used in an Oregon voters' pamphlet.

OCCUPATION: Family physician for 24 years in the Rogue Valley; Oregon State Representative 2001 to present.

OCCUPATIONAL BACKGROUND: Former Chief of Medicine at Rogue Valley and Providence Medical Centers; Director of Valley Family Practice.

EDUCATIONAL BACKGROUND: D.O., 1977; College of Osteopathic Medicine, Kansas City, Missouri. B.A., 1969; Central Washington State University.

PRIOR GOVERNMENT EXPERIENCE: Eagle Point School Board, 1990–2001; Governor's Committee for Excellence in Education, Member (1997–1999); Oregon Health Services Commission (1989–1999, chair: 1997–1999).

MILITARY SERVICE: US Army (1965–1967); Served in Vietnam.

What others say:

The Oregon Business Association ranked Representative Alan Bates among the top ten legislators in Oregon: courageous, smart, thoughtful.

The Oregon League of Conservation Voters gave Rep. Bates an 82% pro-environment rating.

The Oregon Education Association rated Dr. Bates in the 90th percentile for his advocacy of public education.

"As a freshman legislator, he shined as he forged consensus legislation ensuring a healthy and competitive workers' compensation market in Oregon. It was Dr. Bates who kept the interests of the insured and the small businesses first."

—Coalition for Economic Security for Oregon
(Small Business Alert, August 2001)

Because of legislation sponsored or strongly supported by Dr. Alan Bates Oregonians will have:

- increased access to higher education (HB 2521)
- a patient bill of rights (HB 3040)
- reduced prescriptions costs for seniors (HB 3300 & SB 819)
- improved roads and highways (comprehensive transportation package)
- government made more accountable through annual audits (HB 3980)
- a cleaner and safer environment (mercury reduction legislation)

"Representative Alan Bates was one of the most effective and respected freshman legislators in Salem this last session. His success was due to hard work, determination, and his ability and willingness to work with both sides of the aisle.

"Alan consistently placed consensus over conflict, compromise over partisanship, and communities over special interest.

"He deserves our support."

Governor John Kitzhaber, MD

FIGURE 3.12 Example of Voters' Pamphlet Candidate Statement

The brochure is the centerpiece of the down-ballot campaign and should include enough text to inform the voters but not so much that it overwhelms the recipient at first glance. Use photos to evoke emotion and reinforce the text; ones that alone, without text, could tell your story. And never lose sight that the brochure reflects on the campaign in more ways than words and photos: use paper that feels good to the touch and a layout design that is both inviting and compelling.

4

Digital and Social Media

By Sarah Golden

IN THIS CHAPTER
- Understanding Demographics: Who Uses Social Media?
- Ten Tips for Building a Digital Footprint for an Election
- The Minor Leagues: Social Media Essentials
- The Major Leagues: Data-Driven Campaigning
- Tech Trends in Elections

THE DIGITAL AGE IS TRANSFORMING THE WAY WE CONSUME INFORMATION. The days of waiting for a newspaper to land on your front step to find out what's happening in the world are behind us—and with that, the rules of communication have changed. A recent Pew poll revealed that half of online users now get their news from digital devices—more than either radio or newspapers. The diversification of news platforms has made the audience's information-gathering systems less predictable. This creates both a challenge and a great opportunity for campaigns. A well-executed digital campaign provides an unprecedented tool for campaign communication, much of it affordably priced. And candidate and issue-based campaigns are eager to leverage digital and social media as effectively as possible.

A digital campaign entails many considerations—more than can be addressed in a single chapter. Though the tools have changed, the rules of campaigning have stayed the same: You are trying to communicate with people about the candidate or the issue by using a particular message. But the digital world gives you more flexibility to be creative and innovative and has potential for better precision and more thoughtful content. Additionally, the instant nature of social media, combined with the large number of people engaging, means that the impact of a well-run social media presence is priceless. Social media opens up a world of supporters advocating on your behalf—something more powerful, genuine, and personal than more traditional campaign advertising.

This chapter provides a crash course to help you understand the basics of digital campaigning. Some things are mandatory: Facebook, Twitter, YouTube, and a website. These represent the bare minimum in digital campaigning and can be found under the "Minor League" section of this chapter. Should your candidate win the election, these platforms also provide an avenue of continued communication with constituents. They can also provide a solid foundation to begin a reelection campaign.

In the 2012 general election, we saw new depths of what can be achieved with digital media. President Barack Obama's digital campaign illuminated what is possible, foreshadowing the extent these platforms will be used in election campaigning. Though down-ballot campaigns won't have the necessary resources to run the type of tech effort the Obama campaign executed in 2012, knowing about the tools available is important. At the speed the digital world moves, it will not be many years before the types of tools from the 2012 campaign will be more broadly accessible and impactful, and knowing the tools of the past will help anticipate the applications of tools in future elections.

> "Everyone's excitedly watching TV news at 7 PM. We are all 82 years old."
>
> **JASON GAY** @JASONWSJ, *Wall Street Journal* sports columnist, tweeted on election night 2012

This chapter also discusses these next-level technologies. Under "Major League," you will find summaries of tools that offer power and precision when effectively maintained by someone with a high level of technical ability. The technologies are becoming more widespread and user friendly, but it is still important to have the right person to direct a digital campaign. Digital campaigning can quickly suck up hours and resources and, if not done well, won't translate into votes. This section will run through the resources available and where more research might make sense for a particular campaign.

Because of these technologies' virtual nature and recent advent, I used examples from national campaigns as they demonstrate occasions where these tools were used well, but the rules of quality content are the same in localized contexts. Just remember to always be mindful of how you target, as local campaigns must always be geographically specific.

Understanding Demographics: Who Uses Social Media?

As with all campaigning, when you approach the digital world you have to know to whom you're talking. So who is on social media? According to a 2012

Social Networking Sites
% of internet users who use social networking sites

		Use Social Networking Sites
All internet users (n=1,802)		**67%**
a	Men (n=846)	62
b	Women (n=956)	71[a]
Race/ethnicity		
a	White, Non-Hispanic (n=1,332)	65
b	Black, Non-Hispanic (n=178)	68
c	Hispanic (n=154)	72
Age		
a	18-29 (n=318)	83[bcd]
b	30-49 (n=532)	77[cd]
c	50-64 (n=551)	52[d]
d	65+ (n=368)	32
Education attainment		
a	Less than high school/high school grad (n=549)	66
b	Some College (n=519)	69
c	College + (n=721)	65
Household income		
a	Less than $30,000/yr (n=409)	72
b	$30,000-$49,999 (n=330)	65
c	$50,000-$74,999 (n=283)	66
d	$75,000+ (n=504)	66
Urbanity		
a	Urban (n=561)	70[c]
b	Suburban (n=905)	67
c	Rural (n=336)	61

Source: Pew Research Center's Internet & American Life Project Post-Election Survey, November 14 – December 09, 2012. N=1,802 internet users. Interviews were conducted in English and Spanish and on landline and cell phones. Margin of error is +/- 2.6 percentage points for results based on internet users.

Note: Percentages marked with a superscript letter (e.g., [a]) indicate a statistically significant difference between that row and the row designated by that superscript letter, among categories of each demographic characteristic (e.g. age).

FIGURE 4.1 Social Networking Sites

Pew poll (see figure 4.1), the majority—about two-thirds (67 percent)—of all internet users have a social media profile. Furthermore, social networking accounts for 20 percent of all time spent online worldwide—up from only 6 percent in 2007.[1]

Understanding demographics will inform a campaign about how best to communicate with a target audience. For example, the Pew poll shows that more women are on social media than men. Other research found that women who are online spend about 30 percent more time on social networking sites than men.[2] Couple this with information from a 2009 Gallup poll that demonstrated that the millennials, the coveted eighteen- to twenty-nine-year-olds who spent significant time online, generally support Democrats or independents.

> "This latest gaffe is the worst setback for Romney since the time he spent his whole life failing to learn how to relate to people."
>
> **COMEDIAN JON LOVETT** @JONLOVETT, tweet after Romney's "47 percent" comment, in which a hidden camera captured Romney _____ writing off almost half the country

These demographics suggest that there are statistically more young Democrats and women online—but that doesn't mean those are the only people you can target. Most people have an online presence in some way. Research more nuanced demographic information for your area, and determine the best platform to address your target audience. For a general list of demographic breakdowns and digital media, check out the Pew Research Center's Demographics of Social Media Users.[3]

Ten Tips for Building a Digital Footprint for an Election

The digital world is ever changing. It's hard to keep track, and hard to understand how it can best fit in with your boots-on-the-ground campaigning. Here are ten tips and reminders as you wade through the digital world:

1. *Keep up the dialogue.* It's called social media for a reason; it's a two-way street, and people won't pay attention to you if you don't pay attention to them. Answer every tweet, every Facebook post, and every YouTube comment. This is not an obligation; it's an asset. The interactivity of digital and social media offers an unprecedented means for two-way communication, allowing you to listen to your supporters and engage on issues that matter to them. If you listen, you can learn a lot about how to inspire and connect with your support base.

2. *Brand carefully and confidently.* The visual world and multimedia give you the ability to paint a sensory and emotional experience that frames your campaign. Don't take this power lightly. Think about what you post, how you post, and how your online presence looks as a whole. To see the power this can have, look no further than President Barack Obama's 2012 use of emotion in social media at Mindjumpers (mindjumpers.com /blog/2012/11/social-political-campaigns). Through simple images and intentional branding, Obama was able to resonate with the voter through the senses, creating an ethos for his campaign that people associate with him as much as his actual policies.

3. *Develop your voice.* Social media users respond to communication that is authentic, compelling, lively, funny, and smart. In other words, they want to hear your voice. Don't make social media communication sound like talking points or headlines—make them sound like you.

4. *Keep it catchy.* You cannot underestimate people's attention span. Just because the election is the most important thing in your life right now doesn't mean anyone else cares. People are demanding to get more from less time, so keep content short and to the point. Remember: The average page visit is less than a minute, so value your audience's time like a gift and respect it.

5. *Recognize that politics is going visual.* There's been a shift toward sharable visual online content—photos, memes, infographics. Play to this, and think of ways you can tell your story using compelling graphics and pictures. People are more likely to share and remember the information.

6. *Know to whom you're talking.* Be conscious of the demographics using social media in your region. While social media tools are sexy and cool, depending on whom you're wanting to engage, figuring out how to use the most cutting-edge technology may not be as effective as basic digital media and boots on the ground.

7. *Turn social media support into votes.* Keep in mind that the virtual world knows no geographic limits—but voter registration does. While it is great to get buzz in other regions, unless you can find a way to translate that into local notoriety, it doesn't get you any closer to elective office. Remember this as you create and post content. Organize your Twitter followers and Facebook friends by location and try to translate virtual support into a call to action—like getting out the vote or looking for volunteers.

8. *Balance your resources well.* The online world is changing so fast that by the time this book is printed, this information is already dated. The people with the most natural technological skills are being born right now. Digital sensations during the 2012 election either didn't exist or weren't widely used in 2008, presenting boundless opportunities for creativity; if you can imagine it, there is a way to do it. But keep in mind the priorities of your campaign. You could spend a lot of time pioneering digital trails, but it may not be the best use of campaign resources. Be clear about what you want to achieve, and be realistic about what will get you there given your technological capabilities and ability to stay on top of these quickly changing platforms.

9. *Play to social media's strengths.* Keep in mind where the digital world does well and where an on-the-ground effort excels. For example, the internet offers a venue to instantly reach out to the whole world, giving

a campaign the ability to answer attacks and address issues quickly. Use this as a place for rapid response, but remember: All the rules of rapid response still apply. Just because you have a venue for responding faster doesn't mean you can think less.

10. *Remember that these technologies are young.* The tech world has forever changed campaigning. And there are a lot of resources—and a whole lot of data—out there. We saw some great social media campaigns in 2012, but it is far from a science. We have yet to see how these things will evolve, what tools will be used in the future, and how users will respond. There already is a demand for more creativity to rise above the sea of content. While the tips and tricks in this chapter are based on experience and history, no one knows the equation of tapping into the internet perfectly or what will hold true in the future. Know the basic rules before you decide to break them, and analyze things you try to see what's working.

> "I wish they took a break every 2 minutes so I could catch up on Twitter."
>
> **ARIANNA HUFFINGTON**, founder and president of the Huffington Post, tweeted after the third presidential debate in 2012

The Minor Leagues: Social Media Essentials

Twitter

Twitter is a microblogging site that allows users to write messages of up to 140 characters, which then appear in their followers' feed. Tweets are public, so even if people aren't followers, your tweets can still appear in searches and on your page.

Twitter proved to be the new pillar of communication in political campaigning, and knowledge of it is almost ubiquitous—92 percent of Americans are aware of Twitter, up from 5 percent in 2005.[4] The increase in usage is equally striking—on Election Day 2012, Twitter broke its own record with 31.7 million election-based tweets, with some moments reaching 327,452 tweets per minute[5]—twenty-four times more than the peak during the 2008 election.[6]

> "Ha! Thank you for understanding my creative humor & sarcasm Mr. President, the smart ones always do . . . *sends love & support*"
>
> **POP SINGER NICKI MINAJ**, tweeting the president to confirm that rapping a Romney endorsement was a joke, and a great example of how Twitter has leveled the communication playing field

Twitter has emerged as the most direct communication between individuals and candidates, where candidates respond to individuals' tweets and the Twittersphere acts as a real-time public opinion barometer during presidential debates.

Usage is significantly lower than awareness, however. In 2012, 16 percent of internet users had a Twitter account (12 percent in rural areas),[7] with only 60 percent of those users actively posting content (the other 40 percent use Twitter as a means of receiving news but don't contribute).[8] Although the majority of people may not yet utilize Twitter, it still has a powerful ability to influence the conversation. For example, during the 2012 presidential election, Mitt Romney joked that no one had ever seen Obama's birth certificate. Within three minutes, this was tweeted, and within four minutes, was on Politico's website. Buzzfeed had video available after five minutes, and within twenty-one minutes, Romney's campaign was asked to clarify. That means, as Adam Sharp from Twitter told the *Guardian* newspaper, "We have shifted from a 24-hours news cycle to a 140-character one."[9] While a local campaign would likely not be under the same scrutiny, this story indicates the new power Twitter has to shape the political discussion.

It's important to have an account and maintain it throughout the campaign, and it should also be utilized thereafter. Building a following and engaging constituents is a lot of work that you don't want to lose after the votes are counted. If your campaign wins, it's a good way to communicate with constituents; if you lose, it gives your candidate or issue a head start for the next campaign. Twitter use will likely grow in future elections, and an online presence can reach deep into communities by word of mouth in secondary ways that we do not know how to quantify. And although Twitter may not yet be a powerful organizing mechanism in your area, it can reach into communities that traditional media has trouble contacting. But, as always, be aware of the demographics of your area to understand which audience you're talking to.

For example, in my home in southern Oregon, the chances of engaging a significant number of people on Twitter are low. The area is mostly white, older, and rural. All of these demographics indicate low Twitter usage—meaning ability to mobilize through Twitter is difficult. Additionally, the volunteers and people running the local party headquarters are not familiar with the platform, adding another barrier. But this is ever changing, and it is just a matter of time until the next generation takes the reins and can realize this medium's potential in local campaigns. Until that time, however, resources could be better spent elsewhere.

Here is a quick guide on maintaining a Twitter account that will further your issues, voice, and brand locally.

Getting Set Up

- *Username:* Choose a simple, clearly identifiable username. If your candidate has a common name, use both first and last name. If he or she has a long name or one that is difficult to spell, shorten it in a way that it is easy to remember.

- *Visuals:* You need three images—one each for the profile, background, and cover. Use a (professional) photo of the candidate for the profile, and images that are consistent with the campaign's branding for the background and cover.
- *Biography:* You have 140 characters for the candidate's biography on Twitter, so use them wisely. Whatever you say, be sure to include basic information, such as who the candidate is, his or her district, party affiliation (for partisan campaigns), the office he or she is seeking and links to the campaign's other social media and website.

Tools

- *Hashtags (#):* Hashtags are a word or acronym used to describe or add context to a tweet. The best hashtags are short and catchy, as tweets can be only 140 characters. Hashtags can be used in several ways, including satirically and humorously, but their typical function is to make it easy for others to search topics or events. For example, during the 2012 election, election news was posted with the hashtag #election2012 so followers could cut through the noise to election coverage. Hashtags can be newly created or can reference an existing hashtag that communities have informally agreed upon. It is generally more impactful to join an existing hashtag conversation than to start one of your own.
- *@mentions:* An @mention is another shorthand, like a hashtag, that allows you to engage with specific users in a public way. For example, if someone tweeted a message that relates to your organization, @mentions are a good way to acknowledge them. Just like in the real world, people appreciate getting replies and attention. This shorthand also enables followers the ability to follow dialogue between Twitter users. Talk show host Piers Morgan, after tweeting his disappointment that British gold medalist Brad Wiggins didn't sing the national anthem during the London Olympic Games in 2012, famously got slammed by a follower. Piers Morgan tweeted, "And yes, I was very disappointed @BradWiggins didn't sing the anthem either. Show some respect to our Monarch please!" to which a relatively unknown fan, @colmuacuinn, replied, "@piersmorgan I was disappointed when you didn't go to jail for insider dealing or phone hacking, but you know, to each to his own." The interaction was picked up by several news outlets and shared through social networking. Though not a political context, this is a good example of how a private citizen can shine a spotlight on a public figure. This is a line of communication

unknown in yesteryear; the power of Twitter lies in the egalitarian nature of the platform.

- *Retweets:* Retweets are like @replies because they single out a specific user, but instead followers repost, or "retweet," the same thing the original person posted. This is an easy way to post thoughts or opinion without having to craft your own message and engages the user in a way they'll notice.

- *Direct message:* A direct message, or DM, is a private communication with an individual user. Use this if you want to tweet someone privately, but be careful what you do here. This is what Anthony Weiner, then US representative, *thought* he was doing in June 2011, when he tried to direct message a picture of bulging underpants. He accidentally typed an "@" instead of a "D," making the tweet public instead of private—a very costly (if not inevitable) typo for his career, reputation, and marriage. Weiner claimed his Twitter account had been hacked, teaching us another great lesson: Never claim your social media network profile was hacked. People will know.

FIGURE 4.2 Obama's response to Clint Eastwood's appearance at the Republican National Convention, where the actor spoke to an invisible Obama/empty chair, and an excellent use of visuals in a campaign.

- *Favorites:* Twitter gives you the option of "favoriting" tweets, represented by a little star. This is a good way to organize tweets you'd like to keep track of and giving a nod to tweets you appreciate. Though the number of times a tweet is "favorited" is public, only the author and you will know you "favorited" it.
- *Shortened URLs:* Because you get only 140 characters, URLs could really eat up real estate. Twitter now automatically shortens the URL if you paste it inside a tweet, but you can also use a URL shortening program such as Bit.ly, which tracks analytics about how many people clicked the link, giving you feedback about which tweets are getting attention and which ones aren't.

Replying to Tweets

Twitter is a social medium. Again, this means it's a two-way street—you have to give and take. Mention people with whom you'd like to connect, and respond to every tweet written to you. People will give to you if you give to them.

If people tweet negative things about you, react as you would on the campaign trail—that is, acknowledge the tweet (if appropriate), reply, and stay calm and collected. You don't want to come off as snarky, and much can be lost in tone on the Twitter platform.

Your Following

The proliferation of tweets upped the volume in an already busy Twittersphere, and it can be difficult to rise above the noise and be noticed. Many personalities have honed the art of communicating in 140 characters and, spoiled for choices, users have become more selective about whom they follow. But followers you must have—they lend your account credibility, and their presence also indicates to others that you have support. Here are a few tactics to help you get started:

1. Fill out your profile completely—this will help people find you and is a good place to share information about yourself.
2. Ask your friends, family, and supporters to follow you.
3. Find voters and follow them—a certain number of people you follow are sure to follow you back, and you'll see in your Twitter feed what your voters are talking about in real time.
4. Identify community leaders, follow them, and check out what they're talking about. Look for a way to engage, and send a personal tweet chiming into the conversation.
5. There are simple online programs, such as Fllwrs.com, that will keep track of how many followers you've lost or gained. Using one will give

you feedback about what content is pulling people in and pushing them away, and allow you to engage with new and recently lost followers to see if you can get them back.

6. Do not buy followers. It is easy to get fake followers on Twitter, but it is dishonest and inexcusable. It is tantamount to paying people to show up to your campaign rally.

Making Twitter Local

Twitter has some easy tools to find people within your community. First, you can simply use Twitter's built-in advanced search options to filter results to be "near this place." You can put in your city or zip code, along with a radius (in miles) to locate local users. There are also programs to help you put geographic boundaries on your Twittersphere. Twellow.com, for example, acts as a kind of yellow pages for Twitter. You can find people based on location and interests. Other programs help you follow the local Twitter conversation. The program TwitterLocal can keep a constant stream of all tweets coming from a specific location. You can have this running in the background of your computer and find out what local people are thinking and talking about in real time—and engage them.

Content

Tweets are short and sweet, and should be well crafted. You are limited to 140 characters, and it's polite to leave ten characters of breathing space so others can easily retweet you—which makes your job a challenge. There is an art to getting a point across in so few characters, and the competition is stiff. Communicating on Twitter, as mentioned above, is more than just putting out information—you should develop a voice, and try to stay away from politics-ese and talking points. Cory Booker, @CoryBooker, is an excellent example to turn to for a politician who is getting Twitter right—his voice is strong, and he leverages the medium to connect with constituents.

Think about the tone of every tweet you craft. Conversational tweets are great at engaging, but a formal tone might make more sense for an announcement. Remember, your meaning can get lost in tweets, so stay positive, professional, and consistent. When thinking about what to tweet, classify your tweets in seven broad categories. Draft a combination of tweets, and pay attention to what works with your audience. Here is a list of the type of tweets, as outlined in the book *Politics and the Twitter Revolution*.[10]

1. *Campaign trail:* These are tweets about the day-to-day life of campaigning. Write about events, polls, or stories, or live blog from an event. For example, on Halloween 2012, Ann Romney tweeted, "Sharing a tender

moment with this little boy who was dressed up as Iron Man at Nationwide Children's Hospital today," along with a picture of Ann leaning smiling across a hospital table to a little boy dressed in a Halloween costume.

2. *Personal:* This covers all personal details, mainly of a nonpolitical nature.

3. *Candidate ideology:* Tweets talking about the candidate's position on policy or issues. Presidential hopeful Rick Santorum tweeted during the primaries, "I'm standing firm on conservative principles. I'm no Etch a Sketch waiting to be shaken up & re-shifted."

4. *Opponent-focused:* Tweets talking about the opponent in any capacity—such as position or history. Romney was fond of these, with tweets like "Unemployment is higher today than when @BarackObama took office. Think about that. #CantAfford4More." However, be careful about where and when you use these. You should have more of a voice on Twitter than defining yourself by the opposition.

5. *Call to action:* These tweets ask something of your followers—such as volunteering, voting, or retweeting. Add a URL to increase interaction. Michelle Obama reached out to engage and empower voters in the final days of the election with tweets like, "We'll win this election because you were part of it. Sign up for a volunteer shift to help this campaign finish strong," with a link to the Obama website.

6. *Endorsements:* Information about an official endorsement or supporter testimonial is nice to get out there, especially when the endorsement can act as a validator to communicate to a key audience.[11] For example, on October 28, 2012, Mitt Romney tweeted, "We need Iowa to help get America back on track I am honored to have the @DMRegister's endorsement."

7. *Community news:* What's making a splash where you live? Tweet about what's happening locally. Where possible, add your own take on community activities and respond about what's happening in your community.[12]

When to Tweet

For many, Twitter is a distraction from other things in life. So the best time to tweet is when people are most likely to be taking a break at the office or have a free moment over lunch. Retweets are best in the afternoon, from 2 to 6 p.m., and peak around 5 p.m. Click-through rates, the number of people who will actually click on a link you tweet, are highest Monday through Thursday from 1 to 3 p.m. However, there is no magic number for how often you should tweet. Marketing studies have analyzed how many tweets the most influential users and brands post, but if you're new to Twitter, it's best to develop a voice that feels most natural to you. Trying to meet an arbitrary quota will do you few favors. That could mean one post three times a week or ten tweets a day.

Being a regular poster does not mean you have to constantly be in front of your computer. Use a management program like Hootsuite, which will allow you to schedule tweets at specific days and times. Try to give this some attention—you can spend a little time one night a week drafting different types of tweets and schedule them to go out at optimal times throughout the week. Feel free to rewrite the same piece of information in a couple of ways—research shows that tweets have

> "If Obama's message for 2012 is 'Forward,' the message of the Romney campaign has definitely been 'Accidentally Reply-All.'"
>
> **DANIEL KIBBLESMITH,** writer and comedian tweeting in the final days of the 2012 election

a shelf life of around three hours,[13] and marketing tells us it takes several attempts to make contact with the audience,[14] so there is room to reinforce a single tweet's message—if it's in creative or different ways. Remember, though, scheduling tweets is not a replacement for interactions on Twitter—it just ensures you are still maintaining an online presence when your campaign scheduling doesn't allow for more time spent on social media.

Twitter Advertising

Twitter allows you to place targeted ads with flexible pricing plans. You select your audience and choose if you'd like to promote a tweet or the account. Promoted tweets are good if you're trying to drive more traffic to your website or a favorable news piece, for example, whereas a promoted account drives followers. At the time of this writing, $50 in advertising got us 28 website visits, 25 new Twitter likes, and almost 10,000 engagements. Promoting a single tweet with $50 got us 81 clicks, and 1,500 engaged. Though this amount can vary greatly, in this spot test followers cost about $2 each.

Monitoring Twitter

At the time of writing, there is a surfeit of applications and tools to make sense of your Twitter feed. In addition to Hootsuite (mentioned above, which also has basic analytic information), there are programs that cut through the noise to help you easily identify trending topics and hashtags, and what your followers are talking about. Check out up-to-date Twitter tools online—I find Mashable.com to be a great resource.

Facebook

Facebook is still king of social networking. Sixty-seven percent of all internet users have a Facebook account. Older demographics tap into Facebook more than any other social media—including a third of people on the internet age sixty-five and over.[15] People don't use Facebook the way they use Twitter, and Facebook users tend to be more insular and private with content. The network's growth has leveled off and some research suggests its popularity is declining (a recent Pew study showed teenagers don't like how many adults are on the site), but at the time of this writing, there remains no other social media platform with anywhere near the same reach. This means there is more potential to connect with people—but also means there is more competition to get noticed. But the extra effort could pay off. A Pew poll showed that Facebook users who log on multiple times a day are 2.5 times more likely to attend a political rally or meeting, 57 percent more likely to try to persuade someone how to vote, and 43 percent more likely to have said they would vote.[16]

Having a Facebook page for a campaign is a must. Don't try to morph your personal profile—make a group page specifically for the campaign. With that said, your personal page is a great place to start encouraging people to "like" the newly created group and to drive traffic through cross-posting content. Remember, though, who your Facebook audience is—this is a self-selected group of people who "like" you. This is your base. While this can be a great tool for mobilizing and interacting directly with voters, it also is by definition a friendly crowd. It will not be the best venue for reaching the savables.

Your group page is public, meaning people wanting to know more about your campaign will also likely come across it. Because of the Facebook timeline layout, visitors will be able to see the unfolding story of your campaign at a glance. Keep this in mind, and use content that is visually stimulating and will communicate to people at a quick scan.

Getting Started

Name your page in a way that is clearly identifiable as the candidate. For a down-ballot election, include the candidate's full name and position he or she is seeking, so it is clear at a glace. Fill out the profile completely, including information about the campaign and links to other social media profiles. Facebook requires two visuals for the account: a profile and a cover photo. Pick a professional profile picture and a visually appealing cover photo that supports the underlying message behind the candidate's campaign. Avoid cover pictures that look cheesy or like banner ads. Stay consistent with your branding.

When you first set up your page, your URL will be facebook.com/averylongslewofnumbersandletters. Personalize your URL so your account is easier to find. Use the candidate's name, if possible—as in Facebook.com/JohnSmith. You can do this at facebook.com/username.

Getting Facebook Page Likes
This is the equivalent of Twitter followers. For local elections, these can be hard to get. People are careful about what they "like," as that is viewable by all of their friends—which is exactly what makes likes so valuable. Think of these as endorsements from community members—and all they need to do is click. Ask your current friends and contacts to like your candidate's page—and ask them to do the same with their friends. People can be a powerful influence on their friends—70 percent of consumers trust brand recommendations from their friends.[17] If a friend shares information about a politician, the promotion seems more genuine than other forms of advertisement.

You can tap into the resources you have on Twitter, too. Make sure your Twitter followers know you have a Facebook page, and let your Facebook fans know you are on Twitter as well. Once you have a base and are posting content people want to see, people are more likely to "like" your page. It is important to promote the page wherever you can—have a link on your website, on your Twitter account, and any other materials you make, such as emails, direct mail, campaign literature, and advertisements.

Personalized Landing Page: Your Profile's Welcome Sign
Facebook lets you create a customized landing page. By default, users will see your Facebook timeline, but you can customize a tab that visitors who are not yet your fans will see. You can customize this to ask visitors for email addresses, donations, or to "like" your Facebook page.

Crafting Your Message
Facebook mechanics are similar to those of a tweet. You post through status updates, which will appear in the feed of those who "liked" your page. Though you are not constrained by 140 characters, try to keep your posts short and pithy. If something isn't well written or compelling, it likely will get lost between an article about Kim Kardashian and a cat video. As with tweets, your messages must be authentic, compelling, lively, and smart, and have a tone. Try to avoid posting official statements or press releases. Facebook uses a more casual and personal style of communication, so save the stump speech for the stump.

- *Sharing:* You have the option to share others' posts on your group's timeline. Share things that reflect some aspect of the campaign, and make a nice, short introduction that explains the connection. Make this succinct with language that draws in the audience—don't make them do the legwork to figure out the connection.

- *Interaction:* Marketing research shows that shorter posts encourage dialogue, increasing user interaction. Companies find the posts that get the most interactions are between 100 and 119 characters in length—short enough to be a tweet. Asking a question in a post increases the likelihood of interaction, too. The best way to engage users is to plan your engagement over two or three posts in different ways.[18] Because this will all be on your candidate's page, make sure to vary the way he or she talks about topics so it doesn't appear redundant.
- *Likes:* "Liking" posts, the term for giving a post a little thumbs up, is a staple for Facebook interaction. Your group page can *like* others' posts (it can like a fellow group's posts, though), but other users will be able to like your page's posts. "Likes" have a powerful effect. Studies where posts were arbitrarily "liked" showed others were more likely to approve, regardless of quality of content.[19] Don't underestimate the value of a "like"—it could create a bandwagon effect.

Timing Matters

- *Optimal timing:* Getting others to share your post is great PR, so keep in mind how people use Facebook. The greatest number of shares happen on Saturday. Marketers report 32 percent more engagement on Facebook during the weekend.[20] During the week, the best time to share is at noon—think lunch break.
- *Frequency:* The company pages with the most likes on Facebook post on average once every other day. Find a rhythm that works for you. Try not to post just for the sake of hitting your quota or hold back good content if you've got it. You can use a management program like Hootsuite to schedule things to go out at optimal times. Of course, it is best to have content that is current, so post timely things quickly and more evergreen content in advance.
- *Shelf life:* Posts get the majority of interaction in the first sixty minutes and after three hours are essentially irrelevant.[21] In other words, as soon as it gets buried, it's forgotten. Choose your timing well.

Gaining Insight

There are many analytics programs you could use to glean information from your Facebook account, and none more accessible than Facebook's built-in platform, Insights. Insights will automatically appear in your page's Admin Panel once you get thirty or more "likes," and transforms data into feedback for your digital campaigning. As summarized from the *New Media Campaign*, such data will include:

- The demographic makeup of those who like your page
- The best times for posting to your audience, and which types of posts get the most interactions
- The number of people who saw and interacted with a post
- How many times your page has been viewed[22]

Paid Promotion of your Facebook Page

Facebook gives you flexible options for promoting your page. You select your audience, their interests, and a daily price (the precise amount doesn't matter—you could designate as little as five dollars a day) and Facebook will amplify your page or post. A recent spot test of $50 showed Facebook "likes" to cost $2.60 each—although this amount can change greatly.

Syncing Facebook and Twitter

Syncing Facebook and Twitter is easy—a built-in feature allows you to automatically tweet Facebook posts, or to post tweets. I think it's best to craft content that plays to the strength of the individual platforms, so, if possible, leave the two accounts independent.

YouTube

YouTube is a video sharing site, now owned by Google, where users upload videos and share them with the world. It is simple, easy to use, and, now that most cell phones are also pocket-size video cameras, very accessible. YouTube can be a great way to keep users up-to-date with your campaign and message. It is worth mentioning that there are other video sharing sites, such as Vimeo, but at this time YouTube is the most popular and friendly with other programs.

> "I didn't run to make history. I ran to make a difference."
>
> **TAMMY BALDWIN'S** tweet the morning after being elected as the first openly gay member of the Senate in 2012 _____

You can easily embed videos from YouTube on most platforms. Be aware that YouTube requires an active Google account. Establish a dedicated account for your candidate to avoid any confusion with unrelated Gmail or Google activity.

Five Tips for YouTube

1. Keep in mind that people do not have a long attention span. Videos should be short and to the point. Unless you are skilled in cinematography, don't expect viewers to watch more than ninety seconds. If you go over three minutes, you'd better have something good to say. Don't put up unedited

content or things with poor video or audio quality. No one will watch it and it will reflect poorly on your campaign. Basic video editing software is common, so find someone who is up to the task if you want to post videos from the field.

2. Always be mindful of using copyrighted material in anything you produce—including images, music, and video. There are troves of free things you can find online—check out free domain materials through things like the National Archives or Creative Commons—and always be mindful of the material's restrictions.

3. Spend time with a videographer covering important issues in the campaign, post to YouTube, and embed them on your website. This will mean that people can watch videos on your website, but you still keep YouTube as your central location for all videos. Capture the candidate outlining basic positions. YouTube videos provide a quick, easy, and controlled venue for a candidate to convey his or her passion and charisma. A few years back, one local candidate talked extemporaneously on twenty-three subjects he felt were important in the county and posted these separately by subject matter. Besides imparting his depth of knowledge of county business, the clips were incredibly informative for the average person. His site received 65,000 hits—a huge amount for the small market in which it was posted. Use clips such as these on the site on the "Issues" page.

4. If debates are videotaped, extrapolate some of the best moments for your candidate and post them to YouTube. You can then embed them on your Web page and link to this on other social media platforms. Similarly, you could upload anything your opponent may have said that could be damaging to him or her. If the opponent is an incumbent and the official government meetings are taped, go through and pull out damaging moments and place them on your site. These should be kept brief (under three minutes).

5. Create a YouTube channel and link it to your Facebook, Twitter, and website. As always, make sure to fill out the profile completely. Not only will that make sharing content easy and fast, it increases your search engine optimization (SEO), meaning that when people search your candidate's name they are more likely to see his or her YouTube channel—along with his or her Twitter, Facebook, and website.

6. Users can subscribe to YouTube channels and profiles. This means new content will automatically be added to that user's queue of videos to watch.

FIGURE 4.3 Example of a Web Page Header

Websites: Your Digital Front Porch

The website, once the center of the candidate's online presence, plays a different function since the proliferation of social media. Once the go-to location for all information, websites now play the important role of your campaign's library, housing background material, platform nuances, upcoming events, volunteer and contribution opportunities, all news pieces and releases, and your blog, if you keep one.

Use a host that is easy to maintain and is cheap or free. Wordpress is user friendly, intuitive, and customizable. It has a wide variety of templates that can make your site match your brand, and maintenance is easy, so you won't waste man-hours on technological disasters. Figure 4.3 is an example of a Web page header that uses a clean and visually compelling branding that matches the other collateral campaign materials.

You can think of creation and maintenance of your site in two broad parts—the nuts and bolts of the site, which determine look, feel, and functionality, and the content that populates the site. In turn, these can be thought of as the back end and front end of your website maintenance, respectively.

Back End: Under the Hood
1. Keep the site up-to-date and make sure all content is working. The website is like your campaign's front porch: if it looks like a mess and seems unloved, people will make assumptions about what's inside.
2. Be sure to link your website to your social media profiles. Have buttons on your page that easily take the user to your Facebook, Twitter, and YouTube pages, along with an opt-in form for your email newsletter. This makes it easier for people to find you across platforms and increases your search engine optimization.
3. Use a template with a navigation bar with tabs for the different sections of the website. Not only does this add for easy navigability, it lends itself well to Web analytics (see Web monitoring below). Scrolling websites are growing in popularity, but use them with care. They can be difficult to navigate for those looking for pointed information.

4. Include dynamic elements to your site, such as widgets, which are a small application that can appear on the side of pages. These give the appearance that the site is fresh and updated frequently with minimal maintenance. You can insert your Twitter feed, Facebook posts, or newsfeed of local news. You can also embed a scrolling ticker of endorsers of the candidate or issue, which gives a perpetual-motion feel. A slider on the home page with pictures is a simple way to add visuals and movement to your site.

5. If you have pages with multiple sections, you could provide a table of contents with anchor links within the page. This not only lets people know what is on a page without scrolling down, but will also give your audience a better experience. Visitors can easily move between the topics they want to read. Check out any Wikipedia page to see what this looks like (en.wikipedia.org).

> "What's at stake for you in this election? Share what's on your mind—and help shape the conversation moving forward."
>
> **BARACK OBAMA** tweeted, along with a simple form asking what's important to the user this election, in a good _____ example of engaging voters.

Front End: The Showroom

There is no one-size-fits-all for websites, though there is content that is important to include for a well-run digital campaign. Here are a couple tips to keep in mind:

1. Include a bio and lots of pictures. House your television ads, radio spots, direct mail pieces, brochures, voters' pamphlets, newspaper endorsements, everything.
2. Keep a running Q&A section based on questions encountered while canvassing.
3. If there are specific Facebook posts or tweets you don't want to lose in the virtual noise, you can embed them in your site.
4. Be sure to visit other websites and borrow ideas for layout and content.
5. Your website is the venue for long-form pieces. Your candidate does not need to keep a blog, but if he or she feels compelled to communicate in long form, the website is the place to do it. This is where the candidate can set the record straight or point out issues with an opponent's platform.

Website Monitoring

There are some simple analytic programs you can harness to see how people are using your website and responding to content. Free programs, such as

Google Analytics, can get you a substantial amount of data, including (but not limited to):

- What pages are most visited, and how long users spend on each page, giving you valuable information regarding what your voters want to know about
- Which outreach efforts are driving traffic to your site (e.g., a tweet or a Google search)
- What content is losing people's interest—and where users bounce from the site
- Which keywords and phrases are driving people to your site
- The path users take through your site and how many pages they view before leaving
- How many new versus returning visitors come to your site

Alone, these analytics are just numbers—but you can extrapolate feedback that can inform your campaign. Your website traffic gives you valuable information about which outreach efforts are successful, what people care about, and which content is creating a buzz.

You can also think of clever ways to leverage the information you know the analytics will deliver. For example, you could summarize your candidate's positions in bullet points, each with a pop-out window (with a unique URL) with more detailed information. Your website analytics could tell which issues your visitors care the most about based on the volume of traffic and the length of the visit each page.

> "One hour and still waiting to #vote in DC. Women fought 75 years to be able to vote. No problem with standing in line one hour."
> **JANICE NOLEN** @NOLENJE, dedicated voter tweeted on election night

Email

Email blasts have been deemphasized with the proliferation of other, more personal forms of digital communication, but they still play a valuable role in campaigning and fundraising. In 2012, email was more consistently effective for mobilizing supporters, donors, and volunteers than Facebook posts or tweets by a factor of ten.[23] Be thoughtful when emailing en masse. Every busy person's inbox is already overflowing with impersonal emails, so make your emails minimal and be sure you have something to say.

Here are a few tactics and tips to keep in mind when working on email lists:

1. *Collect email leads:* Give people plenty of opportunities to opt into your email list. You could have an opt-in form popup for new visitors on your website, and embed an opt-in widget that will appear on every page within your site. These leads are the most likely to help you meet volunteer and fundraising goals, so don't give up this effort.

2. *Clickable subject lines:* The power of your subject line makes all the difference in opening rates. You must be honest, compelling, and authentic to get a click. Don't be obscure or sensational—people are too busy to open an email with the subject line: "You have to know this!" Write to your audience. More prominent election candidates, such as President Barack Obama in 2012, for example, can get away with more cryptic subject lines, such as "Join me for dinner?" and "Hey!" This campaign's best fundraising subject line was "I will be outspent," which earned the campaign $2.5 million.[24] Be wary of using a similar strategy with candidates who won't catch the eye simply being a household name. But, as with all digital media, if you want to try something, try it—the numbers will let you know if you're on the right track.

3. *Track what's successful:* If you're using an email management system, such as ConstantContact (a paid service), you can split test subject lines—meaning you break your email list into groups and test out what works by comparing open rates. This will help you narrow down what type of communication works with your community. If you don't have the money for a program like Constant Contact, you can still do split tests through generating different URLs for the same site. Through your analytics, you can see which URL got the most clicks and, from that, try to draw conclusions about what messages are most effective for your audience.

"You're literally LAST person I trust on this. RT @algore Confident in saying President Obama is going to carry Florida."

WILL LEITCH, Gawker Media's funding editor tweeted to Al Gore on election night 2012

4. *Keep it short and to the point:* People get a lot of emails. Respect that, and get to the point with a clear message. In 2012 emails became much more personal.[25] Write the way a normal person would talk. Make it fun to read. If you are asking something, make the request clear, accessible, and justified. If you supply a link, clearly mark where it will take you. You don't want to mislead your readers—people don't like feeling tricked.[26]

5. *Personalized landing pages:* You can create a landing page on your website that corresponds directly to your message for better results. If you are promoting donations, embed a link to a donations page that, if possible, relates directly to the content of your email.

Other Platforms

There are many other platforms out there, each with their own benefits and features. You can get very creative and tell an amazing story. But keep in mind that use of these platforms is still minimal—10 percent or less—and the science of doing it well is far from precise. You can struggle for quite a while on these sites without making a splash. With that said, if you use and like another digital platform, by all means use it. Just don't break your back and resources feeling like you have to make these work. Here are some platforms and tools you should be aware of:

- Instagram, now owned by Facebook, is a photo sharing service where users take pictures and apply a digital filter that gives the photo a distinct feel and tone. It can be a great place to house and texture your photo ops, and can be easily shared on other social media. Instagram recently added a video feature, with the maximum video length of fifteen seconds. Per the Pew study above, only 13 percent of internet users are on Instagram, but photos can be shared on other sites to nonusers.
- Vine is Twitter's microvideo platform. Videos are six seconds long, which, like 140 characters, doesn't sound like much. But like all tools on the internet, creative people have harnessed this platform to make powerful video bites.
- Pinterest is a pinboard-style photo sharing site where users keep theme-based albums (primarily repurposed from other sites). It is overwhelmingly used by women (83 percent of all users). The content is visually driven and revolves around hobbies—such as recipes and fashion. The 2012 election was the first since Pinterest's advent, but still was a point of buzz, and even competition between Michelle Obama and Ann Romney. Fifteen percent of internet users are on Pinterest.
- Foursquare is an application where users check into physical locations using their mobile devices. A user could head down to the coffee shop and "check-in," and all followers will be able to see where he or she is. You can also create your own locations—when Obama's October 2010 visit to LA created a massive traffic jam, the "Obamajam" was the most checked-into location on Foursquare for hours.
- Tumblr, now owned by Yahoo, is a microblogging platform. There is no designated length, but the site is visually driven and posts are generally short. Tumblr is characterized by the specificity of the blogs—they usually focus on only one thing. The tone is usually light, and it can be a good place for satire. After Mitt Romney's infamous comment about binders full of women during the second presidential debate in 2012, the Tumblr

FIGURE 4.4 A Meme Posted to the BindersFullOfWomen Tumblr Page

blog bindersfullofwomen.tumblr.com gained 11,000 followers in twenty-four hours, with users contributing comical scenarios playing off that line. Be careful about having the official political campaign dabbling in this kind of satire, lest the candidate come off as insincere. Six percent of internet users are on Tumblr.

- Internet memes are most commonly thought of as an image with big text written across. They are usually funny, poignant, or satirical, and are easy to share on social media sites. A popular meme, as many posted in the bindersfullofwomen example above (figure 4.4), can spread far and wide and can combat months of effective campaigning. But part of their power is that the creators are anonymous and aren't accountable—so again, this is not a technique that the official campaign should approach flippantly.

Search Engine Optimization (SEO)

SEO is the process of improving your search results strategically by choosing words and terms that people are likely to plug into a search engine. Think about how you would Google something when you're creating content—are you using terms the average person would think to search for? You can get help from SEO tools, too. There are plenty of free and paid services that will help you craft your key words to drive your candidate high on search results. For more basic information on how to take advantage of SEO, check out Google's starter guide at bit.ly/googleSEOptimization.

> "On your ballot, enter OBAMA-OBAMA-ROMNEY-ROMNEY-DOWN-DOWN-PAUL RYAN-START-SELECT to vote for the secret Will Smith / DJ Jazzy Jeff ticket."
>
> **H. CALDWELL TANNER** @CALDY CollegeHumor .com illustrator at the intersection of video games, celebrity, and Twitter—a millennial-targeted trifecta

The Major Leagues: Data-Driven Campaigning

The data gathered about each of us in the digital world, and implications of how it can communicate and influence, is unimaginable. Every day we leave digital breadcrumbs of where we put our time, energy, and money. In 2012, we saw the beginning of integrated information from multiple sources, painting a personalized picture of voters from their political, commercial, and cultural spheres. The applications for political campaigns are still being explored, and in elections to come the capability and availability may be impressive.

Take my morning, for example: I get up, head to the corner cafe for a coffee; I swipe my debit card to pay for it. While I wait for my drink, I read a couple of news stories through a customized newsfeed app that knows my interests. While I'm reading an article about India, my iPhone is automatically downloading my favorite podcasts for my commute. I have my Facebook page open and notice I was tagged in a photo of a river trip I'd taken the week before, and my brother posted a link to an *Onion* article. I "like" it. I get in the car for my morning commute, cross a bridge where FastTrak picks up my vehicle identification; I stop for gas after I exit. The gas pump asks for my zip code when I swipe my credit card. As I pump seven gallons, I check on plane tickets to Seattle for the next weekend and a round-trip ferry schedule to the San Juan Islands; I then skip over to a bridal registry. It isn't eight a.m., and I've already left a sizeable digital footprint that indicates I listen to NPR, have a brother and both of us have irreverent senses of humor, that I'm heading to the San Juan Islands for a wedding, love the outdoors, know I probably drive a fuel-efficient vehicle, go to work and the route I take, and that I may be traveling to India in the future. All of that information came to the digital world in less than one hour; imagine the kind of footprint we leave every hour of every day with online purchases and dozens of electronic transactions.

The 2012 presidential election gave us a taste of what future elections may look like. Once the curtain was pulled back in the wake of the election, we were all surprised (none more so than the Republicans) at the impact of Obama's digital machine. The campaign had an unprecedented tech team composed of, in the words of Harper Reed, chief technology officer of the reelection campaign, "100 data scientists, developers, engineers, analysts, and old-school hackers [who] have been transforming the way politicians acquire data—and what they do with it." The team cross-analyzed multiple databases to draw nuanced conclusions to cater to targeted voters' personal tastes. The quantity of data the campaign had on individuals was, aptly put by Daniel Kreiss, professor at the University of North Carolina–Chapel Hill, "creepy."[27]

While 2012 was a big year for campaign technology, we did not get anywhere close to meeting its full potential. But be careful—these technologies are still young—meaning quality and availability of the data can be unreliable and expensive, especially at a local level where campaign resources are not that of Obama's 2012 pool. Every day technology is becoming more user-friendly, but it is very easy to waste time or money on new technologies that may promise the world but lack the sophistication to synthesize data into a clear course of action. Right now we have a lot of data, but conclusions are problematic. We watched this struggle during the 2012 elections as news networks tried to call winners based on social media battles. Metrics are messy, making predications inaccurate.

Finally, if tapping into the fast and experimental world of digital tools makes sense for your campaign, Google it and figure out what is working this campaign cycle. All of this is changing, and it's hard to say what will be most effective in the future. While data-driven efforts will likely become more powerful, there might also be user backlash about privacy concerns—meaning it could also become harder to engage them with some of these tactics.

Tech Trends in Political Elections

In the 2012 campaign cycle, several technology trends emerged, foreshadowing techniques of campaigns of the future. Many of these technologies are young, and it is unclear how to best apply them to local elections but, by 2016, they almost certainly will have adapted to be more accurate, accessible, and affordable. Here is an overview of a couple of the trends changing how we think about campaigning.

Microtargeting

Driven by commercial marketing, digital advertising is a technology where there is much research and progress. The vast amount of data on people out there can be used to predict consumer behavior and can be transformed into tailored messages to activate supporters. Microtargeting allows a level of precision unknown to the elections of yesteryear. You can advertise based on specific demographic and location (see figure 4.5), and the platforms let you get specific with how you want to advertise—Google allows you to advertise by congressional district, and Twitter lets advertisers target keywords in tweets.

These microtargeted ads can be coupled with other successful advertising techniques, such as more general banner ads to influence the broad public conversation, and pre-roll ads, which are videos that play automatically when you

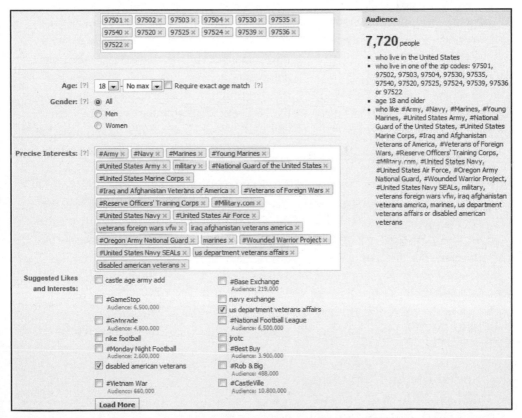

FIGURE 4.5 An example of microtargeting a demographic on Facebook from the 2012 general election. In this example a geographic area is targeted using zip codes, and then categories of "Precise Interest" are checked to reveal a category of voters with interest in the military.

visit a page like YouTube or Hulu, or audio that plays on places like Pandora and Spotify. Pre-roll ads cost a little more but are harder for the user to ignore.

In the 2012 election, it still wasn't clear how much effect microtargeting had on outcomes. It appeared that that social media was powerful when it came to fundraising and get-out-the-vote (GOTV) efforts, but persuading undecided voters was harder—possibly because people seek out online content that aligns with preexisting views.[28] Running targeted ads is only half the battle—to make maximum impact you also need to look at which ones are resonating in which demographics. Analytics are rising to meet this challenge, with the ability to measure consumer attention through how much time a user spends scrolling down or hovering over an object within a particular ad.

Microtargeting is still far from a science. A ComScore survey indicated that adding three variables (e.g., women, eighteen to twenty-nine years old, single) delivers an impression to the target an average 11 percent of the time. [29] Click-through rates on these ads are low (about one in every 2,000 Facebook ads is clicked for top companies), but may still provide better precision than traditional media, making a potential way to get a down-ballot candidate's name out to the right demographic with the right message.[30] This may be a good way to get a down-ballot candidate's name out to the right demographic with the right message. Further, information that existed during 2012, like real-time demographic and ad-buy data, will likely be widespread tools in elections to come, with metrics pinpointing information about which aspects of an online ad pushed donors to give more, or what shifts the polls.

> "It's still early on cable news, but words have opened up a big lead over information. #Election2012 #vote2012 #election."
>
> A tweet from writer **ANDY BOROWITZ** on election night 2012

If you're clever and have resources, there is plenty that can be done with the existing data. Obama's 2012 campaign, for example, with the "Are You In?" application, required users to grant permission to access personal Facebook information, including friend lists. On Election Day, the Obama campaign reached out to Facebook users in swing states and tasked them to urge friends whose ballots weren't in to get to the polls. In this way, Obama found a work-around to reach the prized young voting demographic, who are hard to reach through traditional campaigning such as landlines, TV, radio, or mail.

Social Media Monitoring

All of your social media interactions supply a wealth of information. Some, such as Facebook's Insights, is right at your fingertips. But the built-in mon-itoring tools just scratch the surface. Other applications can delve further into data. Attentive.ly can create infographics based on matching names with social media networks and identifying where your efforts would be most influential. Other programs, such as Radian6, Trackx, and Zingal, offer in-depth social media analysis but can run your campaigns hundreds of dollars per month.

Conversation Monitoring

For highly skilled campaigners, it is not enough to know what people are talking about. They want to know how people are talking about it. Tools have emerged to meet this demand, such as ViralHeat, a social media management platform with the ability to follow conversations in real time. As with many of these things, these monitoring techniques are on a trend to become more user-friendly, more predictive (rather than reactionary), more affordable, and more accurate, especially when gauging whether mentions about your candidate are positive or negative.

Some tools measure pieces of social media conversation, but none, as of yet, bring together both the quantity and quality of conversations. Still, the ability to track in real time what is successful (and what is not) enables a campaign to shift and adapt accordingly. These tools are sure to become essential in campaigns and could make it so any staff member can have his or her finger on the pulse of a quick-moving story or sentiment.[31]

Software

Standard campaign software now has some basic microtargeting features—information that was once prohibitively expensive to local elections. This has great implications for down-ballot candidates—even more so than for large campaigns. Joe Green, cofounder of the campaign software NationBuilder, argues, "Most citizens have no idea who's running for office and are therefore open to persuasion—a significant fact since local elections can be swung by just a few votes."[32] In 2012, the accuracy of microtargeting software was questionable. A spot test done with the Democratic National Committee's database was so wildly inaccurate that we decided against using it in our GOTV effort and relied on tried and true techniques. Soon, however, this technology is sure to mature, so check out what's available and consider its use to your campaign.

Mobile Devices

Smart phone use is ubiquitous. Fifty-five percent of Americans now access the internet on their phones,[33] and 28 percent use a mobile device to get news, up from 14 percent in 2008.[34] Smart phones are full of potential for a campaign.

- *Mobile fundraising:* Apps like Square and eWallet make it possible for people to donate to your campaign via a mobile phone. Note that this is different than text-to-donate—this is more like a virtual wallet that is linked to a credit card. Square has a mobile credit card reader allowing you to run supporters' bank cards anywhere with cell service. Such platforms can be a quick and secure way to get a contribution bump, whether you advertise mobile fundraising in a newspaper advertisement or at an event. The app also collects valuable information about your donors as they donate.

> "If Obama wins I'm leaving the country. If Romney wins I'm leaving the country. This is not a political post I just want to travel."
>
> **@MIILKKK** tweeted in the days _____ before the 2012 election

- *Geofencing:* As many of us carry around a device that tracks our location, a world of location-based advertising is opening up. Companies such as Starbucks and L'Oreal are already using this technology, but it has great potential for local elections, too. If a supporter agrees to receive your campaign's notifications, the campaign could send him or her messages, pictures, or encouragement to vote when they are at a specific location—like event venue, landmark, or polling stations.[35]

- *Quick Response (QR) codes:* QR codes are those black and white pixel squares that work as a matrix barcode. Most smart phones (with the help of an app like Google Goggles) can take a picture of the code and instantly open a particular corresponding website. They're easy to make—QR generators are free online—and you can do things like print a QR code on your lawn signs or brochures that lead to your campaign's Facebook or donation page. QR codes are an elegant way to tie the hard copy world with the digital, while giving you information about what drives people to your online presence. Keep in mind that QR codes are for phones, so make sure the destination URL is a mobile-friendly site.

- *Fieldwork:* Mobile devices can also save you valuable time inputting information while on the go. If your volunteers have access to a smart phone or tablet, simple pieces of software, such as VoterTag or Organize, allow you to collect data from volunteers about voters while canvassing or in the field—including questions and reactions. This saves time, is easy to manage, and gives you information instantly. It can also help you better communicate with your volunteers, with the ability to send directions and talking points.

Managing Online Reputation

The candidate's online reputation is the impression one gets when looking at his or her cumulative digital footprint. In other words, what comes up when you Google the candidate's name? Is there a scandal that dominates the news? Is there a picture of your candidate doing a keg stand in college? Treat Google as your homepage, and manage what people see when they type in your candidate's name. There are online reputation management companies, ranging from somewhat affordable to very expensive,

> "Rock the Vote! Or if you're middle-aged with a sentimental side, Easy Listen the Vote!"
>
> Tweeted political satirist
> **STEPHEN COLBERT** @STEPHENATHOME
> on election night 2012

who will work to get more favorable search results. Unless there is some giant scandal dominating the internet, this probably doesn't make sense at the local level. Instead, focus on SEO terms and run a solid digital campaign to push the right type of results.

Takeaways

Everything in this chapter should be taken with a grain of salt. The digital world moves so quickly that information in this chapter became dated between edits, and there is no telling what the future will look like. But through the confusion and speed, there seem to be some constants and patterns that will likely remain true as tech morphs into its next incarnation.

- If you have an idea, give it a try. Part of not knowing what works means that anything could—if done well. So, if inspired, follow your vision, evaluate, and adjust.
- Remember geographical location. You could have videos going viral, but if your voters don't know about it, it's all for naught. Create content with your target audience in mind.
- Analytics are your friend. If you're putting out content regularly, check in often to know what's working, what's not, and adjust.
- The digital world is fun. The proliferation of voice have spoken, and what people want to read and share is often positive, funny, and poignant. Use this flexibility to show who you are.
- All the other rules of campaigning apply—this is just a new vessel, not a new game.

5

Fundraising

ALTHOUGH THIS HANDBOOK SUGGESTS A NUMBER OF WAYS TO STRETCH your campaign dollars, no matter how many volunteers or friends with special talents you may have, eventually you will have to spend money to get your message out. Production and media buys require up-front, cash-in-hand transactions. The US Postal Service will not send direct mail on a promise, and most places that print anything for campaigns require payment when you pick up the product. Although volunteers can cut your debt load and are a valuable resource not to be squandered, they're not enough.

The bottom line is that if you want to get your message and your candidate's face or name into the public view, you must raise and spend a certain threshold of money to be competitive. What that threshold is depends on your race, the voting population, and which campaign activities you intend to implement.

I have worked on campaigns where money was no object and others where every decision was a financial trade-off, and yes, it's more fun to work on campaigns with ample funds. Most important, money can buy you the opportunity, ability, and freedom to respond immediately to anything coming at the campaign.

While there are always stories of winners being grossly outspent, history indicates that the inverse is more often true, especially as you move up the food chain. According to the Center for Responsive Politics, in the 2002 midterm elections, "just under 95 percent of US House races and 76 percent of Senate races were won by the candidate who spent the most money."[1] Subsequent election cycles reveal little variation in the ratio of winners to losers based on money spent, according to OpenSecrets.com and the Center for Responsive Politics.[2] And this trend continued into 2012, when better than 93 percent of the biggest spenders won House races and accounted for Senate wins 79 percent of the time.[3]

> "Never put your own money into the show."
> *THE PRODUCERS*

However, the down-ballot candidate can often level the playing field with shoe leather and common sense. In 2012 a local city council candidate ran into his opponent while canvassing and they struck up a conversation, during which his opponent revealed that she hated canvassing hills and was sticking to the flatlands of the city; he immediately got in his car and drove to the hills, where he systematically canvassed for the rest of the cycle. He eventually won all the precincts in the steepest parts of the city and prevailed in the election even though his opponent had a robust lawn-sign campaign, had thirty meet-and-greets thrown by her friends and neighbors, and outspent him two to one. No one saw it coming.

Both the message and the quality of candidates (or issues) matter when it comes to raising money. However, campaign organization is a major factor in determining whether contributors are willing to "invest" in your campaign throughout the election cycle. Relationships that develop as a result of the candidate, the campaign team, your message, and your organization will bring in early money and early endorsements from individuals, companies, political action committees, and formal organizations. Indeed, a well-run, well-organized, hardworking, professionally executed campaign does not go unnoticed by the electorate. The voters correctly assess the job a candidate will do once in office by the campaign he or she runs to achieve that office. That is true from president of the United States to the county tax assessor. Further, when voters determine that a campaign is disciplined, they equate that with winning and contribute time and money.

Early Endorsements = Early Money = Early Media Buys

Early money is a way to communicate to the public that a cause or candidate has the necessary support to pull off a win. Also, throughout the campaign, major donors can serve as another type of communication tool with the electorate. For example, in Oregon, individuals who give more than $100 must be listed separately on the contributions and expenditures forms (C&Es) filed with the secretary of state. If this is true in your state, look for well-respected people whose names can draw votes, and ask them to give an amount that will get them listed in a prominent way in the local paper, which in turn may bring in money from their friends and business associates. Obviously this amount varies with the type of race. A $250 contribution may be news for a city councilor or alderman in a small town, but not in a large city mayoral race or congressional district race.

Unfortunately, contributions from individual donors tend to arrive late in a campaign, as things begin to heat up. When supporters see the campaign in the paper and on television or hear it on the radio, they know that this takes money. What they may not realize is that media time must be bought weeks in advance. *Early money is critical to a successful media campaign.* That is why many candidates take out personal loans to get their campaign rolling.

The urgency to raise money for media buys changes with each election cycle and is influenced by other races on the ballot that may be competing for media time. For example, in the presidential cycle, all down-ballot races in our area have to buy television by August to secure time for the general election. In 2008 one local candidate for county commissioner decided not to buy TV, and when he changed his mind in October, basically Saturday cartoons were left. Talk about testing the "trickle up" theory.

> "Big money brings big problems."
>
> —————— BILL MEULEMANS

Know the law: In some states, you may not legally begin collecting money until you have filed with the county clerk, city recorder, elections office, or secretary of state. However, from the moment you decide to run or work on a ballot measure, you can begin calling and lining up pledges that will come in as soon as you file.

Campaign Budget

It is pretty easy to put together a cursory budget sheet based on the activities you intend to conduct throughout the campaign; all it takes is a few phone

CAMPAIGN ACTIVITY	COST IN DOLLARS
Brochure	
Layout and design....................................	110.00
Printing (7,500 full color)	495.00
Lawn Signs	
Design.......................................	100.00
Printing (250 @ $2.24 each- 2 color-two sides)...............	560.00
Wickets@ $1.00 ea	250.00
Voter lists from County for absentee, GOTV or access to voter activation network	50.00
Direct Mail: 1 piece: postcard (saturated)	
Postage, layout, mail charge	3,000.00
Photocopying, misc. office supplies........................	60.00
Candidate Photo Session...............................	165.00
Voters' Pamphlet	300.00
Total	**$ 5090.00**

FIGURE 5.1 Example of a Campaign Budget for a Candidate in a Small-City Race

calls. Figure 5.1 is an actual budget sheet from a local city council race. This race covered a city of 19,000 people and 8,000 homes. There was no TV or radio advertising.

If your budget is tight, consider omitting direct mail; that means you could run a campaign of this size for $2,000. However, if you're intent upon sending direct mail, note that printing costs have gotten very competitive, so go online to find the best deal. Be sure you print only once; multiple short-run printing jobs will really drive up your costs. Figure 5.2 is the budget from a countywide, issue-based campaign. This county covers about 2,000 square miles and has about 180,000 residents (approximately 100,000 registered voters). Because of the size of the county and limited volunteer help, lawn signs gave way to four-by-four-foot and four-by-eight-foot field signs placed along highways.

In 2002, hotly contested Oregon House races came in around $225,000 each for the general election. By 2008 this doubled and then doubled again in 2012. On the high end, a Portland metro-area campaign bumped up against $500,000 in 2002, and on the low end, a couple of races in the outlying areas spent less than $150,000. By 2012 metro races were $500,000 to $1 million *for the primary alone.* Figures 5.3, 5.4, and 5.5 are examples of budget components

Campaign Activity	Cost in Dollars
Direct Mail	
Fundraiser letter: 1,000 pieces, three times	
Design	300.00
Printing and postage, plus remit envelope	1,500.00
General mailer: full color, 50,000 pieces	
Design	300.00
Printing and mailing	10,000.00
General mailer: black-and-white, 50,000 pieces	
Design	300.00
Printing and mailing	9,000.00
Targeted mailer: black-and-white, 25,000 pieces	
Design	300.00
Printing and mailing	4,000.00
Walking/info piece: 5-by-11, color, 30,000 pieces	
Design	300.00
Printing	2,000.00
Precinct Analysis	900.00
Voters' Pamphlet	300.00
Field Signs (200)	5,000.00
GOTV	
Voter registration database from county	100.00
GOTV inactive reports (four reports)	400.00
Data consultant	3,000.00
Media Advertising	
TV ad development: four ads at $1,000 each	4,000.00
Cable buys	6,000.00
Network buys	12,000.00
Radio development: five spots at $250 each	1,250.00
Buys	4,000.00
Newspaper	9,000.00
Facebook and Online Advertising	3,500.00
Other Advertising	
Insert in chamber newsletter	75.00
Car/business signs, 500 pieces	200.00
Campaign Management	10,500.00
Office Supplies	200.00
Celebration Party	200.00
TOTAL	**88,625.00**

FIGURE 5.2 Example of a Countywide, Issue-Based Campaign Budget

Campaign Activity Expense	Amount in Dollars
Direct mail: 11 pieces 125,000	50,000.00
Design	5,500.00
Direct-mail fundraising	3,950.00
Polling	6,000.00
Voter ID (18,000)	7,000.00
Printing cartridges	1,000.00
Letterhead envelopes	704.00
Headquarters	1,500.00
Data services	—
Volunteer support	
Food, refreshments (war room)	600.00
Field signs	
Design and layout	100.00
Printing	2,500.00
Staff	
CPA	1,000.00
Campaign manager	30,000.00
Field coordinator	7,500.00
Activities coordinator	3,000.00
Media (see media budget, figure 5.5)	102,478.00
Office supplies	
Postage, pens, software	500.00
Telephone, fax	1,500.00
Staples, envelopes, etc.	2,500.00
Paper	400.00
TOTAL	227,732.00
Anticipated and available income	158,915.09
Difference (must raise)	68,816.91

FIGURE 5.3 Example of an Expense Budget for a State Senate Campaign

for a state senate race. Figure 5.3 is the expense portion, figure 5.4 the income portion, and figure 5.5 the media detail. In this particular race, we came in on budget and overcame a 4 percent registration disadvantage, winning by 2 percent points.

Interestingly enough, by 2012 direct mail had moved entirely to the back of the bus in part because voters are numb to it but also because of the general expense. Similarly, TV has become so fractured that it too is decreasing in effectiveness. Meanwhile, social media and online advertising have stepped

FUNDRAISING ACTIVITY	COST IN DOLLARS	ANTICIPATED INCOME IN DOLLARS (AND AMT. IN BANK)
Donor/volunteer mailing (600 pieces)	600.00	6,000.00
Physician mailing (500 pieces)	500.00	6,000.00
DO mailing (200 pieces)	200.00	4,000.00
State/nation physician mailing (1,000 pieces)	500.00	1,000.00
Pharmacists	150.00	1,000.00
Medford Education Association		3,000.00
Oregon Nurses Association		20,000.00
Oregon League of Environmental Voters		
Oregon Education Association		
Pledges		14,600.00
Money in the bank		90,840.09
Deposit 8/27		3,475.00
Events		
Chiropractors		2,000.00
Portland physician event		3,000.00
Ashland physician event		1,000.00
Optometrists (20 pieces)		1,000.00
Owed for Medford fundraiser	1,000.00	
Misc. gatherings	1,000.00	2,000.00
TOTAL	3,950.00	158,915.09

FIGURE 5.4 Example of a Fundraising Budget for a State Senate Campaign

up as better tools, especially for the down-ballot campaign. To estimate how much money your campaign will need, consider talking with people who have previously run a similar race. Some will have budgets with predicted and actual money spent. The county clerk or state election office should have contributions and expenditures by race on file, and a little time with these records provides an opportunity to reconstruct what was spent, and where. The following sections show how you might go about determining a budget for specific campaign activities.

Brochure

1. Find another brochure with a design and layout you like.
2. Get a price quote from a graphic designer for something comparable that's camera ready.

MEDIA COMPONENT	BUYS IN DOLLARS
Charter	6,600.00
AFN	4,000.00
FOX	23,400.00
KTVL	25,228.00
Radio	20,000.00
TV production (3 @ $1500 each)	4,500.00
Radio production (3 @ $250 each)	750.00
Print media	8,000.00
Layout and design	1,000.00
Inserts	1,000.00
Facebook advertising	5,000.00
Google advertising	2,000.00
GOTV Post-it notes	1,000.00
TOTAL	**102,478.00**

FIGURE 5.5 Example of a Media Budget Detail for a State Senate Campaign

3. Determine which precincts you will target (you will determine this from your precinct analysis, as described in Chapter 1 and Appendix A); using voter registration lists for those precincts, calculate how many brochures you'll need to print. Remember that the number of registered voters and that of actual homes are two different things. You need enough brochures so that one will go to each home, regardless of how many registered voters live there. To get the actual number of unduplicated households, try calling the county clerk or a mail house if your voter activation network does not allow you to fine-tune this duty. Call a printer and get a price quotation; you can always have more done later, so don't get carried away. But remember: Don't print 300 this week and 50 next week or you will quickly break the budget on printing alone.
4. Call a photographer, and ask how much a photo shoot will cost.
5. Things that affect the cost of a brochure:

   - Color costs; the choices, in descending order of cost, are full color, spot color, and black and white.
   - Paper can have a dramatic impact on cost as well as printed quality. Be careful not to use paper that will absorb the ink too much. I think the feel of the paper is very important, and I tend to spend a little more for

a more professional feel. For a three-up brochure, look at 80-pound vellum Bristol or 80-pound Xerox Digital Color Elite.
- Does it need to be folded or cut? Each of these brings additional charges. Cutting is cheaper than folding. Die cuts for a door hanger also come at a cost.

A few years back, a local candidate had his graphic designer create a brochure that he could email to friends and supporters. The idea was that supporters would print as many as necessary for their own canvassing in support of the candidate. The brochure (obviously, black-and-white) dictated the lawn signs, which were also black-and-white, as were the newspaper inserts.

Lawn Signs

Use steps similar to those listed above for the brochure. First, determine the total number of signs you will need. I have worked on campaigns with as many as one lawn sign for every thirty homes and others where we had as few as one for every hundred homes. It really depends on whether you can get the locations for signs and whether you're in an urban race or one with an urban/rural mix. Does the race warrant a large number of signs? Again, one way to determine the number of signs you need is to call someone who conducted a similar campaign covering the same geographical area and ask how many signs were put up. While you're on the phone, ask for their list of lawn sign locations.

Once you know the number of signs, get the same number of stakes plus a few more. Signs run around $4 to $5 each with stakes and the miscellaneous stuff you will need for them. Unlike brochures, short runs for signs may take as long as two weeks to print, and they can be costly. For example, a run of twenty-five signs costs $13 per sign, whereas the cost for a run of five hundred is $2.45 per sign. Get enough printed the first time.

If you are using H-wickets for corrugated signs, they run about $1 each. If you intend to place your signs on wooden stakes, you will need screws and washers to attach the signs to the stakes; price these items and list the cost. Wooden stakes plus screws and washers to hold them to the sign also run about $1 per sign. Another option that can cut costs per sign is to use smaller stock; if you do this, be sure to keep the design as simple as possible: predominantly featuring the candidate's name, minimizing the office sought, and omitting slogans. In general, try to think of every little thing you will need to do to complete a specific activity. After you have done these tasks, call around for some prices.

Everything you do in a political campaign requires money. While many of the people who work for you will also give you money, the bulk of it will come from people who are not directly involved as volunteers.

I never apologize or feel as if I am begging when I ask for money for a candidate or ballot measure. I assume that the potential contributor wants my candidate in office (or wants the benefits of the ballot measure) and is willing to back up that desire with money. When I ask for money, I think of it as providing an opportunity for the voter to get involved at a level other than the voting booth. I also look at a request for money as less demanding than a request for an individual's time. The reality is this: If you can find excellent candidates to serve in office implementing programs that you support, more power to them; do all you can to help get them there. And money is a lot easier to give than time.

> "It's not how much money you raise. It's how you spend your money."
> **JEFFREY GILDENHORN**, former candidate for mayor of Washington, DC

Figure 5.6 is a template of a budget sheet you can use or modify for your purposes. Many local campaigns are too small and underfunded to have a campaign headquarters (other than in your home) or even staff. However, I included a staff section just in case you need it. Feel free to photocopy or scan this page and modify it to fit your budget needs.

Direct Mail for Money

While direct mail can help create a relationship between your campaign and the voter, it is also an opportunity to raise money where those relationships are established. Given that efficient direct mail requires a mailing list of an already identifiable group of voters, I prefer to see which lists I can get and then formulate a letter or piece that will appeal to those voters. Remember, *your direct mail is only as good as the list to which it is sent.* Carefully match your appeal to the people you are targeting.

In a direct-mail fundraising piece, you might include a targeted letter, a campaign brochure, and a remittance envelope (figure 5.7). Direct mail can be used simply to align your candidate with an issue such as a concern for jobs where unemployment is high, parks and playgrounds where there are none, or antigrowth in a neighborhood where a big development is planned. Be sure to color-code your remittance envelopes with your direct-mail pieces so that you know who is responding to what. That way, you get some feedback on which letters are the most effective. By running a marking pen along the edges of a stack of remittance envelopes, a campaign

Campaign Activity	Amount	Campaign Activity	Amount
Brochure		Lawn Signs	
Layout & design		Design & Layout	
Printing		Printing	
Photography		Field signs	
Staff (salaries)		Printing, shipping	
Treasurer		lumber or metal stakes, etc	
Campaign Manager & other staff		for installation	
Headquarters		Office Supplies	
Rent, phones, etc. (list it all)		Postage, pens, software,	
Web Page		Telephone, fax	
Facebook & Online advertising		Staples, envelopes, etc.	
Direct Mail Television			
(Do this for each piece)		Production	
Layout and design		Buys	
Printing		(Again, use the ad rep	
Postage		of each station to set up	
Lists and labels (or)		a schedule and budget	
Mail house (they handle labels		according exposure you	
& postage)		want. Put total here.)	
Misc. Printing		Radio	
Bumper stickers		Production	
Flyers		Buys	
Body badges (canvassers		Fundraising expenses	
& volunteers)		Staples, envelopes, etc.	
Letterhead, envelopes		Invitations, layout, printing	
Print Advertising		Postage	
(I would run a separate budget		Decorations	
sheet for print advertising and		Prizes	
include the number of ads,		Volunteer support	
the size of ads, and the cost		food, refreshments	
of each with reductions as		GOTV	
to the number of runs.		Voter ID lists	
Polling		Absentee lists	
Benchmark Poll			
Tracking Poll			

FIGURE 5.6 Sample Budget Form

can cheaply, quickly, and easily color-code envelopes. When color-coding your remittance envelopes, stay away from highlighter pen; use bold colors, such as red, black, and blue, that can easily be seen when the contribution comes into the campaign.

Finding Targeted Mailing Lists

Throughout this handbook are tips and suggestions for establishing relationships with special-interest groups in your community or region. Such alliances can really pay off in mailing-list dividends. Think about who would be most interested in seeing you get elected or seeing your measure passed. Will other candidates or officeholders turn over their house lists to your campaign? Consider asking someone who previously ran for the office you are seeking, especially if that someone is an exiting incumbent. Think about other organizations, too: Which ones would sell or give you their mailing lists? Here are some possibilities of lists that could generate money:

- Teachers, especially if you're working for a school or library bond measure or running for school board

Enclosed:	I/we volunteer to:	
____ $1000	____ Canvass	❑ Use name(s) as supporter
____ $500	____ Host event	____________
____ $250	____ Phone bank	❑ email address:
____ $100	____ Stuff Mail	____________
____ $50	____ Display lawn signs	Dr. Alan Bates
____ $25	____ Put up lawn signs	State Senate
____ Other	____ Sign Maintenance	

The following information is required in order to comply with Oregon Campaign Law:

Name ____________ Phone ____________
Address ____________
City, State, Zip ____________
Occupation ____________
Employer ____________
Employer's Address ____________
City, State, Zip ____________

Please make checks payable to Committee to Elect Alan Bates. Contributions may qualify for an Oregon tax credit of $50 per person filing a single return, or $100 per couple filing a joint return.

Authorized by the Committee to Elect Dr. Alan Bates, Salley Jones, Treasurer,

FIGURE 5.7 Example of a Remittance Envelope

Don't forget to include a line for an email address.

- Environmental organizations such as the Sierra Club, fly fishermen, League of Conservation Voters, Friends of the River, clean-water groups, greenway organizations, Critical Mass, or any organization that sends or emails a newsletter to a specific group of supporters
- Women's organizations such as National Organization for Women, or Women's Political Caucus
- Your church
- Civic clubs, firefighters, law enforcement groups
- Historic preservation groups

Ten Tips for Success When Mailing for Money

1. Solicit only targeted lists.
2. Always include a remittance envelope (figure 5.7).
3. Use quality paper stock and printing. Keep graphics and fonts simple and clean.
4. Personalize the letter: "Dear Suzi" works better than "Dear Friend," and always include a P.S. The P.S. should not be a throwaway; this is often the only thing that is read in a fundraising letter, so make it count.
5. Keep the letter short: I use a single piece of heavy-weight paper, laid out in landscape, cut in half, then folded in half. This way each piece of paper will generate two letters of solicitation and looks like a greeting card from the outside. (Note that this size restricts your ability to have the contributor's name and address at the top—only a "Dear Bob and Mary" will fit; that means everything must be kept in order.) The front of the folded half sheet can be simply a picture of the candidate or a list of accomplishments; a report card of sorts (see: "Direct Mail that Works" in this chapter).
6. Use a size of envelope that does not scream junk mail; 6½ by 5 inches (number 6) works best. This size envelope will comfortably hold the folded half sheet of paper and your remittance envelope. You want everything to match, so since the remittance envelope is always white, make both the letter and envelope white as well. Avoid using business-size envelopes (number 9).
7. Personalize the envelope: Have volunteers hand-address them or select a font that gives the appearance of a hand-addressed envelope when printing your list directly onto it. Don't print your picture on the outside of the envelope.
8. First-class stamps get a far better response rate but there are some pretty classy bulk-mail stamps out now. Placing the stamp so it is

slightly crooked also helps with the response. For all other direct mail, I use a bulk-mail permit number that gets printed in the upper right-hand corner when everything else gets printed. Have the graphic designer

> "I have only made this letter rather long because I have not had time to make it short."
> **PASCAL, 1656**

create a sort of canceled-stamp look with the bulk-rate number. Check out the bulk mail stamp I use in figure 3.1.

9. Have the return address printed on the *flap* of the envelope with only the address: do not print the candidate's name or place a campaign logo on the envelope. Printing the return address on the flap gets the recipient one step closer to opening the envelope and potentially giving. Omitting the candidate's name and logo keeps everything clean and unrecognizable as political mail.

10. A direct-mail piece followed up by a phone call from the campaign substantively increases your response rate.

Tone

- People in lower economic groups and those with less education respond in greater numbers to a longer "the house is on fire" solicitation. This group gives less money and votes less, so be sure you have targeted correctly before spending lots of money on a multipage solicitation.
- Wealthy, well-educated Republicans respond to letters that are no longer than two pages with lots of "this is what I've done; this is what I will do." A single page will work fine for them.
- Well-educated, affluent Democrats respond in greatest numbers to short, single-page letters explaining the community needs that you will address and how their contribution will make a difference.
- Once people respond to the first mailing, solicit them again. For those responding the second time, solicit them again. After three letters, go back to your house list.

Determine a Baseline Budget for Direct-Mail Solicitation

1. Decide how many mail pieces you intend to send throughout the campaign.
2. Look at some other direct-mail pieces you like, and get a cost estimate for layout and design.
3. Decide which groups you are mailing to, and then determine the number of households that will receive the piece.

4. Use this number to figure your printing and mailing costs for each piece; 50 to 65 cents each is a good ballpark figure. However, economies of scale do count here.

5. Multiply the per-piece cost by the number of direct-mail pieces you want to send.

"My practice is to go first to those who may be counted upon to be favorable, who know the cause and believe in it, and ask them to give as generously as possible. When they have done so, I go next to those who may be presumed to have a favorable opinion and to be disposed to listening, and secure their adherence. Lastly, I go to those who know little of the matter or have no known predilection for it and influence them by presentation of the names of those who have already given."

BENJAMIN FRANKLIN

Special Events

Special events are campaign-sponsored activities intended to raise money and support for the campaign. Examples are a coffee at a supporter's house or a campaign-organized luncheon, dinner, or picnic. Although I have had many successful special events for campaigns, given the campaign time expended for the return, and the fact that people who attend are usually supporters who have already given and have every intention of voting for the candidate or cause, you will find that the more efficient fundraising effort goes to dialing for dollars. Nevertheless, it is important to stress that fundraisers are not just about raising money. Special events are also for public visibility and education, for involving volunteers so they are more committed to the campaign and candidate, and for promoting "friend-raising" by strengthening the bonds volunteers and guests have with the candidate.

When approached as an opportunity to advertise the candidate and cement relationships, special events can be worth the necessary resources. But don't underestimate the commitment involved. You need to be cautious about the strain special events put on the campaign committee, the volunteers, and the candidate. If someone other than the campaign committee is sponsoring the event, as is often the case with a coffee, you need to be ready to help ensure that the event will be a success.

Ensure a Good Turnout

The one thing you must avoid if you schedule a special event is a poor turnout. If it looks as if a fundraising event will have marginal attendance, I invite all my volunteers to attend for free. Numbers are more important than money when holding a special event in political circles. Whatever the attendance, you need to be certain that the people who do attend don't have a bad experience. If people can't find the location, can't find parking, or were inadvertently left off the reservation list, they are likely to blame the campaign. You never want to lose a supporter over an avoidable organizational error at a fundraising event. Take care of your supporters by taking care of details.

Holding a Special Event

A good rule of thumb for planning special events for fundraising is that it takes one week of preparation for every ten people you expect to attend. Obviously this time frame becomes tight in a three-month campaign, but the rule underscores the importance of ample preparation time for a successful event. The preparation takes place in four stages:

1. You must *define* the purpose or purposes the event is to accomplish and what type of event you want.
2. You must *plan* the event.
3. You must *promote* the event.
4. You must *conduct* the event.

Tips for handling each of these stages are discussed below.

1. Determine the Purpose and Type of Event

Be clear about the purpose of the event. Is it to attract donors, raise money, raise support, thank volunteers and supporters, or just get the word out on the measure or the candidate? Special events can, of course, have more than one purpose, but you need to focus on one purpose before you can pick the event. Focus on the main purpose when choosing the type of event; then see whether other purposes might be accomplished as well.

Dinners. Hosting fundraising dinners at a local restaurant is both easy and lucrative. First, contact a supportive restaurant and ask whether the owner will donate the dinner at cost in the restaurant. Then sell it to the guests at retail. Generally the restaurant can't afford the whole affair, so go to another eatery and ask whether that owner will donate the dessert, ask another for a donation of the coffee, a local vintner for the wine, and so on. Invite a local musician or band to volunteer (for tips) talent to make the occasion special (consider looking at the high school music department for great talent). Restaurants are often closed on Mondays, making it a perfect night for your fundraiser.

Intimate affairs at people's homes can also be fun while raising money. In this approach, the host produces the invitations and provides the food. If the person hosting the event is new to this sort of thing, it's important to check in frequently and help as needed. These events usually involve having a well-known person provide a lavishly catered meal for a well-known candidate at a fairly hefty price. In this scenario, be selective about who is invited, although the price will usually select who will attend, and the invitees know that. We have brought in as much as $6,000 in our small area at this type of dinner.

> "Every experienced campaigner knows that money follows hard work. It is not the other way around."
>
> MARGARET SANGER

When the candidate is unknown, don't suggest a donation amount or impose a cover charge for a fundraising event for two reasons: First, because the candidate is new to the political circuit, people will stay home rather than give money to someone they do not know. Second, if the candidate performs well and the crowd swells behind the candidacy, people will give more than any contribution the campaign might suggest to get in the door. For example, if the admission charge is $25 for a meet-the-candidate event at someone's home, typically many attendees can give more; however, the campaign will get only the $25 cover. To lend credibility to a political newcomer, bring in a well-known political figure, such as the governor, and schedule two events back-to-back in two cities. The first event can run from 6:00 to 7:30 in one city, and the second from 8:00 to 9:30 in another. To make sure there will be plenty of money flowing, arrange for one or two people at each gathering to announce that they have just written a check for $1,000 and would encourage all to give as generously as possible. In one campaign, we raised $10,000 in three and a half hours with this approach; there was no suggested contribution on the invitation, no cover charge to get in, and virtually no one knew the candidate before the events.

Coffees. Coffees sponsored by a supporter can be easy and quite successful. However, they can also be a miserable failure. To be successful, coffees must be closely supervised. Most people do not like attending political fundraisers such as coffees, so the drawing card should be the combination of the candidate and the host of the coffee. The campaign should oversee the invitations and be ready to help with follow-up phone calls to ensure good attendance. A host who invites sixty people, only to have three show up, may feel humiliated because he or she let the candidate down. Or the host may feel the candidate is responsible for the poor turnout. Either way, the candidate and the campaign manager have been deprived of one more night at home or of time that could have been spent raising money by phone, preparing for a debate, or getting volunteers for a canvass.

A few years ago, I started the practice of assigning one person to oversee coffees. More recently, because of the importance of this job, I actually paid someone to do this task. This person works closely with the campaign scheduler and serves as the campaign's liaison to any host who wishes to sponsor a coffee; he or she does not need to attend committee meetings. The coffee coordinator should be well connected in the community and, ideally, have ready access to lists that may help the hosts in beefing up the invitation list. The coffee coordinator helps with invitations, callbacks, and typically attends all coffees, arriving early with campaign paraphernalia and items the host or hostess may need for a successful event. Whether you have a coffee coordinator or not, the campaign can help any house party by securing and providing the hosts with a list of all the registered voters living near their homes; lists of this nature can be attained through your voter activation network or from the voter registration files you secured from the local election office.

Hosts who walk invitations to their neighbors invariably get a better turnout, after all there's nothing like the personal touch in politics. In the same vein, if at all possible, have the candidate call the people invited to the coffee, or at least some of them. This will ensure a donation if they are going, and if they can't make it, it is an opportunity to ask for money or support.

The candidate's call would go something like this:

"Hello, Sam? This is Ben Bloom. Say, I just got a list of all the people invited to Shirley's coffee, and when I saw your name, I had to take a moment to call and tell you how much I'm looking forward to you being there. It should be a lot of fun. Bring some tough questions for me, will you? Great, see you there."

Using coffees effectively will bring in money, but more important, they are a great resource for finding campaign workers and obtaining email addresses and lawn sign locations.

Auctions and Yard Sales. To generate auction items, the campaign can go to businesses and supporters to secure a wide variety of donations, including baked goods to sell to attendees. I recently helped with an auction where a state senator donated a day of fly fishing; as part of the donation he included a lunch of locally produced foods and wine as well as transportation to and from a nearby lake. On the night of the auction one of the volunteers working with the auctioneer came out dressed in hip waders, carrying a fishing pole; the crowd loved it and bid heavily. This particular auction took a year to put together, had five hundred in attendance, and raised better than $22,000, but I've also worked on smaller auctions spanning shorter time frames that raised $4,000. A good auctioneer who is outgoing and funny makes all the difference.

A yard sale is another option. If you're going to plan one, make it an event. Get a huge yard and lots of donations, old and new. Advertise the great stuff in advance. A good yard sale will bring in a couple grand a day and off-load unwanted things in the bargain. However, the setup and cleanup is time-consuming; assign a team to these tasks.

Involve Attendees. One event I held in a small community was a dessert bake-off. I called specific supporters in that area and asked them to bring their very best dessert. I charged an entry fee for all but the bakers. The campaign provided the coffee (donated), and I recruited other locals to serve as the judges. I made up ribbons for different awards, such as "Dessert Most Likely to Keep a Marriage Together," and each entry won a prize. Because it was held in a very small community, all who attended knew each other. Everyone had a great time, and the only cost to the campaign was the building rental.

General Considerations. Whatever the type of event, the location is a big consideration. Is it big enough? Too big? How about the atmosphere? For indoor events, *never* use a huge hall or room unless you are expecting a huge crowd. When selecting locations, I look for places where rooms can be closed off in case of poor attendance. No matter how many people come, I want the event to look well attended and successful, leaving attendees with the impression that just the number expected came. In selecting a restaurant for a dinner, try to find one that has a medium-size room with another adjoining it that can be used or closed off as needed.

Consider your budget when deciding what type of event to hold; figure roughly what it will cost the campaign and what income it is likely to generate. You also need to estimate the commitment necessary from the candidate, the campaign committee, and your volunteers. Don't forget to consider the economic climate in the community. A $50-a-plate dinner in a town where the last factory just closed might not be a very good idea even if it would make you money. When considering an event, always ask: Does this make sense? Does it fit? Does it feel right?

2. Plan the Event

Planning an event is an extension of choosing the event. All the considerations that informed your choice of the event must now be put into an action plan. In other words, it is time to sort out the details. For instance, some events will require licenses or permits from local government. Such requirements can be a factor in the decision to hold an event, but once the decision is made, someone has to make sure the license or permit is obtained. Similarly, the location, which helped you decide on the type of event, must now be secured. The theme of the event, whether it is a candidate luncheon or auction for a school bond, now influences the details of the event.

To run a successful special event, it is critical that you know your audience and how to reach them. For example, are you planning a dinner to support your library? If so, you need to get a mailing list from the Friends of the Library.

Once you know whom you want to reach, you must decide how to reach them. Printed invitations with a telephone follow-up might work well for a formal dinner. However, if the event is a yard sale, just advertise it in the paper or place flyers around town. Whatever the means, people must be assigned to accomplish it. Invitations must be printed; flyers must be designed, printed, and distributed; ads have to be written and delivered. All this takes time and people, and you will need to plan accordingly.

A good way to make sure the details are taken care of is to put the event on a timeline, just like the one for the whole campaign, only smaller. Scheduling in all the tasks and placing the event on a timeline requires someone who is in charge. That person needs to have volunteers assigned to all aspects of the event. Like the campaign itself, successful special events are the product of organization. If you assign the leadership of a special event to one person, provide ample volunteer help, develop a timeline, and plan a budget, you will have a successful event.

While budgets are an extra step, making one will not only help you get a handle on expenses, but also remind you of things that need to be done. For example, listing the room expense may remind you to check the date of the event to see what else is going on in the community at that time. If you're hosting that dinner to support your town library, you don't want to find out right after you printed the invitations and rented the hall that it is on the same night as the American Association of University Women annual dinner at the college. Paying for the ads for your auction may remind you to check whether the hospital auction is on the same weekend. Here is a list of the things that could be included in a budget:

- Site rental
- Food
- Drinks
- Rental (sound system, tables, chairs)
- Printing
- Supplies

- Mailings
- Entertainment
- Professionals
- Parking
- Advertisements
- Decorations
- Insurance
- Fees
- Use permits
- Liquor licenses
- Cleanup
- Awards, door prizes
- Thank-you mailing

Although someone in your organization is in charge of planning the event, when it comes time to implement the plan, provide additional help in training and staffing volunteers. These requirements must be met before the actual setup begins.

In addition to having trained helpers available, you must plan for the supplies you will need. Often supplies must be ordered well ahead of the event—decorations, for instance—and these should go on your special-event timeline. Also, things that will cost you money—here again, decorations are a good example—are listed in your special-event budget. If you keep going back to the budget and to your expense list, you will be reminded of things you might have forgotten.

Keep in mind that in the planning of an event, some things that do not appear in your budget or timeline may nonetheless be critical. For instance, legal issues such as prohibitions against holding political fundraisers in public buildings must be considered. On a more mundane but no less critical level, be sure to have duplicates of essential items. If a projector is needed for an event, it is wise to have two projectors on hand, or at least two bulbs. How about extension cords and an extra microphone? Also have duplicate lists of all the important phone numbers of the people you are depending on, such as the vendors, caterers, entertainers, staff, and volunteers. These lists will also help you remember all who need to be acknowledged at the end of the event.

> "The first thing you naturally do is teach the person to feel that the undertaking is manifestly important and nearly impossible. . . . That draws out the kind of drives that make people strong, that puts you in pursuit intellectually."
>
> —— **EDWIN H. LAND**, founder, Polaroid Corp.

It is helpful, too, to know the earliest possible time you can get into the building where the event will be held. Early access provides an opportunity to set things up and test all systems before people arrive.

3. Promote the Event

To promote a special event properly, you must have a target audience in mind. Consider the income level and age of your target audience. Once these details have been established, consider how best to reach them. Your first task is to determine where to get lists of the people in your target audience. If you have a narrow group in mind, such as teachers, doctors, or human-service advocates, you can often get mailing lists from the special-interest groups these people belong to or support. If your audience is broader, as it would be for a neighborhood bake sale, you can take the list from a general source, such as your voter database. Recently a friend was holding a coffee for a candidate for state representative and asked if I could come up with a list of his neighbors and provide phone numbers as well. Using the voter database and street names near his home, I generated and emailed a list in less than ten minutes.

Once you know whom you are trying to contact, you must decide how best to do it. Some possibilities are:

- Invitations
- Flyers
- Radio and television ads
- Press releases
- Posters
- Newsletters
- Handbills or flyers
- Facebook
- Email

The content and design of announcements must be attractive, professional, and clear. Include the date, place, time (beginning and end), and cost, and provide a map or clear directions for getting there. Note whether any of the cover charge is tax deductible or refundable. For instance, if the event costs $25 for the attendee but your cost per attendee is $10, then the difference, $15, is a straight campaign contribution. Instead of including the math in the ad, simply put a footnote at the bottom stating what amount of the price is deductible.

4. Conduct the Event

Arrive early: The most important thing you can do to ensure success is to set up early. Everything should be ready forty-five minutes to an hour ahead of time. As the organizer, you need to keep focused and calm. Your volunteers will take their cue from you, and the message you convey must be calm efficiency. It's a nice touch to have a packet for volunteer organizers with their names on them. Include the overall plan as well as the names of the individuals responsible for each of the volunteer activities.

Once people start to arrive, your focus is on hospitality. How you greet people and work with them will set the tone of the event. Allow adequate time for the candidate to circulate. Do not schedule or allow the candidate to "help" operate the event. The candidate should not be doing anything other than meeting the supporters. Name tags will help the candidate when greeting the guests. Place the name tag below attendees' right shoulder so it can be read discreetly as the guest moves closer to the candidate's line of sight when he or she is shaking hands.

Remember to thank everyone, even the people who sold you things. Everyone involved—volunteers, guests, and vendors—is forming an impression of the candidate and the campaign, and you need to do everything you can to make a positive impression. That includes a good cleanup, even if you have rented the facility, so make sure there are volunteers assigned to this task. As an organizer, never leave an individual to clean up alone. Stay until everything is done.

Candidate Calls to Raise Money

Direct contact by the candidate remains the quickest, cheapest, and most effective way to raise money. It is critical to a campaign's success. Remember, as the candidate, you are willing to do a job and volunteer your time at a task that few want to do. If people support your core values and ideas, they must show that support by contributing to your campaign, thereby helping you get your name out. Do not sound apologetic. You are doing the community a favor.

While the campaign manager can call for moderate amounts of money, the calls to major donors should be conducted by the candidate or a close family member, such as a spouse, a sibling, or a parent. It is very difficult for people to turn down the candidate on a direct ask.

Set up some time each day to make the calls from a prepared list that includes phone numbers, addresses, party registration, giving history, personal notes about the prospective donor, and a suggested amount for the ask. Be sure to have accurate information on what name the candidate should use when speaking with the donor: Is it Katherine, Kathy, Katy, Kate, or Kay?

Because it is so difficult to get a candidate to actually sit down every day and dial for dollars, assign a person to assist with the task. First put together a three-ring binder that has a list of all those who will be called. Within the binder, include an individual sheet for each contributor. The individual sheets will list name, phone number, work, giving history, and notes of previous attempts

> "A great leader is seen as servant first, and that simply is the key to his greatness."
> **ROBERT K. GREENLEAF**

to call. The assigned campaign worker stays with the candidate throughout call time and makes notes on the call sheet for the candidate.

Calling for Money for Ballot Measures

When fundraising for ballot measures, it is sometimes easier to set up a goal for a specific item, such as a full-page newspaper ad or radio spots. Let people know what you are trying to buy and how much it will cost so they can contribute accordingly. For example, I might tell people that I am trying to raise $1,500 for a last-minute ad campaign and ask what they can give toward it. If you are going to use a phone bank for fundraising, use just a few people who are committed and are identified with the measure in the community. Provide each caller with a list of the people you want to call; the list should include their giving history along with their phone numbers.

Since people prefer to sign on to something that's going to fly, I tell potential donors that we are X dollars away from our goal. Keep track as pledged dollars roll in, and if the campaign hasn't received the check within a week, remind the donor with either a phone call or email.

Voters do not look favorably on campaigns who cannot live within their fundraising abilities, so while waiting for fundraising to catch up with spending, consider setting up business accounts with as many of your vendors as possible. Although TV and newspapers require that campaign advertisements be paid in full before the ad runs, printers, typesetters, and other vendors may allow you to run an account and pay monthly or at the end of the campaign. Although the money is technically spent, it does not show up on your financial reports until the campaign has received an invoice.

Raising Money on the Web

Given the online fundraising success of the McCain campaign in 2000, the Dean campaign in 2004, and the Obama campaigns in 2008 and 2012, as well as online giving during national crises, Web-based fundraising must look like the answer for easy, cheap money. After all, it doesn't involve stamps, printing, folding, stuffing, or any of the items listed on the budget sheet. No clerical team necessary.

Indeed, according to Blue State Digital (BSD), retained by Obama "to manage the online fundraising, constituency-building, issue advocacy, and peer-to-peer online networking aspects of his 2008 Presidential primary campaign," by October 2008 better than half of Obama's eventual $750 million raised came through the Obama website using the BSD online tools suite.[4] However, before you opt out of the inefficient and costly means of raising campaign dollars through direct mail and events, consider this: Although there will always be exceptions, online contributions for down-ballot races are a relatively small part of a campaign's overall income stream.

> "Never think you need to apologize for asking someone to give to a worthy object, any more than as though you were giving him an opportunity to participate in a high-grade investment."
>
> — JOHN D. ROCKEFELLER JR.

In 2008 former Speaker of the Oregon House Jeff Merkley (D) challenged incumbent and Republican Gordon Smith for the US Senate. In that race, Merkley raised and spent a little more than $6 million to Smith's $13 million.[5] In a recent interview, Jon Isaacs, Jeff Merkley's campaign manager, explained that Merkley received less than 16 percent from online donations (compared with Dean's 2004 and Obama's 2008 online contribution percentages of 53 percent) and that this amount was only after the campaign received national attention that Smith was vulnerable. For now, down-ballot campaigns should add the internet to the fundraising toolbox while continuing to employ more traditional fundraising methods such as events, direct mail, and dialing for dollars. The following are ten tips to help your online fundraising efforts. These tips are based on observations by David Erickson of eStrategy Internet Marketing Blog.[6]

1. Make it easy to contribute by allowing supporters to donate small amounts of money, $20 or less. Lowering the barrier attracts more donors.
2. Create multichannel marketing: Place donate buttons everywhere—within internet ads, social networking profiles, or in blog posts. This provides as many opportunities as possible for people to contribute.
3. Use spot color to make the donate buttons pop on the website.
4. The website should be able to reload the donation form with information the donor gave previously (name, employment, address, zip code, and phone number). Small contributors often give repeatedly and do so at times impetuously following an irritating comment by the opposing candidate or in support of something your team has said or done. Make it easy.

5. Include next to the donation form a short video of the candidate underscoring the importance of the donor's support.

6. The design of the donation form is important. Place labels so the donor does not have to look back and forth to fill in data, and include only the information necessary to complete the donation. The submit button should be obvious.

> "I am deeply touched—not as deeply touched as you have been coming to this dinner, but nonetheless it is a sentimental occasion."
>
> **JOHN F. KENNEDY,** at a political fundraiser

7. This is not the time to gather unrelated information about your contributor. You want the donor doing only one task: giving money. Remove all distractions, and omit from the donation page any links that will take the donor away from it.

8. Give donors opportunities to give incrementally, $20 per month or whatever amount they choose, so multiple donations continue to come in with little or no campaign effort.

9. People are more likely to give to a candidate or a cause that their friends endorse, so build in incentives to encourage supporters to "bundle" their friends for giving. Besides bringing in money, it also expands a campaign's money network.

10. Your website is integral to the success of fundraising. People will not give to a cheesy website. It must look professional; colors, font, layout—all this matters. Spend some time and money on the design of your site if you hope to attract money with it. For more ideas, check out "The

> "He who gives early gives twice."
>
> **CERVANTES**

Political Consultants' Online Fundraising Primer" from the Institute for Politics, Democracy, and the Internet (www.ipdi.org/UploadedFiles /online_fundraising_primer.pdf).

Tips for Successful Fundraising

- Campaigns are about emotion, not intellect.
- Be visionary, present a vision, address opportunity. People need to feel that investing in a campaign will make life better, both now and in the future. They should feel that your winning will strengthen the community. Make your case larger than the office you seek or the program you hope to fund.
- Invite donors to invest in leadership, solutions, and vision. Through a candidate or a campaign, people are making an investment in their

community. Generally, people contribute to a campaign or candidate because they believe that they will get something in return. Describe to the donor, the voter, or the citizen what he or she will get with a victorious election. Use issues that are in front of voters.

- Do not look at fundraising as though there is just so much money and no more. Money flows like a river; don't think of it like a pond. There's plenty of money if you can show that the gifts will be used wisely. This applies to money for candidates and campaigns as well as money for schools, libraries, parks, and other issue-based campaigns.

- Sell ideas and hope, not the candidate. You're offering something that the voter wants: opportunity, vision, solutions, parks, better schools, less traffic, lower crime rates, cleaner air, whatever. Look at your campaign as the vehicle for the voters to get what they want. Charles Revson, founder of Revlon, said, "In the factory, we make cosmetics. In the stores, we sell hope." Sell hope.

> "Nobody roots for Goliath"
>
> **WILT CHAMBERLAIN**

- Never think of fundraising as begging. If you're a candidate, you're putting yourself out there, at no small sacrifice, to do a job that people want done. If you're working for a ballot measure, you're creating opportunities for a community to realize a vision.

- There's a difference between an underdog and a losing effort. People want to help an underdog but usually will not help finance an effort they believe will lose. Presenting your campaign as an underdog suggests that people are investing in the American Dream.

- Stay on your message. Your message should always be at the center of every appeal. Incorporate it into the ask while keeping the targeted donor's profile and interests as the focus.

- Be organized. Because people equate organization with winning, by showing a strong organizational core you are more likely to get people to give.

- Think community. Community campaigns are the most successful. Such a campaign presents issues that people understand. It presents solutions, involves volunteers, and encourages investment in the future. Do not talk about the mechanics of the campaign. A campaign and a candidate don't have needs; the community and the people in it have needs and challenges. The candidate or campaign should represent opportunity, solutions, answers, and the ability to meet those needs.

- Don't be afraid to ask for money. Asking for money is how you fund a campaign.

Fundraising Ideas That Take Less Than One Month of Preparation

1. Personal solicitation.
2. Dinner at a restaurant as outlined above.
3. "Sponsored by . . . " dinner or brunch at the house of someone well-known. This is a variation on a theme of a coffee, but whereas coffees are usually free, a dinner has an admission fee.
4. Theme dinner. These are great fun. First and most important, you need an incredible friend who is willing to open his or her home and prepare the food with other friends. A theme dinner usually will focus on a period in history (such as the turn of the twentieth century), an author or a set of authors, an important leader, and so forth. For example, you might have an evening focusing on Jane Austen. One friend would research her life and prepare some text that may be read throughout (or between) courses of the meal. Others would prepare a meal that features the types of foods eaten during that period. A theme dinner can also center on many authors. In this case, your really great friend might prepare favorite dishes of certain authors or dishes featured in books—such as *Like Water for Chocolate*. We have done this with high school girls and boys acting as the servers (dressed in black and white). You will also need different people to read appropriate passages from books that pertain to the courses being served. As these dinners are a real treat—almost like time travel—and lots of work, charge plenty. Make sure you sell enough tickets to make it worth your while before you head out to shop for groceries and spend days cooking. When we do this type of dinner, it is sold as an auction item for a specific number of people; whoever receives the winning bid gets to invite his or her friends to the feast. It can also be that seats are auctioned with a limited number of seats on the block. One theme dinner we conducted was an auction item for public television and sold for $5,500.

   > "You may never know what results from your action. But if you do nothing, there will be no results."
   > **GANDHI**

5. Small auctions. They are surprisingly easy to conduct. You need volunteers who are willing to approach businesses and friends to get donations for a candidate. Combine donations to make more attractive prizes. Auction a pair of shoes from a local shoe store or a backpack from a mountaineering supply store; find someone willing to give tennis lessons or golf lessons; ask a historian to donate a tour of your town's historic district; ask a

pilot to donate a ride in a private plane; a day of fly fishing; a rafting trip; and so on.

6. Softball tournament. This requires lots of work and makes very little money, but is great fun and a perfect project for that guy who wants to help but doesn't quite fit in anywhere else. The admission fees go to the campaign.

7. Birthday party for the candidate. The price of admission in dollars should be the candidate's age in years.

8. Raffle. This requires someone to be completely on top of the event, someone who can really track where the tickets are. You need one to three big prizes and some lesser prizes plus a bunch of people to sell tickets. Again, you can combine things to create a big prize, such as dinner for two, plus two theater tickets, after-theater dessert, and nightcap at a popular spot. A great auction item that's easy to gather is ninety-nine bottles of wine. Supporters can donate single bottles of wine, and wineries and private brewers are asked for mixed cases. A donated weekend in a cabin, at the lake, in the woods, or near a ski resort. Do you know anyone with a condo in Hawaii? If a supporter has lots of frequent-flyer miles, he or she could donate the required miles to get your winner to the final destination.

> "We make a living by what we get, but we make a life by what we give."
>
> — WINSTON CHURCHILL

9. An afternoon with . . . Have a local celebrity or author put together entertainment or a reading. How about asking the governor to pop in as he or she is moving through town? Have some great donated pastries and assorted hot beverages on hand.

10. Tasting and toasting. This is a theme coffee with an admission. It is just what it sounds like: wine tasting with finger food and a couple of big names present.

The World's Smallest Brochure: Direct Mail That Works

Most direct mailings have a rate of return of 3 percent to 6 percent without callbacks. Because a campaign does not want to send a direct-mail piece that costs more money than it brings in, the challenge lies in designing a piece that has a higher rate of return and is inexpensive to produce.

> "Men take only their needs into consideration, never their abilities."
>
> — NAPOLEON

People have become very sophisticated at detecting junk mail. To increase the rate of return, the piece must first get opened; second, it must be read (at least in part); and finally, it must be compelling enough to motivate the reader to give. Anything in a business-size envelope (a number 9) with an address label, a bulk-mail stamp, or a meter mark is suspect and apt to be thrown away without being opened. So the first task is choosing an envelope size that will make it more likely that the piece will be opened.

Years ago, the Reform Party created a direct-mail piece that went out nationwide to 70,000 recipients. By using an oversize (5 by 7 inches) courier envelope and an easy-to-read three-page note, the mailing drew a return rate of 4 percent. This return rate was double the national average, and the piece realized a two-to-one profit.[7]

A mailing this large enjoys an economy of scale that few local elections can attain; in this case, it cost only 67 cents per piece, including postage. The cost of a mailing like this for a short run in a local election could easily be more than twice as much; in fact, postage alone (if using first class) would have come in at 57 cents.

While oversize pieces work well with some voters, they do not work everywhere. Indeed, I've found the size that gets the best rate of return looks like an invitation or a greeting card from a friend; that is, 6½ by 4¾ inches. This size is large enough to hold a remittance envelope (without folding) and will comfortably hold a half sheet of paper folded in half. Given that a shorter letter is more likely to be read, do not make the mistake of folding an 8½-by-11-inch sheet in four.

Once the envelope is open, it is important that the piece offer plenty of information, be pleasing to the eye, and have a weight and feel that says the recipient is important, without looking lavish or expensive. The challenge, then, is how to make it all fit in a small format.

To accomplish such a package, my graphic designer and I created the world's smallest brochure: a half sheet of 8½-by-11-inch 80-pound vellum Bristol, folded in half with a photo of the candidate and a list of his accomplishments and ratings on the front (figure 5.8). The inside had another photo of the candidate and a letter with a P.S. on the state's tax refund policy on political contributions; each piece was personally signed by the candidate in either blue or green ink (never use black). The back had an endorsement from the governor. Given the space constraints, we skipped the usual business-letter practice of including the donor's address in the upper left-hand corner. Some letters had a "Dear Friends" salutation, and on others, we used no other identifier than the recipient's first name to make it a personalized letter; this created more work, but was worth it. To keep everything looking sharp, the letter, envelope, and remittance envelope were all printed on white. To encourage the recipient to turn the envelope over (one step closer to opening it), we had the representative's name and address printed on the envelope flap rather than on the front in the upper left-hand corner.

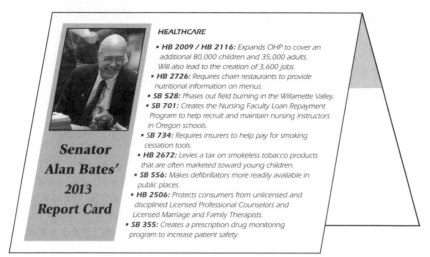

HEALTHCARE

- **HB 2009 / HB 2116:** Expands OHP to cover an additional 80,000 children and 35,000 adults. Will also lead to the creation of 3,600 jobs.
- **HB 2726:** Requires chain restaurants to provide nutritional information on menus.
- **SB 528:** Phases out field burning in the Willamette Valley.
- **SB 701:** Creates the Nursing Faculty Loan Repayment Program to help recruit and maintain nursing instructors in Oregon schools.
- **SB 734:** Requires insurers to help pay for smoking cessation tools.
- **HB 2672:** Levies a tax on smokeless tobacco products that are often marketed toward young children.
- **SB 556:** Makes defibrillators more readily available in public places.
- **HB 2506:** Protects consumers from unlicensed and disciplined Licensed Professional Counselors and Licensed Marriage and Family Therapists.
- **SB 355:** Creates a prescription drug monitoring program to increase patient safety.

Senator Alan Bates' 2013 Report Card

FIGURE 5.8 Front of "The World's Smallest Brochure"

To test a "Dear Friends" salutation versus a personalized one, I divided the mailing into two parts. The first was sent to five hundred people who had canvassed, had a lawn sign, or volunteered time to the campaign in some way. Although some had also given to the campaign, I did not have the donor list at the time of the mailing. This group had a letter that began "Dear Friends," which allowed me to have the whole thing printed, cut, and folded at a local print shop. Using a clerical team of sixteen seniors, we hand-addressed, stuffed, sealed, and stamped the envelopes (using bulk, not first-class postage) in one hour and fifteen minutes. The mailing cost was $425 (85 cents apiece)—for printing, postage, paper stock, layout, and remittance envelopes.

Because the candidate was a physician, I sent the second mailing to one hundred local physicians he knew, either personally or peripherally, using a letter designed to address their interests. This mailing was identical to the "Dear Friends" mailing except for four things: the text of the letter, the personalized salutation, a first-class stamp rather than a bulk stamp, and a computer-generated "handwriting" font on the envelope. A volunteer printed and stamped the envelopes. One side of the letter was printed at a local print shop, and I used my printer to add the personalized salutation and letter on the other side; I cut and stuffed the letters as they came out of the printer. Increasing the postage from bulk to first class increased the price by 14 cents per piece, but saved an enormous amount of time going to the post office and dealing with the bulk-mail process. The cost of the second piece was $1 each, for a total of $100.

For the five hundred "Dear Friends" letters, the rate of return was 19 percent, with an average donation of $61. This $400 mailing brought in $5,795. The mailing with the personalized salutation and first-class postage stamp had a 53 percent rate of return, with an average donation of almost $97. This $100 mailing brought in $5,125. The two mailings combined realized a twenty-to-one profit. We did not make follow-up phone calls for either mailing.

Given the expense of this mailing, send it only to your best list of supporters, volunteers, and lawn sign hosts; any less-targeted list, it will not pay for itself.

Fundraising Through Email

With the introduction of Facebook, Twitter, and donation buttons on Web pages, campaigners have mistakenly moved email to the back of the bus. While Facebook is a fabulous tool for mobilizing large numbers of supporters for your cause in a short amount of time, I've found that email has remained a mainstay for raising money quickly and efficiently. Recently I helped a candidate retire a small campaign debt following a losing bid for a local office. Contacting only those who had previously contributed to the campaign and individuals I knew personally, I sent a two-paragraph appeal that was individually addressed to each of the potential contributors to keep it personal. Of those I emailed, 19 percent said no, 16 percent did not respond, and 64 percent contributed. Within the two paragraphs I placed a date-certain (about two weeks out) when the campaign would be permanently closed; doing this gave individuals

> "It does not matter so much where we are . . . as the direction which we are moving."
>
> **GOETHE**

a sense of urgency to respond. After receiving the contribution, I emailed the individual to acknowledge that the check arrived and thanked the contributor along with the acknowledgment. As with all successful fundraising, email solicitations work best if they are:

1. Short
2. Personalized
3. Personal (the individual making the request knows the potential contributor)
4. Clear about intent (to retire a debt, raise money for a display ad, fund printing of a last-minute flyer—that sort of thing)

5. Finite—that is, they have a timeline. As in the example above, let a potential donor know when the event, ad, flyer, or whatever you're trying to fund will occur.

Keeping Track of Donations

One enormously helpful contribution a campaign volunteer can make is to keep the records of donations as they come in. By having these records complete and in one place, your campaign will save money in accounting fees and will have at hand the information needed for filing with the secretary of state or the elections department. Figure 5.9 is an example of headings you can use in a spreadsheet for keeping track.

Name, last	First: (signer name)	Spouse/ partner	Address/ PO box	City	Zip	Occupation (signer name)	Donation amount	Date received	T.Y.	Phone #

FIGURE 5.9 Example of Headings for the Donor Spreadsheet

For filing purposes, your campaign must have the occupation of the person who signed the check and the date the check was received.

Thank-You Notes

With the introduction of computers and desktop publishing, a printed thank-you note does not carry the same weight as a handwritten note from the candidate, his or her spouse, or the campaign manager. Most people know that computers not only can generate a personalized thank-you note but can also print the candidate's signature. While a campaign should send a thank-you note or receipt for a contributor's tax records, if you are working with a candidate who is willing to scratch a few lines in his or her own handwriting, it really goes a long way. Besides thank-you notes for contributions, it is important to send notes to volunteers who have gone above and beyond the call of duty and to anyone who hosts a coffee or facilitates a campaign event.

Because thank-you notes are fairly expensive to send, I look at them as an opportunity to strengthen a relationship between the donor and the candidate. To do this, I put together a printed, personalized thank-you note for the candidate to sign but will look for some small thing the candidate can add to the note after it is printed. I will go through the lists of contributors with the candidate to identify those he or she knows personally. This doesn't take long and can be done over the phone. I create a printout and make a note next to the names of anyone the candidate knows personally to keep those notes apart from the rest. If the contributor has been involved with the campaign in some small or large way, I attach a Post-it to the thank-you note as a reminder and sometimes scribble what I want the candidate to jot on the bottom. For example, if the campaign receives a contribution from someone who also baked all the cookies for a coffee earlier in the campaign, I instruct the candidate to acknowledge that effort one more time in the contribution thank-you note: "Still thinking about those great desserts you brought to the coffee last month. Hope all is well, and thanks again."

When responding to contributors from a targeted mailing, such as doctors, teachers, dentists, lawyers, or some other special-interest group, I will include in the body of the thank-you letter information that the contributor may want to know because it pertains to his or her field of interest. I also try to make these a little gossipy, so the contributor feels more a part of the inner circle. This is especially important with anyone who gives more than $100. Only a

> "Time is the most valuable thing one can spend."
> **THEOPHRASTUS (300 BC)**

small portion of a thank-you note is about the gift. The real power of it is to curry the donor for the next "give" so that subsequent contributions will come and perhaps even increase. In local elections, personal communication with donors is about investing them in the campaign in more ways than just money.

In all preprinted thank-you notes, be sure to have the candidate sign in an off-color pen. Because blue and black ink are often used in computer-generated signatures, green is best. Avoid colors like pink, red, or purple.

For thank-you notes that do not need a contribution receipt, I have special stationery that I print from my computer. On the front is a picture of the candidate on the campaign trail or a collage of the candidate in different settings. I usually ask my graphic designer to put together the layout and then email it to me so that I can print out the cards as needed. However, if your design uses just one photo, it is pretty easy to drop it in yourself.

To generate this stationery, lay it out in landscape format so that each sheet of paper will make two note cards, and use paper that is slightly heavier, such as 80-pound vellum Bristol or Xerox 80-pound elite, with matching preprinted envelopes (the ones you used for your world's smallest brochure mailing work well). As noted above, to help the candidate, it is a good idea to have the campaign manager or someone from the committee make a short list of who might receive a personalized thank-you note. Have the envelopes preaddressed and stamped so that the candidate need only jot a note before the notes are stuffed, sealed, and mailed.

P.S. If your campaign is short on money, you can also send thank-you notes by email.

6

Lawn Signs

IN THIS CHAPTER
- To Be or Not to Be
- Logo and General Information
- Location, Location, Location
- Assembling Lawn Signs
- Cutting Turf
- Lawn Sign Installation
- Field Signs
- Maintenance of Signs
- Lawn Sign Removal: My Kingdom for a Pickup
- Bumper Stickers and Buttons

To Be or Not to Be

LAWN SIGNS ARE A UNIQUE ANIMAL, SO CONSIDER THE FOLLOWING before deciding to use them:

- Lawn signs work best in nonpartisan races; partisan primaries; and areas of homogeneous populations.
- Lawn signs are *not* about voter persuasion; they're about voter activation.
- Placed in enemy territory, lawn signs can do more harm than good.
- The number of lawn signs placed for a candidate or issue does not necessarily coincide with a win.
- Lawn signs are a great way to increase name or issue recognition in an area that will support the candidate or issue anyway.
- Lawn signs are a high-maintenance relationship.

Because lawn signs are almost entirely about voter activation, they should be used primarily where a candidate or an issue already enjoys support or registration advantage. As outlined in Chapters 1 and 7, Americans are re-locating to communities where political and cultural ideology is shared. In partisan races, if you are not among the majority of the party faithful in a community or an area of your candidacy, you risk—by incessantly reminding people of your candidacy with lawn signs—activating voters who will vote against you.

Oddly, lawn signs are most helpful where candidates or issue-based cam-paigns need them the least, that is, where they will win anyway, by reducing the undervote. They remind voters of pend-ing elections (especially helpful for special elections) and are a public endorsement for a candidate or an issue. These kinds of en-dorsements hold the most sway among small communities and neighborhoods where peo-ple know each other. Most important, because lawn signs are mostly about activation, when placed in areas of overwhelming support, they can increase the margin of a win and moderate an undervote.

> "Few things are harder to put up with than the annoyance of a good example."
>
> **MARK TWAIN**

Lawn sign placement and maintenance is a great campaign activity for those who want to volunteer in a campaign but are not interested in working directly with the public. It is also an ideal task for campaign workers you feel might somehow make an unfavorable impression. Although it's a huge time and money commitment, with enough volunteers a well-run lawn sign cam-paign is an excellent way for a voter to feel involved in a campaign while el-evating candidate name recognition or increasing awareness of a ballot issue. And as indicated above, lawn signs also demonstrate support for a candidate or an issue within a community. However, that is really all they do. Given the expense and hassle of lawn signs plus the demands on your volunteer base, your campaign committee should consider carefully whether to use them. Still, with all that said, if your opponent is using them, you should too.

In my town, lawn signs cannot be placed more than forty-five days before an election. In anticipation of the big day when all the signs suddenly appear, I ask one person from the committee to oversee sign placement and main-tenance. If I am working on a campaign that involves more than one city, I have captains in each town who will oversee these jobs.

There are two schools of thought on lawn sign placement. One is not to worry if you have only a few locations at first, since the final numbers are what matter. This approach gives the impression of building momentum; that as voters learn more, they hop on board. The other school of thought is: *Boom!* Here comes the candidate! Suddenly the name is out, and everyone seemingly supports that person. Until recently I was an adherent of the latter school and worked like crazy to get as many locations as possible for the big day. This approach lends to a big and sudden visual impact and it minimizes work because organization and placement need happen only once.

However, over the past few election cycles I've moved to the slow build, and here is why:

1. Voters are becoming sensitive toward and suspicious of political machines, so when a campaign suddenly appears everywhere—especially with field signs—the signs call attention to themselves rather than the candidate.
2. A slow build has the look of a grassroots effort.
3. Signs placed once with little movement or infill become part of the landscape and lose impact, almost becoming invisible as a campaign moves closer to the election.
4. New candidates will spend an inordinate amount of time trying to get locations before they're known in a community. While this is an important effort early in the campaign, the steep climb from obscurity to public figure dictates a hybrid lawn-sign placement approach: Get as many locations as possible to start and then infill like crazy throughout the election cycle.
5. Infill happens with both the boom and slow-build approach, so it is no more work to do the latter and actually more work to do the former.

When the day arrives to place your first round of lawn and field signs, it is important, as in all campaign-related activities, to have everything ready and organized for the teams. Also note that it is especially important that people work in pairs in this activity: one to drive the car or truck and the other to hop out and install the sign.

Logo and General Information

Lawn signs are basically a campaign's logo and, like trademarks, must easily identify your cause or candidate. You need to develop a "look" that distinguishes your campaign from all others on the landscape. However, there are times when something unforeseen materializes after the sign is printed and everyone is unhappy. So, after you've printed all of your signs and decide that your logo is the worst thing you've ever seen, it can be fixed for a price—all it takes is a run to the dump and money to reprint. However, I would advise a really bad lawn sign to be used in the primary and, should you survive, change it for the general. But remember, make the second redesigned

> "To a large degree reality is whatever the people who are around at the time agree to."
>
> — **MILTON H. MILLER**

FIGURE 6.1 Example of a Lawn Sign Using Logo and Theme: Campaign for the Carnegie

In an issue-based campaign it is advantageous to connect a positive image with the ballot item. This logo was in red, black, and white and was so well liked that voters who had never had a lawn sign before called and requested one for their yard. (Crystal Castle Graphics)

FIGURE 6.2 "Maxwell for the House" Lawn Sign

sign for the general resemble the one you used in the primary—that is, use the same font and similar graphics so the candidate doesn't look new to the world. Once you have a logo, try to use it in all campaign literature and advertising.

Regardless of who does your signs and logo, it is a good idea to visit local vendors who print lawn signs. They usually save at least one of each sign they have ever printed. This way, you can shop for ideas in style and color combinations without any out-of-pocket expenses. When you're designing your sign, keep in mind that using two colors costs a lot more than one but is well worth it (figures 6.1 and 6.2). To save some money, you can get a two-color (or even three-color) look by having almost a solid color printed over the white stock while leaving the lettering with no color (see figures 6.3 and 6.4). This produces white lettering on what looks like colored stock. Then use halftones (a mix of the white sign and the solid color showing through) in the design or part of the lettering for the "third" color. The result is very classy and quite affordable.

Consider placing a Quick Response (QR) code on the lawn sign as well as literature and print advertising to take the smart-phone user to the campaign website. Although only a small number of smart-phone users may actually scan a lawn sign QR code, it implies a mobile-friendly campaign.

Weatherproof Stock

Lawn sign material that is not weatherproof will curl with the first heavy dew or light rain, and your campaign "look" will be one of litter. Political lawn

FIGURE 6.3 **Example of a Low-Budget Yard Sign**

Using one color (deep blue) with half-tones in the silhouetted trees behind the lettering and reverse type on the name, this sign appears to have three colors rather than one. Although the design measured 10x24 originally, the final size was 12x24 with the Web page eventually added to a bottom 2-inch blue-on-white banner. (Crystal Castle Graphics)

FIGURE 6.4 This low-budget sign used a deep blue-green background with half-tones of light green and reverse type on the name for a three-color look. It measured 9x24—half the size of a normal lawn sign and half the price. (Crystal Castle Graphics)

signs are a touchy subject with some voters. Keep lawn signs neat and complete at all times. If you're sloppy about quality, placement, or maintenance, lawn signs may do your campaign more harm than good. But if you do it right, they make your campaign look well organized and supported.

Do not cut costs on your stock; use stock that is weatherproof, such as poly tag or plastic corrugated. The corrugated stock is nice because it is printed on both sides of the same sign, thus eliminating the need to staple signs back-to-back. Stapled signs often come apart and need repair.

There are two types of corrugated signs: one with the interior tubes running horizontally and the other with vertical interior tubes. If your intention is to use wooden stakes, be sure the print shop knows this; if the signs are printed with the tubing running perpendicular and are mounted on wooden stakes, they will bend and flop in the wind. Corrugated signs printed with the interior tubing running vertically require H-wickets, which slide up the tubing, to hold the sign in place.

> "The seeds of political success are sown far in advance of any election day . . . It is the sum total of the little things that happen which leads to eventual victory at the polls."
>
> **J. HOWARD MCGRATH,** former chairman, Democratic National Committee

If you use poly tag, bring in your clerical team to staple the signs back-to-back. This needs to be done before the signs are put in place. Do not staple poly tag signs to the stakes before pounding the stakes in the ground or the sign will fall off.

Stakes for lawn signs are expensive. To save money, call around to those who have run and lost or are not running again, and collect stakes or H-wickets.

This works especially well if you are running a single campaign in the fall and someone you know had only a primary run. If you have no luck, try to get a secondary wood products company or nursery to donate them. Still no luck? Ask supporters in the construction industry to make you some. Still no luck? Just buy them. Four-foot stakes work best.

You can count on your lawn signs plus stakes or wickets costing $4 to $5 each, depending on the size of the sign you print, the quantity, and number of colors. Budget accordingly, and place them carefully.

Obviously the size of your lawn sign can affect the cost of printing as well as the cost of stock. Lawn signs come in all sizes, so while you're visiting the printer to look at past political signs, check out their sizes as well. A typical sign is eighteen by twenty-four inches, although I've seen some very effective signs that were nine by twenty-four inches (figure 6.4). This longer, narrower size works quite well if your candidate has a long name that fits comfortably in that space. Smaller signs do the same work of a larger sign but are more stable against the elements and give the appearance of a modestly funded campaign. Oversize signs are more trouble than they're worth.

If firefighters or other well-organized groups endorse you, they may be able to print lawn signs, with some limitations, such as number of colors or size. It's worth checking; such groups could save your campaign a lot of money. Keep in mind, however, that you may have to post such a contribution under "in-kind" on your campaign financial reporting.

Another style of lawn sign uses a U-shaped metal rod, like a large croquet wicket, that holds a printed plastic sleeve. This type of sign costs as much as or more than the conventional lawn sign, because the wickets, which are practically indestructible, are quite expensive to buy and even more expensive to ship. Still, the sign stock itself does not need to be stapled or attached with hardware to stakes, omitting the advance work to prepare the signs for placement. The downside of these signs is that they are not particularly attractive. One caution: Even a small amount of moisture will cause the steel wickets to rust and get all over your hands and vehicle during installation and removal. Since it is the wickets that drive up the cost, we now save the metal hoops. To store wickets, make a two-bar, modified sawhorse that the wickets simply straddle. Wickets thrown into a pile until the next campaign are a nightmare.

> "Eliminate risk and you eliminate innovation . . . don't eliminate risk; knowingly take it on."
>
> **VAUGHN KELLER**

The most pervasive sign these days is a corrugated sign placed on an H-wicket. The H-wickets are surprisingly flimsy and often need a little help getting into the ground, so be sure your installers have mallets and metal spikes to drive a pilot hole, especially if there's been little or no rain.

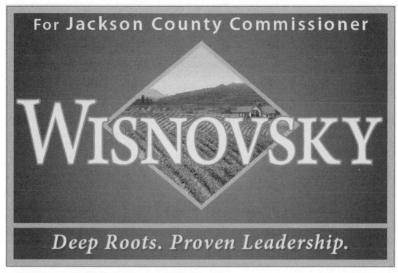

FIGURE 6.5 A Full-Color Lawn Sign Design

In 2010 we developed a lawn sign design to appear like a wine label; it worked well because our candidate was a vintner and ran for office in a predominantly agricultural area. The sign was full-color and wildly expensive but became a huge part of the campaign. Rather than being screened onto the corrugated plastic, it was a laser picture. With lettering in orange, background in blues, and the grape fields in the middle of a full-color picture, it was a gorgeous logo and sign that could be seen forever. (Landeros Design)

Lawn signs should be a work of art. You want the homeowner hosting the sign to be pleased with its look. You know you have a winner when people call and ask for a lawn sign simply because they like how it looks (figure 6.5).

Location, Location, Location

Getting good locations to display your signs is the second half of using lawn signs effectively. Often people who have run for office in previous elections will have a record of where their lawn signs were placed. Try to get such lists, and call those people first. This works best when you share a political ideology with a former candidate. Similarly cold-calling registered voters using party registration as the first filter and then geographic location as the second, is a brutal but effective technique for securing authorization. Indeed, if your objective is to place between 600 and 1,000 lawn signs on the first day, the best approach is to begin the process with phone banks. For this many locations you would need ten people calling for ten nights for 90 minutes per night. And that's with good lists.

Another option is to canvass for lawn sign locations starting on collector and arterial streets to quickly place lawn signs in high-visibility areas first where they will offer the greatest returns. Subsequent canvassing can fill in other less-traveled routes.

Just remember, lawn signs are not campaign buttons; they are a valuable campaign resource and should be used appropriately

Assembling Lawn Signs

Somewhere in the midst of finding locations and cutting turf, lawn signs must be assembled or at least organized. As noted above, be sure to have everything ready for your volunteers. If you're using corrugated signs with horizontal tubing on wooden stakes, you will need electric screwdrivers, screws that are the proper length, washers, and stakes. It's a nice touch to have tables for the workers; I use old doors on saw horses, but if none of that is available, your lawn will do nicely.

To assemble 600 signs you will need ten electric screwdrivers (ask volunteers to bring theirs from home), 1,200 screws and washers, 650 stakes (there's always damage), a couple of trucks (to disperse the signs to installation meet-up locations), and about 30 people to do the assembly.

H-wickets for corrugated signs with vertical tubing are quick and easy to assemble but beware: If the H-wicket is spaced too closely into the sign, the sign will bow a bit. For 600 signs you need about 10 people for a couple of hours and no hardware.

Cutting Turf

Because down-ballot campaigns are generally smaller and more manageable, lawn sign installation can still be conducted without using spreadsheets or mapping programs, but why? Mapping lawn sign locations using Google maps or other mapping programs in voter activation networks is fast and accurate and frankly, anyone can do it. It takes a fraction of the time and the way the little red dots are dropped onto the map directly from the address on the Excel sheet is completely civilized.

If you are working with a voter data network, trust me, the network has a mapping program—there has to be one, as it's what campaigns use to cut turf for canvassing and it's there for lawn sign installation as well. In the 2008 primary I even had one volunteer download some obscure mapping program, and with only longitude and latitude of the city, she was able to drop all the

"Anything worth doing is worth doing frantically."

_____ JANE TOWER

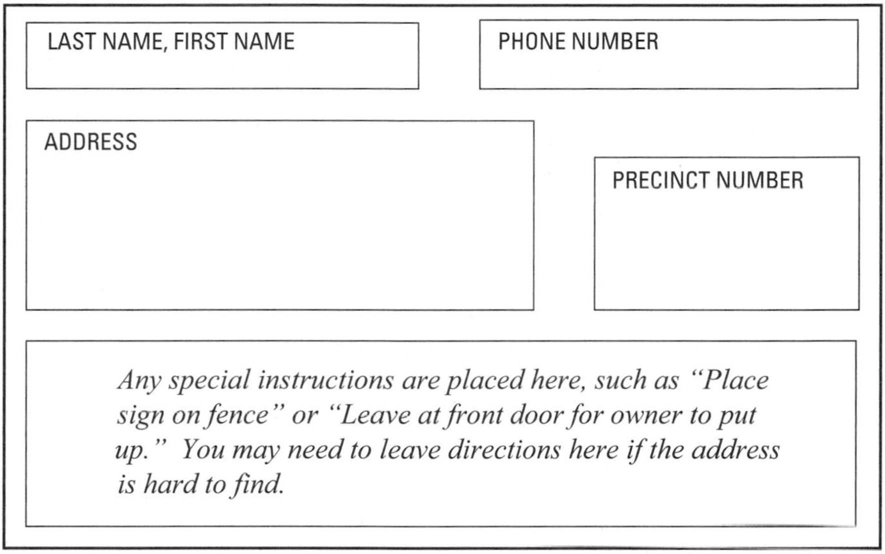

LAST NAME, FIRST NAME	PHONE NUMBER
ADDRESS	
	PRECINCT NUMBER

Any special instructions are placed here, such as "Place sign on fence" or "Leave at front door for owner to put up." You may need to leave directions here if the address is hard to find.

FIGURE 6.6 Example of a 3x5 Lawn-Sign Card

locations from my Excel spreadsheets onto maps. Now all GIS systems are user friendly and easy to find, saving time and angst.

If you're working in a small city where streets are familiar, you can easily use the old-school system of marking locations on a real estate map or precinct maps from the county and accompany those with a list or index card that includes the address, name, phone number, and any special installation instructions (figure 6.6).

For campaigns covering more than one small city, GIS mapping is the only way to go.

After loading your Excel spreadsheet of addresses for your lawn sign locations into your mapping program, you will have a bird's-eye view of your coverage areas, which now must be broken down into manageable units for the installers. Typically I find it easiest to work city by city but in large cities I break it down to east/west, north/south depending upon man-made or natural barriers that could slow down installers. Examples of barriers might be rivers, highways, drainage ditches, parks, or just geographic distance (one city to the next). Whatever your map looks like, you want to minimize the back-and-forth of your volunteers during lawn sign installation. Depending upon distance between locations, installers may be able to cover anywhere from ten to thirty signs in a two- to three-hour time period. Clearly rural areas take longer to get from one location to the next, and some neighborhoods can be thick with signs that will go up quickly.

FIGURE 6.7 Example of a Lawn Sign Map

When I print my map (figure 6.7), I also print information about the home that is included in my Excel spreadsheet, such as name, address, phone number, and installation instructions (if there are any). The list is the detailed information of the map.

Typically I will prepare and attach a list of the location addresses, a map, and door hangers (figure 6.8) to a clipboard and place that on top of the appropriate number of lawn signs for the packet area. Always be sure to add a couple of extra signs to each pile in case one breaks or a neighbor asks for a sign during a team's installation.

Lawn Sign Installation

Placement crews work in pairs. If you are using poly tag signs, crews need a staple gun (to attach the sign to the stake), a stapler (in case the sign comes apart at the corners), and a mallet (to pound the stake into the ground). If they are placing corrugated signs with wooden stakes, they will need only a mallet and maybe a metal pole for making a pilot hole. Similarly, installation teams placing corrugated signs with H-wickets or plastic sleeve signs with croquet wickets also need a hammer and metal spike for pilot holes. In any case, it is a good idea to bring along extra signs.

Assigning crews is then simply a matter of handing them a clipboard with the map and address list along with the appropriate number of signs and stakes (plus extras). Ask as many volunteers as possible to bring tools, or borrow enough ahead of time from friends. Be sure everything the campaign borrows is labeled and returned promptly.

I like installers to bring the map and location lists back to me so I know the task was completed or whether any addresses were missed. If you do not want installers to make the trip back to your launch location, simply number each of the areas and ask installers to sign up prior to installation so you know who did what, and then contact the team by either email or phone to follow up.

As stated earlier, poorly designed, poorly constructed lawn signs can hurt a campaign more than help. If you are going to use lawn signs, they are way too expensive and too labor-intensive to cut corners on design and production. If you can't raise the money to do them right, don't do them.

Even so, sometimes you must deviate from this rule for strategic reasons. In one issue-based campaign, because of a lack of funds, we printed only one-third the normal number of lawn signs. Although they were carefully placed to maximize visibility, they soon began to disappear (it was a very controversial money measure). People who wanted signs were calling, and others were calling to request replacements. We knew it was a close race, and our diminishing number of signs looked as though our support was waning.

So, using the same color of ink as our signs, I hand-painted more signs in my barn on the back of old poly tag lawn signs. In the middle of the night, I placed them throughout the city. I did not want them to be next to each other; rather, I wanted to create the impression that homeowners had taken the

"A problem adequately stated is a problem well on its way to being solved."

R. BUCKMINSTER FULLER

initiative to paint their own signs and put them up. I wanted the look to be one of individual, rebellious support for our side and angry opposition to the money fighting our effort. We won the election by fewer than three hundred votes out of 5,000 cast.

Finally, no matter how careful you and your team are, mistakes happen: Addresses get inverted, people hear yes when no is really spoken, signs get vandalized or stolen. Further, if you have an incorrect address and do not know it and the homeowner pulls in the sign, your maintenance teams may assume it disappeared for completely different reasons and continue to replace it.

In short, the host of your lawn sign must be able to reach the campaign in case something goes wrong. To make this easy, the campaign should include a door hanger for each of the locations where a lawn sign is installed. These

Dear Mark Wisnovsky Supporter,

Thank you for displaying a lawn sign. Your public support for Mark will help raise visibility of his candidacy.

Although we try to contact each and every homeowner where a sign is placed, there is still room for error -especially given that our campaign is largely staffed by of volunteers.

If we have installed this lawn sign incorrectly or if there is any problem with your sign (either maintenance or if it disappears) please call or email us (phone and email address) and we will repair, replace, or remove the sign as needed.

We will return within two days of the general election (November 2nd) to remove your sign.

Thank you,
Committee to Elect Mark Wisnovsky

FIGURE 6.8 Example of an Instruction Door Hanger for Lawn-Sign Hosts

notes are printed four-up on brightly colored paper, usually shocking orange or yellow (you want them to be seen), and then they're cut so that each sheet of paper makes four.

Hole-punch an upper corner, and include enough rubber bands within the packets for the instruction cards. These are hung by your teams on a door knob of each address where a sign is placed (figure 6.8).

In the 2012 cycle I worked on one of the most disorganized campaigns of my career; suspecting trouble, I decided to meet installers in case the campaign manager didn't show (she didn't). Although I had given the manager door hangers the previous week, for some reason they had been loaded in the manager's car and were nowhere to be found on installation day. By the time the campaign manager arrived with the hangers, all of the installation teams were out, and this is what I learned: The accuracy of mapping programs makes the door hanger less critical than when signs were being installed back in the day. So, if you're out of time and feeling overwhelmed and cannot quite get it together to get a door hanger on the knob, don't worry.

Before I leave this section, let me state the obvious: Be sure the signs are installed perpendicular to the street. The point of lawn signs is for people to see them from a distance as they drive by. To get any benefit from lawn signs, you need to attract voters' attention.

Requests

You will find that supporters will call to request lawn signs throughout the campaign. It is important to accommodate them. However, this means that your campaign must be discerning about initial lawn sign placement. Hold some back to replace lost or vandalized signs and to accommodate requests. Avoid placing signs on cul-de-sacs or overloading some streets while leaving others bare. Let supporters know—from the beginning—that the number of signs is limited and that the campaign needs to place them in areas of high visibility.

But be aware of guilt by association.

In 2008 I worked on a nonpartisan campaign of a former Republican, and of the remaining 13 percent of Republicans in my city, every one of them wanted my candidate's lawn sign. But when these same Republicans put up signs for John McCain and Sarah Palin, my candidate had to pull his out or suffer backlash-by-association at the ballot box.

In my neighborhood, which is still relatively mixed politically, I had a lawn sign of the above candidate in my yard, as did a very conservative neighbor down the street. When I canvassed my neighborhood, a half dozen neighbors commented that it was the first time in twenty years they had seen the same lawn sign in front of both my home and my neighbor's. People are always looking for clues to contextualize a candidate, and lawn signs are the easiest way to do that. It can be a good or a bad thing.

Finally, avoid placing your sign in yards already teeming with political signs, and keep away from coupling yours in hundreds of locations with the same signs from other campaigns. Keep in mind that voters are highly sensitive to visual cues. They know their neighbors and look to those they respect for help in making decisions about candidates and measures. They are also likely to spot patterns, and although lawn sign patterning is bound to happen, make it a priority to mix things up. By occasionally coupling your signs with those of candidates running in the opposing party, you give voters "permission" to split their ticket.

> "It's far easier to start something than to finish it."
> **AMELIA EARHART**

Signs

Typically field signs are printed at the same time as your lawn signs and are simply a giant rendition of the smaller sign. Campaigns will often print a portion on both sides and a portion on only one side to save money. One-sided signs can be placed on the side of buildings or become half of a V where two signs are necessary to get maximum visibility.

Although I believe a top-notch lawn sign campaign will beat out a field sign campaign any day, campaigns with more money than volunteers often drop lawn signs in favor of field signs. And indeed, a well-located field sign can be very effective in raising name recognition for campaigns.

With that said, field sign locations can be tough to find. Many cities have restrictions on the size of a sign, which would limit your field sign locations to outside city limits for a citywide race—hardly worth the money. But in races in large geographic areas, locations can be found by contacting real estate agents who have parcels listed along highways or in cities; ranchers; farmers; and owners of large vacant lots. I've even had luck with farmers "renting" me a spot on an edge of their property that abuts the freeway. Also, some counties now list property and owners online, so if you find a location you like, consider looking for the owner through the county tax assessor's office.

The volunteer crews putting up field signs must be carefully selected. These people should have some construction experience so the structure can withstand wind and the weight of the sign. Supply them with, or ask them to bring, metal fence posts, a ladder for height and mallet or post driver to pound in the metal fence post, a screwdriver or hole punch, and zip ties to thread through the hole you just punched. You can also save time and effort by using existing structures, such as established fence posts, to support one side of your field sign. Given the size of field signs, a pickup truck for installers is a must.

Know the law: Be sure to contact city and county authorities to find out size requirements and any other regulations on field signs. In one election, it suddenly came to light that our county had a size limit on large political signs. Although I'd worked for decades in county races, I had somehow missed this, and of the five races I was working on, four were out of compliance in this regard. There was some discussion about making candidates and issue-based campaigns remove all signs that were too big, which would have been financially difficult for many of the races. Luckily, two of the three county commissioners were up for reelection, and since they too had illegal signs, they temporarily changed the law to allow the larger signs.

Another area of potential conflict for field signs is along state highways where a state highway right-of-way may extend as much as fifty feet on either side of the road. Although cities and counties may look the other way when a campaign encroaches on a right-of-way, the state generally does not. To have field signs installed only to have them ripped down by state workers is maddening and wasteful. And when I say ripped down, I mean ripped down. State workers do not take the time to carefully disassemble your field sign for reuse; and good luck trying to locate the sign among various state highway yards. Save the campaign time and money: Call the local office of the state department of transportation, and ask about any locations where you are uncertain of the right-of-way.

Maintenance of Signs

Large or small, campaign signs must be maintained once they are up. Depending on the circumstances, you may use the same crew that placed the signs to maintain them throughout the campaign, or you may use a completely different crew. The maintenance crew must travel with installation supplies—whatever those may be. Ostensibly maintenance crews are ready to repair any ailing sign they see in their normal daily travels but from time to time the crews may need to travel their assigned placement routes for a more systematic check of the signs—such as after Halloween. For this level of maintenance, both lists and maps can be emailed to volunteers.

Besides maintenance, there will be the ongoing duty of filling new lawn sign requests. If there aren't too many requests, you can assign new locations to the appropriate maintenance crew or have special volunteers to do this task on an ongoing basis. Believe it or not, having the candidate help with new location installations is great PR. As the campaign progresses, voters increasingly recognize the candidate and will often honk and wave as they drive by. Such a simple thing makes the candidate appear more accessible and "like one of us." In one campaign I worked on, the candidate, a local physician, went out and helped put up field signs on the weekend. He reported that lots of people honked and waved and that some even stopped to help or say hello. A couple of days later, when the signs that the candidate himself had helped erect fell down, I got a number of calls from people I did not know asking if they could help get the signs back up for "Doc." Ultimately his initial efforts got him a lot of mileage and then brought us some great workers.

In another campaign, there was a street where all the lawn signs disappeared every night. The man who put the signs in that area was also in charge of maintenance and just happened to drive along this street to and from work each day. After the signs disappeared and he had replaced them a couple of times, he decided to take them down on his way home from work and put them back up each morning on the way to work. You can't buy that kind of loyalty.

It is best to get requested signs up as soon as possible. However, if there are too many requests, it may be necessary to organize another day for placement. If you do this, be sure to include all of your current locations so that signs can be repaired if damaged or replaced if missing.

Lawn Sign Removal: My Kingdom for a Pickup

Most localities have regulations requiring that campaign signs be removed within a certain number of days after the election. Whatever the regulations, your crews should be lined up and ready to remove all your lawn signs the day after the election. Although field signs can be removed the weekend following the election, if the lawn signs are left up longer than a day, homeowners begin to take the signs inside or throw them away, making it difficult or impossible for your crews to retrieve them. Field or lawn signs printed on poly tag must be dried prior to storing or the paint will delaminate. If stored properly, both poly tag and plastic-bag signs seem to last indefinitely, which is money in your pocket for the next election. At a minimum, you will want to retrieve the stakes or wickets for future campaigns. Since you have to get the signs down eventually, you might as well look organized and responsible by retrieving them as quickly as possible.

Pickup trucks greatly increase the speed of lawn sign retrieval, so consider an early mass email to party faithful, on your Facebook page, and to the volunteer list, asking for help from people with pickup trucks. This simple request is the easiest way to bring in new workers who would normally *never* volunteer in a political campaign.

Depending upon density of placement, a single team with a pickup can retrieve an area that required two or three teams for placement. Here again, volunteers work in pairs with maps and address lists. When installing signs I try to assign areas close to the homes of my installers, and the same can be done with lawn sign retrieval. Keep track of who is picking up what areas, and whether they've received a map and list directly from you or by email.

During one primary campaign, gas prices went up immediately after signs were installed, and I was disinclined to send volunteers back out to pick up the signs just to have them reinstalled in October. So as an alternative, I mailed a postcard to each house that hosted a sign and asked the host to bring in the sign after the primary. I also indicated on the postcard when it was legal to put them back up before the general. I included my phone number on the postcard in case a sign went missing. It completely worked. Supporters pulled in their signs and put them all back out before the general election on the designated day.

Signs with H-wickets can be stored with the H-wickets still installed—they hang neatly from hooks on a garage or barn wall; however, if the campaign has no intention of using the sign again or you're using wooden stakes or the U-wickets, they should be disassembled for storage and all parts harvested for reuse. This is a great time to get together a volunteer thank-you party to disassemble lawn signs, put them away for the next election, and bundle wickets or stakes in sets of twenty-five with duct tape or twine.

Bumper Stickers and Buttons

Bumper stickers are an inexpensive way to familiarize the community with your name or ballot measure. Although bumper stickers are used predominantly in large city, county, state, and federal races, they can also be quite effective in the small election simply because they continue to be a novelty there.

> "In life and business, there are two cardinal sins. The first is to act precipitously without thought and the second is not to act at all."
> **CARL ICAHN**, investor, entrepreneur

This is one application for which I would relax my strong recommendation to place your campaign logo on all your materials. Bumper stickers are small and hard to read, so clarity is what is important. On a bumper sticker, ideally you want your candidate or measure before the voters, nothing more.

A bonus with bumper stickers is that they are occasionally left on cars and bikes if a candidate wins, giving the community the impression that the individual is well liked in office. People who like to display bumper stickers are often willing to kick in a dollar or two to buy them.

Three points of caution on bumper stickers: First, should you decide to print bumper stickers, be sure to print them on removable stock. If people know the stickers will easily come off after the election, they'll be more inclined to place one on their car. Second, urge people to drive courteously while displaying your name on their cars. If they are rude on the road, the only thing the other driver will remember is the name on the bumper sticker. Finally, keep in mind that the use of bumper stickers, like lawn signs, is an untargeted campaign activity.

Buttons are walking testimonials or endorsements. If supporters actually wear them, this tool further serves the goal of getting your name in front of the voting public. My experience is that very few people put candidate buttons on each day, and these items tend to add clutter and expense for the campaign.

However, since all canvassers should have some sort of official identification with the campaign, this is what I recommend: At a stationery store, buy a box of the type of plastic name holders used at conventions and meetings.

Ask the graphic design artist who put together the lawn sign logo to make a miniature version of it, sized to fit in the plastic badges. Also ask the designer to lay out as many of these as will fit on a sheet of paper. Reproduce on card stock as many as you think you will need, keeping the original to make more throughout the campaign. Cut out your miniature "lawn signs," and slide them into the plastic holders. After the campaign, you can reuse the plastic name badges.

When it comes to using lawn and field signs, don't hesitate to be creative and bold. You never know what will work. Bold, however, does not mean elaborate. Simple signs with a simple theme are the easiest to read, especially when observers pass by at high speeds. Given the work and expense of lawn signs, if you choose to include this activity in your campaign, make it as successful as possible.

7

Targeting Voters

IN THIS CHAPTER
- Finding the Likely Voter
- Partisan Gaps
- Canvassing
- Direct Mail
- Tracking Polls

AFTER USING A PRECINCT ANALYSIS TO DETERMINE THE BEST ZONES OR precincts on which to focus your attention, the next challenge is to determine, within that context, which voters are most likely to vote and how to persuade them. Incorporating individual traits such as turnout history, education, income, gender, race, or social context outlined in Chapter 1 offers a winning strategy for finding and persuading voters at affordable prices.

Finding the Likely Voter

Here are the top six indicators for predicting voter participation:

1. Voting history
2. Education
3. Income
4. Absentee voting
5. Age
6. Social Media

Voting History: The Most Reliable Method of Determining Future Participation

Accessing past voter participation is as easy as contacting the local clerk or election office, your political party, a voter contact service, or even a PAC that routinely helps partisan races or one backing an issue-based campaign aligned with your candidate. Any campaign vendor specializing in direct mail will have access to voting history. Who voted, not how one voted, is a matter of public record and remains the most reliable predictor of future voter participation; indeed, it "exceeds the effects of age and education."[1] And those who vote in a primary are 42 percent more likely than nonprimary voters to vote in the general election.[2]

A voter is typically referred to as a four, three, two, or one, that is, someone who voted in four out of the past four elections, three out of four, and so on. Fours will vote. The others can be a little trickier to pin down. However, with a little prodding, threes and often twos can be activated to do their civic duty. Unless your race is during a presidential cycle, people who went to the polls only once in the past four elections may be a waste of time, effort, and money.

> "You've got to work like it's your first day on the job every day."
>
> —— **NICKI MINAJ**

Education

According to a 1993 Simmons Market Research Bureau study, college graduates were 33 percent more likely to vote than the average adult, and those with a graduate degree were 41 percent more likely to vote. A decade later the Field Institute in California released a study of expected turnout in which it compared the characteristics of the state's voting-age population, its registered voters, and its likely voters. The study revealed that those who have no more than a high school education constitute 42 percent of the state's adults but only 24 percent of registered voters (and likely voters), and those with a college degree constitute just 28 percent of the adult population but 42 percent of likely voters.

> "Campaigns are preparation, organization, execution, and luck."
>
> —— **ELAINE FRANKLIN**

Further, college entrance increases voter participation by between twenty-one and thirty points.[3] Similarly, the Center for Information on Civic Learning and Engagement reports that 70 percent of all voters eighteen to twenty-nine years old come from the subset of the same age group who have ever attended college (57 percent).[4]

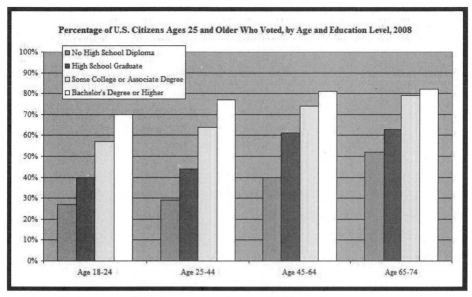

FIGURE 7.1 Percentage of US Citizens Aged 25 and Older Who Vote, 2008.

(US Census)

According to the US Census, of US citizens between the ages of twenty-five and forty-four, 76 percent of those who graduated from college voted in the 2004 presidential election, compared with 49 percent of those who had only a high school diploma. For those between forty-five and sixty-four, 83 percent of college graduates voted, compared with 63 percent of those with a high school diploma. But more dramatic is the voting-rate comparison of those between eighteen and twenty-four. Of this age group, 67 percent who held a college diploma voted, compared with only 38 percent of those who did not go beyond high school (figure 7.1)—twenty-nine points higher.

Income

Turnout can also be predicted by income level, which obviously correlates with education (figure 7.2). According to a 1999 report by the US Census Bureau, people in the workforce with a college degree in 1976 had, on average, an income 57 percent higher than those with only a high school diploma. By 1999 the proportion had increased to 76 percent, and by 2006 people with advanced degrees were earning four times what one could earn with a high school diploma alone.

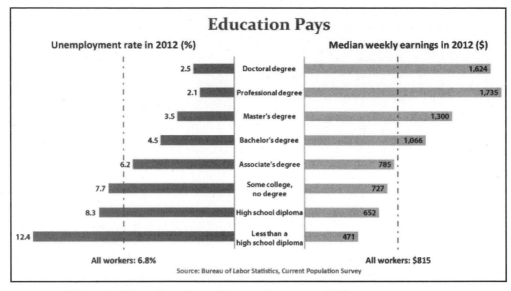

FIGURE 7.2 Education Pays: Correlation Between Income and Education

Identifying these voters early and persuading them to support your candidate or measure is one more component of a win, because they will vote or are likely to vote.

Absentee Voting, Early Voting, and Voting by Mail

Voters who request an absentee ballot have long been among the most likely of likely voters. While the percentage of people requesting an absentee ballot may vary among states and regions, their turnout doesn't. Absentee voters can represent a substantial proportion of the overall turnout. In Oregon, before people could register absentee permanently, those requesting absentee ballots typically ran about 25 percent of all the registered voters. In the 1998 primary election, after voters were given the option to register absentee permanently, 41 percent of the voters did so. In that election, absentee ballots accounted for nearly two-thirds of all ballots cast. Absentee voter turnout was 53 percent, whereas turnout among those casting their votes at the polls was only 22 percent. In the 1998 general election, 73 percent of those requesting an absentee ballot returned their ballot.[5]

> "A great many people think they are thinking when they are merely rearranging their prejudices."
>
> —— **WILLIAM JAMES**

In 2008 the Field Research Corporation of California (www.field.com) reported a record 13.7 million Californians voting. Of those, nearly 42 percent (5.7 million) voted by mail, an increase of 1.6 million over those voting by mail in 2004 and more than twice the 2.7 million who did so in the 2000 presidential election.[6] In 2008 permanent mail-ballot registrants represented better than 32 percent of the state's total registered voters—more than twice the permanent mail-ballot registrants in the 2004 presidential election. And in 2008, 84.9 percent of the 6.7 million registered voters issued a mail ballot returned their ballots, nine points higher than the 75.9 percent turnout of all other registered voters.

By the 2012 general election, 43 percent of California's voters were permanently registered to vote by mail and represented 51 percent of the overall voter turnout—eclipsing (for the first time) poll voters by two points. However, more dramatic is the actual turnout of mail registrants (82 percent) compared with that of those voting at precincts (60 percent), a difference of twenty-two points (www.sos.ca.gov/elections).

Sometimes absentee voters have a regional context a campaign should examine. For example, in 2008, 29 percent of California's mail-ballot registrants were from the San Francisco Bay Area, whereas only 13 percent were from Los Angeles (Field Institute).

And party demographics are typically different. Again in California, in the 2008 general election, 46 percent of precinct voters were Democrats, compared with 30 percent Republicans, whereas Democrats held only a 4 percent margin over the GOP for mail ballots.

Other demographic characteristics should also be studied. The Field Institute of California reports that mail-ballot voters have these characteristics:

- Older, although this margin has narrowed over past elections
- White non-Hispanic (70 percent, versus 23 percent Latino)
- Female (54 percent, versus 46 percent male)
- More conservative (32 percent, versus 24 percent liberal)

Given the potentially high percentage of overall voter turnout that absentee ballots can represent, your campaign should work them long before the get-out-the-vote (GOTV) effort, with a separate, focused campaign. Methods for both timing and reaching these voters will be covered extensively in Chapter 11.

Age

Voters age eighteen to twenty-four essentially abdicate their voting power to older Americans, who both register and turn out to vote in greater numbers.

For example, 75 percent of those sixty-five and older are registered to vote, compared with slightly more than half of the youth vote; and those sixty-five and older outperform the youth vote by twenty points in presidential elections and nearly forty points in midterms (www.census.gov/compendia/statab/cats /elections/voting-age_population_and_voter_participation.html). So although those eighteen to twenty-four outnumbered those sixty-five to seventy-four by 7 million, they represented 1 million fewer voters at the ballot box in 2004 and 6 million fewer in 2006 and 2010.

In Oregon, final activity reports list every voter who participated in the election and include the date local election officials received the ballots. To determine who was voting when, we began tracking ballot returns by age in 2004. While voter turnout among age groups varies between presidential and nonpresidential cycles, the voting behavior of age groups does not. Essentially, the older the voter, the sooner the ballot is returned.

For example, in 2008, 35 percent of those sixty-five and older returned their ballots during the first week of voting and then continued to vote at an even rate up until Election Day. This compares with 76 percent of those eighteen to twenty-four and twenty-five to thirty-four who voted in the final week and 72 percent of those thirty-five to forty-nine. The sixty-five-and-older group outpaced the other age groups' turnout up until Election Day and at times was outperforming the other groups by as much as 30 percentage points.

That older voters consistently vote earlier would indicate that their minds are made up weeks before Election Day.

Other interesting patterns we observed looking at ballot returns and election results as tabulations of each day's return was posted:

- The later the ballot was mailed, the higher the undervote in down-ballot races.
- Nonaffiliated voters not only underperformed party registrants by fifteen points overall but they also voted late, with 42 percent casting their ballot in the last two days.

There is no reason to believe that voters do not perform similarly across the US, and because batches received daily in Oregon are tabulated separately, it gives campaigns a clear road map:

- Get to older voters first.
- In an effort to reduce undervoting in down-ballot races, campaigns should target eighteen- to thirty-four-year-olds and nonaffiliated voters in high-priority precincts with a knock at the door the week before Election Day or the day ballots are due for mail elections.

Social Media

Although much of this is covered in depth in Chapter 4, it bears emphasizing. According to the Pew study "Social Networking Sites and Our Lives," published in 2011:

- The well-educated and the more affluent are more likely than others to participate in civic life online.
- Nearly 70 percent of online US adults used social networks in 2012, up twenty-two points from 2008.
- All adults posting links to political stories increased sixfold between 2008 and 2012.
- All adults following or friending a political candidate or figure on social networking sites increased fourfold between 2008 and 2012.
- Liberals use social media more than conservatives (79 percent versus 63 percent).
- Similarly, liberals use Twitter more than conservatives (25 versus 10 percent).
- Social media is skewed to younger people: 92 percent of those eighteen to twenty-nine, 73 percent of those thirty to forty-nine, 57 percent of those fifty to sixty-four, and 38 percent of those sixty-five and older are engaged in social media.
- Half of the registered voters have watched political videos online.
- The number of those using social networking sites has nearly doubled since 2008 and users have gotten older.

To reach voters, especially young voters, a campaign must have an online presence.

Partisan Gaps

Youth Voters and the Growing Age Gap

Millennials (those born between 1978 and 2000) represented a dramatic change in youth voting and involvement in the 2008 presidential election, with 53 percent reporting for civic duty and adding more than 2.2 million voters to the overall turnout. More remarkable is that the turnout in 2004 represented a 9 percent increase over 2000, when only 42 percent weighed in on the presidential election.[7] One in ten youth voters contributed to the Obama campaign, and many more volunteered. While their overwhelming support of Obama (66 percent) did not make or break the race for him, it certainly helped.[8] In 2000, registration among the eighteen-to-twenty-nine group was almost evenly split between the Democrats and Republicans but the gap widened to nineteen points by 2008 (NBC exit polls). These numbers held in 2012.

In 2012 it would appear that the youth vote did make a difference for Obama. According to Tufts University's Center for Information and Research on Civic Learning and Engagement (CIRCLE; www.civicyouth.org/wp -content/uploads/2012/11/CIRCLE_2012Election_GenderRace_ForWeb1 .pdf) and America Goes to the Polls 2012 (www.nonprofitvote.org), "The youth vote was a determining factor in four swing states: Florida, Ohio, Pennsylvania, and Virginia. If the youth vote in those states had been evenly split, Governor Romney would have won all 4 states and therefore the presidential election."

Scott Keeter, Juliana Horowitz, and Alec Tyson, all from Pew Research, have studied the demographics of the young electorate: "Young voters are more diverse racially and ethnically than older voters and more secular in their religious orientation. These characteristics, as well as the climate in which they have come of age politically, incline them not only toward Democratic Party affiliation but also toward greater support of activist government, greater opposition to the war in Iraq, less social conservatism, and a greater willingness to describe themselves as liberal politically."[9]

"To have doubted one's own first principles is the mark of a civilized man."

_____ OLIVER WENDELL HOLMES

The researchers also described the overarching political result of their findings: "This pattern of votes, along with other evidence about the political leanings of young voters, suggests that a significant generational shift in political allegiance is occurring."

But before Democrats cheer and Republicans hang their heads, consider this: In Jackson County, Oregon, where I've tracked voter patterns for thirty years, a distinct pattern emerged in the 2008 presidential cycle and again in 2012. In the 2008 primary, the Obama campaign aggressively registered new voters and re-registered nonaffiliated voters to the Democratic Party. All in all, voter registration disparity narrowed from an eleven-point Republican advantage to a modest two-point advantage. However, after the votes were counted in 2008, Obama had received 8,000 (8 percent) more votes than any of the down-ballot Democratic candidates and 7,000 more than the Democratic candidate for US Senate. As I indicated above, the youth vote reported late and when their votes were counted, the undervote increased. Compare this with the Republican ticket, where down-ballot candidates received vote totals nearly identical to those of John McCain (within one hundred votes). By 2012 the registration of Republicans grew in my county, but the undervote in the down-ballot races remained at eight points for down-ballot Democrats.

Mobilizing Young Voters: What Works and What Doesn't			
Nonpartisan tactic	*Mobilizing effect*	*Dollars/vote*	*Notes*
Door-to-door	8–10%	$12–20	Tested on young voters
Volunteer phone bank	3–5%	$12–20	Tested on young voters
Professional phone bank	0–2%	$140 and up	
Multiple calls	0–1%	n/a	Tested on young voters
Leafleting	0% (party affiliated voters)	$40 and up	7% effect on unaffiliated
Direct mail	0–1%	$40 and up	

Summary of Alan Gerber and Donald Green's 2001 findings. (Source: Alan Gerber and Donald Green, "Getting Out the Youth Vote," December 2001, summarized by Ryan Friedrichs, "Mobilizing 18–35-Year-Old Voters," John F. Kennedy School of Government, Harvard University, April 2002)

TABLE 7.1 Mobilizing Young Voters: What Works and What Doesn't

This may indicate that first-time or somewhat disengaged voters lag when it comes to other campaigns within communities. Further, it suggests that reaching new registers and nonaffiliated voters with campaign resources should be a top priority for down-ballot campaigns. However, given the ineffectiveness of direct mail, phones, and TV advertisements with these voters, and the comparative success in engaging them by canvassing and using social media, down-ballot campaigns would do well to shift strategies.[10]

According to Joe Green, president and cofounder of NationBuilder, "For local campaigns, most citizens have no idea who's running for office and are therefore open to persuasion—a significant fact since local elections can be swung by just a few votes. And since persuasion at the local level happens by direct voter contact, field organization is the key to victory. The campaign that does it better, wins."[11]

Mobilizing Young Voters

A number of studies have been conducted on how to mobilize the eighteen- to twenty-five-year-olds on Election Day. The Michigan Democratic Party's Youth Coordinated Campaign and two studies conducted by Alan Gerber and Donald Green reported similar findings: This young group of voters responds best to canvassing or personal contact from the candidate or campaign (table 7.1). Also of interest is that while phone canvassing was found to increase young voter participation, multiple calls generated no increase beyond single calls.[12] Subsequent studies by Green and Gerber outlined in the second edition of their book *Get Out the Vote: How to Increase Voter*

Turnout, published by the Brookings Institution Press in 2008, reinforce and restate these findings.

So if you're going to contact these voters by phone, it is better to call more of them than to make repeat calls to the same voter. Also worth noting in these studies was the lack of impact that direct mail had on young voters. Given the cost of direct mail and the annoyance to the voter created by the sheer volume of campaign mail, this is good news for financially strapped down-ballot candidates struggling to get their message out.

> "A candidate or party that can gain the trust and loyalty of young adults now, before their opinions and beliefs are set, can build a generational voting base that will remain for years."
>
> ———— CAMPAIGN FOR YOUNG VOTERS

Two excellent resources for targeting youth voters are George Washington University's *Young Voter Mobilization Tactics* booklet and Tufts University's CIRCLE.[13] The following tips originate from these two sources as well as the above-referenced studies:

- *Personalized and interactive contact counts.* The most effective way of getting a new voter is the in-person door knock by a peer; the least effective is an automated phone call. Canvassing costs $11 to $14 per new vote, followed closely by phone banks at $10 to $25 per new vote. Robocalls mobilize so few voters that they cost $275 per new vote. (These costs are figured per vote that would not be cast without the mobilizing effort.)
- *Begin with the basics.* Telling a new voter where to vote, when to vote, and how to use the voting machines increases turnout. Urge all new voters to register to vote by mail if the state allows for no-excuse absentee voting.
- *The medium is more important than the message.* Partisan and nonpartisan, and negative and positive messages seem to work about the same. The important factor is the degree to which the contact is personalized.
- *In ethnic and immigrant communities, start young.* Young voters in these communities are easier to reach, are more likely to speak English (cutting down translation costs), and are the most effective messengers within their communities.
- *Initial mobilization produces repeat voters.* If an individual has been motivated to get to the polls once, he or she is more likely to return. So, getting young people to vote early could be key to raising a new generation of voters.
- *Leaving young voters off contact lists is a costly mistake.* Some campaigns still bypass young voters, but research shows they respond cost-effectively when contacted.

By largely overlooking eighteen- to twenty-five-year-olds, candidates and campaigns are perpetuating a vicious cycle: Young people don't vote, so no funds are spent informing them, so they do not become invested, and therefore do not vote. Campaigns spend so much time and money focusing on seniors—who would turn out to vote with little or no campaign effort—but spend almost none targeting the youth vote.

There are important similarities between what activates the young voter and what activates the sporadic adult voter.

1. Both groups respond best to canvassing, and when younger voters are canvassed by a campaign, they activate adults living in the same house, creating a "trickle up" effect.[14]
2. Young voters identify the voting process itself as part of the problem for low voter turnout, saying it is designed to discriminate against people who move, are overwhelmed with day-to-day concerns, are poorer, or are living on the edge. Priscilla Southwell's report to Oregon's Vote-by-Mail Citizen Commission, "Survey of Vote-by-Mail Senate Election," showed that those who were younger, worked hourly-wage jobs, were students, were single parents, were minorities, and were registered as independents all turned out in greater numbers in vote-by-mail elections than in polling elections.
3. Young voters respond best to candidates who are genuine, speak frankly and directly, and are involved in community activities. These traits are valued by all age groups.
4. Young voters respond best to GOTV phone calls that inform—such as identifying the polling place location.[15] GOTV work I've conducted in southern Oregon with older voters mirrors this pattern. As a result, the script of our GOTV calls changes almost daily, and always includes some bit of information the voter may not know. "Did you know the county still has not received your ballot?" "This is the last day that ballots can be safely mailed and still make it to the clerk's office by Election Day." "There isn't enough time to mail your ballot; you will now need to hand-carry it to . . . "

Ethnic and Gender Gaps

Make no mistake: There's a shifting demographic in America that was profoundly revealed following the 2012 presidential election. Minorities (Asians, Latinos, blacks), millennials, blue-collar workers, the affluent, the well-educated, and women (both married and unmarried) underscored the power of voting en masse for one side or the other.

Although for many years more women than men have been eligible to vote, it wasn't until 1976 that women actually registered nationally in greater numbers, and not until 1984 that they began to turn out in greater numbers. By 1996 over 7 million more women voted in the presidential election than men. For our purposes, however, it's important to look not only at who votes but also at how they vote.

In a 2006 survey, Public Opinion Strategies found that white men were more inclined to support Republican candidates over Democratic candidates— 53 percent compared with 45 percent. Although this gap has closed considerably since the 28-point spread in 2002 and the 24-point spread in 2004, it remains an important predictor of voting behavior.[16]

> "How few aim at the good of the whole, without aiming too much at the prosperity of parts!"
>
> — JOHN ADAMS

Similarly, the *National Journal* presented an overview of voting demographics by age, religion, marital status, and race in October 2008; some categories were updated after the 2008 presidential election. Each year shows little or no movement toward the Democratic Party by white men, who consistently have given just 36 percent to the Democratic nominee.[17]

The Ethnic Gap

While voting gaps are widely studied at a national level, especially following a presidential election, they also have an effect at state and local levels. For the down-ballot campaign it is important to be aware of other issues on a given ballot that may affect the outcome of a seemingly unrelated ballot item.

For example, in 1997 the Asian vote in San Francisco turned out en masse to oppose a freeway retrofit measure that adversely affected their neighborhoods. In the same year, San Francisco approved funding for the AT&T Giants stadium, largely as a result of the number of minorities voting in predominantly ethnic areas. Whites living in the upper-income sections of the city opposed the stadium but ultimately were overwhelmed by minorities hoping for improvements in a marginal neighborhood and those opposed to the freeway expansion. When it came to approving the stadium, minorities living outside the affected neighborhood indicated that they had supported the stadium in hopes that their neighborhood would be next. Ironically, the very people who supported and voted for the stadium bill are among those least able to afford tickets to the games.

In 2008 the black vote, which turned out in record numbers to support Obama, was ascribed the blame for the passage of Amendment 2 in Florida and Prop 8 in California, which opposed same-sex marriage. And indeed, the math works: In 2004 blacks in California were 6 percent of the California electorate; in 2006 the US Census placed them at 6.7 percent. But in 2008 they jumped to 10 percent of the electorate and voted for the ban on same-sex marriage by 70 percent. If they had turned out closer to historical percentages, the amendment would have failed with a 49.3 percent approval vote.[18]

The Hispanic vote has become the most sought-after, for both parties, both in national politics and in states with Hispanic populations large enough to influence the outcome of a close race. However, for the down-ballot race, there are a few things to consider with any minority vote:

1. Always consider social context first: Minority Republicans and Democrats, like their white counterparts, tend to self-segregate, moving to states, cities, communities, and neighborhoods where people of similar cultural, social, ethnic, political, educational, and economic similarities live. Large, segregated populations, whether white, Latino, black, Native American, Asian, or religious, are best studied and targeted using precinct analysis and the US Census.
2. Fully integrated minorities tend to be more invisible and therefore ignored by campaigns. This results in lower voter performance than that of targeted minorities living in large homogeneous neighborhoods.[19]

The Marriage Gap

Although white men have shown little deviation from their support of the Republican Party candidates, white women have been less predictable. Once marital status is broken apart, however, a more reliable predictor than education, gender, or age emerges for determining voter patterns.[20]

Currently there are as many unmarried women in America as there are married. Although unmarried women constitute 26 percent of the electorate, they did not flex their voting potential until 2004, when they moved from 19 percent of the electorate to 22.4 percent, an increase of about 7 million voters. In 2004 unmarried women voted for John Kerry by a twenty-five-point margin, while married women voted for George W. Bush by an eleven-point margin. These numbers are mirrored by all age groups, including eighteen- to twenty-nine-year-olds. Although white voters supported President Bush in 2004 by seventeen points, Kerry did well among white unmarried women, who gave him an eleven-point advantage.

> "This country will not be a good place for any of us to live in unless we make it a good place for all of us to live in."
> **THEODORE ROOSEVELT**

In 2008 young married women (eighteen to twenty-nine years old) supported John McCain by twelve points, while young unmarried women dwarfed those numbers, giving Obama 77 percent of their vote. Similarly, among white college-educated women, Obama enjoyed a sixteen-point plurality over McCain, but married non-college-educated white women weighed in for McCain with a twenty-seven-point margin.[21]

In the final days of the 2008 election, Democracy Corps conducted a tracking survey of battleground states. The results indicated a forty-one-point marriage gap compared with a seventeen-point gender gap. Of those, unmarried women gave Obama a forty-point lead, compared with married women, who gave McCain a one-point advantage. Following the election, these numbers held, with Obama receiving a dramatic 70 percent of the vote cast by unmarried women. This is the highest margin recorded since marital status has been tracked and a sixteen-point net gain over Kerry in 2004. Of men, Obama split the vote with McCain (49–48 percent) but lost married women by 3 percent.

A full 20 percent of unmarried women voted for the first time in 2008, compared with 4 percent first-time voters among married women and 11 percent overall first-time voters. Of all unmarried women, 41 percent registered to vote between 2004 and 2008. Overall, the 2008 election saw a forty-four-point marriage gap, while the gender gap remained constant at twelve points; these numbers held for 2012.[22]

Economics of Unmarried Versus Married Women

Married women and unmarried women differ in many economic and political aspects:

- Unmarried women are less likely to have a college education (19 percent) than their married counterparts (29 percent).[23]
- Nearly one in five (19 percent) unmarried women are raising children.[24]
- Children being raised by unmarried mothers account for nearly half of the children living below the poverty line.[25]
- Unmarried women make 56 cents for every dollar that married men make.[26]
- All in all, unmarried women live on the edge financially, especially compared with married women and men.

Because unmarried women tend to be less engaged in politics, they are consequently targeted less by campaigns and therefore participate less in politics. In this way, they are just like the youth vote and integrated minorities. However, if reaching unmarried women is one of your campaign's goals, then keep in mind that unmarried women are more inclined to vote early and vote by mail.[27]

Canvassing

Typically to get a vote, you must ask for it anywhere from three to eight times. Newspaper, television, and radio advertising, direct mail, special events, phone banks, social media, emails, and canvassing are the most common ways to ask for a vote. However, canvassing remains the most effective and affordable tool in a campaigner's bag of tricks. In small communities, canvassing is an ideal way to check in with the voting public and can be elevating and gratifying for the candidate. While TV, newspaper, and radio ads target groups, canvassing is about targeting individuals—specifically, voters who are either persuadable or generally inclined to support your efforts.

In areas that historically have supported candidates and ballot initiatives similar to the one you are promoting, canvassing is not as much about changing minds as improving voter turnout and engagement. By going door-to-door in areas of high support but of low to medium turnout, you activate your voters for Election Day.

An example of the effectiveness of canvassing supportive precincts while ignoring precincts inclined to vote against your efforts is provided in figure 7.3. Identical ballot measures were placed before Ashland voters in 1993 and

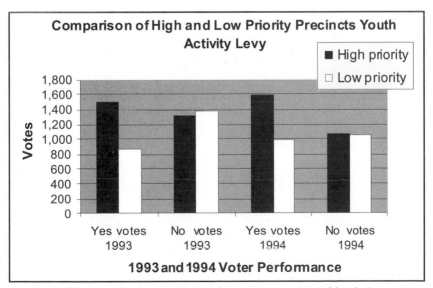

FIGURE 7.3 Voter Performance on a Youth Activity Levy in Ashland, Oregon: A Case for Activating the Right Voters

then again in 1994. Our supporting campaigns were the same, with two exceptions. First, in 1993 both high- and low-priority precincts were canvassed, whereas in 1994, only high-priority precincts were targeted. Second, in 1994 we conducted a voter identification and GOTV effort. The combination of activating only high-support precincts with a GOTV effort worked. The same measure that lost in 1993 by 326 votes passed in 1994 by 447 votes.

A decade later in February 2004, we used this same model after the failure of a January 2003 statewide initiative to backfill state-supported programs with additional income tax revenues. In 2004 we effectively increased support of the second attempt on the revenue measure by decreasing the no vote. To do this, the campaign focused only on precincts where the previous revenue measure narrowly passed or where it failed up to 10 percent. Any precincts where it passed handily or was defeated in large numbers were ignored. Voter identification was implemented in the targeted precincts as well as canvassing. There were no lawn signs and almost no media (outside unions came in and advertised on radio, of all things, before we got hold of them and asked that it stop). A killer GOTV was conducted leading up to the election with neighbors contacting neighbors. In the end, the county vote came in 2 points higher in 2004 than in 2003, but the yes vote was virtually unchanged between the two elections. The improvement came almost entirely out of a decrease in the no vote in the precincts that were ignored. While this may not seem like an overwhelming endorsement, you must consider that statewide, the second measure failed by a 15 percentage point higher margin than the vote in 2003.

When low-priority precincts are activated by canvassing or untargeted activities, nonsupport increases. However, when supporting voters are identified in low-priority precincts, and when only they are activated in a GOTV effort, two important things happen: First, the overall number of no votes decreases because nonsupporting voters' neighborhoods are ignored, and second, the number of yes votes increases because of GOTV activation. While yes votes increased slightly and no votes decreased in high-priority precincts between 1993 and 1994 and again in the 2002 and 2003 election examples, the lower turnout combined with the decline of no votes in the low-priority precincts is what made the difference.

Canvassing Leaning Voters

In areas of medium support with low to medium turnout, canvassing can actually pull votes over to your side. All things being equal, the candidate or cause that gets to a leaning voter first and with the best message has a better shot at winning support. Should these voters already be moved by your ads, brochure, debating prowess, command of the issues, and good looks, then, as with the first group of high-support precincts, canvassing will serve to activate that support—that is, to remind the voter to vote.

Canvassing is a time-consuming, volunteer resource-intensive way to activate sympathetic voters and bring your message to the people. It can also be a great way to get a feel for your chances of winning. In my second bid for mayor, lawn signs for the opposition lined the main street through town, making my prospects appear bleak. However, after I started canvassing, I realized how handily I would win; it gave me confidence and I was more relaxed in all my campaign activities. Canvassing will give you information about voter intentions. It can also help you get additional lawn sign locations in key spots.

If canvassing is done right, you will also get valuable feedback on voter concerns. This information can help you adjust your ads and debate emphases to meet those concerns. For example, in Ashland's prepared-food and beverage tax campaign, a canvasser stopped at a home that already hosted a lawn sign in support of the tax measure. The homeowner told the canvasser that it was fine for the lawn sign to stay, but that she was rethinking her decision to support the tax measure because of all the controversy and seemingly overwhelming support for the opposition citywide. In another campaign, a canvasser reported that the base party voters did not know who was running for the office. In both of these examples, thanks to the canvassers, we were able to address the problems, fix them, and win the elections.

Although there are few, if any, campaign activities that have a greater return on investment than canvassing, it is important to keep in mind that canvassing is not for everyone. Also, some places are too risky for the traditional canvass. Be careful, and know the areas you are going into. Never send someone to canvass alone or go alone yourself, and never enter a house, if for no other reason than that your partner will not be able to find you.

Map Packets

Before volunteers or the candidate can canvass, you must first do a precinct analysis to determine where you're targeting your efforts. Then you must prepare maps of those areas for your canvassers. After these tasks have been completed, the canvassing activity itself begins.

Note: If your campaign is using hand-held devices for canvassing, the canvass map packet (the map and list of voters along with voting history) can be downloaded for easy reference. The turf will still need to be cut but printouts become unnecessary.

Setting up canvass map packets is an important detail to a successful canvass (figure 7.4). Do not wait to do this with the canvassers when they first arrive, or even the night before. Map packets should be organized in advance, and a generous amount of time should be allotted for the task.

Setting up map packets for canvassing begins with great maps. You can get them from the clerk's office or online from your voter data network, which, by the way, should also have a program to help you cut turf. *Cutting turf* is simply assigning areas on your map that can be canvassed by two people in a two-hour canvassing session. When possible, use maps from the county clerk's office or the county geographic information system (GIS) department so that precinct lines are identified. In fact, GIS mapping programs (such as ESRI's Arcview and ArcGIS software) are a great option for canvass maps. With GIS programs, you can list which doors to knock on according to income, the number of voters living there, how many of the past four elections the occupants have voted in, marital status, registration, and more.

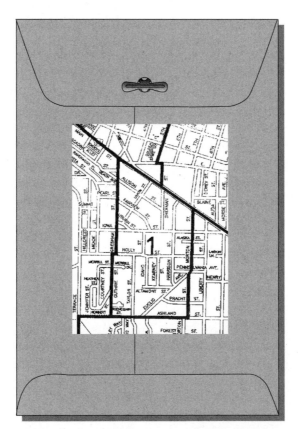

FIGURE 7.4 Example of a Canvassing Map Packet

If your canvass is a *knock* (actual knocking on doors to speak with people), you can count on canvassers covering anywhere from ten to fifteen homes in an hour. If it's a *lit drop* (leaving literature at the door without knocking), you can figure thirty-plus homes an hour for the canvassers. The time it takes depends on the density of housing and the steepness of the terrain. If it's your campaign, you should know your precincts better than anyone. If you don't, hop in the car, take a little drive around, and get to know them.

When dividing precincts for canvassing teams, it is best to use one team to cover both sides of a normal city street. Doing so may require that portions of two or more precincts be included on the same map. Remember: Efficiency is more important than precinct lines; if a precinct jumps a major thoroughfare, do not expect your canvassers to hop across four-lane highways while canvassing.

For each of your teams, make two identical map packets, with the assigned area for canvassing highlighted (figure 7.4). If you do not have access to a program that cuts turf for you and you're going at this old school, it is sometimes helpful to line up your team maps on a window, or at least side-by-side, to check that streets haven't been missed or highlighted on two packets of adjoining canvass areas. Canvassing houses twice wastes both the volunteers' and voters' time and is annoying to both. It's bound to happen, but do your best to minimize it.

No matter how well someone claims to know an area, every canvasser needs to work with a map. No exceptions. That is why two identically highlighted maps must be created for each pair of canvassers. Have canvassers mark off the blocks they complete on their map. This information helps you keep track of both the areas already canvassed and the work of your canvassers.

Once the maps have been prepared, tape each one to a manila envelope, which will then be used to keep brochures protected in bad weather and looking fresh by the time they reach the doorstep. Manila envelopes are fairly cheap, but they are also easy to find used. If you tell friends and coworkers that you need manila envelopes from their mail trash, you'll have more than you can use in a very short time especially if your friends work in government.

Remember, you have two identical packets. People work in pairs, so the two packets must stay together. To make sure the duplicate packets are not separated from each other, fold and place one inside the other, or staple the two together. If they get separated, you are bound to have two different teams pick up the same packet and canvass the same area twice, so pay attention to this detail. Also, be sure to number your packets so that you can quickly see if any are missing.

Place the materials necessary for the type of canvass you are conducting into each envelope. If you are doing a GOTV canvass or using walking lists to contact specific people, this is the packet in which you place those materials. Just put the voter lists and the matching envelope inside one envelope. The canvassers will separate out the walking lists when they divide up how they want to work. You may either place a bunch of brochures into the packet or leave them loose in a box by the door for the volunteers to pick up on their way out. Either way, volunteers should take additional brochures to avoid running out before they have finished their areas.

I always tape an index card to the back of the manila envelope. That way, if someone canvasses the home of a strong supporter, he or she can write the information on the card so it can get to the campaign. For example, supporters may tell a canvasser that they want a lawn sign or would like to be in an endorsement ad or to contribute money if the candidate calls. When packets are returned, all cards with notes are quickly pulled from the packet and processed accordingly. Having it there also reminds the canvasser that you're looking for more than just a knock at the door and an exchange of campaign materials. Each canvasser will need a pen, so have plenty on hand. I remind people to bring pens during the callback before the canvass, but there will be those who forget. It's a nice touch to have your canvassers write on the front of the brochure "Sorry we missed you" for people not at home. Have them do it in a color that stands out, like red or green.

Consider posting a large map of your city or county on a wall where you can mark off areas as they get canvassed. Color-code the wall map according to high, medium, or low canvass priority. As volunteers complete streets, mark off the streets in different-colored inks. That way, volunteers get to see their collective work and know they are part of a bigger effort.

As mentioned before, number the map packets to make sure they all come home. It's also a good idea to have one master map for each city, color coded with each of the canvassing areas marked. This allows easier replacement of a missing map.

In 2004, the Oregon Bus Project (busproject.org) came to help us canvass. One of the agreements with the organization is that the campaign matches every canvasser the Bus Project brings on the bus with one from the campaign. On its first visit, the organization brought fifty canvassers to southern Oregon from the Portland metro area. This meant that we needed to provide fifty volunteers and assemble one hundred canvassing map packets and attach them with the walking lists to a clipboard. However, clipboards for that many people would not only be too expensive, but also difficult to store after the canvass. So I called a local lumber store, and they offered to cut three pieces of four-by-eight-foot, eighth-inch Masonite into ninety-six clipboard-size pieces. To this we added metal clips to hold papers secure. The whole thing ran the campaign just over a dollar per clipboard. And after removing the oversize metal clips, the Masonite stores neatly in a box because nothing protrudes.

Let me repeat: Make and keep a complete duplicate set of maps that you can quickly copy should one go missing or for the next canvass or campaign. Don't give in and use your backups when you're in a hurry, or you'll be sorry the next time you need them.

Organizing the Volunteer Force

Have your volunteers arrive fifteen minutes early if they have not canvassed for you before. The moment they walk in, ask them to read the brochure to familiarize themselves with the contents. Generally I have a plate of cookies, brownies, or some little thing to eat, plus juice and water. For morning canvasses, I have coffee on hand if someone asks for it, but I do not set it out; after coffee, people will have to go to the bathroom the minute they get out the door and usually go back home to do it. Coffee or not, urge people to use the bathroom before they head out to canvass.

In training canvassers, I tell them never to talk issues. That's for the candidate or the campaign committee to do. However close a canvasser is to the candidate, none can possibly know how a candidate stands on all the issues. When asked a question at the door, canvassers can say, "Why don't you give [the candidate] a call and ask her [or him]?"

Unless otherwise directed by the candidate, canvassers should not offer to have the candidate call to answer a question. Instead, leave a phone number, and urge the voter to contact him or her. Too often, when a phone call from the candidate is offered, the message doesn't get through or the voter can't be reached, which makes the candidate the flake. If a voter truly wants an answer to a question, he or she will take a

> "There are very few people who don't become more interesting when they stop talking."
> **MARY LOWRY**

moment to pick up the phone. And for those who prefer not to call, include in all of your material a Web address that will get a voter to an email contact for the candidate or campaign.

Canvassers can and should tell people why they are out working for the candidate. It might be because of the candidate's stand on the environment, development, timber, air quality, transportation, education, taxes, jobs, libraries, public safety, health care, guns or human resources. Every person who works for you will have a reason for volunteering. Urge your volunteers to think what that reason is before they head out to canvass. This directive should be part of your pre-canvassing spiel. Be sure to include things like "What would motivate you to get out and canvass on a beautiful

Saturday when you would probably rather be home with your family?" This is a nice way to let volunteers know you understand what they are giving up to work for you and that you appreciate it. I also include in my pep talks or training how difficult the odds are of winning the campaign, and how important it is that we, not the opposition, win. This brings out the best in your workers.

Scheduling the Volunteers

More than anywhere else in the campaign, I try to accommodate volunteers' schedules for canvassing. Generally I set up four time slots for people on a given weekend. However, if none of those times work, I will send volunteers out whenever they can go. Nine times out of ten, there will be someone else who can or must fit into the same time slot, so I can usually provide a partner. If no other volunteer is available at that time, I'll send the candidate or will go along myself. I do this because it's safer for canvassers to work in pairs and because it's good for the candidate or campaign manager to canvass from time to time. Personally, I love canvassing; it's exercise with a purpose and I think the best job in a campaign. Not only is it a great stress reducer, but you also become more empathetic about the efforts of your canvassers and get out to hear about voter concerns. But most of all, it demonstrates your willingness to work as hard as the volunteers. Volunteers love to canvass with the candidate or campaign manager.

It is important to accommodate your canvassers in other ways, too. If a canvasser prefers to walk her neighborhood or canvass flatlands over steep grades, let her know a packet will be set aside just for her; once promised, be sure to follow through. This further reduces the possibility of no-shows. Box 7.1 summarizes some good rules of thumb for your canvassers to follow.

A big part of a good canvassing effort is placing the right volunteer in the right precinct. For example, if you have an area with a senior population, place your oldest canvassers in that area or other elected officials or well-known local personalities. Canvassing works best if it is about community talking to community; neighbor talking to neighbor.

If you have canvassers whose manner of dress is new age or in some way inappropriate for a given neighborhood, put him or her in a more progressive area or have the person work lawn signs. People should canvass their peers. Whomever you assign, remember that when they knock at the door, they represent the campaign. Let people know before they canvass that they must present themselves well to the public and look nice, because for that moment, they are the face of the campaign. Also, keep in mind that canvassing young voters will often activate adults in their home.

Canvassing Directions

1. Split the street with a partner (opposite sides of the street; or wraparound method).
2. Walk fast; talk slow.
3. Respect property and lawns.
4. Look for clues, and look at the list for information.
5. Smile; be friendly.
6. "I'm a volunteer." Say it and wear it.
7. Say their name, say their name.
8. Sincerity counts—deliver the message sincerely.
9. Say the candidate's name.
10. Ask, listen, and write things down.
11. Get a commitment: email addresses, lawn sign location, bumper sticker, endorsement ad.
12. "Pitch and lit"—after listening.
13. Get IDs.
14. Take good notes.
15. Move on—don't drag it out.
16. Use good literature placement—no mailboxes.
17. Be aware of stranger danger—be careful; never go inside a house.

BOX 7.1 Canvassing Directions

These guidelines will help your volunteers have a successful canvass. (Jefferson Smith, Oregon Bus Project)

Sometimes you will have volunteers in areas of swing voters who are overwhelmingly registered with one party over another. (Remember, swing voters are those who do not always vote along party lines.) In such cases, try to place a canvasser who has the same party affiliation as the voters being canvassed. For example, if you want to swing Democrats, use a Democrat; Republicans, use a Republican. That way, when you hit a voter who says he or she always votes party, the canvasser can confess to being registered like the voter while explaining that this candidate is different and deserves attention.

Bad Weather

There are bound to be days of bad weather when volunteers are scheduled for a canvass. But think of this: When it rains, more people are home, and your campaign gets bonus points for getting out in bad weather. When people open the door, they feel empathy for you and admire your dedication. I have also noticed that volunteers don't mind canvassing in marginal weather, which makes sense: If it is a sunny, glorious spring or fall day, wouldn't you rather be in your yard working? Up to a point, if the weather is lousy, canvassing is a good thing to do with your time while getting some exercise. However, canvassing in really bad weather doesn't help your cause: Canvassers will hate it, and voters will wonder about the campaign's judgment.

A very effective technique for getting more people to canvass is to ask every person who has agreed to walk to bring a friend. This makes it more fun for those who do, increases your volunteer numbers, and helps reduce the possibility of no-shows. Since canvassing is conducted in pairs, it is an ideal activity for friends or couples.

Canvassers often ask if they can bring their children to help. If the kids are old enough, it should be fine. I started canvassing for my mom when I was in middle school. I believe in children having a hand in campaigns, not least so that they can celebrate the win with their parents. I especially like to have kids along with canvassers when I'm working for a library or school funding measure. After all, they have a stake in the outcome, and it doesn't hurt for the voters to have a stakeholder at their door. Very young children, however, can be a distraction and can really slow down a canvasser. If you are the candidate, you should not tow your kids along unless, of course, you're a man with a baby (figure 9.1).

Remember, don't put any campaign literature in or on mailboxes, and be sure your campaign material does not become litter. When residents are not home, volunteers should wedge the brochure or walking piece into doorjambs, screen doors, and trim boards so that it cannot escape into the wind. If it appears that the residents are out of town and campaign literature and newspapers are already littering the doorstep, consider skipping that home.

Candidates should always get out and canvass along with the volunteers. Because it is much more effective for the candidate to knock on the door, cover as much ground as possible. Start early in the campaign to canvass as many homes as possible. The personal touch really works. Lots of voters have told me and the candidates I work with that they will vote for any candidate who knocks on their door. It's shocking, really. The only drawback of a candidate's knocking is that he or she often gets hung up talking with voters,

> "The reasonable man adapts himself to the world; the unreasonable one persists in trying to adapt the world to himself. Therefore all progress depends on the unreasonable man."
>
> —— **GEORGE BERNARD SHAW**

so be sure a partner goes along to help cover the area and prod candidates out of doorways. You can always tell which candidates are canvassing because they lose a lot of weight. On a recent campaign, one candidate I was working with lost forty pounds; another lost thirty; and another, twenty-two. A few years back, one of my candidates had to buy new clothes because he had lost so much weight. Apparently there *is* a relationship between exercise and weight.

Occasionally other campaigns, party headquarters, or a special-interest group will contact your campaign and offer to include your literature in a neighborhood canvass. This is a tempting prospect for any campaign lumbering under a big canvassing schedule. However, the downside is that your brochure is dropped at the door in a pile along with others and loses the purpose and impact of canvassing a piece to a home; I've even seen bunches of candidate

> "Sometimes you can observe a lot just by watching."
> **YOGI BERRA**

brochures bundled with a rubber band at doors. Although this may make it convenient for the canvasser, it also makes it easier for the homeowner to drop the lot in the recycling. Canvassing is about getting a person to the door, not the brochure.

Get to Know Your Voters by Where and How They Live

When you canvass, you are moving about in neighborhoods that have supported candidates or causes like yours in previous elections. You can learn a lot by studying the neighborhoods that have popped out as your top- and medium-priority areas. Are the homes historic or modern ranch? Are they well cared for? Is the neighborhood made up largely of working-class or retired people? Minorities, single parents, college students, mill workers? Look for clues as to why these voters may have trouble getting out to vote. Are they simply overwhelmed with life, children, work, school, poverty? As Jim Gimpel, a professor of political science at the University of Maryland, has remarked, neighborhoods tell us about the voters who live there. They "reveal housing preferences, spending habits, racial and ethnic composition, lifestyles, levels of geographic mobility, voting habits and other traits relevant to predicting political participation and attitudes."[28]

Direct Mail

Vendors who specialize in direct mail often serve as campaign strategists, so it is in their best interest to send as much direct mail as an endorsing PAC or your bank account can afford. This section is not only about what works, but also about rethinking the idea that more is better when it comes to direct mail.

If you have a high-turnout and high-support voter, that is, one who always votes and lives in an area that votes for your party or issue by overwhelming percentages, why would you send him or her twenty pieces of mail? It's a waste of money and resources.

Similarly, if a voter is registered in the opposing party, always votes, and lives in an area that overwhelmingly rejects issues or overwhelmingly supports candidates in the opposing party, why would you want to spend money there? Even worse is to communicate with someone who is low-support and medium or low turnout. Why activate a voter who will cast a vote against your cause if summoned to vote? The best you might get out of these voters is an undervote. To facilitate an undervote, you want to minimize communication so they will hopefully leave the decision up to others—like your saints.

A few years back, I worked with a vendor from another part of the state. He presented to me a mail plan for my candidate that appeared to be a little thin on strategy. Based entirely on issues that polled well in the benchmark, it exclusively targeted voters on individual traits, with no consideration of social context. Although the benchmark had been broken into zones, there was no acknowledgment or awareness of the unique voting patterns of the small local cities within the district.

For example, Ashland polled favorably on any question dealing with schools or education, while thirty miles away another city, similar to Ashland in income, tourism-based economy, education levels, and support of historic preservation, polled poorly on schools. But not just poorly; this city liked its school—just not the larger district the school was a part of. Nor did the city like the state system that oversees the entire system. Further, it didn't like higher education, back-to-work vocational programs, or Head Start. Understandably, the Oregon Education Association had a negative net-favorable rating in this community. And yet the mail plan included several education pieces that were to go to all Democrats, nonaffiliated voters, and women Republicans throughout the district. I knew better. Indeed, all in all, the vendor's plan had twenty-one pieces of mail to be sent—that is, 800,000 printed—to every Democrat, nearly every nonaffiliated voter (irrespective of where he or she lived), and nearly every Republican woman. It was a recipe for disaster especially considering that my candidate was at a registration disadvantage.

> "I never vote for anyone; I always vote against."
>
> — W. C. FIELDS

Included in the mail plan were twenty-one pieces to be sent to Ashland, a city with a Democratic registration advantage of fifty points (seventy points in one precinct) that never deviated from party. At the time, I explained that two mail pieces would be adequate for Ashland plus a brochure; just enough to remind the base what a great guy their candidate was. Any more, I explained, would result in angry phone calls slamming the campaign for wasting money and resources. But when I said this in a conference call, the vendor bellowed over the phone, "You send only two pieces, you'll lose; you'll *lose!*" They never say, "Send twenty-one, you'll win; you'll win."

Small cities generally have their own distinct signature with shifting demographics creating a more homogeneous and politically extreme constituency; wherever one party completely dominates another in registration, all voters, irrespective of party, will move in that direction. Further, residents in small rural communities often get their mail exclusively at post office boxes where direct mail is tossed before patrons head out the door. Although these voters behave differently at the polls and should be studied within their specific context and voting history, mail vendors communicate with them just as they would urban and suburban votes.

Indeed, the biggest challenge facing the down-ballot campaign is the undervote from the party faithful in small homogeneous cities where direct mail is not the answer. Direct mail is expensive and wasteful; it increases voter activation by less than 1 percent; it has little or no effect on the disengaged voter and a negative effect on the youth voter. In fact, it pretty much does not work on any voters.[29]

But if you're running for the state legislature or working on such a race, it will be sent; the push from the lobby and legislative leadership is simply too great to overcome. Both have money to spend and no longer will give directly to campaigns; instead they give it directly to vendors whispering in their ears extolling the benefits of direct mail and how it will engage the voter.

I have not found one scholarly study that says direct mail works, and I have long argued against sending it; but between the lobbies, legislative leadership, and vendors who serve as strategists, candidates cave with the reasoning that it's free to their campaigns and who believe at worst it's benign. If the candidate or campaign manager resists sending it and the campaign does not win, the loss will be ascribed to insufficient quantities of direct mail going to voters. I have never heard of a loss attributed to too much mail being sent to voters—never.

In 2010, in the final days of a close legislative race I was managing, I pulled the plug on the direct mail and said "no more." Nevertheless, state senate leadership sent it; I found out about it only after the final expenditure reports when it was listed as an "in-kind" to our campaign. When our win was extraordinarily narrow, I was told it would have been bigger had I just agreed to send more mail.

Because the mail will be sent with or without your blessing, you'd best keep a place at the table and have a cursory knowledge of everything you will never need to know about direct mail.

By way of background, direct mail typically falls into three categories: advocacy, comparison, and attack. Advocacy is just that: It states what a terrific person the candidate is; comparison draws distinctions between the two candidates. Attack goes after a candidate on a personal or public level.

Advocacy ads are the weakest in terms of voter activation and work best for an incumbent. Challengers really cannot use advocacy, as their mission is to explain why the incumbent should be relieved of duty.

Comparison works the best on mobilizing voters in part because voters see comparison as the most truthful.[30]

The most credible studies on the influence of attack advertising on performance (turnout) and persuasion found the following:

1. Strong attack advertising can demobilize the electorate.
2. Pure attack advertising reduces turnout and harms the *sponsoring* candidate's share.
3. Attack is weakly and negatively related to turnout (advocacy is weakly and positively related to turnout).[31]

Whereas canvassing is about activating voters who, according to past precinct voting patterns, are inclined to vote for your candidate, direct mail is about activating voters around specific issues that transcend voting tendencies.

Direct mail aims at cultivating a relationship between your campaign and the voters based on issues. These issues should resonate with your base vote and the swing vote. Again, the goal is to lock in your base vote and move swing voters your way—regardless of party affiliation or prior voting tendencies.

The strategy used here is the same one you used in an issue-based campaign. With an issue-based campaign, a campaign looks for ways to package a single issue (such as building a new library) so that voters will identify with it. With candidates, direct mail is used to package issues as a way to move voters both away from the opposition and toward your candidate. Although there will be specifics on which competing campaigns disagree from the outset, such as taxes, choice, or gun control, the issues used in direct mail are often the result of things the opposition said or did during the election process. These things may not be readily apparent at the beginning of the campaign, so pay attention. Once the game begins, look for anything that will pry support away from the other side. By offering voters simple, additional information, the campaign provides a shortcut to a decision. Direct mail is a way to get a specialized message to individual voters, regardless of where they live or how their precincts tend to vote. Although campaigns are relying on direct mail to do more of the communications with

> "Be the first to not do what nobody has ever thought of not doing before."
>
> — **BRIAN ENO**

the electorate, remember that it is just one part of a campaign. Direct mail is marginally useful only when it augments the more comprehensive campaign.

Direct mail is more than a letter or brochure stuffed into an envelope. It is the most selective of all media forms, and because of its selectivity, it offers distinct advantages over TV, newspaper, or radio ads. Using direct mail, a campaign can align an exact issue with an exact voter in a specific house. Doing this effectively requires research on the part of the campaign. You must know your opponent's stands on specific issues as well as specific issues that will influence specific voters. It requires a well-constructed and well-organized

> "The art of persuasion depends mainly on a marshaling of facts, clarity, conviction, and the ability to think on one's feet. True eloquence consists of truth and rapid reason."
> **JOHN ADAMS**

database. Besides party registration, it is helpful to know the person's voting frequency, age, gender, neighborhood, marital status, general economic category, and educational level and whether there are children at home. It can also be helpful to have access to information about whether a hunting or fishing license was issued; whether the voter belongs to the National Rifle Association; is a veteran, a union member, a teacher, a police officer, or a firefighter; or works in a medical facility. Basically, you want any information that will help categorize likely voters based on demographics (individual traits) and areas of interest—that is, "universes." Direct mail targets specific universes of people who may be moved or activated by new information that is related to an area of personal interest to them.

Direct Mail to Persuade Voters

Through direct mail, you aim to move the leaning voter or to create "ticket splitters." Remember, these voters will split the ballot between parties, voting Democratic for one office and Republican for another on the same ballot. Ticket splitters are moved by emotion and issues rather than loyalty to party. Any of the items listed in "The Cardinal Sins of Campaigning" at the beginning of this book will potentially create ticket splitters.

The following are examples of issues that could be used to move voters to cross party lines. Each of these examples actually happened in local campaigns.

Military votes. You are running against an incumbent who was one of two no votes in the state senate on a bill designed to protect the job security of National Guard volunteers after a military rotation. This is information veterans should have.

Libraries. Your opponent voted to close the public library during tight budget years while voting to increase his salary. Friends of the Library, district schoolteachers, volunteers associated with the libraries, and faculty and students at a local college should know this.

Women's right to choose. Your opponent voted against sexuality education in the high school curriculum while serving on the school board, and the number of teen pregnancies increased. Supporters of NARAL, the Women's Political Caucus, the American Association of University Women, Planned Parenthood, and the Presbyterian and Unitarian Churches should know this.

Environmental issues (timber, rivers, deserts, parks, and wildlife areas). You are running for county commissioner against an incumbent Democrat who worked outside her office purview to reduce the acreage of a federally designated monument. The federal designation was the result of nearly two decades of work by local environmentalists. The city representing the incumbent's base polled five to one in favor of the monument as designated. Furthermore, in an effort to reverse the federal designation, your opponent, along with her two fellow county commissioners, skewed numbers on public testimony to make it look as though fewer people supported the designation than opposed it. Getting this information to people in the city of the incumbent's base support and to environmentalists countywide could induce voters to vote against their party or to undervote in the election. Unseating an incumbent generally requires capitalizing on key constituencies that have been alienated.

Lying to the voters. In the above example the incumbent is also vulnerable because of the role she played in misrepresenting data in public testimony. It is not a huge leap to suggest to the voters—whether or not they are environmentalists and whether or not they support the monument—that if she lied to get her way on one issue, she might lie elsewhere to do the same.

State- or area-specific issues. There may be area-specific issues that are not openly addressed in a campaign. For example, in the 2002 Georgia gubernatorial race between incumbent Democrat Roy Barnes and his GOP opponent Sonny Perdue, an underlying issue appeared to be Barnes's replacement of the state flag with one that did not have a confederate emblem dominating it. In Oregon, the mere suggestion that a candidate supports a sales tax is akin to touching the third rail. Voted down by Oregonians in nine elections by overwhelming numbers, a sales tax polled only 35 percent, even as Oregon was in economic free fall in 2002 and again in 2008.

Flip-flopping. Your opponent tells a school group that she will support a sales tax, after emphatically saying in debates that she would not. Voters look for consistency in candidates. If candidates express support for an issue while speaking to one group and opposition to the same issue while speaking to another, it will catch up with them. If your candidate genuinely changes his or her mind on an issue, hang a lantern on it. Make it clear why, and turn this potential liability into an asset. ("I am committed to studying issues and basing decisions on sound information. If new information should come to light after I've made a decision, I will weigh it carefully, and if it is in the best interest of my constituency, I may change my mind.")

Other issues that create ticket splitters. A wide variety of other issues can engender enough concern among voters that people may be willing to split their ticket:

- Air quality
- Traffic (congestion, bikes, pedestrian walkways, mass transit, and so forth)
- Airports, especially general aviation
- Seniors, especially health-care issues
- School funding, teacher salaries, and school infrastructure
- Unions
- Small businesses
- Land use, development, and parks
- Taxes
- Gun control
- Changing registration from one party to another; candidates who recently switched registration often leave votes behind that are problematic for their new profile

Although you may intend to use these issues to differentiate yourself from your opponent, your opposition can do the same to you. Your team must carefully examine where you may be vulnerable to losing your base or leaning voters. For example, if the campaign committee counsels a candidate to avoid an issue—say, sales tax—when the candidate is open to the idea, or even supports it, there is potential trouble. It is not enough for the committee members to tell the candidate to "avoid" an issue, especially if it is bound to be brought up in a campaign; it is their job to help the candidate resolve this internal conflict and to prepare him or her with answers for any questions on the subject.

Effectiveness of Direct Mail

Direct mail basically has two forms. The first is a fundraising letter mailed in an envelope, designed to move the voter by the way an issue is presented in the copy or by the effect of the person who sent the letter (or both). Long ago, such letters capitalized on the personal relationships the author of the letter had with the recipients. However, they now include mass-mail letters sent from movie stars and current or past office holders from larger or different arenas, including former presidents. The former personal solicitation from one business colleague to another has morphed into something that casts a huge net in hopes of capturing many small contributions. Although direct mail for fundraising purposes is covered more thoroughly in Chapter 5, it bears repeating here that your piece is only as effective as your mailing list. For smaller, local campaigns that work within tight budgets, each direct-mail piece designed to make money must do just that. And the best way to raise funds is to use lists of individuals who have a history of giving to your kind of candidate or issue-based campaign.

> "A word once let out of the cage cannot be whistled back again."
>
> ———— HORACE, first century BC

The other type of direct mail generally comes as a glossy, full-color, flat or folded, oversize piece of paper that is issue- and voter-specific. This type of direct mail is not about raising money but is similar to fundraising direct mail in that it goes, theoretically, to targeted voters, specifically swing voters with particular issues that will influence voting behavior. Knowing who these voters are and where they live is often enough to bring before them an issue that will make them split their ballots.

For direct mail to be effective, you need to work an angle with the voter. In one election, an Oregon House candidate mentioned that he would raise taxes on SUVs because of the impact they have on the roads and air quality. The opposition used that opportunity to send a mailing to soccer moms—women over age thirty-five with school-age children—who voted in two of the past four elections. In another campaign, one candidate made a damaging remark about health care. The opposition sent a direct-mail piece to alert people over the age of fifty-five who voted in two of the past four elections.

A few years back, a governor from one of the northeastern states suggested banning disposable diapers because they were adding tons to landfills each year and were considered a health hazard as they contain untreated human waste and could potentially contain live viruses from vaccines. Understandably, people with small children were not pleased. However, the diaper manufacturers, seeing trouble, immediately introduced biodegradable disposable diapers, which satisfied the governor.

When I told this story to a friend of mine who had very young children and who was a well-educated progressive and a strong environmentalist, she leaned forward, looked me in the eye, and, her voice dropping, slowly said, "No one is taking my disposable diapers from me." Truly effective direct mail aims to touch a nerve that elicits that kind of emotion in a voter. You're hoping for a swing vote or at least an undervote on the opposition.

Direct Mail to Hit Your Opponent: It Takes Research, Opportunity, and Timing

Direct mail is often based on your research of the opposition. Many candidates hype their background in community service and draw inferences from that experience. So if a candidate claims to be in tune with and committed to education because she served on the school board, your job is to see how well she served. Did she miss a lot of meetings? Was she effective? Likewise, does your opponent claim to be a rancher but keeps only a mobile home on a small piece of dirt while traveling extensively throughout the year? Does your opponent claim that you are out of touch, yet he or she spends more than half the year at a second home in another state?

A few years back, a direct-mail hit piece went out on a state senate candidate, Phil Warren, who claimed to be a farmer. The full-color piece had minimal copy that appeared below each of six simple pictures: a garage door, labeled "A barn"; a push mower, labeled "A harvester"; a square of grass, labeled "A crop"; a poodle, labeled "Animals." The last two pictures were one of the candidate and one of a dollar bill.

Below the candidate, the copy read: "Phil Warren grows no crops, milks no cows and sells no cattle. So why does he call himself a farmer?"

Then, below the dollar bill, it said: "So he can get a $42,000 break on his property-tax appraisal. Phil Warren in the State Senate? All fertilizer. No farm."[32]

Still, there are some pretty despicable direct-mail pieces that come out each cycle. In 2004, a Republican strategist from the Portland, Oregon, area hit Democrat Rob Brading with a direct-mail piece suggesting that Brading defended the right to pornography over the rights of children because Brading served on the library board when computers were brought in for public use. The disclaimer at the bottom of the piece was a website (probably generated for that piece alone) called Friends for Safer Libraries. It worked.

Pointing out how your opponent has voted while serving in office does not constitute negative campaigning, and juxtaposing actual votes with campaign claims in direct mail can be very effective. To do it well, however, your team must do its homework. Did your opponent claim to support education and yet vote down the school funding package? Did she claim to support people with mental illnesses but vote no on the health and human services budget? Did she vote no on contraceptive parity? Did he receive obscene amounts of money from right-to-life organizations and then vote against a bill that would cover a morning-after pill for rape victims? Is your opponent bought and owned? Show the voters the bread-crumb path.

Know where the opposing campaign's money comes from. For issue-based and candidate campaigns alike, follow the money and follow the endorsements. Look at the principles on which the opposition is basing its campaign—that is, the campaign message. If the voting record directly contradicts the message, you can raise the question of integrity. Campaign themes, like voting records, are fair game.

A voting record is not only a verifiable set of facts, but one that goes to the very essence of why we have elections. Have at least one volunteer dedicated to researching your opponent's voting record. What the research turns up may be useful not only for direct mail but also for debates.

Direct mail should be both clever and simple. Democrat Jeff Barker, a candidate for the Oregon House, faced Republican Keith Parker in the general election and found that the voters were having trouble differentiating the two because of their similar surnames. To help voters, Barker incorporated into the mail pieces a barking dog that strongly resembled his family dog, which was in campaign photos. Barker won by 44 votes out of 15,720 votes cast.

Being clever can also backfire. A few years ago, a special election was held in Oregon to backfill falling revenues in the state budget. Opponents of the tax measure said that government, like everyone else, needed to tighten its belt. In response, proponents of the tax measure sent a direct-mail piece featuring the gut of an overweight man with a belt cinched

"Washington is a city of southern efficiency and northern charm."

_____ JOHN F. KENNEDY

about as tight as possible (figure 7.5). The message was to underscore the difficulty schools were having with budget cutbacks as Oregon faced monumental budget deficits that biennium. However, in the context of the criticism leveled against the measure, one look at the photo brought to mind the *opponents'* message: Cut the fat.

Reference Your Comparison Pieces

I usually mail or walk a comparison or persuasion piece to voters the week before the election. During my last run for mayor, I did so, as I had in previous elections for other candidates and issues. Each point I listed about my opponent had been said during one of the five debates we had or was part of

FIGURE 7.5 Example of Direct Mail That Can Reinforce the Opponent's Argument

Be sure the image you present to the voters is the image you want to communicate.

the public record of his voting history on the school board. However, I made a fundamental mistake: I did not reference any of these items. When the piece came out, voters felt it was unfair to bring these quotes up at the last minute when they "did not come up during the campaign." At that late date, no amount of my saying when and where they were said really mattered. I could have avoided this simply by putting dates and events next to each item.

Direct Mail on a Budget

If you are campaigning in a relatively small area, combining direct mail with canvassing can save a campaign a lot of money and is far more effective than mailing a piece to the voter. Some years back, I ran a campaign in which we canvassed direct mail attached to the brochures. In that campaign, we were trying to get approval for an open-space program designating where future parks and walking paths would be in our city. Each neighborhood of the city was slated for a park in the plan. So we drafted a specialized campaign piece pointing out what kind of park each specific neighborhood would get and asked four to six supporters from that neighborhood to allow their names to be printed on the specialized piece. Volunteers hand-carried it into the appropriate neighborhood as part of our canvassing effort. With this approach, the campaign piece became both a personal letter and an endorsement. We also had neighbors canvassing neighbors, an extremely effective canvassing technique.

> "Words that come from the heart enter the heart."
>
> —————————— ANONYMOUS

Walking direct mail to the door is also a good way to time your mailing. For example, in the above-mentioned campaign for the open-space program, the voters approved the open-space program but turned down the funding proposal. The city council immediately sent another proposal out to the voters, and it went down as well. At this point, the entire voter-approved park component would be threatened without a funding package. In a narrow vote, the city council presented the public with a proposal for a prepared-food and beverage tax to fund both parkland acquisition and Department of Environmental Quality–mandated upgrades to our wastewater treatment plant.

However, no city in Oregon had a tax on prepared food and beverages, and the industry did not want a domino effect starting in southern Oregon. As a result, our opposition included all but one eating establishment in Ashland, the Oregon food and beverage industry lobby, local businesses, and Realtors who did not want land taken out of the inventory for parks. Again, our campaign had little or no money for lawn signs or advertising, and because of the controversy, people told us they were reluctant to write letters to the editor.

The weekend before Election Day, we hand-delivered a direct-mail piece to every home in the city. In the piece, we pointed out nothing more than who was financing the opposition. This tactic worked for two reasons. First, it clearly showed that our side was rich with volunteers: Close to one hundred people walked the streets for that canvass. Second, we canvassed the city on the same day the opposition coincidentally took out a half-page ad in the local paper underscoring who opposed the funding and who paid for the ad, reinforcing what our flyer said. Given that our measure passed by 150 votes out of 5,000 votes cast, I'm convinced the flyer played a part in the winning effort. This program—both the parks component and the funding mechanism—won state recognition in the Cities Awards for Excellence Program.

To save money, you might also consider a mailing of postcards. One sheet of card stock can make four postcards, saving your campaign money in paper stock, printing, and postage.

Another option for saving money is to change the size of the universe you are mailing to. For example, rather than mailing to voters who voted in at least two of the last four elections, just mail to those who voted in three of the last four elections. This approach is most effective in nonpres-

> "A test of a man's or woman's breeding is how they behave in a quarrel."
> **GEORGE BERNARD SHAW**

idential elections. Still too costly? Select only those precincts with the most swing voters, or mail to the difficult-to-walk rural precincts and then canvass the incorporated areas with volunteers.

However, be aware that when you narrow the universe you can actually increase the postage rates, so money saved in printing may well be expended in postage. Given that voters are relocating to live near those who share similar political and social attitudes, campaigns can actually save money on direct mail by saturating a city (or postal route). A saturation piece goes to every mailbox regardless of whether a registered voter lives at the address or intends to vote; while this may drive up the cost of printing, it can be worth the savings in postage. In 2012 we sent a saturated mail piece to a city of approximately 10,000 homes for just under $2,000 (less than half the bid by a local mail house). To save money we did not mail to post office boxes, and a campaign worker delivered the mailing to the local post office rather than using a mail house. The postage ran just under $1,400; the brochure design was $165; and printing for the 10,000 pieces cost $460. Because a saturated piece is delivered to every mailbox in a given postal route, there was no need for bulk-mail permits or for printing addresses on the pieces—which explains in part why the printing was so cheap. For candidates, this method works well

> "The first and great commandment is, Don't let them scare you."
> **ELMER DAVIS**

in nonpartisan races and for partisan primaries in small cities of homogeneous populations that are overwhelmingly registered with one party. It is also effective for just about any issue-based campaign where there's broad support with a need to remind and activate voters regarding an upcoming issue on the ballot.

The Urban Versus Rural Divide

As you have undoubtedly discovered from your precinct analysis, voters have very different attitudes within an incorporated city as opposed to rural areas outside the cities. Small cities provide great opportunities for the campaign.

1. There exists far more area-specific information available through the US Census for small cities than for their rural neighbors in the same county.
2. Many small cities are a single postal route, so a saturated mailing to a city is more affordable than mail sent to rural voters.
3. Small cities are easier to canvass and easier to get volunteers to canvass.
4. Small cities often have many citywide elections covering issue-based and candidate elections that provide additional information to your targeting model.

Remember, too, that as the campaign progresses and your issue or candidate looks like a winner, more money will come in to support your efforts. Even if you have a very limited direct-mail budget, chances are there will be additional opportunities before Election Day, especially if you target small, distinct universes.

Mail Preparation

A lot of money can be saved by having a group of dedicated volunteers willing to repeatedly prepare and send your direct mail. Be sure to have the bulk-mail stamp printed on your piece to save time and effort. If you have no bulk permit number, which generally runs about $100, and plan to do a lot of mailings, that initial outlay will quickly pay for itself. If not, your party or even an organization you're working with for an issue-based campaign may have a bulk permit number you can use. Return address should always be part of the printing to save time.

> "No matter what side of an argument you're on, you always find some people on your side that you wish were on the other side."
>
> —— **JASCHA HEIFETZ,** musician

Once you have decided what you are going to do and the direct-mail piece has been written and printed and is back at your home or headquarters in boxes, here's what you do:

1. Organize a clerical work team to assemble or label your direct-mail piece; have everything lined up and ready to go when people arrive.
2. If the mailing is not a flat or postcard, it must be stuffed and addressed. Hand-addressing increases the number of people who will open the piece and look inside. However, printing envelopes with a font that appears as though it were handwritten is almost as good and saves a lot of time. Do not use labels or recipients will throw them away unopened.
3. Visit the post office or go online to get all the particulars for bundling and preparing your bulk mailing.

4. Once everything is together according to their standards, take your bundles to the post office to fill out the paperwork and place the appropriate post office stickers on the front of each bundle. The post office will provide stickers and forms. Be prepared to stand in line three times. Often at the end of a campaign, when the committee suddenly decides to create and send another direct-mail piece, the grassroots campaign cannot pull together the people to get the piece out on time. This is a great time to consider a mail house. Again, if you're activating your base and the swing voters to vote, go to the county and ask for the full registration list for the targeted precincts.

The mailing house can download which parties you want, eliminate household duplicates, and print the name and address directly on the piece. Be aware, however, that mail houses are often flooded by last-minute requests from political candidates, which can affect timing.

As noted above, direct mail is different from targeting neighborhoods for canvassing in that you are directing your pitch for voter interest rather than for voting patterns. Also keep in mind that by using direct mail, you can address subjects that, if put in a more public forum, might activate a lot of heated letters to

> "For purposes of action nothing is more useful than narrowness of thought combined with energy of will."
>
> —————— **HENRI-FREDERIC AMIEL**

the editor. Well-targeted direct mail reaches potential friends of the campaign and lets them know where you (or your opponent) stand and where to send money.

Tracking Polls

Tracking polls are generally brief, with only a handful of questions, and are most helpful when conducted regularly throughout the campaign. Conducting a tracking poll on a tight budget is covered in Chapter 3.

A tracking poll may be used to do several things:

- Track candidate or issue support
- Fine-tune a campaign message
- Tell you whether a particular campaign event or ad has left you or your opponent vulnerable
- Determine whether negative campaigning, on either your part or that of your opponent, is helping or hurting (this is generally tracked in a quick response poll following an ad)
- Indicate what groups are still undecided

Tracking Polls Without the Poll

If you cannot afford a tracking poll, there are some telltale signs that will give you an idea about the progress of your campaign and that of your opponent. Here are just a few examples:

"Candidates have to fight back hard, or else voters don't believe they'll fight for them."

—— **SID BLUMENTHAL** (former Clinton aide)

Attendance at debates. At the beginning of a campaign, while voters are still undecided, attendance at debates is often high. Once voters have decided how they will vote, they tend to stay home. This phenomenon will vary from city to city. If it happens in a city in which you enjoy support, that's great. If voters are still coming out in droves to hear you and your opponent in an area that does not belong to you, that's bad news for your opponent.

Your opponent, who had been straddling the fence, suddenly moves to the extreme of his or her base. Chances are, when a candidate moves toward the base, it's because information has come in that the opponent's base is not secure. Remember, just because you are not polling does not mean your opposition is not polling. Trying to lock your base late in a campaign is difficult and can be a sign that a campaign is in trouble.

A week before the general election, canvassers report that people still do not know your candidate. In general, astute canvassers bring back valuable information about your candidate or issue-based campaign. If they report that many people still don't know your candidate, you must find a way to go back and grab your base without losing swing voters. Not ideal, but it can be done.

Targeting voters for persuasion and activation is central to winning a down-ballot campaign. By taking advantage of the wealth of available data that examines voter habits, a roadmap emerges revealing how and when to reach voters effectively.

"When I hear another express an opinion which is not mine, I say to myself, he has a right to his opinion, as I to mine. Why should I question it? His error does me no injury, and shall I become a Don Quixote, to bring all men by force of argument to one opinion?"

—— **THOMAS JEFFERSON**

8

Media

CAMPAIGNS ARE ABOUT SELLING A PRODUCT. THAT PRODUCT IS A candidate, library, school, parkland, civic building, water system, or whatever. But just as the local skateboard shop would not waste money placing an ad in a senior center newsletter for an upcoming sale, you should not waste campaign money trying to solicit individuals who will never buy your product. If you have not conducted a precinct analysis, stop what you're doing and get it done. You're about to spend a lot of money, and you want every penny to count.

Remember, your precinct analysis will give you a road map as to which neighborhoods, precincts, and communities will support—or not support—your candidate or issue-based campaign. From this information, you can generate a message to target swing voters. Message discipline is the foundation of your media campaign.

As with other campaign activities, your theme and message must be at the center of all media efforts. No matter what comes at the candidate or the spokesperson for an issue-based campaign, he or she must be disciplined about staying on message.

Print Media: Paid and Unpaid

Americans have become as divided over their opinions of the credibility of news sources as people have become isolated by partisan leanings in their neighborhoods and cities. Democrats watch their networks and listen to their

205

radio programs, Republicans watch other networks and listen to other radio programs, and each group believes that the other's news sources are biased and lack credibility. Further, the programs people listen to and watch break down by age as well. For example, nearly six in ten young voters get their news online, while older Americans receive news from more traditional venues—such as newspapers and network television news.[1]

> "The charm of politics is that dull as it may be in action, it is endlessly fascinating as a rehash."
>
> ———————— EUGENE MCCARTHY

Newspaper readership, which has been in steady decline for over a decade, now hovers around 29 percent.[2]

More problematic, however is the relationship between newspaper credibility and partisanship (figure 8.1). This relationship plays out when it comes to newspaper endorsements for candidates and issue-based campaigns; not receiving one hurts a candidate or cause more than receiving one helps. Newspaper endorsements do, however, continue to influence voters in primaries and citywide races of communities with overwhelming Democratic registration.

Still, no matter what presence your daily newspaper holds where you live, issue-based campaigns and candidates on either side of the aisle should never

News Organizations' Credibility Ratings by Party 2002-2012

% giving each believability rating of 3 or 4 ...	------Republicans------						------Democrats------						R-D Gap			
	02 %	04 %	06 %	08 %	10 %	12 %	02 %	04 %	06 %	08 %	10 %	12 %	02	08	10	12
CNN	72	64	58	55	48	40	84	83	73	79	78	76	-12	-24	-30	-36
60 Minutes	74	61	58	61	60	51	85	77	73	79	77	81	-11	-18	-17	-30
CBS News	70	53	49	48	51	45	80	71	65	68	71	77	-10	-20	-20	-32
ABC News	67	54	58	55	53	43	80	73	69	72	76	77	-13	-17	-23	-34
MSNBC	70	56	60	52	46	32	80	75	65	74	79	69	-10	-22	-33	-37
NBC News	68	57	56	51	51	41	82	72	71	75	77	74	-14	-24	-26	-33
NPR	63	44	53	50	51	48	64	63	60	68	69	59	-1	-18	-18	-11
Daily newspaper you know best	63	52	54	61	58	49	73	59	64	70	71	65	-10	-9	-13	-16
NY Times	--	50	43	41	40	37	--	70	62	70	76	65	-20*	-29	-36	-28
Local TV News	72	64	61	70	67	68	72	67	65	68	71	70	0	+2	-4	-2
Wall St. Journal	86	65	67	66	67	57	75	67	66	68	68	65	+11	-2	-1	-8
USA Today	70	57	54	55	48	50	70	65	59	59	64	54	0	-4	-16	-4
Fox News	76	71	76	75	77	67	67	55	51	51	43	37	+9	+24	+34	+30

PEW RESEARCH CENTER July 19-22, 2012. Percent giving each news organization believability ratings of 3 or 4 on a 4-point scale. Based on those who could rate each organization.
* New York Times from 2004.

FIGURE 8.1 Credibility Ratings of Various News Sources

Source: http://www.people-press.org/2012/08/16/further-decline-in-credibility-ratings-for-most-news-organizations/

squander opportunities with local papers. Thoroughly prepare for interviews, editorial boards, and any campaign events that will be covered by the media.

Unpaid Print Media

I recently had a candidate announce his intention to move from the state house to the state senate during an interview regarding the incumbent who was resigning midterm. Naturally, the announcement was buried in the article that covered the real story—a thirty-year veteran leaving office. If the candidate had waited even one day, his announcement would have received front-page coverage. As a campaign manager, you must be ready for the candidate who is so excited about running that the person gets ahead of himself or herself. In general, a candidate who wishes to seek an office that is being vacated by an incumbent who has either resigned or died must give an appropriate amount of time and space to the exiting office holder. It's just polite. If this is not done, at best it will cost the campaign money to come back in and fabricate an announcement event, and at worst it leaves the public with the impression that the candidate wishing to seek the office is lying in wait politically, is ambitious, or is arrogant.

> "What we are voting on is far more important than buying cereal. The last thing we should be doing is advertising that dumbs us down."
> **CINDY WILSON**, freelance public relations and marketing specialist

The announcement of your candidacy or your issue-based campaign is the first piece in your free-media tool kit. Announcements should be timed to have the biggest impact and the best news coverage. The following tips should help make this exciting day more successful.

Have your campaign team gather as many supporters (cheering throngs) as possible for your announcement: Make the announcement in a public place that is both well-known and well-liked by your community. Just as candidates seeking state office go back to their hometown, and presidential candidates to their home state to announce, you should choose a place that is significant to you and your community.

Know the law. Avoid announcing on publicly owned property, such as a school or a civic building, and do not involve people who are on taxpayer-funded payrolls (such as school or government officials) during the workday, even during the lunch hour. While an announcement may be legal on publicly owned property, collecting money for a political cause may not be, and it is typical for people attending an announcement to hand the candidate a check.

Know the schedules of the press. An announcement should be held at a time and place that is convenient for the press, even if it is not convenient for your supporters. Call the local papers, and ask what time would work best for them, given their deadlines. If you know that some of the media cannot attend, have printed news releases emailed to those who will miss the announcement. Be sure to include a photo.

Schedule the announcement at the convenience of television crews rather than newspapers. Getting your face in front of the camera is important, and the print media can be covered with a press packet. Keep in mind that television news crews typically work late at night and are not available until late morning.

"Never argue with people who buy ink by the gallon."

— TOMMY LASORDA

If your announcement is too late for the newspaper reporters to attend, provide them with the needed information before their deadlines. You want your announcement to be covered everywhere on the same day. If you are putting together a press packet, include a photo of the candidate and another of the candidate with his or her family, a list of supporters and their phone numbers that the press can call for quotes (don't forget to give these supporters a heads-up), your announcement speech, a bio, and a brochure if you have one.

Find a good date and time to announce a candidacy or to kick off an issue-based campaign. You have to know what else is going on in the community. Avoid major holidays, as people don't watch the news or read the papers as much on those days. For the same reason, don't announce on a three-day weekend or on a Friday, as fewer people read Saturday's paper or watch Friday evening news. If it is a nonpartisan race with only a general election, announcing in June gives you the opportunity to participate in Fourth of July parades and to let people know before summer vacations. The objective is to do whatever you can to get your name out in an inexpensive and effective way.

Have everything ready ahead of time. I recently witnessed a candidate announcement that was well attended with a retired congressman and dozens of community leaders who stood and waited while the candidate and his wife erected a banner of his candidacy with masking tape. The attached banner fell just as the last piece of tape was attached and the process began anew.

Keep announcements short, know what you will say, and rehearse it over and over so you sound natural and well-spoken.

Line up supporters to write letters to the editor immediately after your announcement. Letters should be short and simply say how glad the letter writer is to see that you decided to join the race. The letter writer should also mention one or two things that are central to your theme.

Letters to the Editor

If you don't have the funds for a sustained paid advertising campaign, letters to the editor can carry a campaign until paid advertising begins. Depending on your area, using the letters-to-the-editor section of the local paper can be a very effective media tool. Letters show that a voter cares enough about a candidate or ballot measure to take the time to write a letter and get it to the paper. E-letters are limited in length, which is good, because short letters are more likely to be read, are often the lead letters, giving them prominence, and newspapers tend to run them more quickly than more traditional letters to the editor.

Once published, letters are in the public domain, so the campaign can often pull nuggets from them to use in endorsement ads, on a Web page, and in a brochure. Referenced quotes in advertising have more credibility.

As noted in Chapter 2, assign a committee member to oversee letters to the editor. This coordinator should be willing to write sample letters, provide general instructions and tips to potential letter writers, and be prepared to constantly remind supporters about getting letters to the papers. It is the most difficult job of a campaign, so choose this person carefully, and do not assign any other campaign tasks to him or her until after the deadline for letter submissions.

Early letters get read. Later in the campaign season, readers become numb and rarely read the last-minute opinions of their neighbors. Also, because long letters are not read as much as shorter letters, remind all who may write on your behalf to be brief. A good rule is for a letter to cover one subject and to be no longer than one or two short paragraphs. As important as a letter may be, the heading placed above it is more important.

> "A test of a man's or woman's breeding is how they behave in a quarrel."
>
> **GEORGE BERNARD SHAW**

Shorter letters mean more boldfaced titles, which will be read, even by those just scanning the page. As noted above, short letters, like e-letters, are often printed more quickly, and sometimes they are printed after the paper has said, "No more letters." Figure 8.2 is an example of a letter to the editor. Remind supporters to send copies of letters to all the local papers, as you never know who reads what.

Many papers have cutoff dates for letters to the editor. Get this information for each local paper, include it in the letters-to-the-editor sheet you prepared for your committee (in the campaign committee packet), and place the date on the campaign plan, calendar, or flowchart. Most people procrastinate, so keep supporters apprised of the deadline as it approaches especially if letters to the editor are a critical component. Because many papers must

Vote for Daniels

Elle Daniels would be an excellent school board member. Elle has devoted her life to education as a volunteer in the classroom.

We need people in decision-making positions who know first-hand what is going on with our children. Elle Daniels has my vote.

C. Golden,
Ashland, OR

FIGURE 8.2
Example of a Letter
to the Editor

Letters to the editor are most effective if they are short and appear early in the campaign cycle.

verify authenticity of mailed letters before printing them, hand-carrying a letter usually results in an earlier publication. Letters that are typed, emailed, and faxed also get printed faster.

Other Free Media Coverage

Many newspapers have a public interest section that serves as a community chalkboard. If your candidate is speaking at the Rotary Club or the League of Women Voters, or if one of your committee members is giving a presentation on your ballot measure, be sure it gets into the community activity section of the paper. Figure 8.3 is an actual example from a local paper in my town.

Press Conference

If there is an opportunity to call a press conference, do it. When I was working on our food and beverage tax campaign, members of the opposition called a press conference to announce an alternate funding scheme for open space negating the need for our proposed controversial tax measure. They gathered a broad range of local and prominent people to show support for their argument. To counter, we called a press conference as well.

We also had a broad range of local leaders represented at our press conference. We took advantage of the occasion to point out why the funding proposed by the opposition would fall short of the community's needs. We

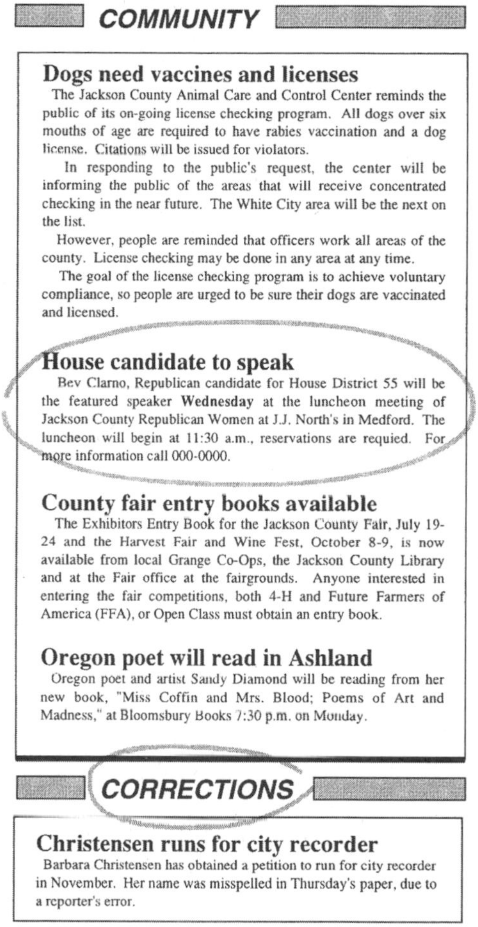

Dogs need vaccines and licenses

The Jackson County Animal Care and Control Center reminds the public of its on-going license checking program. All dogs over six months of age are required to have rabies vaccination and a dog license. Citations will be issued for violators.

In responding to the public's request, the center will be informing the public of the areas that will receive concentrated checking in the near future. The White City area will be the next on the list.

However, people are reminded that officers work all areas of the county. License checking may be done in any area at any time.

The goal of the license checking program is to achieve voluntary compliance, so people are urged to be sure their dogs are vaccinated and licensed.

House candidate to speak

Bev Clarno, Republican candidate for House District 55 will be the featured speaker **Wednesday** at the luncheon meeting of Jackson County Republican Women at J.J. North's in Medford. The luncheon will begin at 11:30 a.m., reservations are requied. For more information call 000-0000.

County fair entry books available

The Exhibitors Entry Book for the Jackson County Fair, July 19-24 and the Harvest Fair and Wine Fest, October 8-9, is now available from local Grange Co-Ops, the Jackson County Library and at the Fair office at the fairgrounds. Anyone interested in entering the fair competitions, both 4-H and Future Farmers of America (FFA), or Open Class must obtain an entry book.

Oregon poet will read in Ashland

Oregon poet and artist Sandy Diamond will be reading from her new book, "Miss Coffin and Mrs. Blood; Poems of Art and Madness," at Bloomsbury Books 7:30 p.m. on Monday.

▨▨▨ *CORRECTIONS* ▨▨▨

Christensen runs for city recorder

Barbara Christensen has obtained a petition to run for city recorder in November. Her name was misspelled in Thursday's paper, due to a reporter's error.

FIGURE 8.3
Example of the "Community" Section from a Local Paper

On this day, two candidates got some free ink.

also went one step further and used the press conference as an opportunity to promote our campaign. We were thus able to prevent any damage the opposition's proposal might have caused and to use the opportunity to advance our own campaign goals. We kept our campaign message out front. Politics is motion: Take energy that is coming at you, and redirect it at your opposition.

In general, don't invite the media to coffees or fundraisers. If for some reason an event is poorly attended, media coverage could work against your cause. Furthermore, supporters need time with the candidate without the press around. If the media are there, many will have the sense that everything is staged and that those attending are merely props. Do not, however,

"Of course the game is rigged. Don't let that stop you—if you don't play, you can't win."
ROBERT HEINLEIN

hesitate to include the media if a big-name politician or movie star is willing to endorse you or your measure on your home turf. A big political figure can get you the only page of the paper that is not for sale—the front page—not to mention all the leads on the evening news.

A number of other tricks can be used to get your campaign on the front page of the papers. Challenging your opponent to a series of debates is a time-honored way to get local coverage. Another is to announce that you are challenging your opponent to campaign on a limited budget. If you issue the challenge, you get to come up with the amount; set it at a level you can live with but doubt that your opponent can. If you're an incumbent, this can really work to your advantage. In small-city elections, incumbents are better known and don't need to spend as much as outsiders to get their names out. Because the public tends to think incumbents are compromised, this has the effect of making them seem more pure. However, one caution here: If you propose a spending limit and your opponent is unwilling to go along with it, you have a problem and should be prepared to drop the idea. Campaigns require an enormous commitment of time and energy by many people, so do not needlessly hobble your campaign with a tight budget when no one else is doing so.

Press Events

Whenever possible, create press events. This is where your research can really pay off. Examine what the opposition is claiming, and then look for inconsistencies in past actions, voting records, and money trails. Dribble this information to the press so that it comes out in increments. Look for where your opposition is getting money and support, and if their sources are inconsistent with their message, get this information to the press either directly or in letters to the editor. You want to have a game plan—and a "hammer"—ready should your opposition take the hook. For example, you are running against an incumbent who claims to be a clean-air advocate. You point out how his voting record is inconsistent with that claim, knowing full well that his record contains other, favorable clean-air votes that he will pull out to make you look silly. That is OK; the hook has been taken. If he doesn't respond, your accusation stands, but if he does, you have a hammer. In this case, you hook him with his clean-air voting record and then hammer him with a history of contributions from polluting companies and other non-air-quality votes of his that would suggest that he is bought and owned by these companies. Hold the opposing campaign accountable to his or her voting record and message.

If you find ten inconsistencies with the opposing campaign, use them for ten press releases or press conferences, not one press conference with a list of ten. Use supporters to point out your strengths as well as the problems with the opposition. For example, the Board of Realtors endorses you, an antigrowth candidate. Call a press conference for this announcement, and help the Realtors with a reason. In their endorsement they should include not only why they are endorsing you, but also why they are not endorsing your opposition. Campaigning from a third party appears less self-serving.

Take advantage of events that are already happening, like a Fourth of July parade. Plan to attend events that are likely to get media coverage, and let the press know you will be there. When considering what these events might be, look to your persuadable vote and not your base. Sending a candidate to events that reinforce his or her stand on a particular issue or to an event that is already largely supported by the base takes precious time and energy from the candidate.

It is also important to look at a possible downside of attending an event: Who will be influenced to vote for the candidate because of his or her participation, and at what cost? One great example of this occurred in 1994, when George W. Bush was running for governor of Texas. He decided to attend the opening day of dove-hunting season to show that he was one of the boys and supportive of a liberal gun policy. Of course, the press was invited by Bush's team. When Bush finally did pull down a bird, however, it was not a dove but a bird under protection. This did not play well, and he was fined on top of it. One must question whether this was an appropriate outing for this candidate in the first place. Was this a group of persuadable voters or part of his base? At what cost did he participate?

Fielding Questions from the Press

If the press calls with a question you have not considered or feel unprepared to answer, don't answer on the spot. Explain that you're busy, and ask if you can call back in a couple of minutes. Be sure to ask for their deadline, and don't end up crowding it. If the question asked is about a complicated issue and the story will not appear for a couple of days, take the time and do some research before calling back. If the reporter says he or she is on deadline and needs something right away, ask for five minutes. Even a short amount of time can be enough to get your bearings on the issue. Call your media adviser, your campaign manager, your partner, or a supporter with specific expertise, and come up with an answer. Be creative. Recently a state representative from upstate called because a wastewater pipe had broken in her district and was dumping sewage into a nearby stream. Uncertain about what to say to the press, she called me because she knew that Ashland has its own wastewater treatment system, and she correctly assumed that I had dealt with such problems while I was mayor.

It's a good idea to write down specific points you want to touch upon before returning the call. Make these short and quotable, but deliver them with spontaneity. For example, even though the answer is in front of you, pause from time to time as though you're thinking. It's OK here to throw in a few "uhs" and "you knows."

One important note: If you ask a reporter to "go off the record," he or she must agree, or you are not officially off the record. It does not work to say something and then tell the reporter, "And by the way, that was off the record," or "Please do not print that." Sometimes, after the interview is over, reporters will engage a candidate or a representative of the ballot issue in small talk. You may be thinking that the interview is over, but it's not, so watch what you say. Some argue that nothing is off the record and that a good rule of thumb is to say nothing that you do not want to see in print at the breakfast table.

> "Speak when you are angry and you will make the best speech you will ever regret."
>
> _____ **AMBROSE BIERCE, 1842–1914**

If you're upset about an issue, cool down before you head out to face the press. I cannot stress how important this is. Because tempers can flare when you're in the midst of a political campaign, think about how what you say or do will read the next day in the paper, and choose your words carefully. I hear people say that the papers took their comments out of context or distorted what they said, but I have rarely found that to be the case. More often, I have wished I had been misquoted.

Top Ten Media Tips

1. As the candidate, you want to project the image of a credible community leader. You must remember that reporters do many interviews and miss very little. What kind of clues are you giving that speak louder than your words? Avoid nervous behavior. Don't click your pen repeatedly, jingle change in your pocket, or twist your hair. Avoid verbal ticks, such as "like," "um," "if you will," "quite frankly," "you know," and "to be honest." Toeing the ground—looking down and moving your foot in a half moon with your toe—signals insecurity. So does crossing your feet while standing. Stand with your feet no farther apart than shoulder width. Don't cross your arms. Don't put your hands on your hips. Stand with arms at your sides, or use your hands as a way to emphasize what

you're saying. Speak in a clear, firm voice, and look directly at the reporter. Keep your hands away from your face; this is a hard thing to remember when you're sitting behind a desk.

2. Be sure you know your subject well. Practice with family members or campaign supporters. Discuss talking points around the campaign table, and repeat these to yourself until they come out in short, concise sound bites. Reporters do much better if you're to the point and they don't have to do a lot of work to figure out what you're saying.

> "It's better to recall something you wish you'd said than something you wish you hadn't."
>
> **FRANK A. CLARK**

3. Although you may have the reporter in front of you at that moment, it is the voter who will be reading what you say the next day. Think about your audience, and talk to your base and swing voters.

4. I try to keep a positive spin on everything. Reporters like to print controversy, but if that will hurt your cause, do not go there. Remember, you do not have to answer the question being asked, you just have to sound as if you're answering it.

5. Even so, unless it's your intention, don't answer a question that hasn't been asked. Candidates, especially new ones to the arena, tend to talk on and on. They often will hear one question when another is asked or want to offer up more information than is necessary. Shorter is better, always. Keep on your message, and do not let a reporter pull you off.

6. When the press calls, take a moment to think about what you will say, call someone for help if you need it, jot down some notes, and then return the call.

7. In general, return all calls promptly. As a rule, the earlier you're interviewed, the higher up you will appear in an article.

8. Avoid going "off the record."

9. Never speak when angry. Calm down, and then do the interview.

10. You get to select where the interview takes place. Think about the backdrop and whether its visual effect can further your message.

Paid Print Media

With declining readership, newspapers have increased rates for display advertising to the point that they are out of reach for the down-ballot campaign. Considering the dwindling numbers that read newspapers, the lack of credibility they have with Republicans, and that newspapers miss most voters under the age of thirty, campaigns should think long and hard whether they want to spend limited campaign dollars in this medium. Still, should you choose to do so, there are three advertising formats that work well in newspapers: emotional, informational, and testimonial (endorsement). None of these ads are mutually exclusive.

- Emotional ads are just that: ads that use pictures or other images and copy that will elicit emotion in the voters. Children at school, a couple talking privately, a child drinking clean water from a hose, a river, backdrops of your city, congested streets, historic buildings, kids engaged in school activities, seniors, and so forth.
- Informational ads are generally used with issue-based campaigns and are designed to let the voters know some bit of important information, such as the impact a tax measure will have on their yearly debt load; for candidate races, comparison ads are an effective information format.
- Finally, testimonials or endorsement ads use a third person to speak on behalf of a candidate or ballot issue. While those listed or quoted may be movers and shakers in a community, testimonials and endorsement ads can also feature the average person. The testimonial approach is especially effective in a candidate race, as it is more effective if someone else says you're smart and hardworking than if you say you're smart and hardworking.

Advertising Formats for Newspapers

Between literature drops, lawn signs, direct mail, and advertising, political campaigns tend to look like clutter, a sort of strip mall of democracy. Whenever possible, organize your efforts, and give a sense of continuity and neatness to your campaign. Use your logo in all campaign literature, or bring some thread from one medium to another to create continuity for your campaign. If your lawn sign is an especially good design, use it as an identifier in print ads, television spots, direct mail, in social media ads, and on badges for canvassers. It's your trademark, and it should be used just as a major corporation would use its trademark.

> "Poor ads disengage consumers from the category. They make you feel like the category is not worth entering. Consumers ask, 'Is that all the category of government is?'"
>
> **JOEL DRUCKER**, Oakland, California, marketing and communications consultant

Although there are many formats for newspaper ads, here are a few examples that have helped move campaigns forward in the print media.

CATHY GOLDEN ON INDEPENDENT MANAGEMENT AUDITS

Cathy
GOLDEN
FOR MAYOR

"Ashland city government is long overdue for a management audit by an outside professional firm. It just makes good economic sense.

Management audits consistently pay for themselves in money saved, improved service, and higher staff morale. And they let taxpayers know exactly what they're getting for their money."

Building a Better Community

FIGURE 8.4 Example of Candidate Ad Made to Look Like a Newspaper Article

(Crystal Castle Graphics)

JuSt The FaCtS
Cultural and Recreational Levy 15-3

If the levy passes, will my property taxes go up?

No. They will continue still downward, as mandated by Measure 5, but just not as much. Each of the next two years, they will drop by $1.53 per thousand, instead of $2.50 per thousand.

Authorized by United Ashland Committee, Linda & Joe Windsor, Treasurers, PO Box 2000, Ashland, OR 97520

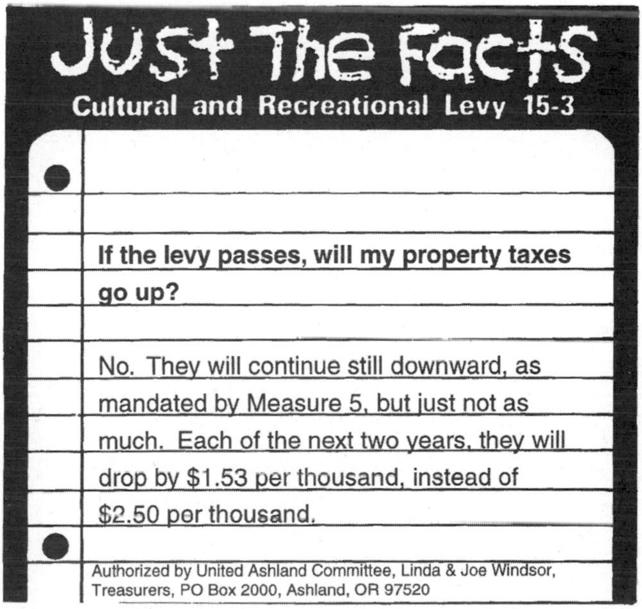

FIGURE 8.5 Example of an Information Ad

This ad uses graphical cues that we typically associate with schools to help the reader identify the ad with the tax measure. (Crystal Castle Graphics)

Create newspaper ads that mimic a news story in layout. Place the candidate's picture as a fairly prominent part of the ad. Select and place a headline with copy alongside the candidate picture. Ad copy should be no more than three paragraphs long, should cover only one subject, and should include the campaign logo and slogan. Figure 8.4 is an example.

This format can be rotated with five or six different headings and copy, and the picture of the candidate should vary to alert the reader that the content is different. This format works well as a *two-by-four*—two columns wide by four inches high. Smaller ads like this are more affordable and tend to be placed on top of other ads and directly under newspaper copy. I have seen local races effectively place ads, daily, on each page of the paper.

A two-by-four lends itself well to informational and endorsement ads. Informational ads for issue-based campaigns should also adopt a uniform look that is recognizable to the public. Figure 8.5 is an example of an ad used in an issue-based campaign for school funding. The font, layout, and design intentionally lead the voter to connect the ad with schools. Similarly, the endorsement ad shown in figure 8.6 uses the same two-by-four format and visually links itself to other ads advocating for the same school tax measure.

Testimonial or endorsement ads are among the most effective you can use anywhere in a campaign, but they lend themselves especially well to newspaper advertising. Unfortunately, too many campaigns attempt to cram too much into this format. Remember, newspapers are inherently cluttered, so do all you can to help your ads breathe. Keep the pictures simple and mem-

FIGURE FIGURE 8.6
Example of a
2-by-4 Newspaper
Endorsement Ad for
an Issue-Based
Campaign

By design, this ad links itself to schools and other ads for the same tax measure. (Crystal Castle Graphics)

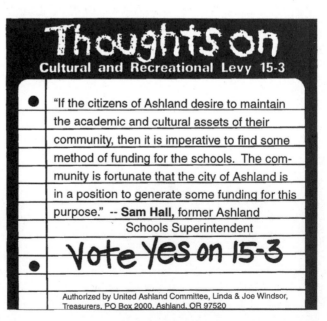

orable. Pictures in small-format ads are difficult to see and work best with a close-up of only one person. Resist the temptation to show the candidate shaking hands with the person lending the quote. Keep all ads as clean and simple as possible.

This format can also be set up with text of a community leader or prominent citizen endorsing the candidate. Be sure to use a picture of the candidate and not that of the person who gave the quote: It's important to get the candidate's face in front of the public at every opportunity.

As the campaign progresses and the candidate gains endorsements, some of these candidate ads can be recycled to emphasize a point. For example, in my first run for mayor, I was characterized as a no-growth candidate. My feeling was that growth itself wasn't the problem, but rather the effects it had on our quality of life. Some would say it is too fine a distinction, but I argued that our objective should not be to stop growth but rather to mitigate its negative effects. One of my small candidate-information ads referred to building moratoria resulting from inadequate planning for growth. Later, when I was endorsed by the Board of Realtors, I enlarged the building moratorium ad and included a banner highlighting the Board of Realtors endorsement. By coupling this endorsement with my advocacy of planning for growth, I took the bite out of my opponent's "no-growth" charge and replaced it with a responsible-growth view. Remember, you do not want to get on your opponent's message. Instead lead the voter to your message—in this case, "planning for growth."

Issue-based campaigns generally do best with ads that tug at emotion. You can and should run some information ads, but in general, information ads tend to be off message. Expanding a library, adding curriculum options for a school, and acquiring parkland are not about how affordable the projects are but rather about what the projects will do for your community, society, and future generations. There is no price for that. Stay on message: You are not selling fifty cents a pound; you are selling apples, and if voters want apples, they'll buy apples. Your job is to keep people focused on what they're buying, not on how much it will cost.

For example, in Ashland's open-space campaign, we ran ads that juxtaposed pictures of open fields filled with grazing sheep with more recent photos showing the same fields filled with housing. The caption urged the voter to help leave some of the community's open space untouched by voting yes. Similarly, we ran other ads comparing pictures of wooded hillsides before and after development (figure 8.7).

Ashland's Youth Activities Levy was designed to pick up dropped extracurricular and co-curricular activities, and we needed to convey the importance of these programs to the future success of our students. To do

TIME IS RUNNING OUT!

YOU DECIDE

OR

The revenues generated by Measure 15-1 will help preserve the land that gives Ashland its unique character.

Paid for & authorized by the *Good for Ashland!* Committee, Hal Cloer, Treasurer, PO Box 0, Ashland. OR

IT'S GOOD FOR ASHLAND! VOTE YES ON 15-1

FIGURE 8.7 Example of an Emotional Ad

(TAO Productions and Crystal Castle Graphics)

this, we had one ad that juxtaposed two transcripts of the same student. One transcript had an excellent GPA; the other was identical in grades and GPA, but also included a list of all the student's ancillary activities, showing co-curricular activities in leadership, debate, and sports. The caption read: "Which student would you rather hire?" Another ad was identical except for the caption, which said: "Which student is more likely to get into a great college?"

> "Victory goes to the player who makes the next-to-last mistake."
>
> ___ **SAVIELLY GRIGORIEVITCH TARTAKOWER**

In these ads, without a lot of print, we were able to get to the heart of the challenges facing students if they are to get ahead. You're selling opportunity, not twenty-five cents per thousand; if you're discussing the impacts the measure will have on the homeowner's property tax, you're on the opposition's message.

When local restaurants opposed a food and beverage tax for funding parkland acquisition and upgrades to the wastewater treatment plant, they argued that the tax was on the tourists who visited our city each year to enjoy the Shakespeare Festival. We agreed. They then said it was a tax on locals. We agreed again. To say this dramatically, we ran an ad with a picture of the city's central plaza on the Fourth of July, when more than 30,000 people drop in for the day. The caption pointed out that 150,000 visitors each year use our parks, have their bedding laundered, and flush toilets (figure 8.8). We took what was coming at us and redirected it back at the opposition, implying that tourists, like residents, should help pay for the systems they use.

Endorsements and Endorsement Ads

Endorsements from support groups, editorial boards, and business and community leaders can mean both money and votes for your campaign. As you get endorsements, place them on your Web page and Facebook page, and incorporate them into your brochure, direct mail, and newspaper, television, and radio ads. Craft them into press releases, and send them to the local papers and newsrooms.

Endorsement ads or testimonials can take many forms. You can list the names of hundreds of people who support you, hopefully showing a broad cross-section of your community; you can

> "Charm is a way of getting the answer yes without asking a clear question."
> **ALBERT CAMUS**

150,000 VISITORS TO ASHLAND A YEAR:

• FLUSH TOILETS

• TAKE SHOWERS

• HAVE THEIR SHEETS AND TOWELS LAUNDERED

This creates considerable sewage flow.

Visitors should share in the sewage solution.

The revenues from Measure 15-1 will come from a good blend of locals AND visitors.

Paid for and authorized by the Good For Ashland! Committee, Hal Cloer, Treasurer, PO Box 0, Ashland, OR.

Photo by Christopher Briscoe

IT'S GOOD FOR ASHLAND! VOTE YES ON 15-1

FIGURE 8.8
Another Example of an Emotional Ad

Whenever possible, use what is coming at your campaign and redirect it to the opposition.

FIGURE 8.9
Example of an
Endorsement Ad

This ad was made
more striking by
adding shading and
placing it at an angle
in a box. (Crystal
Castle Graphics)

pull quotations and names from letters to the editor; or you can have a page of logos from businesses that endorse you, with a caption identifying you. Figure 8.9 is an example of an actual ad that included the endorsement of a newspaper's editorial board.

Endorsement ads listing hundreds of names are routinely postponed by campaigns, forcing everyone to scramble in the eleventh hour to amass a list long enough to impress the voters. Whether or not you intend to run this type of ad, you should prepare for one from the beginning. Ask everyone you talk to whether his or her name can be used in an endorsement ad. This not only makes producing an endorsement ad much easier, but also tells you whether the person you are contacting is in fact a supporter and how public he or she wants to go with that support. Some campaigners believe that endorsement ads are ineffective and I would agree that their impact is less than one might suppose. But when you hear that your opponent is doing one, suddenly everything gets dropped while your volunteers start calling lists of people who might be willing to lend their name to an ad. This leaves your workers with the impression that the campaign is disorganized. It also takes time away from other campaign activities at the end of the campaign, when volunteers are stretched to the limit. The last hours of a campaign are precious, so don't needlessly burden yourself: Take care of this as you go.

Ages ago, I worked on a campaign in which the candidate said early on that he thought endorsement ads were silly and ineffective and that he did not want to do one. Accordingly, we never collected names. Then, at the end of the campaign, his opponent came out with one of the best endorsement ads I have ever seen. The ad had great pictures of the candidate, a few tasteful lines about America and community, and a full newspaper page of names. And as if that weren't enough, he bought the back page of the paper for his ad. Even if we had the time and started calling then and there, we couldn't have pulled together an ad that would have even approximated what our opposition had done. The ad went unanswered. We narrowly lost that election.

When preparing an endorsement ad, keep a separate list of names in a computer, or create a field in your campaign database for an endorsement-ad sort. Use the computer to sort names alphabetically to help you find duplicates. However, when it comes time to run the endorsement ad, do not put the names in alphabetical order. A random listing of names pushes people to read through more of them, looking for familiar names. Also, random order allows you to put your big names in prominent locations, like at the top of columns or just above a prominent quote.

In my first mayoral campaign, we ran the endorsement ad on bright yellow paper with a die-cut (a hole at the top) so it could hang from doorknobs. On the front at the top was the logo and the phrase "Join us in voting for Cathy Golden." Below this was a list of hundreds of names, which continued on the back to cover both sides of the door hanger. At the crack of dawn, the Saturday before the election, about sixty volunteers covered the city in two hours. No matter where voters traveled in the city that day, these yellow endorsement door hangers could be seen hanging from doorknobs.

After the food and beverage tax passed, funding parkland and wastewater treatment plant upgrades, restaurant owners began placing a postcard on every table in every restaurant in town. On one side, it asked patrons to let the city know what they thought about the meals tax, and on the other side of

We *LIKE* the Meals Tax

We've been coming to Ashland since 1970. OSF is the impetus, but we've come to love the charm of your city/area. We make three trips a year into your economy. Since the ambience of the area attracts us, we don't object to contributing to ambience things like park areas, and mundane things like sewers. We're not paying the total cost with our 5% meal tax, just a contribution (maybe $25 a year). It's a small price to pay for the joy we get in return. How would the critics finance these things? And if you don't have them, folks like us wouldn't come. Don't be foolish, there's no free lunch – and we had a picnic in the park last night. 5% was only $1.50.

– R.S.
Eugene, OR

I applaud the wisdom of your voters in implementing this tax. I hope it continues.

– B.C.
Edmonds, WA

As frequent summer vacation visitors to Ashland, my wife and I are pleased to make a small contribution to the well being of your beautiful city through the tax. We feel it to be a good idea, not unreasonable.

– J.R.M.
Portland, OR

Paying 5% on our meals is a small price to pay to help keep Ashland the lovely city it is.

– T.W. **Talent, OR**

As a frequent visitor to Ashland, I welcome the opportunity to help pay for parks, open space and water treatment. The 5% tax seems appropriate to me.

– K.R.D. **Corvallis, OR**

I think you would be <u>CRAZY</u> <u>NOT</u> <u>to</u> collect this tax. These services benefit tourists, like us, therefore we should pay for them. This tax should focus more on visitors who put demands on your open space and utilities. Restaurant oriented taxation does that.

– J.H.J.
Winters, CA

I think the restaurants are foolish to oppose this tax. I support it and think we should have one in Eugene.

– G.S.
Eugene, OR

Good for you! Deal with your real problems ... I'm glad to chip in my share.

– M.P.
San Luis Obispo, CA

Although I work at a local coffee shop and am surrounded by opposition to the meals tax, I still support it. Please stick with your aims and goals no matter what pressure the restaurant owners put on you. '<u>Good Job</u>!'.

– **Ashland, OR**

We have been annual visitors to Ashland for the past 16 years, and we do not feel burdened to support this sales tax for Ashland's parks and sewers (both of which <u>we USE</u>).

– R.K.
Los Altos, CA

Save our funding for park acquisition
VOTE NO ON 15-1 and YES ON 15-2
Paid & authorized by the Good for Ashland Committee, Jean Crawford, Treasurer

FIGURE 8.10 Another Example of an Endorsement Ad

Again, whenever possible, redirect back to the opposition what they send your way. (TAO Productions and Crystal Castle Graphics) the card was my name and address at city hall. Obviously the idea was to have patrons tell me that they hated the tax. Naturally, some postcards said just that; however, many came in with glowing remarks about Ashland and how happy the visitors were to contribute in some small way to the beauty of our community. I saved all these cards. Eventually the people who opposed the tax pulled a petition and referred it back out to the voters through the initiative process. Once the referral qualified for the ballot and it was clear that we would have to run another campaign, I took the postcards supporting the tax and printed them verbatim in an endorsement ad (figure 8.10). Because I had not asked permission to use the names of the people who sent me postcards, I just used the initials. As mentioned throughout this manual: Take what is coming at you from the opposition and redirect it against them.

Use both endorsements and published letters to the editor in online advertising. For a campaign website, assign a campaign committee member to troll the newspaper for letters and then select a memorable sentence from each. This sentence is what goes on the site with a "more" link that will open the full letter for those who want to read it. Prominent endorsements are scattered throughout the pages of the campaign website, and of course all endorsements scroll on the page. The scrolling names follow the visitor from page to page.

One caution on endorsement ads for those running for a judge or district attorney: Listing a disproportionate number of attorneys and those making a living in law enforcement can backfire. I understand the tendency to do so, as it underscores both respect and credibility for the candidate. However, voters need to know that a judge or DA will be impartial once elected and when too many who potentially will work with or come before the individual seeking office, voters become wary. One way around this issue is to simply omit identifiers that might typically be used to precede or follow a name such as "atty.," "JD," "Capt.," or "Lt."

The avenues with which campaigns communicate with the voters are fairly standard. Lawn signs, advertising, debates, voters' pamphlets, brochures, walking pieces, Web pages, social media, and direct mail are standards used in a political campaign, whether it is issue-based or candidate-based. However, the difference between a winning campaign and a losing one is really how the campaign communicates through these different instruments. In product advertising, there seems to be little concern about whether someone remembers the product because the ad was irritating or because the ad was clever. This is not true in politics. In politics, where the period during which you must attract the voters' attention and move them to support you—and vote for you—is so short, irritating ads can hurt more than help. You want to create ads that have people saying to their family and friends, "Hey, check this ad out; it's really good." Your campaign must "pop" in a memorable way to break out of the clutter.

Years ago, I was involved in a campaign for a circuit judge. In the campaign war room was a local newspaper columnist who had been riding me and city hall for years. From time to time, I had responded to his missives with guest editorials that were as hard-hitting as those he had aimed at me. Our ongoing feud was well known in the community. One evening in the war room we happened to sit directly across the table from each other. Everyone in the room knew the backstory and the tension was palpable. While we were discussing possible newspaper advertising, I suggested that the columnist and I be photographed back to back, arms crossed, looking directly at the camera. The caption would read: "They can only agree on one thing: Phil Arnold should be elected circuit court judge." We ran the ad. People in our community loved it and commented on it for weeks.

> "Few people can see genius in someone who has offended them."
>
> —— ROBERTSON DAVIES

Brochures that breathe with pictures that have movement and that elicit emotion will distinguish yours over the opposition's. Lawn signs should be works of art, and slogans clever and memorable. A creative and memorable political campaign costs no more than one that is indistinct in every way.

Campaigns are the most fluid segment of the advertising market, and nowhere is it more important for your campaign to adapt to changing circumstances and new information than in advertising. One easy way to differentiate your campaign from others is in timing.

Timing Your Ads

Campaigns typically continue with advertising once they've begun, gradually increasing the number, size, and frequency of ads as the election draws near. However, for challengers there is a strong argument to begin advertising well in advance of the immediate pre-election period, when the market is saturated. Early ads allow candidates time to introduce themselves without the distraction of other campaign advertisements. Early ads also give a candidate an initial bump in the polls. Further, in this era of Super PACs where hundreds of thousands of dollars are thrown at TV and radio for up-ballot candidates, early advertising—away from all the clutter—is absolutely the way to go.

This does not mean your campaign should begin advertising in March and keep going until the May primary. Rather, you would do ads one or two weeks at the end of March and then none until three or four weeks before the election. Television and newspapers may have specials in the spring to encourage people to spend money on advertising. Take advantage of this and jump in.

Your first ads can make the biggest impression, so choose them carefully. While an early advertising splash helps establish a challenger, if it will seriously cut into your media budget for the final push, you must consider this decision very carefully. Once you hit the final days, your campaign needs to maintain a presence until the end. Generally, I ask campaigns to buy the time closest to the election first and to work backward from there.

Although timing for a mail-in election and in states with early voting and no-excuse absentee voting is slightly different, for all others a media campaign should work like the fireworks on the Fourth of July. Start with a little at first, then add more and more, climaxing with the finale just before the election. Your money determines when you can start advertising, not when you will end.

Placing Your Buys

For newspaper advertising, talk to the person who sells display ads for your local papers. Although newspapers often include ad layout as part of the package, it is best to have your ad designed by a professional outside the newspaper. It is also worth paying extra to choose where in the paper the ad will be placed. Requesting placement typically adds 15 percent to the cost of the ad. Salespeople will tell you that it is not necessary to request placement and that they will do all they can to get you what you want for no extra money. This works about half the time. I have found that the personal bias, at least on small papers, gets your ad placed where they want it, not where you want it. If you can afford it, pay for placement.

The best spot for ad placement is opposite the editorial page, which some papers no longer allow for political ads. Pages 2 and 3 are also good choices. Stick to the outside of the page, not the fold. Much farther back in the paper, and your ad is at risk of disappearing. Don't forget the television listings section. In many papers, this section is tabloid-sized, and a full-page ad there costs a third as much as a full-page ad in the regular paper. Plus, people, especially seniors, keep the TV section around all week. In my first run for mayor, I ran a full-page endorsement ad in the TV section that contained the logos of all the businesses that were supporting my candidacy; naturally, the businesses loved the free publicity. Following the theme of the campaign, the headline read: "Planning for Ashland's Growth Is Good for Ashland's Businesses."

Don't forget the sports section, local high school newspapers, and college newspapers. Also, consider placing an ad in the help-wanted section:

"Hardworking, energetic businesswoman seeks position on the County Commission. Willing to work long hours in community service. Vote [the candidate]." Finally, if you have the money and the space is available, a full-page or half-page ad on the back of the newspaper can work wonders. One local woman running for state representative bought the top half of the back page. Most of it was a color reproduction of a watercolor by a local artist of the hills surrounding our city. It was the best newspaper ad I had ever seen. She won by a handful of votes.

By December 2008, Pew reported that those receiving national and international news online (40 percent) had passed those receiving the same from a daily (35 percent). More problematic for the health and longevity of newspapers in America is that more "traditionalist" voters, that is, those who receive a vast majority of their information from newspapers, tend to be older. Of the thirty-and-younger crowd, Pew reported in 2008 that 59 percent were receiving national and international news online. So the future of newspaper readership rests with those who are declining in numbers while those coming up through the ranks are not conditioned to receive news in a daily.[3]

Further, classifieds, which have contributed to newspaper income, have moved online, where people can sell their wares for free. Couple this with the struggling economy and a depressed ad market, where there are fewer businesses and fewer still with the ability to expend large amounts of money for print advertising, and the picture for newspapers becomes even more bleak. The income to support newspapers must come from someplace, and that appears to be from the remainder of those still advertising in the paper along with subscribers. But as rates climb, both subscribers and advertising dollars drop off. Further, as outlined above, newspapers hold less sway with Republicans and tend to speak to the base for Democrats. Given the sharp increase in costs of display ads in print media, campaigns must decide whether this is a good expenditure of scarce campaign dollars.

One way to mitigate the high cost of media advertising yet still reach newspaper readers is to pay your daily to place an insert in its paper for your campaign. Given that newspaper readers are more likely to vote and are better educated, older, and more inclined to support schools, parks, and civic endeavors, this may be the happy compromise for getting the word out for a candidate or an issue-based campaign at a reasonable cost.

Radio and Television

To be successful in a campaign, it's important to have a mix of media. When you first sit down to assess your preliminary budget, research the cost of radio and television, and consider what it can do for your campaign. Generally speaking, candidates seeking an office in a small town might be well advised to discard radio and television, focusing on mixes of the other media discussed above. On the other hand, candidates running for a countywide seat, state senate, state representative, mayor of the county's largest city, or further up the food chain should consider television and radio.

Radio

I grew up in the San Francisco Bay Area when Don Sherwood was a huge radio personality. I recall one evening at the dinner table my father sharing a story that Don Sherwood told on the radio during his morning commute into the city. He said that following the story he looked across at the fifteen lanes of drivers queued up to pay their toll on the Bay Bridge, and said everyone was laughing; they were all listening to the same station. In my area that is true today where conservative radio talk shows are the shared experience.

> "Placing TV ads based on cost and running them as often as possible may build voter immunity."
> **MALCOLM GLADWELL**

Morning and evening drive time is still the most coveted of all time slots on radio and has arguably the largest reach. However, equally important is that many workplaces also pipe in radio stations all day for workers and patrons. How many of us have gone to a secondhand store, auto parts dealer, grocery outlet, or another small business and heard a local station in the background?

Needless to say, radio stations know and track their audience for advertising purposes, so reaching certain segments of the population through radio is pretty easy.

Whereas TV ads are broadcast, driving campaigns and advertisers to reach a demographic through a particular program (not network), "radio ads are narrowcast, targeted toward particular audiences with distinguishing characteristics."[4] Listeners choose a station that appeals to their sensibilities: Christian rock, oldies, classical, country/western, hip-hop, NPR news and information, Latino, or contemporary music formats. Because radio listeners' loyalty is predicated on a specific format, listeners do not surf and campaigns can actually target one audience on one station with a specific message and target a completely different audience on another station with a completely different audience.[5]

> "I watch a lot of baseball on the radio."
> **GERALD FORD**

Because radio paints a picture with words and sounds, it should be treated differently than television. Nevertheless, a few years back, one of my clients ran a sixty-second radio spot from two thirty-second television ads we had produced. Because the ads were rich with Foley work (background sound) and had scripts that could stand alone without the TV images, it completely worked. As a side benefit, the ads playing in two media reinforced each other and cost nothing for production.

Radio spots are generally sixty seconds long, which allows the campaign plenty of time to tell a story and, partly due to the length of radio ads—sixty seconds versus a typical thirty-second ad on television—"radio ads really do impart more information."[6] Plus research indicates that the more voters are "exposed to campaign ads on the radio, the more importance they attach to the information they receive from such ads."[7] In one local primary, a candidate running for circuit court judge ran a very effective radio campaign. He had inadvertently missed the deadline for the voters' pamphlet in the primary and was facing a well-heeled opponent who was everywhere, including on television. The voters' pamphlet is one of the most respected and effective tools a campaign has in Oregon, and not appearing in it is a death knell. To overcome his opponent's money and organization, the candidate saturated radio stations with a great ad reminding voters that he was the one who *wasn't* in the voters' pamphlet. It was enough to help him barely survive the primary and eventually win in a runoff in the general election.

> "Politics is short, very focused. To compete with all the commercial advertising you have to punch through."
>
> **LEO MCCARTHY**, former California lieutenant governor

But let's be clear: Radio is not for everyone; as with all media buys, a campaign must know whom they're targeting. For example, "Republicans report higher levels of exposure (to radio) than similarly situated Democrats" and "men are significantly more likely to find radio ads important than are women, and more religiously active citizens rely significantly more on radio ads for campaign information than do otherwise similarly situated secular citizens." Also, Caucasians report "less influence from both radio and television ads than do non-Caucasians."[8]

Indeed, campaigns should not overlook the power of radio in communicating with Hispanic populations, especially in more rural areas where Spanish-language radio and television stations are limited. According to Laura Sonderup (*Hispanic Marketing: A Critical Market Segment*):

- Radio is a proven, effective medium in targeting Hispanics.
- The most unique aspect of Spanish-language radio stations is the amount of time spent listening.

- The Hispanic population often listens to the radio all day.
- The entire family may listen to one station and tune in, on average, twenty-six to thirty hours per week. This ranks more than 13 percent above the general population.

Television

Before deciding to advertise on television, your campaign must first determine whether the medium is within your financial reach and whether it is worth it. If you're running for office in a small city or down-ballot in a countywide race, such as a tax assessor, there are much better ways to spend your money than buying television time, such as video ads on your website or within social media. And if you're involved in an issue-based campaign, a couple things may help make this decision both easier and harder: First, television is a great way to brand a community service (like pools) but issue-based campaigns do not enjoy the same political rate break as candidates.

> "The press always has the last word."
>
> **TOM OLBRICH,** campaign media adviser

Is It Worth It?

Television once had a vast reach, especially in rural areas, which often had access to only a few local stations and limited cable penetration. But with DVRs, Netflix, and digital set-top boxes, television's best and most reliable reach now is to older voters who watch upward of seventy hours per week and in some markets as many as ninety hours per week. Middle-aged voters are best reached by mail and millennials through the internet and canvassing.

But if a campaign has the resources, television can legitimize a candidate or campaign issue more quickly and effectively than any other medium. And once cut, a television ad can also play on the internet to reach younger voters who may visit your Web page or watch it on social media.

Although the costs for television ads near major media markets can be prohibitively expensive, that is not necessarily true in more rural areas. For example, in my market production for a thirty-second TV spot runs from $500 to $4,000 and anywhere from $8 per spot on cable to $3,300 for a thirty-second ad on a network, top-ranked program. Spending $3,300 for a thirty-second spot is completely unnecessary for the down-ballot race, as any campaign can get equal reach with increased frequency on cable or on network television during the day or close to prime time.

Cable Television: A Better Buy

In larger media markets cable remains affordable. And in small markets, it can be the cheapest tool in your media tool box. For example, in small markets a campaign can buy a thirty-second spot on cable for about $10. While $10 sounds cheap—and it is—remember, you're typically buying six spots per day on six to seven cable channels for three weeks. It adds up, and you haven't even bought network.

Campaigns buy six spots per cable station because cable advertising is often available only on rotators. That means you buy six spots, and the station will rotate your thirty-second ad through a time slot, like twenty-four hours or (for a little more) from 6 p.m. to midnight. I've never found this to be a problem and research my buys with that in mind. People watch at all times of the day and night; the trick is to line up your buys on a daytime rotator with shows that people watch during the day and an evening rotator for cable networks and programs that tend to get watched more at night.

> "If there's more than one person—including yourself—in a room, consider anything said to be on the record and a probable headline in the morning paper."
>
> — JOHN F. KENNEDY

Be sure to check with your local cable station to determine whether they can target specific cities with advertising; buying time within a few cities versus an entire region can save the campaign a lot of money. One other advantage of cable is that much of it has become narrowcasting with networks that cater to specific viewer interests, such as the History Channel, the Weather Channel, HGTV, and cable news like Fox and MSNBC.

Finally, in addition to Pew Research be sure to check out the Television Bureau of Advertising (www.tvb.org) website for demographics on cable network viewing. Also, Nielsen Online (nielsen-online.com) has examined Web audiences by site, size, demographic profile, and behavior. Once a campaign knows its audience, a small amount of time in research can help target both internet advertising and television audiences and save money.

Fat-Free TV

As noted above, in smaller media markets, television is a relatively affordable asset in your media budget. In one general election, we advertised on four daytime network stations, nearly every hour for one week, for the same price as developing and sending one direct-mail piece. But to keep television affordable, attention to detail must be practiced at every level.

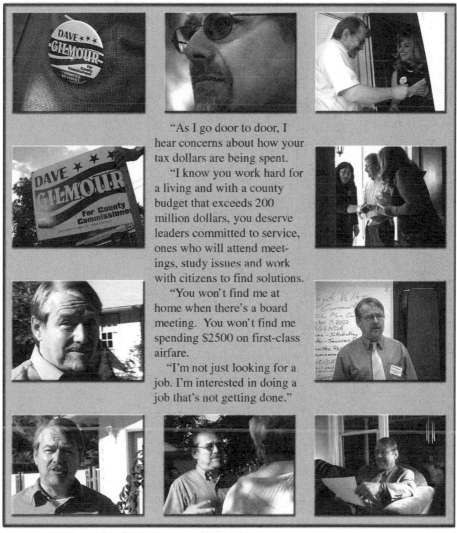

"As I go door to door, I hear concerns about how your tax dollars are being spent.

"I know you work hard for a living and with a county budget that exceeds 200 million dollars, you deserve leaders committed to service, ones who will attend meetings, study issues and work with citizens to find solutions.

"You won't find me at home when there's a board meeting. You won't find me spending $2500 on first-class airfare.

"I'm not just looking for a job. I'm interested in doing a job that's not getting done."

FIGURE 8.11 Example of a Comparison TV Ad

County Commission candidate Dave Gilmour was running with an eight-point registration disadvantage against a popular incumbent. The incumbent had been somewhat remiss in the use of public funds and had received damaging press regarding drug and alcohol abuse and marital problems. We felt that going straight after the incumbent's personal problems would be needlessly unkind and could backfire. Instead, as shown in these stills from the TV spots, we used images to portray the two candidates' differences: Gilmour projected a healthful image (walking door-to-door) and a sound family relationship (his daughter and his son narrated two of the three ads). And the ads spoke to integrity, referencing only his opponent's indiscretion with use of tax dollars. (rickshaw productions)

Although production for television should be left in the hands of a professional, the more you know about the process, the more input you'll have in the finished product. There are a number of ways to stretch your campaign dollars if you decide to use television advertising.

Whether you're cutting the ad yourself on Final Cut Pro or have hired a media consultant, it's important to do as much front-end work as possible. Research both your candidate and the opposition. Anyone creating your ads should know the strengths and the weaknesses of your candidate. While the strengths may be accentuated in ads that establish a candidate, if everyone has a clear idea where the candidate may be vulnerable, then the team is better prepared to quickly respond to attacks—whether on TV or online.

Your campaign should also research the strengths and weaknesses of the opposition. Even if you do not intend to run negative ads, by researching the opposition's flaws, you can juxtapose your candidate's strengths with your opponent's weaknesses even though they're never directly mentioned; they simply become implied: "Jane Doe will not miss important votes" implies that her opponent has (figure 8.11).

Gather as much background information about your candidate: images in the form of newspaper articles, childhood and current family photos (especially ones that help underscore what you want to project), career history, and a list of names and phone numbers of close family and friends the media consultant can contact. This small effort not only makes for better ads but helps your consultant do his or her job efficiently. Also, collect newspaper clippings of the opposing candidate for possible use in advertising.

As an aside, the local community-access station is often hungry for programming and may be willing to produce shows for a candidate at little or no charge. Such productions can provide some outstanding material for your producer to use in an ad or a portion of an ad.

Finally, don't forget to check what is available within your community: In one election, we did not have enough material for a particular ad a candidate wanted, so an appeal was put out in the community for any video on the candidate. One local resident had footage of all the candidates in a Fourth of July parade. Although the quality was marginal, converting it to black and white and slowing the motion gave it a timeless quality, and it added a great deal to the ad (figure 8.12).

Production

Before you hire someone to produce your ads, check to see what level of expertise already exists within your campaign team. Digital cameras can capture video of amazing quality and the average consumer is becoming incredibly

As a Peace Corps volunteer Dave Gilmour learned what it means to serve—a commitment to service that deepened while working on the Zuni and Navajo Reservations.

As a school board member, planning commissioner, city councilor, and physician, Dave emerged as a leader of integrity and dedication in the Rogue Valley.

Now he's running for County Commissioner. Dave Gilmour is committed to service, he's hard working and a great father,

I should know I'm his daughter and campaign manager.

Elect Dave Gilmour
for County Commissioner

FIGURE 8.12 Example of an Establishing TV Ad

All ads should tell a story, but your first one should tell a story of the candidate. Effective ones reveal who the candidate is and not only touch on history but also tug at emotions. (rickshaw productions)

adept at editing and producing short works. Volunteer producers can also be found at local cable access stations, where fledgling producers may be willing to work for the experience and exposure. One note of caution: Contact the local TV stations beforehand so you can meet required formats.

Finding Outside Talent

Finding a good production team can be as easy as noting which locally produced ads you like—whether they're political spots or for commercial businesses. I am continually amazed at the poor quality of local ads in my area; the picture quality is poor, graphics are too small or difficult to read, and sound is uneven. But from time to time one will stand out and include rich visuals and Foley (sound) work. By simply calling or visiting local stations, you can find the names of producers whose ads stand out.

> "Wisdom oftentimes consists of knowing what to do next."
>
> —————— HERBERT HOOVER

Make Ideas Your Own

Spend time reviewing other political spots online for ideas and script inspiration. There is no reason an agency cannot model your ad after another campaign somewhere else in the country. Stanford University's Political Communication Lab has archived thousands of political ads: http://pcl .stanford.edu/campaigns.

Keep It Simple

Be sure the final product does not include unnecessary or distracting motion like clever swirls and bizarre dissolves. Avoid a voice-over that is trying to cram in as many words as humanly possible; a thirty-second television spot should have no more than eighty words, and it is always preferable to have the script written by the campaign team. If it is written by the producer, the campaign team should review and approve the script. On-screen type should reinforce what's being said rather than introduce new thoughts.

A filmlike softness can be created with lighting. Movement adds a great deal—whether it is the candidate walking door to door (hopefully toward the camera) or panning across a still. Frankly, if you have enough still photos, you can use just those with a great script and a professional voice-over to create a fabulous ad at affordable rates.

Local stations may also pitch you their own studio production. These ads are usually in a cookie-cutter, talking-head format with a studio backdrop and are best reserved for a candidate who is responding to an attack or for featuring local stars or incumbents with clout who are willing to publicly endorse a candidate or cause. If the talking-head format can stand on its own for your particular application, it can be a very effective and an inexpensive ad to produce.

B-Roll

B-roll is supplemental footage that can be inserted into an ad to enrich the story being told. There are plenty of occasions for the media team to attend events that include both candidates, providing a venue to capture footage of each. Seizing opportunities of this nature allows your campaign to study both candidates and pick up material for additional ads or for use to intercut with the main shot in an interview format. Anytime a candidate attends a debate, send someone to catch it on a digital video camera, and if a local station or public access channel has a debate or candidate forum, purchase the DVD of the recorded show. After all, they do have professionals lighting the stage and working the cameras. We have cut a number of thirty-second spots from recorded candidate forums. B-roll can also be purchased online where a campaign can purchase shots of ordinary people doing ordinary things to cut into and enhance your ad; just Google B-roll.

Streamline Production: Ten Tips to Save Money and Improve Your Television Spots

Many producers don't press for multiple takes or worry much about mistakes made during filming out in the field, because most can be fixed in production. However, minimizing the amount of time the editor spends on your ads saves money.

1. As a candidate, if you're delivering a speaking part, know your part, and be fully prepared.
2. Bring a change of clothes. Typically a production company will get all of the shots for multiple ads in one day and will attempt to create or re-create events and settings that are quite different. So the candidate may be featured (supposedly) at a day care center, a business, or a senior center, and so on. If the candidate is wearing the same clothes in each of the settings, viewers will notice and the ads will lose the very thing they hope to frame. If you are going from woods to senate chamber, dress appropriately for each setting.
3. If the ad involves testimonials, impress upon those involved that they need to know what they will say, and provide them the lines. Email the scripts to people well before the shoot to provide enough time for them to learn the lines. When it comes to a shoot with testimonials, schedule all the people at a location that can create many different looks. Be sure you do not have to deal with traffic noise. And remember, there's a reason advertisers use actors for testimonials. It is more effort than you can imagine getting an average person to sound plausible in advertising.
4. Find locations that convey message and image. Think about these ahead of time—for example, a backdrop of traffic congestion for a candidate underscoring indiscriminate development. That sort of thing.

5. Use of candidate and community photos or newspaper headlines with a professional voice-over reading a great script will create a credible and very affordable ad with a professional look. Check out online pros who can email you the voice-over.

6. Get enough baseline footage so that more ads can be cut without sending the crew out again.

7. Try using just music and no voice-over. Because TV is so noisy, if a thirty-second ad appears with only music, everyone looks.

8. Consider using stock photos and film clips. For a relatively small cost, your campaign can purchase stock images to convey a message or create an emotion. This is especially important when your ad covers delicate issues such as domestic violence. Rather than send a professional photographer to an old-growth forest or a wastewater treatment plant, buy footage already available on the Web. The great halls of government, people shaking hands, crowds, a child with the American flag, piles of money, orchestras, you name it, are already available and professionally done. The Image Bank is one source, but there are others.

"Tolerance is a virtue of a man without conviction."

—— G. K. CHESTERTON

9. Send a professional photographer or talented amateur to early campaign events, for both your candidate and the opposition. You'd be amazed at how handy this footage can be.

10. Buying television and radio is not a complicated prospect in a small media market, especially if you're willing to do some research, have a clear idea of whom you want to communicate with, and have a good sales rep at the local station. This small effort will save a campaign 15 percent on the buys—a price break that is normally given to the production company making the buys. Do not fall victim to agencies that make your television spot for free knowing they will make their money, and then some, on the buys. Once an ad is made "free of charge," a campaign feels disinclined to ask for changes and feels obligated to use it, especially in a small market where agencies are headed up by friends or acquaintances.

In one campaign cycle, I received a call from a candidate who was working with a local advertising agency. The candidate had gone heavily into debt in the nonpartisan primary race, outspending the opponents nearly three-to-one, and he wanted to know how to get to a win for the general election. After looking over all his materials, which were rather rudimentary, I looked at his TV spot. It was awful. I told him he had to ask the agency to make a new one. He said, "But it was done at no charge to my campaign." I pointed out how much money the agency made placing the buys at his expense; still he could not bring himself to ask for a better ad. He lost the general even though he outspent his opponent better than two to one. A bad ad—free or otherwise—is just that: a bad ad.

Great Ads Don't Just Happen: Be Creative, Organized, Focused

In television and radio campaign advertising, there are generally three types of ads: establishing, comparison, and response/attack. Whatever the format of your ad, certain overriding principles apply to all.

A good ad begins with a good script. The fewer spoken words the better; aim for eighty. Although you're buying 30 seconds of ad time it is actually 29½. Too often, campaigns compensate for long scripts by having the narrator read faster. Remember the quip: "I would have written you a shorter letter if I had the time"; take the time. This is a little like backpacking: Lay out everything you're going to take, and then reduce it by half, and then half again.

The first question to be asked and answered before a script is drafted is, "What is our objective with this ad?" If your objective is to establish the candidate, that is, to tell a story about who he or she is, your ad must stay focused on that aspect of the candidate. An establishing ad, for example, should really tug at emotion; it's a voyeuristic glimpse into the candidate's personal life, past and present. It's a time capsule of what this potential community leader will bring to the table in terms of experience and core values. Is she a fighter? Has he volunteered for country or community? Has the candidate had unique challenges in life that have shaped who he or she is?

The media team must look at the candidate's bio and decide what should stay and what should go. An establishing ad is a good place for the old photos you had the candidate dig up; it is also an excellent venue for stock photos (figures 8.11 and 8.13).

Use language that reflects that of your voters. Don't talk over people's heads, and don't talk down to them. Talk about issues the way real people would talk about them.

Show clear comparisons between the candidates. This can be implied, as shown in figure 8.11, or it can be more direct, as in figures 8.15 and 8.16.

Make the ads believable. Whether you are attacking your opponent or promoting your objectives, be accurate about accusations and specific and realistic

FIGURE 8.13 Another Example of a Comparison TV Ad

In the Maxwell for the House campaign, the Democrats drafted Shayne Maxwell after the primary, setting her considerably behind schedule. With this late start, with little money in a conservative district, and with a seventeen-point registration disadvantage, we knew the first ad had to be bold. It also had to establish the candidate and draw comparisons with her and her well-heeled opponent. (rickshaw productions)

about promises and programs you want to bring to the voters once you are elected. Be sure your goals are achievable. Making unrealistic claims or promises insults people's intelligence.

Look at other political ads—lots of them. Political ads are available on many university websites, as well as candidate sites. As I said before, there are thousands of political ads dating back to 1994 at the Political Communication Lab at Stanford University with more posted each election cycle.

Let others do your bidding. Using family or prominent, respected community leaders can be an effective tool for an outsider to establish authenticity and credibility of a candidate. Using on-the-street people can show that an incumbent is still connected to everyday people.

Use black-and-white. What color does for direct mail, black-and-white does for TV. It's an effective tool to get noticed and to create mood, intimacy, and a sense of history for the candidate or issue-based campaign.

Ads should be easily distinguishable from one another. In a recent election cycle, a local ad firm cut four ads, each with the candidate sitting in a large leather chair talking directly to the camera. Other than the script, they were identical. Given that the opposition was making age an issue, the candidate could have met that criticism without actually acknowledging it by showing images of him fly-fishing knee-deep in a river. Instead, what he got were four ads that looked identical to the viewer.

Use still photography and create motion by zooming in or panning pictures. By mixing childhood photos with more current images, you can tell a story about the candidate in a controlled, evocative way. Still photos work well for issue-based campaigns (figure 8.14).

Carefully select the ad's music. Do not think you can simply use images or music because you downloaded it off of some secondary site on the internet. Copyright infringement is a serious business where campaigns may be fined up to $150,000 in statutory damages for willfully infringing on copyrighted material—that includes instances where there is no actual proof of damages.[9]

Don't risk getting your campaign on the front pages of the local paper for the wrong reasons: There is an abundance of copyright-free music available for purchase. The Music Bakery has a great selection, but many online services are available. Most sites do not expect payment for a piece until you download it for use. Heads-up: Selecting music takes a lot longer than you can imagine.

A few years back we made a spot for a candidate who wanted different music, so we sent him to Stanford Media's website to view other political ads and find something he liked better, which he did. We were then able to very closely match what he liked. You want to be involved in your production; you should always feel you can tweak an ad so it is more to your liking.

Hundreds of men and women found that Rogue Community College allowed them to pursue their dream and prosper in a now very uncertain economy.

RCC's expansion plans provide exactly what we need at the right time: a technical training center so our workers can learn new skills without relocating.

By voting for Measure 17-85 you support the economy of this region.

Support RCC. Vote yes on Measure 17-85.

It's a vote for all of us.

FIGURE 8.14 Example of an Issue-Based TV Ad Using Still Photos

This ad juxtaposed still, black-and-white photos with the brilliant red field sign used in the campaign. The producer brought the field sign to life in the last frames of the ad by cutting out each of the characters in the still photos and layering them on top of the silhouettes featured in the field sign. Using captivating music, the ad ran for ten days with no voice-over, to pull the viewer in and to pop the ad from all the other political clutter. We then came back with the identical ad and a voice-over. Because of the nature of the community-college-bond measure, we chose for the voice-over a student who had a great deal of experience in public speaking and an engaging voice that, although deep, had a youthful quality to it. (rickshaw productions)

Use professional equipment, good camera operators, proper lighting, and thoughtful settings. The settings should all have a purpose. You're spending a lot of money and time, so don't cut corners here (figure 8.15).

Make video look like film. The look of film brings both a reflective and timeless quality to your ads but only those seeking high office would even consider using it. However, lighting can go a long way toward softening images and creating a filmlike look. Ask your production company what techniques they can use to soften video.

"Jackson County has a great history of communities working together for a common economy that works for us all.

"But too often our elected officials forget that development anywhere affects the quality of life everywhere.

"Dave Gilmour believes that we need a commissioner willing to listen to what people want in their neighborhoods even if it means slowing growth in some areas.

"Let's elect one who understands that along with our other spending priorities we should consider protecting a little bit of what makes this place special.

"Please join me in voting for Dave Gilmour."

FIGURE 8.15 Example of a TV Ad with Purpose

Late in the Gilmour for Commissioner race, canvassers reported that voters still did not know Dave Gilmour. We knew we had to go back in and lock his base without losing any swing voters. To do this, we took an issue that was problematic across all communities in southern Oregon—development—and used it as the anchor for the ad. By incorporating progressive environmental images embraced by Gilmour's base with countywide concerns about development, we accomplished our objective. The voice-over was done by the candidate's son. (rickshaw productions)

Use motion. When a candidate speaks directly to the camera, have him or her moving forward, either to a stationary camera or to one that moves with the speaker. This conveys the message that the candidate is someone who is going places, moving forward.

Answer attacks. Years ago in a general election, we were helping a candidate who was being outspent seven to one, had very little money, and had a huge registration disadvantage. However, tracking polls showed our candidate closing in on her opponent, and as his double-digit lead dwindled to the margin of error, he went on the attack through a direct-mail piece sent by Oregon Right to Life. With only a few thousand dollars in the bank, the campaign could not respond through direct mail, so we generated a television ad that brought back to the forefront the unprecedented nasty primary the opponent had run against the incumbent he unseated. "He's At It Again" aired for a week in closely targeted television markets (figure 8.16). In airing the ad, however, we made a couple of mistakes. First, Oregon Right to Life had used a mailing list targeting a select group of voters within that district. The television ad, however, went out to a much broader audience and gave our opponent a reason to use TV ads and automated phone calls to defend himself in a very believable way. Because most people in the district had not seen his hit piece, it looked as though we had gone negative on him rather than the other way around; to add insult to injury, our campaign was scolded by the local newspaper for going negative. In general, attacks should be answered in the same medium in which they were made; so attacks made on TV are answered on TV; those made in letters to the editor are addressed there; direct mail/ direct mail; and so on. We would have served the client better in this case by leaving the charge unanswered.

> "There is no nonsense so arrant that it cannot be made the creed of the vast majority by adequate governmental action."
>
> —— **BERTRAND RUSSELL**

Remember, television is about emotion, not information.

Placing Your Buys on Television: Research, Research, Research

The advantage of television, like radio, is that the market has been thoroughly researched, offering the campaign ample detail about where to best target specific voters. There are many sources you can use to research who views what, such as Cabletelevision Advertising Bureau, Rocky Mountain Media Watch, Simmons National Consumer Study, Nielsen, and Doublebase Mediamark

FIGURE 8.16 Example of a Response/Attack TV Ad

(rickshaw productions)

Research. Industry-tracking firms know who is watching what according to age, education, voting history, income, geography, and gender.

What is helpful for the campaign is that by using industry resources, you can develop and run ads that speak to an audience that is more likely to vote and one with highly specific demographics. Knowing who watches what helps a campaign avoid over-targeting a particular demographic group as well as reach the kind of voters who, with a little information, will support your efforts. Indeed, if your campaign can produce great TV ads for around $500, why not run a different ad on different cable stations at the same time? After all, the air time is the same, so the campaign is only out the production costs.

Every two years Pew Research conducts nationwide polling to determine where Americans get their news. In the report released in September 2012 they compared trends in news consumption spanning the previous decade. The report provides enormous detail and information regarding current news-viewing trends. So by reviewing this report, a campaign would know the age, party, political leanings, education, and gender of who gets their news where.

For example, if you wanted to communicate to less-educated women, you would know they're less likely to get their news online; that they compose relatively large shares of the regular viewers of daytime talk shows, such as *The View* or *Ellen* (73 percent), and morning news shows (62 percent); and that better than half of them view local TV news, MSNBC, and Fox News.[10]

Zeroing in on a specific demographic and delivering a message that resonates with the audience is key to moving swing voters and locking your base.

The Buys

Political candidates must be offered the lowest unit rate. However, be aware that if you come in at this rate, your time is "preemptable" by other buyers.

> "Television allows you to be entertained in your home by people you wouldn't have in your home."
>
> — **DAVID FROST**

This means you can be bumped by someone who is willing to pay the full price. Usually you will be moved to a "comparable," that is, a spot with similar demographics. A second tier, at a slightly higher rate, is "preemptable with notice." At this rate, the ad rep must let you know you're about to be bumped so that you can pay more to secure the spot. Finally, the most expensive rate is non-preemptable. You pay for this rate, and you're gold: No one moves you.

If you're working on an issue-based campaign, there may not be any price break for TV ads. If that is the case, add at least 20 to 50 percent to your television budget buys. Even so, one campaign where I was helping a school tax measure, I talked to a sales rep of one of our three local stations and argued that "local" issue-based campaigns were quite different from statewide initiatives, which often came fortified with millions in special-interest money. Convinced, the station gave us the same break that candidates received. I then called the other stations and told them what their competition was doing for the community and got similar breaks across the board.

Because most campaigns run their media with greater frequency as the election approaches, open time slots for media buys become scarce. Unlike a newspaper, which can add more pages, television and radio have limited amounts of time to sell. Depending on the popularity of the show, the time when you might consider a buy can be even more restricted. If you do not secure your media buys early, there could be nothing available as the election deadline draws near.

That does not mean you have to deliver finished products the day you buy ad time. All the production work can be done later. But it does mean that in August or September, if you're going to buy thirty seconds on *60 Minutes* for November, you must have the cash in hand.

Make your buys early, and make them at non-preemptable rates. This is done for two reasons: First, you lock in the time so no one can bump you, and second, you also lock in the rate. As an election approaches and demand increases, so do rates. One local sales representative told me that during the 2008 season, a statewide issue-based campaign called from Portland with $64,000 to spend in three days. She said that by then, our region was commanding Portland metro rates. Buy early if you know you're going to do television. And even if you end up changing your mind, you can always sell the time back to the station down the road.

> "Political ads are giving Americans a choice between bad and awful, distorting and undermining debate, increasing campaign costs and driving voters from the polls."
> **CURTIS GANS**, Committee for the Study of the American Electorate

With that said, if you're working in a campaign cycle with little competition, such as a special election or a midterm primary, a campaign may well be safe buying television at preemptable rates.

Buy Smart

There are a few ways to reach your targeted audience and hit that critical mass if dollars are short. Television costs are based on the size of the audience: The bigger the audience, the higher the cost. For example, a 30-second ad in *Breaking Bad* finale cost $400,000. However, by purchasing less expensive time slots, when the audience is smaller (smaller-rated), a campaign may air ads more frequently for less money and still meet the desired reach and frequency.

If you know you will be advertising on television but really don't have the funds to keep a critical presence for more than a week, buy your television time starting closer to the election and work your way back. As money becomes available, you can buy ads for more and more days preceding the election. Also, by purchasing

> "We all learn by experience but some of us have to go to summer school."
> **PETER DE VRIES**

the time closest to the election first, you don't run the risk that this highly coveted time will be unavailable later. Smaller-rated "avails" (available time) are usually the last to go, so there may even be some opportunity for in-fill close to Election Day, but don't count on it. Buy early. However, the timing of ad placement changes dramatically when elections are run entirely or almost entirely with vote by mail (VBM). Although this is covered more thoroughly in the VBM section of this manual, ad timing for television, like everything else, moves up with VBM.

Rules and Regulations

The following are general rules and regulations as they apply to political advertising. Nevertheless, be sure to get media packets from your local stations and familiarize yourself with individual station requirements.

- You must be a qualified candidate for public office or an authorized campaign organization to promote a person's candidacy for office. Political action committees and noncandidate campaigns (issue campaigns) do not fall under the political advertising guidelines.
- Reasonable access for political "use" will be provided to all legally qualified federal candidates during the forty-five-day period before a primary or primary runoff election and the sixty-day period before a general or special election.
- While candidates may request specific programming, the station reserves the right to make reasonable good-faith judgments about the amount of time and program availability to provide to particular candidates.
- All ads must comply with the visual sponsorship identification requirements of the Communications Act. In other words, they must all have a disclaimer. The disclaimer ("paid for by . . . ") must last at least four seconds and be at least 4 percent of screen height. Who or what follows the disclaimer depends on who paid for the ad and whether or not the candidate authorized it.
- Any spot for a political candidate or on behalf of an announced candidate must include video or audio use of the candidate's image or voice, or both. In many areas, political ads may not be placed just before, during, or just after news programs.

"If you don't know what to do, call the media and at least give the appearance of doing something."

—————————— **DAVID PETERSON**

As populations become more segregated by political ideology, it follows that Democrats believe and are swayed by some media just as Republicans believe and are swayed by other media. Knowing your audience will lead to smarter media buys that target both your base vote and the potential swing vote while avoiding media that may activate your opposition.

9

The Candidate

ONCE YOU DECLARE YOUR INTENTION TO RUN FOR OFFICE, YOU BECOME part of the public domain and fair game for just about any criticism people might feel inclined to level at you. Should someone write a letter to the editor with an outright lie in it, you essentially have little recourse. You can defend yourself, but unless you can prove malice, you cannot sue. Some political analysts think candidates should ignore attacks and lies. Far more, however, think that unanswered allegations imply truth. Either way, it's a problem. You can defend yourself, but when you decide to run, you give up your right to whine. It is great preparation for holding elective office.

This chapter is about projecting a positive image before the voters and thereby minimizing the potential nitpicking that the public might do. You will also find suggestions on how to redirect negative questions at your opponent, turning the ammunition back on him or her. For a candidate, this is not a time to be defensive. Take criticism as a gift and an opportunity.

The Lay of the Land

Each elective office has specific powers and duties associated with it. For example, my city's charter says the mayor is the chief executive of the municipal corporation and will closely oversee the workings of city government. Laced throughout the document are other stipulated duties associated with the office, such as appointing department heads and duties in relation to the city council. The charter sets up a strong-mayor form of government. In a nearby city, the charter establishes a weak-mayor form of government giving the appointment powers to the city manager and city council; the mayor runs the council meetings and cuts ribbons.

> "A mayor does not create a new vision of a city from the inner workings of his own mind. Rather, he collects it from scattered hopes and buried dreams of people he has listened to in the course of his own political journey."
>
> **FORMER BOSTON MAYOR RAY FLYNN**
> in his 1984 inaugural speech

Before running for mayor of Ashland, I spent a great deal of time familiarizing myself with council business and city documents, but I never read the charter. Then, within my first six months in office, the city council members set about stripping the powers of the office of mayor. Their intention was to do it through simple resolutions, which, unlike an ordinance, do not need a public hearing and cannot be subject to a mayoral veto. As they put it, they didn't want to "take" the powers; they merely wanted to "share" them with me and to "help" me do a better job. I was young, just thirty-five, and felt both attacked and betrayed. No help came from the administrator, who was probably equally concerned about my ability and wanted the power to appoint department heads to fall under the jurisdiction of his office. Furthermore, no support came from fellow councilors, who in fact had initiated the coup and wanted equal say on city board and commission appointments.

Department heads, who did not want to work for a woman—especially one as young and inexperienced as I was—aligned with the administrator even though they technically worked for the mayor. Word came back that many at city hall were saying disparaging things about me, including name calling—my favorite was "the meddling housewife." I represented a change of the status quo. The problem wasn't necessarily that I would wreak havoc on the city or that the existing system wasn't working all that well. There is just a general suspicion, especially in government, when moves are made from the known to the unknown. The council's overall proposed action would result in moving Ashland from a strong-mayor form of government to a weak-mayor form of government, all without going to a vote of the people.

Things heated up quickly. I did not want to go down in history as the mayor who lost the powers of the office. I floundered in meetings as I tried to find footing. I simply could not figure out how to stop the train. Then another southern Oregon mayor told me he thought his city's charter was modeled after Ashland's, and if they were the same, what the city council was doing was illegal. He said, "Read your charter." Simple, obvious, good advice. I did just that.

At the next meeting, armed with information, I held my ground, recited the powers of my office, and threatened to take the council's actions to a vote through the initiative process if the council members persisted. They backed off. Four tumultuous years followed, during which time three department heads, and the city attorney went. By the time I left office, twelve years

> "If you get to be a really big headliner, you have to be prepared for people throwing bottles at you in the night."
> **MICK JAGGER**

later, there had been a complete changeover in all department heads and the administrator and I had moved from a relationship of suspicion to one of trust, understanding, and mutual respect.

Before you run for office, know the powers and duties of that office; attend meetings and familiarize yourself with the lay of the land. Wouldn't you prefer to know before you run whether you're suited for the kind of work that goes with the office? You should also know something about the system: how land-use laws work, how property and other taxes are distributed, the revenue stream, the expenditure stream, and which follows which.

It's also important to know the lay of the land of your community. In one election a candidate appeared in a debate at the Rotary Club. Prior to making a point, he asked if there were any businesspeople in the room. He was not joking.

So what do you do if you make a mistake? Own up to it. A while ago, the Southern Pacific Railroad divested some very important real estate in the heart of our city. We had hoped for a portion of it to create a pocket park, but the option to buy was quickly secured by a developer. The neighborhood was upset. After many calls from the city trying to cut in line without success, I gave up. I explained to the neighbors that it was hopeless and that we needed to look elsewhere for a park. But they would not give up. Finally, somehow, they got the parcel for the park. Sometime later, at a council meeting, I was chastised by this group for giving up and calling the situation hopeless. I had to admit it was the best crow I ever ate, and I acknowledged the group for its success where I had failed.

More recently, former mayor Willie Brown of San Francisco attacked a *San Francisco Chronicle* reporter for exaggerating a problem regarding vandalism and drug abuse on the part of homeless people. When later reports corroborated the reporter's allegations, the mayor apologized and said he wished he could retract his words.

Many people are propelled into the public arena as a spokesperson for an issue that has the electorate enraged. Often, in the heat of the fight, these individuals decide to take on public office to further champion the cause. A word of caution for such individuals: Single-issue candidates generally make bad elected officials. Government has become a complex business that needs office holders who are engaged and attentive to the many facets of the public corporation. Too often, single-issue candidates have trouble with the wide array of duties of a given office and, once elected, sit disengaged until the governing body hits a topic that connects with their issue. It can be unsatisfying and frustrating for the office holder, fellow office holders, and the community.

One final thing to keep in mind is that while you are a candidate, you should never work on other campaigns, either issue or candidate based. Voters are suspicious of candidates who appear to be manipulating an outcome in too many arenas. Your only task is to get yourself elected; once in office, work on as many campaigns as you please.

Packaging the Candidate

A political candidate is selling a lot more than political views. People are looking for an individual who will represent their community, city, school, county, or country in a professional way. Elected officials fulfill the role of continually answering to the public trust. If the community believes in the candidate, then it will believe that its money is in good hands.

"Beware of all enterprises that require new clothes."

——————— HENRY DAVID THOREAU

To meet voter expectations, the candidate must always look the part. If you have a spot on your clothing, no matter how small, change clothes. You should not have any holes in your clothes; your shoes should be polished, and your clothes buttoned, and the buttons should not be pulling or strained from a poor fit.

Because people associate weight loss with happiness and success, an overweight candidate may choose to diet and lose weight during the campaign. It's actually helpful to be disciplined in all things while campaigning, and a good diet helps keep stress levels down and appearance at an optimum. Canvassing can really help in this area. Whatever improvements can be made in your appearance and dress, make them. Attention to appearance will project a positive image, and you will look and feel the part. You cannot afford to cut corners on your personal appearance and dress. A crumpled look may be endearing at home, but not to voters. Inattention to personal appearance translates into inattention to detail and incompetence.

Dress in a consistent style. This gives the community the impression that you are stable and know who you are. Do not do things out of character. We all remember the picture of Michael Dukakis in the military tank. Cowboy hat and boots worked for Ronald Reagan but not for Bill Clinton. When Bob Dole began dressing in khakis and running shoes in an effort to appeal to younger voters in his bid for the presidency, he looked silly. Somebody got to Bill Clinton, who began his first term in office jogging in shorts and a T-shirt that hung below the bottom of the shorts. By his second run, he had moved to the golf course, a more presidential activity. While off the course, he was rarely seen in anything other than a black suit. He was *the* president and looked the part of a president. One candidate in eastern Oregon who wore Pendleton shirts changed to three-piece suits midway through the campaign because his numbers were sagging at the polls. After his makeover, the numbers dropped further. Behave and dress in a way that is consistent with who you are.

> "If you look good and dress well, you don't need a purpose in life."
> **ROBERT PANTÉ**

Barack Obama wears only gray or dark blue suits in an effort to pare down the number of decisions he has to make in a day.[1] While selecting your clothes may seem inconsequential, it all adds up when it comes to the day-to-day grind of running for or serving in office. Finding ways to minimize stress is central to a win and to service.

Image Over Ideology

The uninterested, undecided, and persuadable voters will decide on a candidate according to who they think the candidate is (image) over what the candidate says (ideology). In 1984 polls indicated that more Americans embraced the ideology of Walter Mondale over that of Ronald Reagan, and yet they voted for Reagan in overwhelming numbers. People in this important and elusive group are making their decision based on a feeling they have about each of the two candidates.

Ideology comes into play with your base support. While a candidate may craft theme and message to get at the persuadable voter, he or she must not forget the base and what issues are important to this group. If there is any hesitancy on the part of the base to support the candidate, it must be addressed quickly and within the parameters of your theme and message. So in creating theme and message, leave room for this possibility. For example, again, in the 1996 presidential race, California's environmentalists were upset with Clinton's policies on the issues they cared about most—so much so that many were threatening a move toward the Green Party candidate, Ralph Nader. To lock in these voters, Clinton set aside 1.7 million acres of southern Utah, the Grand Staircase–Escalante National Monument, under the Antiquities Act. For Clinton, Utah was a lock for the GOP. Nothing he could do or say would move that voter base to him, so the giveaway cost him nothing there while locking in his electoral-rich California base and drawing in much-needed campaign workers from the environmental community.

> "In politics as in sport, you take a grave risk when, instead of playing to win, you play not to lose. Running not to lose (means) running on your résumé rather than your vision . . . people don't elect résumés. They elect candidates with an agenda."
>
> **FORMER US CONGRESSMAN LES AUCOIN**
> in a letter to Oregon Democratic
> gubernatorial candidate Ted Kulongoski

"I Yam What I Yam" — Popeye

People running for office often are embarrassed about their résumés and eager to beef them up in an effort to present a more credible image as a community leader. What may feel like a painful biographical note to the candidate can actually be an asset. For example, if a candidate is embarrassed because she dropped out of high school, she is overlooking the possibility that having earned her GED followed by working her way through college carries more weight because of her early struggles.

Candidates and campaigns committees who are tempted to embellish personal history should think long and hard before doing so. It's a crime to place any false statement into a voters' pamphlet and takes only an accusation by the opposition to activate an investigation.

In 1994 Wes Cooley was elected to the Second Congressional District of Oregon. During the campaign, he had claimed in the voters' pamphlet that he was a member of Phi Beta Kappa academic honor society. When that statement was found to be false, the secretary of state gave Cooley the benefit of the doubt and let it go. However, in Cooley's reelection bid two years later, he made more claims. He listed "Army Special Forces, Korea," among his qualifications, although he was never in Korea. During the investigation, he claimed that it was a top-secret mission and all very hush-hush. It didn't let up. Because of his constant denials, the press took on the investigation and in so doing turned up far more than the Korea fabrication. He had failed to get building permits for home improvements, the contractor had not been paid, and he and his wife were secretive about their marriage date so that she could continue to collect benefits as a marine's widow. Cooley backed out of the race and later was indicted.

What is particularly instructive about this story is that more voters could probably relate to someone who was simply drafted and never went anywhere than to someone who claimed to be part of a secret special mission. More people do average things than the opposite. More have attended state-owned universities than private and graduated without honors than have, and most never made the football team.

> "What shall it profit a man, if he should gain the whole world and lose his own soul?"
>
> **MARK 8:36**

Don't miss the opportunity to build relationships with the average citizen by instead trying to make yourself look "more qualified."

Manners Matter

As important as dress and appearance are, there is more to looking the part of a serious public servant. The candidate must adopt the kind of manners a mother would be proud of. Do not chew with your mouth open, pick your nose, clean your ears, or floss in public. Most people remember George W. Bush chewing with his mouth open. Cover your mouth when you yawn.

When appearing as a dinner speaker, you should eat only moderately at the event or, better yet, have a light meal beforehand and skip the public dinner. When people are nervous, digestion slows down. You cannot afford to have a stomach upset from nervous energy and certainly can't afford to burp through the speech. One candidate I worked for who had atrocious eating manners would eat a full meal at the head table before rising to give his speech. During the speech, he would need to burp, but for some reason, he always burped by turning his head sideways, calling more attention to it. In general, eating and greeting don't mix well for candidates, which is ironic, given that food and drink are often the bait used to pull potential supporters to a political event.

Avoid drinking alcohol while running for public office. Besides the fact that alcohol adds empty calories and affects one's ability to deal with stress, people have tons of issues around alcohol, and it's not worth the grief or uncertainty of how drinking, even as little as one glass of wine, will play. Similarly, if you're a smoker, keep it closeted.

Bring along a sweater or light jacket to cover up possible nervous perspiration. Wear deodorant and clean shirts. Previously worn clothes can carry body odor that might be activated with nervous perspiration. Avoid perfume

While Jeff Golden chats with supporters, daughter Sarah Beth gets an eyeful of photographer.

Photo courtesy of SOHS

Golden celebrates wi̇
New commisioner's daughter accompanies him

Candidates each bring their own style and special approach to politics, sometimes they carry a lot of political baggage.

But only Jeff Golden carries a baby on his back.

For much of Tuesday evening – ev live TV interview – the Ashland D wore a baby backpack that held hi daughter, Sarah Beth, born a year giving.

FIGURE 9.1 A Candidate with a Baby

When it comes to children, there is a double standard in society, and the standard carries over into campaigning. Whereas women are penalized for campaigning with their children, men are rewarded.

and aftershave. Do not chew gum. Place a few breath mints in your pocket for easy and unnoticed retrieval; don't be a candidate who pulls out the little bottle of breath freshener and squirts it midsentence. In fact, avoid all public grooming: hair combing, lipstick, and the like. Also, you can avoid problems if you think ahead. For instance, when I get nervous, my mouth gets dry, so I always go to the podium with a glass of water. Marco Rubio's impromptu water break during his GOP State of the Union response in 2012 would have gone unnoticed if he had a glass of water with him from where he was speaking. Similarly, if you have a tendency to sweat when nervous, bring a folded handkerchief to wipe your brow.

As I said before, a woman candidate should leave her children at home. Not only does that enable her to be more focused, but it also meets the voters' need to see her in a professional role. It is difficult for many people to accept a woman as a leader if the only image they have of her includes children clinging to her asking for attention. This is absolutely not true for men. In fact, men are given bonus points for being seen with their children. Society assumes that men are professional, and seeing a man with his children gives the voters the idea that they are getting a glimpse into his private life. He seems warmer (figure 9.1).

Groomers

Given the importance of image, it's a good idea to have a "groomer" for the campaign. As a candidate, recruit a friend whose only campaign job is to let you know how you look and to make suggestions on what to wear and how to better project your image. In all three of my campaigns for mayor, I had a groomer who proved to be invaluable. In my second run for mayor, I was

"You'd be surprised how much it costs to look this cheap."

DOLLY PARTON

to be on television in a debate with my two male opponents, and my groomer advised me to dress conservatively. Both of my opponents showed up dressed very casually and looked less than professional to the television audience. The show repeated seven or eight times throughout the campaign cycle.

The next campaign debate was covered by the media but not broadcast live. My groomer predicted that my principal opponent, having looked casual for the televised debate, would try to make up for that mistake by dressing conservatively for this one. He advised me to wear my hair differently and dress in a brightly colored dress I had rarely been seen in. The idea was that I should stand out to the live audience.

I did as I was told. My primary opponent, as predicted, wore a three-piece black suit and appeared quite intense, severe, even funereal. I had time before the debate to say hello and chat with members of the audience and to enjoy myself. My appearance was friendly, and I was clearly having a good time. My opponent did not smile and seemed out of place, strapped in his television armor. The difference between us was dramatic, and the debate proved to be a turning point in the campaign.

When I work for other candidates, I usually assign a groomer and look for a man or woman with an eye for fashion and detail. If my candidate needs a haircut, I encourage him or her to get the best one available. Have the campaign pick up the cost of a studio photo shoot. The groomer and I will often discuss the kind of look we want out of the shoot and share those ideas with the candidate and the photographer. For example, if I have a candidate who smiles very little and is somewhat hesitant, I look for a photo where he or she leans into the lens. Whatever may be a weakness of your candidate in personality or appearance, your photo shoot is an opportunity to make it look otherwise. Many believe that a photo starting low, looking up at the candidate, projects power and one from above angled down, the opposite. Personally, I think nostril shots are unflattering and don't use them. I like the photographer to work with the camera coming straight on. Chapter 3 presents examples of candidate photos that work well.

> "Nonverbal cues are as or more important than verbal cues."
>
> **MALCOLM GLADWELL**

A groomer must be willing to attend early debates and public gatherings to observe the candidate's behavior. I usually like to talk with the groomer after an event to discuss how delivery can be improved; we then talk to the candidate and discuss adjustments. All such suggestions, however, should be cushioned with lots of praise. Candidates' egos can be fragile, and you don't want them to be self-conscious at the next event.

A few years back, I was running a campaign for a very capable, well-educated, professionally successful candidate. However, after a debate, I was called by the groomer, whom I had asked to attend to observe the candidate in action. She did not have much to say about his dress but told me that his answers were rambling, that he continually said he agreed with his opponent, and that his opening and closing statements were weak.

I immediately called the candidate on his cell phone and asked if he could exit the freeway and return to my home. Although the candidate and I had previously gone over all issues and discussed possible answers, he had not yet made debate cards as he had been instructed. So for two hours we revisited the issues and made debate cards together. (Note: This is not something you can do for the candidate; the candidate needs to be in on this task.) In addition to issue cards, we discussed how no candidate should ever say he agrees with his opponent and why. Finally, we prepared opening and closing statements. No matter how great your candidate, this kind of coaching is invaluable to his or her success. For the campaign manager, getting the candidate's speaking and debating skills in order is every bit as important as printed materials, ads, lawn signs, and letters to the editor. As the candidate left my home, he said it was the best two hours he had spent since the beginning of the campaign. After that he became focused and had a level of comfort I had not seen before.

Stay on Message

Don't let your opponent pull you off message. Ever. The candidate's image is important, because voters need to be able to identify with him or her. However, the candidate and the campaign team must know who will support the candidate and why. The reason people vote a specific way will become the basis for your campaign message. Develop that message to build relationships between the candidate and the voters. A benchmark poll can really help here.

If you have no money for a benchmark poll, then with the team list all of the candidate's positives and why the team feels voters will support this individual. The list might include programs the candidate has been involved with, stands on controversial issues, votes in previous offices, vision, character, and experience. It might be nothing more than a clear list of issues and beliefs that the candidate embraces.

You must also develop a list of issues and concerns that might hurt the candidate's support. (There should be a fair amount of overlap between the lists of positives and negatives.) It is this list that you will use in preparing the candidate for negative questions and in formulating strategies to defuse negative perceptions. For example, if the candidate has an image of being slick, the team

> "No man ever listened himself out of a job."
> **CALVIN COOLIDGE**

sends him to neighborhood meetings, where he can be seen as one of the people. This requires a candidate who is open to observation and criticism, and a close campaign team to develop the campaign message.

Once you have developed your campaign message and strategy, stick to it. When your opponent hits you, respond and move the discussion right back to your message. When appropriate, go after your opponent's campaign inconsistencies and weaknesses.

The campaign team will work only as hard as the candidate or campaign leader. So work hard. Keep in mind that the public, besides looking for a community representative and leader, is observing everything during the campaign: your stand on issues, your presence and composure, your appearance, how you handle stress, and your ability to answer their questions. In particular the public is looking for how well you react under pressure and how hard you work to get into office. That will tell them something about whether they can expect you to keep your head and work hard once you are in office.

Staying on message can be particularly hard for candidates under attack. It's important to respond to attacks, but how you do translates into whether you're on your campaign theme and message or have moved over to that of your opponent. In a recent local campaign for district attorney, the incumbent's opponent was accusing him of running an inefficient office. The incumbent had an increasing caseload with a stagnant tax base. The challenger had left the DA's office a few years before to go into private practice and now wanted back in as boss.

The incumbent, being the first to speak at the debate, stood and said, "I would take issue with anyone who says I'm not running my office efficiently." Boom, he was on his opponent's message. The following day, the debate was covered in the local paper. The headline: "DA denies allegations of mismanagement." Instead he should have promoted his achievements while preempting any criticism that his opponent might be tempted to wage, and he could have done it all without sounding defensive. He would be safe under the umbrella of disclosure.

While looking professional, minding your manners, working hard, and being on message, you must find some way to minimize stress. As noted above, stress can be reduced by eating well, exercising, getting your personal attire together, eliminating alcohol, and developing issue cards for public debates and appearances. Another is to do nothing that, once done, will lead you to tell a lie.

One dramatic example of a lie gone bad occurred a few years back, when a county commissioner was undergoing a recall in another part of the state. The recall looked dead, even though its proponents were able to gather the signatures and actually get it to a vote. It was a vote-by-mail election, and as is often the case in vote by mail, the computer spit out a few ballots whose signatures did not quite line up. One of these was the wife of the county commissioner targeted in the recall. The local elections office, in conjunction with the secretary of state's office, asked the county commissioner if the ballot had, in fact, been signed by his wife or someone else. The commissioner said his wife did indeed sign it. They checked again, and it still came out as a no-match. They asked the commissioner and his wife again. Both said she signed it. The secretary of state's office continued to press. Finally, the commissioner confessed to signing his wife's ballot because she was in the hospital and had directed him to do so. While the commissioner had easily beaten the recall, he now had to resign and was charged with and convicted of a Class C felony. Obviously he shouldn't have signed the ballot to begin with, but had he said from the get-go, "My wife asked me to take care of it for her while she was in the hospital; isn't that OK?" the secretary of state told me he very likely would have said, "No, don't do it again" and dropped the matter. It is rarely the act that gets candidates in trouble but rather the lie that follows the act.

If a candidate is caught in a lie while on the campaign trail, it is sudden death. As one of the ten commandments of campaigning and one of the cardinal sins, being caught in a provable lie is about the worst thing that can happen to a candidate.

A few years ago, a Democratic candidate for the Oregon house was to attend and speak at a Coalition for School Funding Now meeting. The campaign between the Democratic challenger and the Republican incumbent had been very friendly, and in fact it had been the incumbent who had suggested that his opponent jump in the race and run against him. As a candidate, the Democrat was a dream: She was involved in schools, church, and other community groups. She was well organized, articulate, and hardworking. She had a supportive extended family and a great campaign team. She was such a good candidate that in a poll conducted in the last days of the campaign, she was ahead of the incumbent by twenty points.

Consequently, the campaign was confident of the election. So when the coalition meeting was in conflict with another gathering, the candidate and her campaign manager split the duties, with the manager attending one while the candidate attended the coalition meeting. Unfortunately, the candidate, who had a full work and volunteer schedule in addition to her campaign, got away a little late. She then misread the directions, got lost on the way to the meeting, and arrived later than comfortable for all concerned. As a result, the candidate was flustered and off center, and the coalition group was irritated.

After the meeting, the state Republican Party sent a direct-mail piece to the house district, saying that the Democrat was in favor of a sales tax to resolve Oregon's budget shortfall. Since the allegation was attributed to the Coalition for School Funding Now meeting, the campaign committee asked the candidate whether she had said anything that would lead the other party to believe that she supported a statewide sales tax. The candidate, who had been repeatedly schooled by her committee never to talk about a sales tax, said no. Just to be sure, the campaign manager called a couple of people who she knew had attended the coalition meeting and asked them if the candidate had said she supported a sales tax during any part of the meeting. They said no.

The candidate and her campaign committee were outraged at the attack and so, along with the Democratic campaign office, registered a complaint with the secretary of state's office. The investigation uncovered an audiotape made by a staff member of the Republican Majority Office who had attended the coalition meeting. On the tape, the candidate could clearly be heard saying that she would support a sales tax if all other avenues were exhausted and if it included a reduction in the state income tax. The comment was made after an audience member and school advocate repeatedly pressed the candidate to make a stand on a sales tax. The twenty-point lead disappeared after the tape hit the airwaves, and the Democrat lost the election by 92 votes, out of 11,418 votes cast.

Set aside the whole sales tax issue: If the voters do not understand a lie, they will not forgive it. Being caught in a provable lie is a cardinal sin; it's death to a campaign. While the general response would be to focus in on the mistake made by the candidate, many mistakes leading up to the original mistake should not be overlooked, either.

First, it is not enough for a campaign committee to tell a candidate never to discuss a topic. While that can be the directive, there should also be a what-if scenario that the committee works out with the candidate. In the above example, a red flag for the committee would be that the candidate personally was not against a sales tax. If the candidate holds an opinion that could cost support if openly expressed, the issue must be addressed in the war room. The team and the candidate should have covered all appropriate responses should this occasion ever arise, such

> "The question, 'who ought to be boss?' is like asking 'who ought to be the tenor in the quartet?' Obviously, the man who can sing tenor."
>
> —— HENRY FORD

as: "Once elected, I will look at every revenue stream just as I will look at every expenditure. Without the opportunity to first examine where we are spending money, it would be premature for me to talk about revenue streams to remedy the budget deficit." Further, I have sat in many war rooms where a difficult issue was brought up for discussion and had the candidate say, "We don't need to go over that; I have an answer." Whenever a candidate says this, ask to hear the answer.

Second, a committee member should always be present at public forums. Even if it cannot be the campaign manager, someone must go with the candidate or meet the candidate at an event. What typically happens in the final days of a campaign is that good candidates who are really very trustworthy are left to cover ground on their own. But things happen, and you need someone from the committee to help communicate with the war room.

Third, candidates must allow enough time to get to an event. It is the responsibility of the campaign to get clear directions and a phone number to call should any mishaps occur en route. Ask a volunteer to drive the route if it is new to the candidate and report directions and distances. Print out a map and directions for the candidate. Buy the candidate a GPS. Whatever it takes, getting to an event should not be stressful for the candidate. I had one candidate who always ran late and would almost always get lost on his way to anything, no matter how many maps we gave him. Whenever he was en route, there had to be someone near the phone to talk him into his destination because he would completely freak out when he got lost. Finally, I assigned a staffer to pick up the candidate from work and drive him to his events. After the election, when I no longer had someone to "get him to the church on time," I found that reviewing the map with him, prior to departure, really helped. Eventually we got him a global positioning system for his car. Once he figured out how to use it, it saved everyone time and aggravation.

Fourth, once the candidate is late, he or she should still take some time to gather composure and acknowledge to the group that she has made them wait. In other words, "center the audience." Start with a personal and warm story. Something that happened on the campaign trail that the group would love to hear. If I know the candidate is running late, I will call the host with a heads-up and a reason that can be shared. Either way, someone must get the room centered. If you don't, you run the risk of having hecklers—especially among your saints. In politics, teams love to eat their own.

Fifth, a candidate must be aware of what he or she says and not hang the committee out to dry. In this example, if the candidate had remembered what she said, she could have brought this back to the committee, and damage control would have been implemented. Unfortunately, candidates are so overloaded that their memories cannot be trusted. (See the second item above.)

Sixth, supportive groups need to cut a candidate some slack. People running for office are spending insane amounts of time to secure positions that typically result in a pay reduction while they serve—not to mention huge amounts of time away from family. For a member of a group supportive of a candidate to choose to press and press and press an inflammatory issue is both stupid and counterproductive.

Finally, one must question why, for example, a candidate who as a school official was loved throughout the education community accepted an invitation to speak at a Coalition for School Funding Now meeting in the first place. Going to the saints pulls time and energy from other activities—and might even cost you the election. Even so, candidates love to speak to groups who are supportive. So much of campaign work is difficult and stressful, and attending a meeting of "friends" feels good. The flip side is that when candidates go to a supportive group in the final days, they are often very tired, they let down their guard, and they say something they shouldn't. It happens all the time.

Folks, if you're a member of the "team," give candidates a break; make as few demands on their time as possible. Your job is to give money, write letters, volunteer, deliver the votes, and help the candidate woo the savables by spending time where it is most beneficial to a win.

Outsider Campaign Versus Incumbent Campaign

If you are in government already, you are an insider; if not, you're an outsider. Insiders and outsiders typically run very different campaigns, because the voters expect the insider to defend what government is doing and the outsider to challenge it with a fresh outlook. In reality, however, skillful politicians who have been in office for years have, when the need arises, waged outsider campaigns against first-time candidates. Insider or outsider status is as much a state of mind as a fact. Whatever the actual status of the candidate, insider and outsider campaigns require distinctly different strategies.

> "You better start swimmin'
> or you'll sink like a stone."
>
> **BOB DYLAN**

Whether you are the incumbent or the challenger, you should list all personality characteristics of both the office holder and the challenger, both strengths and weaknesses. Your objective is to contrast your strengths with your opponent's weaknesses.

Outsiders

To run an outsider's campaign, you must first legitimize yourself through establishment endorsement (no matter how tangential the endorsement might be). The public record the incumbent has amassed while in office actually defines that person—but in terms of image, not specifics. If you're an outsider, it's important for your team to define the test the voters will apply. Obviously you want to stay away from experience, since an incumbent would easily pass that test. Your best hope is to define the test the voters will apply as that of "time for a change." Ultimately, as an outsider, you will find that it is more important to present sound reasons for why an incumbent should be cast out of office than to explain why you should be elected.

Attacks on the system are effective if they plant seeds of doubt about how things are being done or where attention and public money are being focused. You cannot just throw complaints against a wall to see what sticks. You have to know what you're talking about. Research how things have worked or not worked, and explain them to the voters. Remember,

> "Leaders are people who step forward,
> who influence thinking and action. They
> emerge to meet the needs."
>
> **WILLIAM GORE**

you must sound like a potential office holder rather than a malcontent. That requires offering solutions, not just criticizing. This is where your homework really pays off.

Before my first run for mayor, I went to the local college library, checked out ten years of city council minutes, and read them all. I also checked out every current report on every system for which the city had hired a consultant. I read the city's comprehensive plan and the downtown plan. This put me at a decided advantage: Because it was so fresh in my mind, I could recall the information more quickly than my opponent, who had been a sitting city councilor for ten years. Incumbents who live through the events compiled in such reports while in office will find it difficult to recall the details, and they make matters worse by believing they can. Typically an incumbent will underprepare for an election.

Incumbents

If you are an incumbent, you must show that the average citizen still supports you and show how, working cooperatively with other elected officials, you have made a positive contribution. In other words, your campaign should make the test applied by the voters that of experience and accomplishment. This is a strong theme when voters have a grasp of the complexities of government. Again, your public record defines who you are. But avoid looking at each vote individually. This definition is more about image than specifics. Although you may not actually use the word, stick close to a theme of "proven" leadership. Make your record the focal point of the campaign by using examples that the average person will understand and that apply to the day-to-day lives of those being served. Avoid speaking in governmentalese—that is, using acronyms and jargon that only those in government would know.

Your Opponent

You may breathe a sigh of relief when you discover that you are unopposed in your election or groan when you find that at the last minute, someone has filed to run against you. However, an opponent in any campaign is a blessing. Without an opponent, your race will be ignored by the press, and the programs and issues you want to get before the voters will be that much more difficult and expensive to get there. If you are involved in a hotly contested race, the press will more likely provide front-page coverage, which greatly reduces the amount of advertising you will have to buy. Just compare the Republican presidential primary of 2008 with the Democratic presidential primary. Barack Obama and Hillary Clinton were lead stories every day, whereas John McCain could not get the attention of the press.

This inattention contributed to McCain's loss just as Obama's primary momentum contributed to his win.

If you have a primary race in which you are unopposed, you may never build the momentum and party support that are necessary to win the general election. Do not lament if someone declares against you. Thank your lucky stars, and organize a great campaign. Bring forward programs you want to begin or to maintain, and use the election as a mandate to muscle these into place. Use the campaign as a reminder of who you are and what you stand for and as a rallying point to get people behind your efforts.

"What is noble can be said in any language, and what is mean should be said in none."

— MAIMONIDES

Some voters need something to vote for, while others need something to vote against. Voters who are more motivated by one candidate's negatives than the opposition's positives lie at the heart of negative campaigning. Average voters watch the debate unfold in the paper and on the news and listen to see who makes sense and who doesn't. Others get outraged by a candidate's track record or by inane arguments from the opposition and decide to vote for your cause although they normally would not.

Debates

Don't use debates to attack your opponent; rather, use them to share what you know and would do once elected. Keep on the sunny side.

Debates can be turning points for a campaign or amount to nothing. I've seen amazing mistakes made during debates that had little or no effect on the campaign and seen other items that should have gone unnoticed blow up. There are a number of ways you and your campaign committee can minimize the risk factor and make a debate work in your favor. Small precautions include familiarizing yourself with the room before the event and making sure that some friendly faces are in the audience. However, preparation is your best tool for positioning yourself. When you are well prepared, political debates are surprisingly easy and great fun. As a political candidate, you should welcome the showiness of debates, the pressure, and the opportunity to get your opinions in front of voters. When you have successfully positioned yourself as a candidate, people recognize who you are and what you do. You make sense to them.

"Public officials are not a group apart. They inevitably reflect the moral tone of the society in which they live."

— JOHN F. KENNEDY

The central rule of debating is that the voters should know more after the debate than they did before. Come armed with lots of information. In my third run for mayor, I had the advantage of being well versed in city matters—and even though I was the incumbent, I studied like crazy to prepare for all six of my debates. In the first debate, I was shocked at how uninformed my opponent was in city matters. He had seemingly done little or nothing to prepare for the event. I thought, boy, this is going to be easy. But with each debate that followed, my opponent took, verbatim, statistics and anecdotal examples that I had used in previous debates and presented them to each new audience as though they were his thoughts and his research. It really threw me. I couldn't say, "Hey, you sound just like me," or "That's exactly what I said last week," without sounding like I was petty, whining, accusatory, or on the attack. Every debate was before a new audience who had never heard either of us, so they assumed he was delivering his spiel, not mine. In hindsight, I should have had a campaign supporter who would, as the pattern unfolded at each event, call him on it.

Preparation

To get ready for a political debate, choose eight to ten subjects that are important to you or the community. You should include among them issues that are part of your campaign platform. For each of the subjects you have chosen, list on one side of a five-by-eight-inch index card the information and points that you feel are relevant. Use only one card per subject and only one side of the card.

For example, development in the forest interface is of great concern in my community. As an incumbent, I would list on the left side of a card all that government (with my help) has done to limit development in these fire-prone areas as well as fire mitigation implemented on existing structures. On the right side, I would list remaining concerns of fire danger and what government still needs to do to make the forest and the community safer. If I were running an outsider's campaign, for the same subject I would list all that is being done, how this is not enough, what has gone wrong (being specific), and exactly what I would do to correct the course. This information is just listed on the card, not written out. The idea is to be very familiar with the information before the debate and to use the cards to focus on specific points you want to make, not exactly what you will say.

> "There was a gap between what went on in his mind and what came out of his mouth."
> **JAMES M. CAIN**

Once you have the subject cards filled out, choose a separate color for each card, and color a single stripe along the top of each card in a particular color. For example, your card for budget issues might be red; for forest interface, brown; for park issues, green; for recycling, yellow; for air quality, blue; for transportation, black; and so on. Once the cards are color-coded, they can be placed in a tier in front of you during the debate with just the color bar showing and the appropriate card can be found at a glance. By color-coding in advance, you can avoid disorienting yourself looking through all the cards to find the one you want. And once you have the card you need for a particular subject on top of the stack, you can glance at it while looking around the audience. When looking at the cards, you should appear to be collecting your thoughts rather than reading.

Do not kid yourself that you can guess all the subjects or questions that will be asked in a debate. You will undoubtedly prepare for areas that are never addressed and have nothing for areas that are covered. Even so, with the preparation done ahead of time, you will be much more relaxed and "on" during the debate because some of the answers will be in front of you. Be sure to bring extra blank cards to jot down thoughts during the debate. This will help you remember on rebuttal what you want to say.

Familiarize yourself with any ballot measures or propositions coming before the voters or any initiative petitions being circulated. Either the press or your opponent may ask you about your position on these issues, so have a clear idea of where you stand and why.

The importance of your image and how you present yourself cannot be overstated. Smiling and speaking clearly and slowly enough so those in the audience can hear and understand is very important. A certain amount of tension surrounds a campaign in general and a debate in particular, and people will notice how you deal with that tension. Be aware that your image gets projected in a hundred ways.

> "The palest ink is better than the most retentive memory."
>
> —— CHINESE PROVERB

Fielding Negative Questions

Think of everything as a gift or opportunity.

You will very likely get nasty questions and innuendos during a debate. Look at such questions as an opportunity to demonstrate how well you respond under fire. People know that being subjected to negativity is part of serving in public office, and they will want to see how you handle it. Never be defensive. If possible, be humble and self-effacing; if you can come up with a little joke that turns the attack to your advantage, so much the better. Find anything that uses the ammunition of the opposition and redirects it at them. If you redirect attacks, it is important to do so with class, without sounding defensive or mean-spirited. This is your opportunity to sound smart. Being quick on your feet is not a function of IQ but of preparedness, confidence, and poise.

Grace Under Pressure

Let me repeat: Your campaign committee members should help you list everything that is a weakness—every vote, every misstatement, every missed meeting, all of it. They should also list everything on which your candidate may appear vulnerable: past voting re-

> "Thomas Jefferson once said, 'We should never judge a president by his age, only by his works.' And ever since he told me that, I stopped worrying."
> **RONALD REAGAN**

cords, who is paying for the campaign, special-interest support, inconsistencies in statements and personal deeds, such as missed child-support payments. Once this level of homework is done, you will be much more comfortable.

In general, there are four options for responding to an attack:

1. I did not do it.
2. I did it, but it's not how you think.
3. I did it, I'm sorry, I won't do it again.
4. Attack the source.

If you are attacked and do not respond, you are presumed guilty, especially if the attack is considered fair. When you do respond, you should do so on the same level as the attack. For example, if you were attacked in direct mail, respond with direct mail.

Fatal Flaws

One way to prepare yourself for attacks is to sit with your campaign team and brainstorm on every possible negative question that might come your way. Practice responding to questions concerning your weaknesses. Listing the "fatal flaws" of a candidate or mea-sure allows your support group to de-liberate on the best possible responses. These responses may be placed accord-ing to topic on your five-by-eight-inch cards for handy reference during the

> "All reformers, however strict their social conscience, live in houses just as big as they can pay for."
> **LOGAN PEARSALL SMITH**

debate. Even if the attack is not exactly what your team predicted, this level of preparation lends comfort, poise, and organization to the candidate, re-sulting in better responses in high-pressure situations.

In my second bid for mayor, I responded to criticism of city budget increases by explaining that I was the only member of the budget committee who voted no on the last budget. Later in the campaign, my opponent pointed out (during a debate) that when this same budget came before the city council for final approval, the council vote was split. He went on to point out that I failed to cast the tie-breaking no vote and instead voted yes. Why, he asked, if I was *so* opposed to the budget during the budget process, was I unwilling to vote no at the council level?

Until that moment, I had forgotten that the budget had come before the council when two members who would have voted yes were away and two had unexpectedly voted no. That had left only two voting yes. As mayor, I had been obligated to cast the deciding vote. As I went to the podium to respond, I pulled out my color-coded budget card.

From the card, I was able to outline the exact issues on which I had concern as a budget committee member. After relating those concerns to the audience, I explained that I had lost my appeal to the budget committee to delve into those issues further and explained that the committee ultimately had adopted the budget. Having been outvoted at the committee level, I suggested to the audience that it would have been disingenuous to, in effect, veto the budget by casting a no vote in a tiebreaker. I had therefore voted to put in place the will of the majority of the committee and council, even if I personally disagreed with some budget provisions.

Because I was prepared, my opponent gave me what I could not get on my own: the opportunity to show that I had good reasons to vote against the budget during the budget process and that once outvoted, I was able to set aside my differences with the budget committee. As an incumbent, I was able to demonstrate that I was still willing to challenge the process and yet be a team player.

At another debate, one opponent brought up a program I had initiated to use volunteers to clear fuel (dead and dying brush) from the forest interface. He cited how the program had been a miserable failure and had placed the city at risk of potential litigation because of possible worker (volunteer) injury. I picked up my forest card and took the microphone. I said that while the outcome of the program had been different from what was first envisioned, it raised community awareness of the need to mitigate fire danger. Moreover, the voters needed to make a decision for the future: Did they want leadership that never tried anything out of fear of failure or leadership that solved problems creatively at the risk of an occasional partial success?

By using this attack as a gift, I was able to direct attention to the limited success of the program and then shift back to my message, which was strong, creative leadership: leadership willing to take risks.

Another approach to leading or negative questions is the "Yeah, so?" response. For example, the opposition might say, "Since you became mayor, the city has acquired more and more programs that should be run by the private sector." Your "Yeah, so?" response might be, "I'm sorry. How is this a problem? The proof is in the pudding. We are extraordinarily successful at providing a broad range of outstanding programs, programs that our community may never have enjoyed if left to the private sector. And we do so while saving the taxpayers money." While you may not use these exact words, this is the tone: "Yeah, so? What's your point?"

> "Earlier today the senator called a spade a spade. He later issued a retraction."
>
> **JOE MIRACHI**

In Debates, Attacks Can Backfire

Hitting your opponent with a negative during a debate is somewhat unpredictable and ill-advised. More often than not, attacks waged in debates can backfire and strengthen the candidate under attack. For example, I worked for a candidate whose opponent, an incumbent, was receiving lots of PAC money. My candidate wanted to hit the incumbent for taking special-interest money. Because the campaign team had heard rumors that the incumbent had a story to die for whenever he was hit on PAC money, the campaign team felt that an attack was dangerous.

At the next debate, however, our candidate went after the credibility of the incumbent, because of the PAC money coming in. Our candidate implied that the incumbent was bought and owned because so much of his money came from the lobby and so little from citizens. True to the rumors, the opponent stood up and said that when he was first elected, a supporter who had given a $3,000 campaign contribution visited his office at the capitol. According to the story, the contributor was looking for a particular vote on a bill and felt that the size of the campaign contribution warranted this vote. Our opponent went on to say that after hearing the demand, he went to the bank, took out a personal loan, and returned the money to the contributor. He concluded by saying that no one owned his vote.

> "Ninety percent of the politicians give the other ten percent a bad reputation."
>
> **HENRY KISSINGER**

In about thirty seconds, our opponent showed that he was of modest means like everyone else in the room—after all, he had to take out a personal loan to pay back the $3,000 contribution—and that he had integrity. In hindsight, with our candidate so insistent about using this issue, we would have served him better if research could have unequivocally established a cor-relation between votes and money; if there were none, he may have dropped the attack, and if there were many, it would have called his opponent's cred-ibility into question.

In debates, you just never know how your opponent will turn an attack around. So, unless you are armed with concrete information, avoid rehearsed attacks. If, however, your opponent leaves himself or herself open, seize the opportunity. For example, a few years back, a Democrat and a Republican were facing off for a US Senate seat. The Democrat had been criticizing the Republican for using federal superfund money to clean up industrial waste in his family-owned business. During a debate, the Republican, who was worth millions, was challenged by the Democrat to pay back the money to the taxpayers. The Republican stood and said, "I'll pay it back just as soon as you pay back the honoraria you said you would never take when you ran for Congress." In a very flustered voice the Democrat said, "Why . . . why, you've insulted my integrity!"

This is an opportunity that doesn't come along very often. The Democrat should have seen this coming and been ready. He missed an opportunity to reach into his pocket to pull out a checkbook and say, "Deal! I'll pay back all the money I received for giving speeches. You get out your checkbook and do the same for the federal cleanups, which amounts to $XYZ. And while you're at it, make it out to the federal deficit, because the only way we're going to get our arms around it is if those who have, stop taking from those who don't." While the Democrat had received thousands in honoraria, the Republican had received millions—an easy exchange.

Developing Your Public Speaking Skills

Before my very first debate as a candidate, I was genuinely excited about what was ahead of me. I was charged up and armed with enough information to handle any question thrown at me. Afterward, I thought I'd done a great job. So when someone from the audience handed me a slip of paper, I was certain it would be the name and phone number of a potential campaign volunteer. The note said: "You said 'um' 48 times during your speech and the question and answer pe-riod that followed. Why don't you join us at Toastmasters?"

"The Constitution gives every American the inalienable right to make a damn fool of himself."

— JOHN CIARDI

Unless you're a top-notch public speaker—either a natural or an actor, you need to get some skills, and you need to get them quickly. Even after three campaigns and twelve years in public office, I still got nervous before a speech; it didn't matter how perfunctory it was or how young the audience. But remember, it isn't what you say that's important but rather how you say it. Given how quickly people form opinions of candidates, the candidate who gets some early help in giving speeches will have a longer shelf life than the candidate who receives none. Training in public speaking does not need to take a whole lot of time and can ultimately make the journey much more enjoyable.

The following are ten simple things the candidate and team can do to improve speech-giving, debates, and public appearances.

1. Prepare your introduction. Few will remember anything you said, but most notice how you are introduced. Prepare a strong introduction that gets read at each venue you attend; include your experience and specific qualities you will bring to the office.

> "He can compress the most words into the smallest idea of any man I ever met."
> **ABRAHAM LINCOLN**

2. Keep speeches short and end on a positive note. Tell the audience what you will say, say it, and then tell them what you just said. Always keep on point.

3. Practice topics on-camera. Have a friend or campaign worker with a video camera ask the candidate questions that might come up in the campaign. After the interview, the candidate and someone with experience in public speaking should go over the video. Look at everything: Does the candidate have verbal tics ("you know," "quite frankly," "like," "um"); does he scratch his chest, toe the ground, stroke his chin, fluff his hair, or jut the chin? Does she hold her hand to her cheek when seated? Does she do a nervous yawn? Tap her foot? Click a pen?

4. Be aware of your surroundings. Before giving a speech, familiarize yourself with the room ahead of time. For TV interviews think about where you will position yourself and know what will be behind you. If seated, choose the chair carefully; avoid overstuffed chairs, which can affect delivery and make a candidate look slouchy.

5. Look the part. Clothes, mannerisms, eyes, hair—everything.

6. Don't overload the audience with too many facts. Use facts to make a point, no more.

7. Be authentic. The candidate's job is to appear likeable, so smile and visually engage with the entire room. Show passion.

8. Practice your stump speech again and again so the delivery is both fluid and authentic. Never read a speech. If you cannot remember everything; use the back of a number 9 (business) envelope to jot each point you want to make.

9. Start small. One way to help candidates find their feet is to start with coffees before they head out on the speech or debate trail. A coffee may draw unknown faces, but they're usually a forgiving crowd. Send committee people or those with public speaking skills to give feedback following the event.

10. Share an experience that happened to you on the campaign trail. "The other day, while I was canvassing . . . " can be an effective way to make known that you canvass and care what voters think; plus, it provides an opportunity to communicate an important idea that is part of your platform. Remember: Campaigns are not about the candidate; they're about the voters.

Mock Debates

Mock debates are fun and very helpful for a candidate. For a successful one, you must have a moderator, an opponent, and an audience. High school government teachers, newspaper reporters (though not those who will be covering the campaign), and people who are politically active and involved make the best audience. Your objective is to have seven or eight people who are well versed in public speaking and politics, are smart, and can communicate suggestions without offending the candidate. Rearrange the furniture in the living room so that it looks more like a classroom. Use bar stools for the real and the pretend opponent to perch on. The moderator should be armed with questions that most certainly will come up in a campaign. This is the time to focus on your questions. Let all involved know that everyone will be in character throughout the mock debate. The moderator should be dressed up, and whoever is playing the opposition candidate should study how that candidate dresses, moves, answers questions, and attacks in real life. This does not take long: Read the literature, and watch him or her on a commercial, interview, or public appearance, and you're there.

> "(They) leave the impression of an army of pompous phrases moving over the landscape in search of an idea; sometimes these meandering words would actually capture a straggling thought and bear it triumphantly, a prisoner in their midst, until it died of servitude and overwork."
>
> **WILLIAM MCADOO** regarding President Harding's speeches

Have everything in place when the real candidate and the pretend opponent arrive. Establish guidelines and time the answers, just as they would be in a real debate.

After the debate, questions are taken from the audience and answered by both the real candidate and the pretend opponent. If the campaign is concerned about how the candidate will respond to a question, this would be the time to have someone in the audience persist in asking it.

This is followed by a frank discussion of the candidate's performance, which questions posed problems, and what made the candidate defensive. Cover body language, the brevity and clarity of answers, hairstyle, and clothes.

Most public speakers are best when they have a command of the material and can talk off the top of their head. However, if you are working with a candidate you have told time and again not to read speeches because he or she is horrible at it, be sure to send the debate questions ahead of time. In general, candidates read because they feel uncertain of their ability. If you provide the questions ahead

> "Experience is a hard teacher. She gives the test first, the lesson afterwards."
> **ANONYMOUS**

of time and a clear directive that reading is not a choice, the candidate will prepare content and fret only about delivery. Helping a candidate gain confidence works best if specific aspects of a debate or speech are isolated and worked on one at a time. You don't teach someone to swim by throwing the person in the deep end of the pool.

Have someone videotape the mock debate. This way, the candidate and team can review it later.

Recently we set up a mock debate for a novice candidate. The candidate was given questions ahead of time, and the audience was also prepped. The reporter who attended was smart and direct with questions, as were a US history teacher from the high school, a teacher from the middle school, and an assortment of people from the war room.

The whole debate took over two hours, including the question-and-answer period that followed. It was very successful except for one thing: The candidate was furious with the individual playing the role of her opponent, who

> "From you. And let me say something about the tenor of that question. I look around this room and I see privileged people. It's easy to sit back and criticize government efforts to help ordinary people, but helping them is our responsibility."
> **ROBERT F. KENNEDY** at an elite medical school responding to a student who asked him where he was going to get the money for the solutions he proposed to fix a deeply troubled country

was in character right down to vaguely answering questions and subtly going after the candidate, as we had seen the opponent do in real debates. The candidate was so upset she never watched the video of the mock debate.

However, at her next debate, when the real opponent seemingly reenacted what had occurred at the mock debate, our candidate was brilliant. Her response to a demeaning comment made by her opponent brought the conservative crowd to a round of boisterous applause. She was so good and her opponent so bad that we cut a TV ad by simply juxtaposing the two candidates answering a question at the debate.

Write-In, Third-Party, and Nonpartisan Candidates

In some circumstances, you may be running at a distinct disadvantage as a write-in or third-party candidate. In other situations, depending on the laws of the area, the first election the candidates face might be the deciding election. All these situations require some unique approaches.

The Write-In Candidate

After the sudden death of a city councilor just weeks before one general election, a few of us got together to help a write-in candidate. This turned out to be a great campaign. There were lots of volunteers, plenty of money, great ads, well-placed lawn signs, an excellent brochure, and a solid candidate—one who was both hardworking and willing to do anything her campaign committee asked, from walking districts to modifying her "look." She had been actively involved in city politics and had served on volunteer boards and commissions, she was smart and well spoken, and she did her homework. She got strong endorsements from both local newspapers. She was also a very progressive Democrat running for office in a community with an overwhelming registration advantage.

> "I have always found paranoia to be a perfectly defensible position."
>
> — **PAT CONROY**

The opposition really ran no campaign other than two or three ads and about as many lawn signs. The opponent was a conservative Republican, a political category that in terms of registration in the city, comes in third behind Democrats and nonaffiliated voters. We made no mistakes during the campaign, and still we lost.

Write-in campaigns, under the best of circumstances, are tough to win. Can it be done? Absolutely. There are examples everywhere of people pulling it off. Washington state elected a congresswoman on a write-in ticket. Write-ins are really no more work than a regular election. However, depending on the ballot type, voting for a write-in is more complicated for the voter. In the case of our write-in candidate, our county was using a punch-card ballot, requiring voters to do more than just write a name next to a position.

First things first:

1. You must know the ballot type used by your county and what it looks like.
2. Find out precisely how a write-in vote must be cast at the ballot box. Does the voter have to write in the full name and the position of the office?
3. Know the law. Laws for financial disclosure are the same for a write-in as for a candidate on the ballot.
4. Know when the absentee ballots are mailed. You must both identify support and turn out your absentees on or before Election Day. This is crucial for a win.
5. Know what percentage the absentees are of those who vote—not the registered voters, but of those who actually vote. For example, although 25 percent of all registered voters may request and vote absentee, on Election Day, they may represent 50 percent or more of the voter turnout.
6. Run two campaigns: one for absentees and one for poll-voters.
7. In your campaign literature and advertising, even on the lawn signs, illustrate and reinforce what voters will see on their ballot.
8. Get your candidate on the speaking circuit with the opponent(s).
9. Conduct all other business as you would for any other campaign, keeping in mind item 7 above.
10. If your state has one, get in the voters' pamphlet.

You might think this sounds convoluted, but write-in campaigns are actually more fun than running a regular campaign. No one really expects a write-in to win, so everyone is rooting for you. Also, because write-in campaigns are so rare, the media gives the campaign more attention with feel-good stories during the news, especially if the candidate is working his or her tail off in an obvi-

> "Word of mouth appeals have become the only kind of persuasion that most of us respond to anymore."
> **MALCOLM GLADWELL**

ously well-organized effort. This kind of campaign creates a sense of urgency that brings out the best in volunteers, so they really go the extra distance for the campaign.

It is usually difficult to raise money for a candidate who appears to be losing. With a write-in, however, people don't perceive being behind as the fault of the candidate but rather of circumstances beyond the candidate's control. As a result, if you have a strong write-in candidate, it is surprisingly easy to raise money.

Finally, because people know the odds are long on a write-in winning, when you lose, your efforts get far more attention than they would in a more traditional race. Depending on the kind of campaign you run, the candidate ends the race with more stature, power, and respect in the community than before the campaign and, ironically, is not portrayed as the loser. Next election cycle, get on the ballot and you will win.

In our write-in race, we had a punch-card ballot, perhaps the most difficult type for a write-in. On the punch-card ballot, made famous by Florida, our voters had to write "city council," the actual position number of the council seat, and the candidate's name in an area completely separate from where the actual punch position was on the ballot. They also had to remember not to punch the corresponding number of the opponent on the ballot itself. The name had to be the same on all write-ins. For example, my name is Cathy, but if someone wrote in Kathy, Cathie, or even Catherine, our clerk would not accept it.

To visually reinforce what was required of the voter, we re-created a ballot to use as our campaign logo and put it on everything: lawn signs, the brochure, and direct mail. Still, according to the county clerk, the voters made so many mistakes—such as failing to put the proper council position or any position on the ballot, writing only the position number without specifying "city council," and so on—that hundreds of write-in votes did not count.

Third-Party Candidates

As in all campaign activities, a third-party candidate can be a blessing or a curse. If you're a third-party candidate, you will benefit most by presenting the Republican and the Democrat as one and the same. You and you alone provide an alternative. To win as a third-party candidate, you must be able to pull votes from both major parties, all age groups, and all income levels.

Most often, third-party candidates act as spoilers by splitting the vote of one party and thereby increasing the likelihood of a win by the other. Voters registered as nonaffiliated will track the party of greatest registration within their precinct, so the candidate running as an independent has little claim to any voter and will pull votes from either the Democrats or the Republicans, depending on how he or she stands on the issues. In 1990 a very conservative independent went on the gubernatorial ticket in Oregon. He ran on an anti-choice, anti-sales-tax, anti-land-use-planning platform and successfully pulled conservative votes from a very popular moderate Republican and, as a consequence, effectively gave the Democrat the win.

In New Mexico, Republican Bill Redmond won a congressional seat in 1996 in a district registered heavily Democratic by using a third-party candidate to pull support from his Democratic opponent. Redmond's win was due primarily to three strategies: target the Democrat with negative ads, boost the Green Party candidate to split the Democratic vote, and turn out the Republican base. Redmond's campaign even sent literature to registered Democrats for the Green Party candidate.

In 1999 in California, Audie Bock became the first Green Party candidate elected to state office in the United States. Her rise began with the resignation of Democratic Congressman Ron Dellums, who left office in the middle of his fourteenth term. A special election was held to fill his seat in the US House for the remainder of his term, and another to fill that of Barbara Lee, the California state senator who won Dellums's seat. Yet another special election was held to fill the Sixteenth District Assembly seat of Don Perata, the successor to Lee's senate seat. It was dominoes, with everyone in office moving up the food chain.

Two Democrats weighed in for the Sixteenth District: former Oakland mayor Elihu Harris, who had also served twelve years in the California State Assembly, and Frank Russo, who also had a long list of party credentials behind his name. No Republican entered the fray, as this district had a Democratic registration advantage of fifty-one points. Because California law forced the top vote-getters of each party into a runoff if no one received a majority of total votes cast in an open primary, either Russo or Harris had to pull in more than 50 percent of the votes to lock the win.

Seeing a potential opportunity for a runoff, the Green Party recruited Audie Bock and hoped that neither Democrat would garner the necessary votes for an outright win, thereby forcing a runoff between the Democrat and Green Party candidate. That is exactly what happened. Harris beat Russo but attained only 49 percent of the vote.

In the runoff, Bock ran on a platform that focused on the Democratic Party machine and suggested that the machine was responsible for the series of special elections, beginning with the midterm resignation of Congressman Dellums. While the Harris campaign packed up the headquarters in Oakland and Harris went to Sacramento to select furniture for his new office, Audie Bock hit the streets. Her team of forty primary volunteers grew to one hundred; they walked, phoned, and targeted voters. She had five hundred lawn signs and enough money for one mailer—a postcard.

Harris's consultant ran a late poll and became so concerned that he dropped a dozen mail pieces in the last two weeks. But it was too much and too late, and the last-minute flurry served only to reinforce the Bock campaign theme urging voters to shun big-party politics. Having spent only $40,000 against Harris's $600,000, Bock won by 327 votes with 30,000 cast.[2]

Nonpartisan Races

There are typically two kinds of nonpartisan races: The first matches all candidates in a primary and requires a runoff of the top two only if no one receives 50 percent or more of the votes cast. The other is when all the candidates face each other in a single election, usually the general, and whoever receives the majority of votes cast wins.

If your election is the first animal, that is, you must get 50 percent or have a runoff, your mission is to accurately predict voter turnout for each of the parties in the primary and employ strategy accordingly. Not all primaries are the same. Depending on what is on the ballot, there could be more Democrats or Republicans weighing in.

> "There is no conversation so sweet as that of former political enemies."
>
> ————————— **HARRY TRUMAN**

Therefore, predicted voter turnout is a function of other ballot noise. The goal is to lock in the party that will perform the best in the primary, and then come back and get the other in the general. Even if the campaign does not garner the requisite 50 percent to win the primary outright, the general will be more winnable with this strategy.

Let me give you an example: By the time the 2008 Oregon primary rolled around in May, John McCain already had a lock on the Republican nomination, but Hillary Clinton and Barack Obama were still in full tilt. That presented an unusual opportunity for nonpartisan primary races in our county, where the Republicans, who held a three-point registration advantage (3,400) underreported for their civic duty with a 53 percent primary turnout. Meanwhile, a whopping 75 percent of the Democrats turned out to vote. The net result was 7,400 more Democrats who voted in the primary than Republicans. That translates into nearly an 11,000-vote advantage the Democrats would *not* have in the general. With 7,400 more Democrats casting a ballot in the primary than Republicans, any Democrat looking to garner the 50 percent vote in a nonpartisan race should have been able to pull off a win—as long as the voters "sort of" knew which candidate was which. Although nonpartisan races are just that, voters generally know which candidate is the Democrat and which candidate is the Republican. If they don't, it's the campaign's duty to provide the clues.

Media and the Candidate

You and your campaign team may suspect bias on the part of the local media, and you may even have those suspicions confirmed, but there is no way to use something like this while campaigning. Complaining about the press makes a candidate look weak—and it's political suicide. The best revenge is to win.

> "If you think gun control, abortion, and gay and lesbian civil rights are controversial issues, try a stop sign, a speed bump or a tree that needs trimming."
>
> **ANTONIO VILLARAIGOSA**, former mayor of Los Angeles

Although I'm amazed when I see candidates go after the media, especially presidential candidates, who should know better, it's understandable why they do. In recent years, the media, especially in talk radio, have become more vicious and combative. They can be merciless in their treatment of elected officials—who have volunteered time to serve the community—and then wonder, editorially, why so few throw their hat in the ring for the next election cycle.

Although candidates should respond to attacks from the opposition, they would do best to ignore any bait that the press floats on the pond. Even so, if the editor of your local paper is coming after you, call supporters to come to your defense in letters to the editor.

Blogs

Blogs are a very real part of promoting and attacking political candidates and causes, and because the websites of local papers often allow bloggers to be anonymous, people really have at it. Any time a print article comes out on your race, your team must be prepared to respond to the online comments section that immediately follows the article. The team should defend the candidate on any attacks, and even if there are none, the team should weigh in with positive comments, such as: "Great to see Willie in the race; I volunteered with him at the school and he's an excellent man." Someone must be on top of this medium and protect and promote the candidate.

Negative Campaigning

Negative campaigning is inherent in the process. After all, you are running because you embrace issues or values that differ from those of your opponent. You are working on a campaign—whether for a candidate or an issue—for a reason, and as you define that reason, you define both your campaign and that of your opposition. The inverse is true as well.

Although the thought of being attacked in public can cause panic for a candidate or campaign team, remember that it is yet another opportunity to get your message out and to show how you comport yourself under pressure. As I said before: Do it with grace, and an attack can actually help.

In listing the strengths and weaknesses of a candidate or an issue-based campaign, you are preparing for the inevitable attack. Candidates who have reviewed all the possibilities with the committee and drafted responses will have confidence and strength under fire. By preparing, the committee and the candidate can handle attacks immediately, succinctly, and deftly. If no response comes from your side, an attack often gains credibility.

If your campaign goes negative, keep in mind that numerous studies conducted on the impacts of negative campaigning indicate that only four areas consistently fall in fair territory when it comes to attacks: actual voting records, current ethical problems, business practices, and money received from special-interest groups. Finally, do not think you can win in a direct-mail war; your campaign must be smarter and have scores of volunteers assisting your efforts.

So what do you do if you are attacked? The University of Maryland conducted a study, the Campaign Assessment and Candidate Outreach Project, that looked at the effects of negative campaigning on voters. Charges that voters considered unfair placed the attacking candidate in serious trouble, whether or not the opposition responded and regardless of whether the voters considered the counterattack fair. Charges that were deemed fair (such as a voting record) caused problems for the candidate being attacked, especially if he or she did not respond or did so in an unfair manner. The best outcome for the candidate under attack is to counter with a "fair charge" in return.[3]

> "I don't care if he did it or not, just get him to deny it."
>
> —————— LYNDON JOHNSON

Do's and Don'ts of Attacks

1. Don't start a campaign with an attack.
2. Define yourself before going on the attack, especially if you're running against an incumbent the voters respect.
3. Candidates must be forthcoming on anything in their past that could be used against them. This allows the campaign manager and committee to develop a response to counter the attacks.

4. Don't mix together a lot of unnecessary arguments.

5. Don't mix positive and negative issues within the same ad or directional piece.

6. Avoid inconsistent, misleading, or unconvincing arguments.

7. Be sure that any attacks are believable and fair: Anything questionable will lead the voter to doubt everything.

8. Do your homework so that you can back up any charges you make, and be prepared for a counterattack.

9. Do not attack using revelations uncovered from divorce proceedings. Voters assume things are said (and done) during a divorce that may not be true or representative of the individual in normal circumstances— whether it is child or spousal abuse, being arrested for back child support, or restraining orders.

10. And, in a related topic: Avoid themes that may be related to a potential attack. For example, if the candidate was arrested for failure to pay child support, even for a good reason, do not run him on a "greatest dad" platform; leave his current wife and children out of the campaign literature and run him on his experience, record, or leadership abilities; if a candidate has declared bankruptcy, do not present her as a financial wizard; and so on. Too often the failing itself does not sink a candidate but rather the perceived hypocrisy.

11. Not all candidate indiscretions are treated equally. For example, there's a difference between Mark Sanford's affair and Anthony Weiner's tweeted crotch shots. Voters understand an affair; they do not understand aberrant behavior.

12. If you're caught, fess up. For example, Weiner's initial lies (compared to Sanford's immediate confession) also reflected poorly on him and further brought into play integrity and judgment. Voters forgive mistakes long before exaggerated self-opinion or lies.

13. Look for patterns. Behaviors don't change. If a candidate is accused of unnecessary roughness in intramural sports, chances are it happened in the past and in other areas than on the playing field. Corruption doesn't usually happen just once. If a candidate embellishes in one arena, he or she probably has done so in others as well. Follow the behavior for more examples to establish a pattern to the voters.

"Never insult anyone by accident."
ROBERT A. HEINLEIN

14. Time your attack carefully. An attack launched too early in a campaign may not have the intended impact, and one launched too late may not have enough time to sink in with the voters.

Recall

As with the initiative and referendum process, recalls require a number of signatures of registered voters equal to a specific percentage of those who voted in a specific election. For example, the number of signatures for a recall for a state office might be equal to 8 percent of the number who voted in the last election for governor, whereas a recall of a city official might be 10 percent of those who voted in the last mayor's election. Once a petition is pulled, it must be filed within a specific time (depending on the state or local statutes), and a special election must be held within a specific number of days after verification of the signatures. In Oregon, the whole process can last no more than 140 days: 90 to gather the signatures, 10 to have them verified, and 40 to organize the special election. You cannot begin a recall until someone has been in office for six months after his or her *last* election. This goes for those who are in their second or third term of office as well.

From my experience, recall attempts are often prompted by one specific action that, coupled with the personality of the office holder, means trouble. The recall attempts often focus on strong, smart, outspoken women and strong, smart, soft-spoken men with an overriding theme that the office holder doesn't know who butters his or her bread. If you find that you are the subject of a recall, remember: You only need to survive; they need to conquer. A failed recall attempt generally leaves the office holder in a politically stronger position than before. Whether you believe enough signatures will be gathered is really not the point. Once the attempt has begun, do not hang your head: Fight back. There are lots of people who do not believe in recalls—76 percent of black voters in California, for example, according to data from the 2003 recall of Governor Gray Davis.

Fighting a recall is no different from running a regular campaign. As soon as you hear of an attempt being waged against you, organize a campaign committee. If the organizers of the effort against you claim that you are supported by only one segment of the population, or one community in the county, then be sure that you have representatives from every city and people from all walks of life. If you're being thrown out because of your connection with special-interest groups, then be sure they are nowhere to be seen in the campaign; show broad-based support.

"Fatigue makes cowards of us all."

— VINCE LOMBARDI

Begin by fundraising. You want to amass a war chest that will scare the opponents before they file the papers. Depending on the circumstances, fundraising events for office holders subjected to a recall are often surprisingly easy and raise lots and lots of money. A bonus is that because you're undergoing a recall while serving in office, no one expects you to do more in the campaign than just show up. So enjoy: Raise money and support, and marginalize your opposition as the small-minded, self-serving people they are. If you cannot find a way to say this yourself, have it said by others in blogs and letters to the editor, and do it again and again and again.

The campaign defending an office holder is actually made easier because the recall communication is all negative. Obviously, little is positive about a recall—all communication, TV, direct mail, and radio will be on the attack. After all, the recall proponents must make the case of why someone should be thrown out of office in the middle of a term. Negative campaigning tends both to disengage voter participation and to create support for the person subjected to the public execution. Further, if voters feel the attack is unfair, you're gold. Unfair recall attempts can generate a lot of money for the subject of the recall. Use the opportunity to raise money for your next run.

If you're thinking about recalling an elected official, stop and reconsider. Recalls are almost never warranted. They generally take on the atmosphere of a public flogging. Recalls also scare off other qualified, honest, hardworking people, the kind of people we need, from serving in public office. If you're mad enough to want to recall an office holder, get over it and run a candidate or run yourself in the next election.

A Petition Is Pulled!

Whether you are fighting a recall, an initiative, or a referendum, once a petition has been pulled, there are lots of things you can do to prepare for the inevitability that the petitioners will get the required signatures. Do not make the mistake of waiting to see whether it actually happens. If you do, the momentum will be with the petitioners, and you will not have enough time to mount a viable campaign. Remember, the best way to prevent signatures from getting collected is to organize,

> "If it is a blessing, it is certainly very well disguised."
> **WINSTON CHURCHILL** after losing the 1945 elections

fundraise, and line everything up for a full-on frontal assault. You want petitioners to believe that you're really enthused, delighted, and looking forward to the possibility of going toe-to-toe with them.

Here's what you do:

1. Organize a campaign committee.
2. Send at least one mailing and email blast to your house list explaining what is going on, and alert your Facebook followers.
3. Set up phone banks, and begin voter identification work immediately in all swing precincts. Know who is opposed to the recall or referendum,

as getting them out on Election Day will be critical to survival. Start with older voters, who typically do not support recalls, who vote, and who will actually answer their phones.

4. While you're on the phone, secure lawn sign locations and names for an endorsement ad. It will be important to show broad community support for your side. Secure field sign locations as well.

5. Whether the movement is local or statewide, when it comes to referrals and recalls, voters are hugely influenced by their neighbors and community. The best way to fight a recall or referendum is to focus in close. The battle is waged neighborhood by neighborhood. Show individual support if you're facing a recall, and show individual opposition (rebellion) if your tax measure is being targeted.

6. Establish a speakers' bureau, and put the speakers on the circuit immediately.

7. Do not let petitioners define you. If your efforts are backed by unions, they should stay in the closet. If your efforts are backed by big business, keep it at a distance.

8. You must go on the offensive; define the opposition, and communicate that those referring the tax measure are self-serving, outsiders, or supported by special interests. Have proof.

9. As soon as a petition is pulled, start fundraising, especially if the opposition's campaign is being bankrolled by special-interest groups. If the law does not allow fundraising until petitions are verified, then ask for pledges you can call in the moment the opposition qualifies for the ballot. But remember, if you have kept your campaign bank account open, you do not need to wait until your opposition gets the signatures. Supporters can give to your existing committee. If you closed your campaign account, simply reopen it under your same committee name. Since committees are often called "Committee to Support Whoever or Whatever," you can continue to use that committee name to fight the recall.

10. Line up letters to the editor and supporters to monitor and respond to newspaper blogs. Remember, while your opponents are gathering signatures, you are, too—signatures for letters, contributions, endorsement ads, and the get-out-the-vote effort. As a campaign, review these letters and decide when they go to the paper(s). Letters need a mix of emotion, pragmatism, and ridicule of the petitioners. Keep 'em short and post them on your website after they're published.

11. Get TV and radio ads made.

12. If you're fighting a recall, sing long and hard on accomplishments and service, but make the messenger the average person. If you're fighting

a referendum, do not fight the actual referral, but rather promote and protect what is being referred. Remember, you are selling hope, opportunity, independence, and investment in our future. Don't get on their message by defending how little money the program costs.

13. Know your audience, and ask sales reps in both television and radio to set up schedules for air time. You don't actually have to buy, but you want to know the cost, penetration, reach, and frequency that will get you what you need. The nice thing about recalls is that they happen at a time when other campaigns are not competing for air time, so you can purchase time up to the last minute.

14. If you don't already have them from the previous election, design your lawn signs and brochures, and have the camera-ready art at the respective printers with a directive to wait for your phone call.

15. The moment the petitions are filed and certified, you want to be able to make five calls and quickly move the whole process into high gear.

As a candidate, think beyond just selling political views. Voters are looking for leaders who are committed, exude honesty, and ones that both look and act the part. Voters want individuals who will represent their city, county, state, or nation with class and integrity. The only real qualifications a candidate needs to run and win elected office is a willingness to work hard, communicate honestly, and present an image that meets the voters' expectations of leadership.

The Issue-Based Campaign

IN THIS CHAPTER
- Initiative and Referendum
- Local Preemption
- Polling and the Issue-Based Campaign
- Speakers' Bureau
- Saving Our Libraries
- Special Districts
- Investing in Education
- Packaging the Issue-Based Campaign
- Flies in the Ointment: The Double Majority, Independents, and the Super Majority
- The State Initiative and Referendum Process

Initiative and Referendum

THE INITIATIVE AND REFERENDUM PROCESS AROSE OUT OF THE FUNDA-mental controversy about whether government should come directly from the people or through representatives to the various levels of government. Although some direct democracy existed in the early years of US government, during the first hundred years, it was almost exclusively representative. It wasn't until the late 1800s, when dissatisfaction with government and distrust of the state legislatures became prevalent, that citizens enacted the initiative process. Primarily a western-state phenomenon, the initiative process began in reaction to laws that benefited a few powerful interests rather than the body electorate. Its effect was to enlarge the role people have in policy decision making.

Ironically, today it has become a tool for special-interest groups with agendas related to natural resources, morality, minority rights, taxation, and so forth. As Oregon's former secretary of state Phil Keisling said, "At key moments in our history, the initiative has held up a mirror to who we are as [a society], reflecting our pettiness as well as grand visions, our mean-spiritedness as well as our generosity, our perils and possibilities as a political community."[1]

The state initiative process enables citizens to bypass the legislature and directly place proposed statutes and constitutional amendments on the ballot by gathering signatures. Each of the twenty-four states with citizens' initiative authority has different criteria to activate the process. Before you begin an initiative campaign, contact your local elections office or secretary of state's office to learn all the necessary details.

The referendum process, by contrast, serves as a check on the governing body by forcing adopted legislation to a vote of the people, allowing them to accept or reject it. The signature requirement for referring legislation out to a vote is usually less than the initiative process.

Increasingly the initiative process is being used to amend state constitutions in an effort to keep legislative bodies from tinkering with a voter-approved initiative. The result is that state constitutions and city and county charters are needlessly cluttered. However, in defense of this practice, in the 2003 legislative session alone, the Oregon legislature tried to undo a number of voter mandates. One mandate, a measure to increase the minimum wage in the state, had received voter approval just three months before the Republican house majority advocated undoing the law at the behest of the business interests that funded their campaigns. Another mandate attempted to undo a ban on the use of bait and traps for cougars and bears; voters had previously affirmed the mandate on two occasions. Also, during each session, legislators revisit voter directives related to reproductive rights.

> "To be successful, grow to the point where one completely forgets himself; that is, to lose himself in a great cause."
>
> **BOOKER T. WASHINGTON**, American educator (1856–1915)

Initiative and referendum processes are also available in many local jurisdictions, and their requirements and scope usually mirror state requirements. Local initiatives can be very useful tools for school districts, libraries, and municipal and county government.

In a local initiative, although most of the guidelines are established by state statutes, the percentage of signatures that need to be gathered varies by locale. Voters may also refer (through referendum) any legislation passed by the local governing body to the voters. As with the state, the number of signatures required is some percentage of the number of people who voted in a specific election—for example, 10 percent of those who voted in the last mayoral election.

The local referendum process differs from the initiative process only in the number of signatures required for qualification and in a time limit; that is, the referendum must be referred within a certain number of days after adoption by the governing body. However, if enough people are opposed to a law, it can, in essence, be repealed through the initiative process at any time. Because both the initiative and the referendum process circumvent the legislative body, they have some inherent problems. If you're not working in conjunction with the local elected officials, be prepared: They have more tricks in their bag.

> "I pay my taxes gladly. Taxes are the price of civilization."
>
> —— OLIVER WENDELL HOLMES

Who drafts the ballot title may have a decided advantage. Some titles are prepared in such a way that you cannot tell whether a yes vote is actually a yes or a no (for example, "yes, repeal it" versus "yes, don't repeal it").

Also, some states have limitations, such as allowing only a single subject to be covered in a measure. Meeting this limitation can be a little more difficult than it sounds. Often citizens are eager to throw in a couple of ideas, each of which may strengthen the other and are quite related, and then, after collecting the signatures or running the winning campaign, the participants find that their wording covered more than one subject. It really isn't for the local governing body to determine whether you have more than one question. If you intend to do all this work, hire an attorney—a good attorney.

There are many restrictions on initiatives and referenda. In Oregon, for example, local government cannot put land-use matters to a vote, only legislative matters. So before spending a lot of time and money, learn what your parameters are.

Another caution: Those signing the petition must be registered within the jurisdiction of the area that will be affected by the proposed legislation. For example, if your school measure is to be voted on by those within your school district, then only those registered within the school district will qualify as signers on the petition. Similarly, if your proposed legislation affects your city, then only those registered within the city limits would qualify. In this way, only those affected get to weigh in on the decision.

Also, in a statewide initiative or referral, the people whose signatures are on the petition must be registered in the county in which they signed the petition. This requirement stems from the fact that signatures are verified at the county level where voters are registered.

Be sure to get at least 10 percent more signatures than is required for qualification.

Of the states with no statewide initiative process, many have provisions for initiatives and referenda at the local level.

Competing Measures

Competing measures have two forms. The first, which results from a legislative body's responding to a qualifying initiative, is designed to give voters an alternative to the citizen-drafted law. In this case, the governing body places before the voters legislation that is linked in some way to an initiative or a referral generated by the public. A competing measure is a powerful tool that can be used effectively. For example, Ashland voters approved a prepared-food and beverage tax to fund an open-space land-acquisition program and state-mandated upgrades on its wastewater treatment plant. It was a divisive campaign that had local restaurants, Realtors, and the state food and beverage industry on one side and the parks commission, environmentalists, and citizens buckling under potentially astronomical utility bills (should it fail) on the other. Although the proponents were outspent five to one, the voters approved the tax by a narrow margin. Opponents decided to immediately refer it back to the voters.

In the meantime, the state legislature decided to place a statewide sales tax for school funding before the voters. The timing was such that the referral of the meals tax would appear on the same ballot as the sales tax proposal. I assumed the proponents of the food and beverage tax repeal would use the scare tactic of suggesting that the food and beverage tax would be added to a statewide sales tax. Although a statewide sales tax was unlikely to pass, given that it had been defeated at the polls eight times already, Ashland had always been supportive of such a tax. While the voters might approve a 5 percent local food and beverage tax, few would stand still for a 10 percent tax that would result from the two combined. To head off this predicament, the city placed a competing measure on the ballot along with the food and beverage tax referral. The competing measure said that (1) if the state sales tax passed, Ashland's food and beverage tax would be repealed, and (2) if people voted in larger numbers for the competing measure than to repeal the tax, it would override the referendum on the food and beverage tax. Citizens chose the competing measure over an outright repeal of the tax. The statewide sales tax was defeated three to one, with Ashland supporting it two to one.

Just a note: Measures approved by voters, no matter how narrow the margin, are rarely overturned when re-referred. Voters historically come back on the referral and reaffirm previous intentions by even larger margins.

The other type of competing measure occurs when two or more unrelated money measures appear on the same ballot. They can come from the same governing body, such as two county measures requesting funding through the property tax, one for juvenile services, the other for adult detention, or from different governing bodies placing money measures on the same ballot, such as a county, city, school, or special district.

These days, counties and cities often place competing measures on ballots, because so many needs are falling by the wayside. However, doing this increases the likelihood that all will fail. For example, in one election, our county placed three bond measures before the voters, and all went down. The reason is fairly simple. Among voters, some will vote no on any new taxes, and others will vote yes. Of the yes voters, some will vote for more than one money measure, and some will choose between the measures, effectively splitting the yes vote. They compete with each other.

That counties and cities would place two measures on the ballot at the same time might suggest that some muddled thinking was involved. In some situations, however, it cannot be helped. For example, your school district is trying to pass a bond measure for a new gym, the city needs money for new fire stations, and the county needs the library system upgraded. Three governing bodies, all with the right to place items on the ballot, separately create a competing-ballot-measure scenario. Ideally, they would be talking to one another and working together to spread these items out, but that doesn't always happen.

> "A life spent making mistakes is not only more honorable but more useful than a life spent doing nothing."
>
> ———————— GEORGE BERNARD SHAW

The survival rate of competing measures is further complicated when statewide initiative-driven legislation is placed on the ballot and inflames one group over another, such as legislation dealing with gun control, reproductive rights, or sexual orientation. Issues of this sort will bring out a voter who might otherwise stay home, and as long as they're at the voting booth, they'll weigh in on your issue-based campaign.

Despite these problems, there are times when a competing measure can actually help. If one of the money issues on the ballot is poorly constructed, the campaign is poorly conducted, or fatal flaws have been committed right out of the gate, voters may choose to overwhelmingly dump it. When they do, there is a fairness doctrine that kicks in, and other measures get a little more of the swing vote than they might normally receive.

Local Preemption

State legislatures love to preempt local government. Having served twelve years as a mayor and witnessing two Oregon legislative sessions as chief of staff for a state representative, I find it remarkable that an assembly that could not organize a sock drawer would have the cheek to prevent local governments from solving issues within their jurisdiction. However, moneyed interests have discovered that fighting targeted taxation and legislation is much easier in a state capital, where money is king, than in a hundred municipalities. For example, in 2002, two statewide grassroots initiatives on the Oregon ballot went down in flames. One, a proposal for universal health care, was outspent thirty-two to one, and the other, which would have required labels on genetically modified foods, was outspent sixty-one to one. The latter prompted the agricultural industry, which dumped $5 million into defeating the food labeling measure, to get legislators to introduce a bill prohibiting local government from implementing any food labeling laws.

During my last term in office, the city of Ashland, which owns the electric utility, brought in high-speed data services and cable television as part of the electric utility system upgrade. By doing so, the city was able to provide high-speed, direct-connect internet access to homes, schools, libraries, and the university for pennies. It was also a boon for our software industry and graphic design businesses. Although the private sector had no intention of providing high-speed data services before the city stepped up, cable companies urged the Oregon legislature to introduce legislation prohibiting other cities from doing what Ashland had done—and tried to make the law retroactive in an effort to undo Ashland's system. Government participation in creating this kind of infrastructure is no different from when it participated in state highway systems or rural electric development in days gone by, and it may be one of the best tools for strengthening local economic development. However, when moneyed interests knock on legislators' doors, those answering are often willing to do the bidding for special interests on the house or senate floor.

> "It doesn't make sense to talk about successful corporations in a society whose schools, hospitals, churches, symphonies, or libraries are deteriorating or closing."
> **CLIFTON C. GARVIN JR.**

Polling and the Issue-Based Campaign

Political consultants and pollsters generally agree that to make it through the campaign process, an issue-based campaign must begin with polled support of at least 60 to 70 percent of voters. While this is certainly the case for any issue in which something is requested of the citizens, such as a tax increase or restrictions on where cows can graze, issues that restrict government, such as term-limit legislation or mandatory sentencing for certain crimes, track a different polling pattern.

In my experience, legislation proposing to restrict government, such as disallowing parkland divestment without a vote of the people, restricting city-owned water sales outside the city limits, or imposing term limits, need only show a voter preference in initial polls to successfully pass on Election Day. Typically issues that appear on the ballot through the initiative process stem from angry voters who have been poked in some way. When this happens, the issue need only cross the finish line to win.

Further, there are other considerations in reading polls than a simple majority in favor of or opposed to the polled issue. For example, a statewide poll looking at proposed legislation to reintroduce term limits in Oregon showed voter support at 56 percent and opposition at 30 percent. At first glance, it looks as if this proposal does not meet the 60 to 70 percent threshold for passage following a heated campaign. But comparing the support and opposition numbers shows almost a two-to-one voter preference for term limits. The other thing to consider is the "hard" support and "hard" opposition of the proposed issue-based campaign. In this term-limit example, the hard numbers in favor (definitely for) came in at 35 percent, and the hard numbers in opposition (definitely against) came in at only 20 percent. These numbers suggest that term-limit legislation would be approved by a proportion similar to the Oregon 1992 constitutional amendment, which passed with 69.6 percent.

Here are some things to consider before embarking on an issue-based campaign:

1. It must be simple and straightforward.
2. It must have voter appeal and speak to emotion. Remember, you are selling an idea, not a person, so there are some inherent challenges. Issue-based campaigns that sell hope and opportunity tend to do best.
3. It must be self-serving. The voter must feel that he or she will personally get something upon passage: a park, better schools, a library, reduced taxes, or a shifted tax burden (e.g., to tourists, business, or the wealthy).
4. For fundraising purposes, it must have populist appeal. Remember: Money is thy savior.
5. Timing is everything. Will you be in a midterm or off-year election, when turnout is lower, or in a presidential cycle, when everyone participates? Will the election be a primary or a general?
6. What else will be on the ballot? Has government or a citizens group placed on the ballot legislation that will induce one segment of the population to turn out more than another?
7. Will your issue-based campaign hurt or help candidates you want to support or need to keep in office by turning out an "against" vote?
8. Is there enough time to make your case to the voters, and do you have people willing to head up the campaign?
9. Who will be drafting the ballot title and summary—a friend or a foe?

10. What are the polling numbers? If you're working on a losing campaign from the beginning, you will finish the race exhausted and will have actually set your cause back.

11. Who will carry the measure? Who will carry the opposition? The chair, speakers' bureau, endorsers, and opponents of an issue-based campaign are often the biggest clues the voters have for supporting or rejecting an idea.

12. Have mistakes been made that could sink your efforts even before a decision to place the issue campaign on the ballot?

13. Finally, an issue-based campaign designed to raise taxes must answer four questions: (1) How high will (can) the tax go? (2) Where will it be spent? (dedicate the funds) (3) When will it go away? (sunset clause) (4) Is there a nexus between what is being taxed and where the revenue will be spent? An example would be a cigarette tax to fund health care. If there is not a logical connection, your campaign must make one. For example, in the prepared-food and beverage tax, we pointed out that tourists and residents alike use city parks and flush toilets, so both locals *and* visitors should help improve these systems.

Speakers' Bureau

When organizing campaigns for ballot measures, set up a committee of supporters whose sole job is to serve as speakers; collectively, they are the speakers' bureau. If it is a countywide proposition or measure, the speakers' bureau might be quite large or a single person. In an individual city, those willing to speak at public events regarding a ballot proposal rarely number greater than two. Whatever the size, the group's job is to seek opportunities to speak and to make sure someone is there from the committee to explain the ballot measure and answer questions in a knowledgeable way. These should be people with a command of the issue.

> "I should have dropped the Math and English Departments and study hall. Then no one would have known about it."
>
> **JAMES TAYLOR**, College of Southern Idaho president, reacting to outcries against his dropping three sports and five coaches to solve a financial crisis

A speakers' bureau is a terrific way of publicly involving big-name people who want to be aligned with a campaign. It is also good for the ballot proposal. Whereas an election with a candidate depends on that candidate and his or her ability to build relationships with the voters through political stands and ideology, ballot measures typically encompass only one idea. Often with a ballot measure, the people who attach their name to it create

FIGURE 10.1A Historical Photograph of Ashland's Carnegie Library

This photo was used on the front of the "Campaign for the Carnegie" brochure. (Photo courtesy of Terry Skibby, Ashland Historian)

FIGURE 10.1B Inside the "Campaign for the Carnegie" brochure, we used this image to show voters what they were buying. In issue-based campaigns, use a mix of the old with the new. Civic buildings reflect who we were as well as who we are.

the relationship. You might have the president of the college, the president of the Rotary Club, the mayor, the leaders of every church, and so on. Each will bring a following. Their names have come to represent something in the community, and it is their reputations that help draw attention to the vote.

Saving Our Libraries

In the age of technology, voters often look at libraries as a throwback and consider funding them a frill. Unlike new wastewater treatment plants or water pipelines, both of which can be funded through revenue bonds, libraries have suffered under taxpayer revolts and a lack of understanding. If your mission is to get money to build a new library or to remodel and expand an existing one, there's plenty of hope.

Library campaigns must be set up a little differently from other bond measures, in part because it is more difficult to convince some of their importance. There are basically three steps involved in setting up a library bond campaign for capital improvements and a number of choices within each of those steps.

1. Establish a committee to examine needs, opportunities, and direction. Your first step is to gather a select group of community members to usher your project through. Although some may end up working on the campaign, that is not the purpose of this committee. Its members' job is to serve as liaisons with the community and the project. Assemble people who represent the many sides of your community and are well respected in their circle. You may select an individual from the immediate neighborhood, a businessperson, representatives of influential city boards or commissions (such as planning and historic), a builder, a librarian, a member of the Friends of the Library group, and a liaison to the city council. It is also important to have city or county staff there for guidance and administrative support. It doesn't matter if all the committee members are not 100 percent on board for the project at the beginning; it's actually better if opinions are spread. Don't worry, people will come around or the project won't fly anyway.

   > "We shape our buildings; thereafter our buildings shape us."
   > WINSTON CHURCHILL

2. Once you have the committee in place, working with the local government, hopefully municipal, you will need to select an architectural team. The architectural team should be committed to community process and inclusivity. You want architects who are interested in what the community wants, not what they think is best for the community.

Through community visioning, in which citizens are invited to attend a half-day workshop, a clear idea of what people want will emerge. From this the architects can draft architectural renderings and come up with a money figure to place before the voters (figures 10.1A and 10.1B).

3. Obviously, you want your governing body to place this on the ballot for you. If they don't, see the section above on the initiative process, and consider running for office next time someone in the governing body is up for reelection. Using the money figure generated by the architectural team and backed by your committee, the council should place the matter before the voters. You now have to convince the voters.

Here you might consider who gets to vote on this issue. In my area, those who live in the unincorporated areas—that is, outside city limits—tend to vote no on such things, so I prefer to leave them out of the decision and limit the vote to the city. It's also much easier to turn out the vote if it's just citywide. Don't forget, those who use the library the most live closest to it.

If you think you'll have trouble convincing the city council to place the measure on the ballot or you want additional public input and direction, consider having your Friends of the Library group print flyers with questionnaires and canvass the city. One part of the flyer can be dedicated to what the community proposed in the visioning process, and another part could invite community members to join the Friends of the Library. You would be surprised at how much money you can bring in with this small effort. Keep in mind, if your Friends group is a 501(c)(3), this money and effort can never touch your campaign. It must be kept separate and distinct.

> "This nation cannot afford to maintain its military power and neglect its brainpower."
>
> —— JOHN F. KENNEDY

If the cost estimate of your library project comes in on the high side and sticker shock among voters is a concern, here are some suggestions to get the price down:

1. Have local donors or organizations financially sponsor different rooms, fixtures, floors, rugs, and so forth. Determine how much the children's section, the young adult section, and reference area will cost, and ask civic groups to fund a room with a promise of having their name placed over the door. Go to likely organizations that might pick up the computer component.

2. Have either local organizations or the historical society consider funding and placing all the artwork for the library. Have the walls tell the story of your library or town through pictures.

3. If it's a historic structure, are there local, state, or federal historic renovation grants available for some portion of the remodeling?
4. Consider writing grants for some portion of the expansion, such as community meeting rooms or a kitchen.
5. Reduce the size of the expansion but maintain quality. Nothing is more permanent than a temporary building.

Typically there are two kinds of issue-based campaigns when it comes to libraries, schools, or government efforts: operating and maintenance, and facility upgrades (capital improvements).

If your initiative is for operation and maintenance, it will typically be supported by a property tax levy, which goes out for voter approval. When it comes to "selling" operations and maintenance (O&M) to the community, the test placed before the voters is one of hope and opportunity. When asking voters to fund facility upgrades, the test is one of need. Are books being damaged by a leaky roof? Is overcrowding so bad that for every new book brought into the collection, an old one must exit the shelves to make room? How many people a day use the facility? You are basically making the case that improving the facility is a good way to spend taxpayer money and that it will actually save money in the long run.

There are two ways that facility upgrades can be funded: One is through revenue bonds; the other is general obligation bonds (GO bonds). With revenue bonds, the government entity guarantees payment of the bond through a reliable revenue stream. For example, you want to upgrade your water treatment facility, so you sell bonds on the bond market and the repayment of those bonds is guaranteed through the revenue stream of water rates. The government may raise water rates to pay back these loans.

If you intend to fund your project through GO bonds, then the repayment of those bonds comes from the property tax. Depending upon your state and local guidelines, GO bonds usually require voter approval whereas revenue bonds do not. Also of note is that GO bonds typically get a better interest rate because property tax is seen as more stable than a revenue bond's income stream. Obviously some publicly held interests—like schools and libraries—make no revenue, so they must go to the voters for approval as a GO bond.

Special Districts

One option for funding, operating, and maintaining libraries, public transportation, historic preservation, water, sewer, agricultural extension services, and such is through a special district. States may differ on what is or is not allowed through a special district funding mechanism, so check with the special district offices at the state level of government for guidelines.

If you're sick of begging the county elected officials to keep libraries open, consider a special district. To understand how they work, you only need think of school districts where an elected board, an administrative arm, and citizen budget committee oversee revenues and expenditures, and you have the model for any special district. Typically special districts are set up similarly in that an elected board and paid manager oversee the revenue and expenditures for the voter-approved district.

With increased demands on county revenues from law enforcement, elected officials are gutting library, historic preservation, public transportation, and agricultural extension services funding. In other areas where water is scarce, money is being moved from libraries or law enforcement to find more water. The only way to ensure ongoing and permanent funding for programs your elected officials choose to defund is through a special district.

Typically any city within a proposed district must decide at the municipal level whether it wants its citizens to even vote on a special district; and similarly, your county elected officials must be willing to allow voters in unincorporated areas to participate in the election. If neither the city nor the county government is willing to cooperate, then the interest group must take the issue through an initiative process. Keep in mind, when it comes to special districts the bar is set very high; in fact, I would argue too high for success in this regard.

However, proposing a district to keep an established department open is in the best interest of all concerned and should be presented as such to elected bodies in both city and county government. After all, their expenditure requirements are increasing in the face of stagnant revenue streams and you're offering a solution that will free up funds for other uses. It's a win-win. And with the help of county government, a special district is easily within the reach of a motivated group of citizens. One small caution: Pushback may come from county officials who would rather not lose control of the new revenues and, therefore, will urge or demand that special district proponents support a *service district* instead.

A service district funds more than one type of program (such as historic preservation, libraries, and water combined) into one service district. Under a service district the elected board, administrator, and citizen budget committee determine how the revenues will be dispersed. It's a bad exchange. A service district model denies you of your most persuasive campaign argument: dedicated funding. Selling a special district is much easier because voters know that the new revenues will be used for one and only one voter-approved entity.

Passing a Library District

If you live where there is little hope of a special district passing countywide for libraries, propose a smaller district that you believe *can* pass.

To determine this, first look at the election returns of the last (likely failed) library tax proposal for operating and maintenance money; you're looking for the percent by precinct of yes and no votes. Next, determine predicted voter turnout. As noted in Chapter 1 and Appendix A, predicted voter turnout can be calculated by using percent

> "A coupla months in the laboratory can save a coupla hours in the library."
> **WESTHEIMER'S DISCOVERY**

turnout of similar election cycles (midterm primary, presidential general, special election, etc.) and multiplying that by the current registration numbers, precinct by precinct. Finally, multiply the predicted voter turnout by the yes and no vote percentage from the last tax proposal. This will give you predicted yes and no numbers for all the precincts in the county if a measure were placed before the voters today.

Next, use the predicted yes and no vote to propose a district as large as possible but one that will still pass. Obviously, not all of the precincts in the proposed district will vote yes, but with enough support from other precincts, you want it to pass overall. The proposed area may include both urban and rural (unincorporated) voter precincts.

Once the smaller district passes, go to the remaining incorporated cities outside the district and invite them to annex in through a vote of the municipal registrants. Make clear that if they do not join, their library will close. Voters who oppose libraries in general rarely vote against closing their own library. It is the same mentality that gives Congress a 10 percent voter approval rating by a nation that reelects incumbents 98 percent of the time.

In the end, this approach will leave most unincorporated voters out of the vote and may create some animosity from city dwellers that those living in the rural precincts get to use the libraries without paying. Your response: "Yeah, so what's your point?"

Investing in Education

The biggest obstacle that public school districts have in passing measures for operation and maintenance money or construction bonds is that schooling has evolved beyond the kind of education much of the electorate received. As a result, some voters may still see computers in the classroom as a luxury, extracurricular activities such as debate and business programs as unnecessary, and connection to the Web as a frill. I can't tell you how many times

I have heard how we need to get back to the basics of reading, writing, and 'rithmetic. The reality our students face has to do with screen-based literacy, collaborative learning, and critical thinking.

For voters to support the changes needed in our schools, we must educate the populace to understand that our schools are training students for more than trades and specific jobs. Instead, students are trained, and need to be trained, to work with people, to be flexible in an ever-changing job market, and to think creatively and freely with access to data. Most of the jobs for today's elementary school students do not yet exist.

> "All who have meditated on the art of governing mankind have been convinced that the fate of empires depends on the education of youth."
>
> — **ARISTOTLE**

The bulk of America's schools were built in the early 1950s or earlier and either are falling apart or are inadequate for the electronic demands of the computer age. The task of rebuilding them or constructing new ones, on top of all the other costs of public education, is almost overwhelming to taxpayers, leaving them immobilized. In southern Oregon, however, we have had great luck in this sphere. Here are some tips that we found useful from our experience:

1. Again, set up a committee that represents a good cross-section of the community. The last time we proposed major improvements to our schools, we started out with about forty citizens, all invited, who then worked in focus groups to design a plan and figure out a dollar amount that would work for our community. However you decide to do it, just remember to start broad and continue to widen involvement all the way to the campaign.

2. An architect will need to be selected. Obviously you can't use a large group to select this individual or team, but this is a really important step and needs the right people. Too often, in an effort to save money and make public buildings salable at an election, corners are cut. We should construct civic buildings with materials that suggest permanence, are compatible with the community, and will be objects of civic pride. It costs no more to build a beautiful building than an ugly one. Look closely at what the architect has designed before. Do the buildings all look the same? Have past contractors had trouble working with the architect? Do a lot of research and homework here, or you'll be sorry.

3. If you think you'll have trouble getting this sort of thing to pass district-wide, ask the council to float it to city residents.

4. Do not confuse issues. For example, if the school wiring is faulty and a fire hazard; heating systems work only when it's hot outside and cooling

systems work only in the winter; if boilers are exploding or mold covers portions of the walls and rooms, then make that case to the voters. Do not confuse the issue by bringing in a message of classroom size for a better education experience. Need must be fully demonstrated, and underscoring that crumbling infrastructure expenses pulls dollars out of the classroom is a powerful message.

Packaging the Issue-Based Campaign

In an issue-based campaign, the message is the messenger. You want those in your community who have broad support and leadership standing to usher your project through. I have touched on issue-based campaigns throughout this handbook, but there are many specifics that bear emphasis.

1. Set up a "committee to support" of movers and shakers. This committee is separate from your campaign committee and comprises people whose name will appear on ads, in direct mail, and on the brochure.
2. Find the right chair (or co-chairs) for this committee: someone who embraces the many sides of your community. This is an opportunity to use an individual who will bring along the savables, not the saints.

   > "Education makes a people easy to lead, but difficult to drive; easy to govern but impossible to enslave."
   > **BARON HENRY PETER BROUGHAM**

3. Remember, with schools' and libraries' operating and maintenance, you are selling opportunity. You are not asking people to fund needs. This means you must educate the electorate on the changing world. The aforementioned idea of contrasting the high school transcripts of two straight-A students, only one of whose transcripts lists extracurricular activities, resonates with voters. It asks voters to ensure the success of their children and grandchildren in the future. There is also an element of self-interest to consider. As an aging society, we must position ourselves to improve the education of those who will take care of us in our old age.
4. With facility upgrades, you are making the case for need. Failing roofs, time wasted mopping up after rain, exploding boilers, poorly heated classrooms, unsafe water, meeting federal requirements for in-stream dumping, books ruined by mildew or moisture from leaks—these concrete images can influence voters in ways they can easily grasp.
5. Talk about reinstating libraries as information hubs. Our libraries have become as historic on the inside as on the outside, and the pathways and opportunities they can open to a community, young and old, are often overlooked, even by librarians.

6. In designing libraries, be sure to have areas that can be used after hours for community needs apart from the books. These areas might include meeting, reading, and study rooms as well as computer labs that members of the community can use to become more computer literate or simply access a computer and the internet if there is no access at home.

7. Conduct a precinct analysis that closely tracks who has voted for similar measures. If you are looking for funding for a library, look at census data to determine who has school-age children, and then target them. Remember, schools are moving more toward training our students to work in groups, and these groups need to gather somewhere to do projects and research. What better place than the public library?

8. Acknowledge the changing face of libraries and schools. For example, because of the Web and digital technologies, reference sections are actually getting smaller.

9. Use teachers, PTAs, and parents to volunteer for this effort.

10. Pay close attention to any fatal flaws. For example, in a nearby school district, a bond measure for schools failed because voters discovered that it included money to pave the parking lot. At no time did the committee tell the voters that federal track-out laws require paving if remodeling occurs.

11. Have a speakers' bureau of people who can speak to civic groups. This should not include teachers or librarians, who have a vested interest in the bond's passage.

12. Create a strong theme and message, and stick to them. Remember, a theme is strategic, not tactical. Aim at the souls that can be saved, and use the theme as a focus point for your campaign team and committee to support.

13. In campaigns, timing and context are everything. In general, the further away from a presidential election, the more conservative the vote. However, distance from a presidential election means a lower voter turnout and fewer competing measures that typically get placed in a presidential general election. A low voter turnout offers more weight to the campaign with a strong voter identification and GOTV effort and thus can translate into a win, which otherwise could not happen with a higher voter turnout. There's a case to be made for both. Find out whether there will be other issue-based campaigns that will compete with yours. To have a ballot on which only one money issue is presented to the voter allows that single issue to get lots of light, air, dialogue, debate, and media attention. Plus, it gives those working for them a chance to turn out the support without another election poking a sleeping dog somewhere else.

In 2006 I was hired to help pass a $189 million school facilities bond for the largest school district in southern Oregon. The city of Medford, where the bulk of the schools needing repairs and the majority of the voters in the district lived, had not passed a money measure in a midterm cycle in the twenty-five years I'd been working elections in our area.

By the time I was called in, the lawn signs had been ordered, the logo was done, the Web page was up, a poll had been conducted, and the committee had a number of white papers with different campaign messages that were distributed to parent-teacher organizations. Problematic was that their literature felt defensive and even a little scolding. On the upside, the committee was full of smart, hardworking, energetic community leaders, businesspeople, school board members, and teachers. Although they had little campaign experience, there was enormous talent in the well-balanced group.

In a facility bond, the voters must be made aware of the needs and convinced that money should be spent to meet these needs. As mentioned above, it cannot be something that would be "nice" to have, like smaller classrooms or computer labs, but rather more fundamental. As it turned out, that was not so difficult to convey. In this school district, boiler rooms were exploding; wiring was old and dangerous; water pipes were breaking under playgrounds, causing unexpected geysers; some of the buildings—over one hundred years old—lacked proper insulation and had antiquated heating and cooling systems that were stealing education dollars from the classroom. Some classrooms were forced into closets because of space issues. At one elementary school, the well failed and water had to be brought in by truck, or the children were without bathroom facilities and drinking fountains. Although the city water was

> "Human history becomes more and more a race between education and catastrophe."
> **H. G. WELLS**

within feet of the school, there were no resources to hook into it. We weren't talking about bringing district buildings into the twenty-first century or frills of any sort; we needed to bring them into the nineteenth century.

The committee essentially had six weeks, in which time the message needed to get focused, decisions had to be made on advertising on TV and radio, spots cut, and a precinct analysis conducted to focus canvassing and GOTV efforts. The team also needed to be convinced to leave the lawn signs in the boxes; untargeted activities in such a difficult race could hurt more than help.

Harnessing the team and moving it in the right direction was surprisingly easy. Although money was short, we did put together a television spot. To give the ad intimacy, we used the high school chamber choir for background music and did the first ads with no voice-over; after a week or so, we brought in the same ad with a voice-over. Nearly every image used on television was provided by the committee, although some video was beefed up with stock purchases. (To see the ad, go to YouTube, search by Oakstpress, and scroll down to "Medford Oregon School Bond.")

Essentially, no mistakes were made. Everyone on the committee was disciplined, focused, and hard working. We put together a killer GOTV effort, in which forty volunteers per night called for eight nights straight. And although we went to bed behind by 150 votes, by morning the campaign prevailed with a "landslide" margin of 315 out of 31,000 votes cast. How cool is that?

Flies in the Ointment: The Double Majority, Independents, and the Super Majority

The Double Majority

Under a *double majority*, there must be at least a 50 percent voter turnout before ballots are counted to determine if a majority of those casting a ballot actually support the proposal. This means that the challenge becomes one of turning out at least 50 percent of the vote, not just a majority of support. Those opposing taxes under a double majority understand that not voting and urging their friends to stay home as well, can defeat tax measures quicker than if they actually participate in an election and vote no on a proposal. In counties and states that do not routinely update voter rolls, those who have died or moved get a de facto vote, making it more difficult to reach the 50 percent turnout threshold.

> "We are continually faced with a series of great opportunities brilliantly disguised as insoluble problems."
>
> —————————— **JOHN W. GARDNER**

Independents (Nonaffiliated Voters) and the Double Majority

In nonpresidential primary elections, when even party loyalists underperform, independents stay home in huge numbers. They do so because they are often not allowed to participate in the primary elections of either party. If you are working an issue-based campaign under double-majority constraints, there is little you can do to meet the required 50 percent turnout in a midterm primary election unless the campaign covers a small area (city or school district) with an active electorate. Save your money. You will win the vote but lose the election because of turnout. Ironically, these same campaigns, coming back for a second shot in the midterm general election, often lose because of support. It is almost as though everyone who stays home in the primary votes no in the general. A postmortem analysis on a primary will not give you solid predictors for a general, because the primary support numbers simply do not carry over. To predict these elections, you must take another general midterm election for an issue-based campaign that lost in a primary.

The upside of a double-majority midterm primary election is that if 50 percent turn out, it almost always results in a win. A double-majority requirement creates a sense of urgency on the part of the protax voter as well as the volunteers needed to prod them, and it has the added benefit of scaring away competing measures on the ballot. One small note: Double-majority elections work best in cities.

> "The absence of alternatives clears the mind marvelously."
> **HENRY KISSINGER**

Some states, like Hawaii, require that the majority turnout carry over to all those casting a ballot. In this way, even though 50 percent may turn out to vote, if voters undervote a double-majority tax measure, then the ballot issue fails.

Keep the Vote Within City Limits

Those living in the unincorporated areas can be the most conservative of American voters and often want little or nothing to do with what government has to offer. They have wells and septic drain fields, and many heat exclusively with wood or some other fuel shipped directly to their homes. Oh, they love to drive on paved roads, use libraries, have the sheriff and fire patrol appear promptly, and have their kids attend great public schools, but when it comes to being taxed, they're a loud and strong no vote. People living in cities, however, tend to want what government offers and are willing to tax themselves to get it. If you have an opportunity to run an election under the double-majority rule without the unincorporated vote, do it.

The resounding no vote of the unincorporated voter can keep city residents from getting what they want. There's a disparity in how we pay taxes: County residents pay only for county services; city residents pay for both city and county services. If you want programs for your school district or library system and can keep the vote within the city limits, your chances of passage increase significantly. Here are five reasons to keep the vote within city limits for programs benefiting both those in and out of town:

1. The assessed valuation (per acre) is often greatest within the city, so even if you include county residents in the overall funding scheme, it won't have a huge impact on the cost per $1,000 of the property tax.
2. People within city limits have a higher voter turnout than those in the county, so you're already ahead if you have to meet a double-majority rule.

3. It's easier to run an election and bring in votes within city limits because of the population density.
4. The percentage of people favoring taxes for anything is higher within city limits than in the unincorporated areas.
5. By holding your voting district to the city limits, you eliminate a greater proportion of nonsupporters because of the voting tendencies of those living in unincorporated areas.

Think Creatively

There are all kinds of things that have to go to a countywide vote or a vote larger than the city, but schools and libraries aren't among them. Be creative. If you're an elected official, you are in a unique position to help constituencies realize programs that they want in the community. When roadblocks are placed in your way, keeping your community from having great schools, open spaces, and libraries, don't take that road. Find another path.

For years, our community leaders had been advocating for upgrades to the county library system. Each library had unique challenges for meeting long-overdue improvements to the point that a systemwide upgrade would easily run tens of millions of dollars. The county commissioners were reluctant to put it to a vote prior to other county improvements they felt were more important. The county Friends of the Library group also seemed hesitant, as a countywide vote could ultimately be turned down by the voters, leaving them with dilapidated buildings that no longer could house the incoming books or the volume of patrons availing themselves of the system.

The Ashland Friends of the Library was dogging the county to move forward, but to no avail. Finally they came to me and asked whether the city could help. Because the Ashland branch of the library was actually owned by the city, we were in a unique position to step up. After the first meeting with the Ashland Friends of the Library, it was clear that a general mistrust existed between the Ashland group and the county. There were concerns that Ashland would not get from the county the quality of renovation that the local community wanted and that Ashland would be put on the end of the list after areas that were walking in lockstep with the county.

I proposed that the Ashland renovation move ahead of the countywide upgrades, but the county officials wanted no part of this proposal. They believed that Ashland voters would not support county system upgrades on top of the Ashland branch renovation and expansion. The county also felt that without a strong Ashland vote, the countywide tax measure would have more difficulty surviving an election. Those in the Ashland contingent were concerned about a countywide measure passing, period, with or without Ashland, and were further concerned about meeting a countywide double-majority requirement, which would be very difficult. Meanwhile, county election officials were not moving.

To get all the parties what they wanted, we moved Ashland's city library upgrades to be voted on ahead of the county vote. However, should the bond measure pass in the city, we agreed to hold off on issuing bonds to pay for the project until the county had an opportunity at the polls. This approach had many benefits. First, it got us off our knees begging the county to do something, as a citywide initiative required only the Ashland city council to vote to place the tax measure before the voters—an easy prospect. Second, it would guarantee Ashland voters that a specific amount would be spent on our branch and that the renovation outcome would reflect what citizens had agreed upon in the community visioning process. Finally, for those who did not want to pay twice, holding off on issuance of bonds for the project negated those concerns. To underscore this, we agreed to communicate with the voters that a vote for the county system upgrades would result in lowering the debt load for the Ashland improvements with our taxpayers. The latter is important because the first vote held in the city would mean that only city residents would pay for upgrades, while folding our improvements into the county bond would mean that those surrounding the city would also share in the tax burden. In this way, we locked in how much money would be spent in Ashland and exactly what the upgrades would look like. The countywide vote simply became reaffirming what Ashland wanted but for less money.

> "Experience is not what happens to a person, it is what a person does with what happens."
> **ALDOUS HUXLEY**

In the spring, the city bond measure passed easily and with an ample double-majority turnout. In the fall, when the county put the whole system before the voters, it was approved and the double-majority requirements were also met. Eighty-five percent of those casting a ballot in Ashland voted for the countywide upgrades, more than twenty points higher than typically vote for county library measures. Given that the second vote actually lowered Ashland's tax on the library upgrade, one would have to wonder what the 15 percent who voted no were thinking.

The worst thing we could have done would be to place an Ashland library upgrade before the voters at the same time as a countywide library upgrade, where the two would become competing measures. Although these two sides had plenty of history and suspicion of each other, we were ultimately able to craft an agreement that met all concerns. And given that the city would hold off on floating the voter-approved bonds only until the next election, it pushed the county commissioners into action.

The Super Majority

The super-majority rule, applied to tax measures, requires that either two-thirds or 60 percent of those voting approve the measure before it may take effect. Here your objective is dramatically different from when your constraint is a double majority. The best defense you have to pass anything with a super majority is to place your money measure on an election with the lowest voter turnout possible and no competing measures. Then you must identify your supporters and have a top-notch GOTV effort to get them to the polls or to mail their absentee ballots.

A few years back, in Marin County, California, supporters of a school facility plan used an interesting tactic to pass their bond measure under the super-majority rule. The supporters of the measure determined that those sixty-five and older were both a no vote and likely voters. To move this age group over to the yes column, the bond measure excluded them from having to pay, but did not exclude them from the vote. The campaign then worked hard to turn out the sixty-five-and-over age group, who had nothing to lose by voting yes. The facility plan passed. Given that many seniors are two generations away from having children in public education and have probably already paid enough, this seems like a happy compromise.

The State Initiative and Referendum Process

There are three types of initiatives:

1. *Direct initiative:* The completed petition places a proposed law or amendment directly on the ballot, bypassing the legislative process.
2. *Indirect initiative:* The completed petition is submitted to the legislature, which then may enact the proposed measure or one substantially similar to it. If the legislature fails to act within a specified time, the proposal is placed on the ballot.
3. *Advisory initiative:* The outcome provides the legislature with a non-binding indication of public opinion.

There are four kinds of referenda:

1. *Mandatory referendum:* Requires the legislature to refer all proposed amendments to the constitution as well as measures regarding tax levies, bond issues, and movement of state capitals or county seats.
2. *Optional referendum:* The legislature may refer to the citizens any measure that it has passed. This is often called a referral.

3. *Petition referendum:* Measures passed by the legislature go into effect after a specified time unless an emergency clause is attached. During that interval, citizens may circulate a petition requiring that the statute be referred to the people either at a special election or at the next general election. If enough signatures are collected, the law is not implemented, pending the outcome of the election. The signature requirement is usually lower and the time allowed to gather signatures less than for a straight initiative.
4. *Advisory referendum:* The legislature may refer a proposed statute to the voters for a nonbinding reflection of public opinion.

Initiative and Referendum Procedures

1. *Preparing the petition:* Preparing the initiative petition and organizing the collection of signatures is the responsibility of the chief petitioner(s). The text of the proposed measure is drafted by the chief petitioner(s), with legal assistance if desired, and filed with the secretary of state for state initiatives and the local election office for local initiatives.
2. *Filing the petition:* Any prospective petition must include the names, addresses, and signatures of the chief petitioner(s), a statement of sponsorship signed by a certain number of registered voters and verified by county election officials, a form stating whether the circulators of the petition will receive payment, and the complete text of the proposed measure.
3. *Obtaining the ballot title:* State statutes usually provide strict timelines for moving a filed petition through the process to obtain a ballot title. For statewide initiatives, all petitions are filed with the secretary of state, and two additional copies are sent to the attorney general, who prepares a draft of the ballot title.
4. *Preparing the cover and signature sheets:* The chief petitioner(s) must submit a printed copy of the cover and signature sheets for approval prior to circulation. The cover sheet must include names and addresses of the chief petitioner(s), the proposal itself, the ballot title, and instructions to circulators and signers. The cover sheet must be printed on the reverse of the signature sheet and contain instructions to signature gatherers. Notice of paid circulators must be included.

"It is the same story here as in every state, people for it, corporations against it, politicians trying to straddle the issue and save their scalps."
GEORGE JUDSON KING, National Initiative and Referendum leader after initiative provision was dropped from New Mexico Constitution, 1910 _____

Signature sheets must never be separated from the cover sheet and the measure's text.

5. *Circulating the petition:* As soon as approval is obtained from the election officer, the ballot is certified and may be circulated for signatures. Usually you can withdraw the petition at any time. Any registered voter may sign an initiative or a referendum petition for any measure being circulated in a district where the registered voter resides. All signers on a single sheet must be registered voters residing in the same county.

6. *Filing the petition for signature verification:* There's a deadline for signature verification statewide (usually four months) and locally (usually less time).

7. *Filing campaign and expenditure information:* Within a specified period after filing petition signatures for verification, the chief petitioner(s) must file a statement of contributions received and expended by the petitioner(s) or on their behalf.

Before a political committee receives or expends any funds on a measure or proposition that has reached the ballot, the committee treasurer must file a statement of organization with the secretary of state, and subsequent contributions and expenditures must be reported. Sometimes this must be done even if a petition is withdrawn.

There are few things you can do, including serving in office, which would impact on your community more than running and passing an issue-based campaign. Seeking and receiving voter approval for such things as public buildings, parks, education, municipal water systems, and the like is very rewarding. And, conversely, stopping elected officials from heading in the wrong direction through referral is empowering. If you live in a state where initiatives and referrals are not allowed, then run for office, win, and once sworn in, seek voter approval for programs that will last long after you're gone.

"If you're explaining, you're losing."

————— **RONALD REAGAN**

Getting Out the Vote (GOTV)

MAKE NO MISTAKE; EVERYTHING YOU HAVE DONE UP TO THIS POINT is about the get-out-the-vote (GOTV) effort. Everything. You've canvassed, mailed, advertised, phoned, raised money, and communicated with followers and friends on Facebook and Twitter to deliver your message again and again. Why? To move swing voters and activate your base for support on Election Day. But voters get busy: Kids get sick, cars break down, food boils over, an old friend calls. . . . In short, life gets in the way, and somehow, 8 p.m. rolls around and best in-

> "The final days are the longest."
> **BILL MEULEMANS**

tentions to vote are out the window. Now, after months of campaigning, your job, your one and only job, is to remind your supporters, remove obstacles for them, and motivate them to do their civic duty.

The Essentials

Activating Your Base

Regardless of whether your campaign conducts voter ID, you must know where your base lives and activate them to increase voter turnout among the saints. Although your base vote, that is, party loyalists or those loyal to

Brian Freeman

your issue, has not received the same level of attention as potential swing voters have received, it has not been neglected, either. When it comes to the GOTV, this group is extraordinarily important. Your precinct analysis has told you who among your base will vote with very little effort from the campaign and who needs to be reminded before Election Day.

> "Persistence in the face of adversity is what wins an election."
>
> **PATRICIA SCHIFFERLE**, former assistant to the Speaker, California

Those who need a little prodding can actually be quite different, depending upon their context. With these voters there are generally two groups. The first are those who live in areas of equal or slight registration advantage (up to ten points) but are disengaged. The second group is also disengaged, but these voters are embedded in neighborhoods where their party (and that of the candidate) is greatly outnumbered.

For our purposes, you will have three strategies for your base:

1. Your hard-core voters, those who traditionally have high turnout rates, will need little effort from the campaign. It is a good idea to canvass them with a drop piece on Election Day, and track the returns from these precincts, because you are really counting on them. If it looks as though their turnout will be down, the campaign should be ready to activate them with a knock on their door.

2. For your lazy yet loyal voters (high support and low to medium turnout), your campaign has canvassed, mailed, called, and canvassed them again. If you're in a state that doesn't exclusively conduct elections with vote by mail, your GOTV team will closely watch the polls and absentee lists to make sure these voters do their duty. If they don't, you will need to call them or knock on their door. These are the voters you must continue to activate in the days leading up to the election; remind them that voting early helps your volunteer efforts, and emphasize that their vote and their vote alone will make the difference in a win. For the precincts that are loaded with lazy voters, organize canvass teams to go in and rattle their cage on Election Day. In vote-by-mail elections, send canvassers in to pick up ballots and return them to the drop boxes for the voter.

3. The third group is a little trickier. Voters registered in your party but who live behind enemy lines will need very specific attention, as they are often the most difficult to activate. These voters should be treated like swing voters: They must receive attention directly from the campaign, and the best way to move these voters is by canvassing them. Although this is labor intensive and time consuming, few other campaign activities will activate them as successfully—especially if it is the candidate who knocks. It is critical that these voters be part of your voter ID effort, as they are the least predictable. Your swing analysis will tell you what percentage will always vote party. Voter ID will tell you, by name, whom you can count upon.

Swing Voters

The next group of voters your campaign will identify are those who live in precincts with high numbers of swing voters. Recall that the precinct analysis has told you exactly which precincts they live in and how many of the voters you need to win. Because the campaign must have a clear reading of who will be supporting you, who is undecided, and who will not move, use the candidate, volunteers registered in the opposing party (validators), neighbors, and your best canvassers to knock doors in these areas. Your campaign must keep track of the voters who say they will support you so they may be activated to vote on Election Day. If a swing voter tells the campaign they will vote for the candidate or issue for which you are working, be sure to get some sort of confirmation. Generally it is easiest to ask if his or her name can be used in an endorsement ad or placed on your Web page listing supporters. Whether it is by doing this or by hosting a lawn sign, you want the swing voter to go public. If the voter is unwilling to lend a name to the effort—or host a lawn sign—then, depending on the reason, you should assume that you have been told what you want to hear rather than given a guarantee.

"You know, back in 2000 a Republican friend of mine warned me that if I voted for Al Gore and he won, the stock market would tank, we'd lose millions of jobs, and our military would be totally overstretched. You know what? I did vote for Al Gore, he did win, and I'll be damned if all those things didn't come true."

—— JAMES CARVILLE

The Pleasure of Your Company

Other candidates and ballot issues can affect who turns out to vote. If you're involved in an election in which a controversial measure is also on the ballot, there may be a high voter turnout that significantly affects your efforts. For example, a few years back I was working for a candidate who was on the ballot with two measures intended to limit the rights of a targeted minority. Our campaign had a well-organized GOTV, and we had conducted voter ID from September through November. The committee working in opposition to the two ballot measures also had a great GOTV effort, which helped ours even more. Tracking polls indicated we were neck and neck with our opponent and that the two ballot measures were going down statewide. What we had not anticipated was the huge turnout of the sinners' precincts to vote yes on these ballot measures, and as long as they were there, they voted against our candidate as well.

Unfortunately, we realized too late that we spent far too much time identifying and getting out the vote where the proponents of the two ballot measures were also working. Had we left this portion of the electorate to the other campaign, more volunteer time and energy could have been freed up for voter ID and GOTV of our persuadables.

Disorganized and uncoordinated GOTV efforts can enrage hard-core voters. In Ashland, largely because of the statewide passage of the double-majority requirement in 1996, we have had a GOTV machine that rivals any in the state. Voters are conditioned to vote early if they do not want to be bothered with activation calls and knocks at the door during the week leading up to the election. However, in the 2000 general election, other well-meaning campaigns, specifically those working for candidates running for state and federal office, duplicated the efforts of hundreds of volunteers working on our campaign. Making matters worse, a local teacher, eager to involve students in the electoral process, conducted yet another GOTV effort. As a result, voters were called three or more times in a single evening. It was ugly.

This kind of voter harassment must be minimized if at all possible. To avoid it, conduct cooperative GOTV efforts with other campaigns, or at the very least, call and see what other campaigns intend to do. Call all campaigns that may inadvertently duplicate your efforts, and carve up the voting area so there is no overlap in calling or knocking. Contact high schools, and let leadership and government teachers know how, when, and where their students can help.

> "One thing the world needs is popular government at popular prices."
>
> **GEORGE BARKER**

Identifying Your Voters

Whether identifying voters by phone or by canvassing, you will need walking lists. Walking lists are used because your precinct analysis indicated communities, neighborhoods, and precincts where the base, swing, and opposition support lives; in other words, where attention should be focused, as a result of social context. These lists can be generated from the registered-voters disk you bought from the county, from a voter contact service, or from an organization that is endorsing your efforts.

Since you do not want to waste time on households where registered voters do not participate, prepare your lists so that only the two out of four voters—those who voted in two (or more) of the past four elections—or better are listed. These lists will need to be organized by precinct and then by street and house number.

The lists should be prepared so that streets are separated by page. Across the top of each page have columns labeled "Supporting," "Leaning support," "Undecided," "Leaning no support," and "Not supporting," or use a 1–5 number rating system that corresponds to the categories from "Supporting" to "Not supporting." Once you have the walking lists, you will ID voters by canvassing, phoning, or both. All of this is done more easily and without paper if your canvassers have smart phones. There are apps that allow the canvasser to access voter lists and maps that go with those lists. Then all data is transferred electronically at campaign headquarters.

Canvassing for Voter ID

If you intend to ID voters while canvassing, you need to include registered voters in your canvassing packets, outlined in Chapter 7. If you're using a voter activation service, linking registered voters with maps is part of the package and will save a great deal of time.

At the door, each of your canvassers must ascertain whether the house will be in favor, opposed, undecided, or leaning in some way. If voters are leaning toward support or undecided, your campaign should be ready to follow up with literature, a knock, or a phone call to bring them into your camp. If you're canvassing with a smart phone you can access campaign videos and candidate or issue ads from the website, plus other information that may be helpful to push the voter over to support. In one campaign I only needed to show a voter the endorsement list from the website with two of her friends to get both an endorsement and a vote. If no one is home, you must have cleanup teams going out to re-knock.

> "A citizen of America will cross the ocean to fight for democracy, but won't cross the street to vote in a national election."
>
> —————— BILL VAUGHAN

The idea here is to identify individual voters who support your candidate or cause and to compile a list of these supporters. In this way, your campaign can track them on Election Day and remind them to vote if it looks as if they might be a no-show.

Voter ID by Phone

Although it is easier to get volunteers to phone than canvass, contacting voters and identifying their intent by phone is really a thing of the past. Caller ID, cell phones, and voter resistance to reveal ballot intentions makes identifying supporters by phone challenging. Still, if voters recognize a friend or neighbor's name on the caller ID, the job becomes easier and still has some efficacy. To achieve this I generally ask volunteers to bring their cell phones and use them during the phone bank.

> "This 'telephone' has too many shortcomings to be seriously considered as a means of communication. The device is inherently of no value to us."
>
> INTERNAL MEMO,
> —————— WESTERN UNION, 1876

Also note that the closer a campaign is to Election Day, the less inclined a voter is to reveal intent. Therefore, a campaign must get to voters in a narrow period, when the voters have enough information to make a decision but are still willing to reveal intent.

Whether your voter ID is by phone or canvass, your goal should be to target 10 to 15 percent of the total number of votes you need to win. Always start with the precincts that will give you the most return for the effort. For voter ID, that means going into swing voter precincts to look for swing voters and calling your embedded party registration living behind enemy lines.

If you decide to identify all voters by phone and use canvassing only for activation and persuasion, you might as well prepare your calling lists in a format that will work best at the phone banks.

Pull precincts where you want to ID voters, and sort by last name alphabetically and by phone number. If you sort only alphabetically, you risk repeating calls to households where people have different last names. If you sort by name and phone number, you improve your chances of catching and organizing duplicates in a way to prevent repeat calls.

To identify your supporters, systematically call every registered voter in the identified precincts. Remember, you are first calling areas that have a high swing voter tendency, so you will be calling as many voters as you can reach. Often registration lists do not have all phone numbers listed, so plan ahead and get these from a voter activation network, the party, or a supporting political action committee. If none of these options are available to you, you may need to set up clerical teams to get phone numbers before your phone banks begin.

Last-Minute Efforts to Activate Voters

1. Mail or walk a door hanger to your high-priority precincts reminding them to vote.
2. To swing precincts, mail or walk a persuasion piece that features an individual or a group that normally would not support your cause or candidate (validators) to encourage voters to split their ballots. A comparison piece works well here.
3. Mail pieces designed to give the voters useful information such as polling places, how to mark a ballot for your write-in candidate, or whom to call if a ballot needs to be picked up or for a ride to the polls. These are very effective and often rise above other direct mail clogging mailboxes in the last week.
4. While mail is easier, showing that your campaign is rich with volunteers can be far more effective, especially given the huge amounts of political mail seen in the last days of a campaign. Any big canvassing effort is bound to draw positive attention.
5. Although volunteers and candidates should not stand on street corners and wave signs or banners, adding new lawn signs in key high-traffic

areas may signal to voters growing support as well as remind them of the upcoming election. People get desensitized to lawn signs, but if a new one goes up in a neighborhood or, better yet, ten new ones appear, voters will notice.

6. Attach helium-filled balloons to lawn signs located on busy streets.

7. Hand-paint specialty signs for a specific neighborhood, and place them the week leading up to the election. "Re-Elect Mayor Daniels for a central bike path." "For sidewalks on Oak Street, vote for Bobby." You want a personalized message for just that neighborhood that will present the look of an upwelling of new support. (I have used the reverse side of old lawn sign stock for this.)

8. Have the local paper place a three-by-five-inch Post-it note on the front page of the paper reminding people to vote for your candidate or cause. Use a yellow Post-it, red ink, and a style and size of font that looks like handwriting yet is very easy to read. Our local paper has done this from time to time for local businesses—usually for oil changes. The first time I saw one, I could not believe how it popped out at me as I unfolded the paper in the morning. So we did one for a GOTV on a double-majority issue-based campaign. Although the Post-it notes must be printed somewhere else, our local paper did the insert for $142 per thousand. It was very effective.

9. Some local papers that place the daily in a plastic bag will sell advertising space on the bags. Like the Post-it note inside the folded paper, this "message on a bag" goes to people who subscribe to and presumably read the newspaper—some of the more likely voters. Check with the newspaper to see whether it can use different messages for different cities or areas within your voting district.

Avoid Untargeted Activities

A GOTV effort is most effective in elections where low voter turnout is expected due to voter apathy. If you are not facing a double-majority election, apathy is your friend. Through the GOTV, you bring up the turnout of one segment of the population while leaving the support for the opposing camp alone. That means any activity targeting all voters, not just those supporting your candidate or issue, should be avoided, including standing at the entrance of the county fair, waving signs at commuters, wearing sandwich boards on a busy street corner, or handing out

> "To do great and important tasks, two things are necessary: a plan and not quite enough time."
>
> — **LEONARD BERNSTEIN**

flyers in front of a grocery store. Do not confuse motion with progress. Unless you live in Hawaii, where there is a time-honored tradition for candidates to wave to drivers from the edge of the highway on Election Day, avoid untargeted activities. With the exception of areas with overwhelming support, untargeted activities can actually work against your GOTV effort. Remember, GOTV is about getting *your* voters to the polls, not all voters.

Candidates who advocate doing an untargeted activity on or near Election Day should be redirected to a phone and instructed to call special volunteers and supporters to thank them for their time and money.

The GOTV: A Raft in a Storm

There comes a point in a campaign where you and your team have done everything you could possibly do. You have run a tight, well-organized campaign and raised enough money to get a clear, resonating message across to the voters. You may have been outspent by an opposition that had better television ads, brochures, press, and direct mail. But as the election draws near and you prepare for the GOTV, remember that both your campaign and your opponent's are headed into the same storm. If your efforts have placed you within striking distance, the GOTV is a great equalizer, often making the difference between a win and a loss. In the end, the odds are best for the team that is better prepared.

I have found that by the final three weeks of a campaign, most voters have made up their minds. While campaigns send copious amounts of direct mail, especially toward the end, if you have not made your case three weeks prior to Election Day, no amount of money or direct mail will change that. Don't misunderstand: There will still be voters struggling with the decision of whom to vote for, which is one reason a comparison piece is best left until last. But they are few

> "Let me tell you the secret that has led me to my goal. My strength lies solely in my tenacity."
> **LOUIS PASTEUR**

and far between. By the end of a campaign, the effort is really about who can rally the most troops out of the bunker, regardless of how many happen to be in there. Effective last-minute direct-mail pieces are more about relocking your base and rallying your troops to get out and vote than about moving voters from one bunker to another. Although there may be last-minute revelations that will swing campaigns twenty points, those are the exception, not the rule.

After the recall of Governor Gray Davis in California, voters were surveyed and asked (among other things) what impact the last-minute allegations of sexual harassment charges had on their support of Arnold Schwarzenegger. The surveys "showed that more than two-thirds of the voters had made up their minds more than a month before the election. As a result, the intense publicity in the last week of the campaign about accusations of Mr. Schwarzenegger's unwanted sexual advances appeared to have had little effect on how women—and others—voted."[1]

In the last month before the 2000 presidential election, polling numbers showed Al Gore and George W. Bush bouncing into and out of the lead. At the time, this was attributed to voter whim. However, after analyzing fifty-two polls conducted by seven polling firms, Donald Green and Alan Gerber found that the "preferences toward the candidates changed little" and that "the failure of certain polls to predict the closeness of the actual vote reflects sampling bias, not the electorate's capricious preferences."[2]

After the 2002 general election in Oregon, one political consultant attributed Democratic losses in house seats with close registration numbers to insufficient direct mail and a general unwillingness among Democrats to send hit pieces. But on closer examination of the eleven close house races, only four of the winning races sent more direct-mail pieces, and only five of the winning races sent more negative pieces than the opposition did.[3]

After the 2008 general election, Rasmussen Reports found that 70 percent of those polled said they made up their minds a month before Election Day, with an additional 14 percent deciding within the month leading up to Election Day. Of the 5 percent still undecided in the week prior to the vote, they were evenly divided between John McCain and Barack Obama.[4]

While each race has its unique signature requiring specific action, the overriding features of losing campaigns are that they (1) did not communicate a clear message and (2) did not give due attention to the GOTV among last-minute campaign demands.

From day one, all communication with the voter should be about getting your base to care enough to vote and to move swing and undecided voters to your camp. Keeping track of who moves (voter ID) and getting your base and persuaded voters to the polls (GOTV) is what wins elections, not mounds of direct mail.

As the final week before the election approaches, everything about the campaign should shift to the GOTV effort. That does not mean media, direct mail, social media communication, or solicitation stop, but everyone on the team must focus on filling the phone banks and lining up volunteers to knock on the doors of voters who will support your candidate or cause if engaged. Like fundraising, GOTV should have its own team leader and timeline. To run a successful GOTV, a campaign must accomplish a few tasks:

1. Have 10 to 15 percent of the registered voters identified, including, hopefully, most of those outside the party base in identified precincts of swing voters.
2. Have enough volunteers to phone or canvass apathetic or lazy voters in precincts with high support and low and medium turnout.
3. Have a well-organized data system, and have someone other than either the GOTV coordinator or the campaign manager supply the campaign with canvassing and calling lists generated from registration rolls. For absentee voters and vote-by-mail states, this person would also be responsible for getting daily updates from the clerk's office of inactive voters (those who have not yet returned a ballot) for the week leading up to the election. Typically county clerk offices keep track of ballots that have been received, or active voters.

> "I wanted to look nice if we won, and if we lost this would be nice to be buried in."
>
> **BOB BORKOWSKI**, assistant coach, on why he showed up for a game in a black pinstriped suit

To get a list of inactive voters, remove from voter registration lists those whose ballots have been received; the difference is the inactive voter. It is the same process for absentee—the county keeps track of the absentee-ballot return and your campaign keeps track of that list.

Once you have identified your supporters, your campaign must track them to see whether they've voted. Tracking for vote-by-mail elections, early voting, or absentees can be done electronically. However, if you are tracking voters at the polls, you have a couple of choices: One is poll watching, and the other is working your list by phone and asking voters whether they have cast a ballot.

Poll Watching

Poll watching is a labor-intensive campaign activity that requires plenty of preparation. It cannot be put together at the last minute, so prepare ahead of time. Find someone who will oversee this activity, and support that person with your volunteer base. Each poll watcher will need lists of people who have been identified as supporters sorted alphabetically and by polling station. Ideally you would use a list of all members of the candidate's party, with supporters highlighted, although a list that includes only your identified supporters is fine.

Things to Do for a Successful Poll Watching Effort

1. Before the election, ask your county clerk or election official what is required of poll watchers. Are there forms that must be filled out and returned? Does the clerk require training conducted by his or her staff? In my area, before the introduction of vote by mail, it was legal for poll watchers to review the poll book, as long as they didn't interfere with the work of the election board. In some areas, however, poll watchers can only listen for names as they are being called out.

2. Provide poll watchers with an alphabetical list, a clipboard, pencils with good erasers, and a cell phone. It is also a nice touch to send them out with a folding chair or stool. We used to provide each poll watcher with more than one list so that when volunteers come to retrieve the list to start contacting no-shows, time wasn't burned transferring names, but with the advent of cell phones, names can be called in. With smart phones, the poll watcher has the list on the screen and can note supporters when they arrive to vote.

> "It's not so important who starts the game, but who finishes it."
>
> **JOHN WOODEN,** former basketball coach at UCLA

3. Place your poll watchers in high-priority precincts (that is, where high numbers of your supporters have been identified), and direct them to note which of your identified supporters have voted throughout the day.

4. As the name of the voter is called out, the poll watcher will check the list of supporters to see whether that individual is among those who have been positively identified.

5. Relay this information back to phone banks or for door-knockers, and approximately four hours before the polls close, supporters who have not yet voted get a call or a knock on their door from a volunteer urging them to get down to the polls. In vote-by-mail states, volunteers can pick up the ballots and take them to an official drop box for the voter.

6. Regardless of what you think about the outcome of the election, impress upon the voters how important it is that they get to the polls, that you predict a very close election, and that every vote will count. The supporter who hasn't yet voted must feel a sense of urgency to get to the polls and vote.

7. Offer rides to get supporters to and from the polls. With the poll watcher, the phone bank, canvassers, and the transportation effort, you will have a lot of people involved, and you may find that the best hope for pulling it off is to combine efforts with other campaigns.

Precinct Captains

Each precinct where poll watching is to take place must have a precinct captain, who is responsible for the precinct team. Each captain has three specific duties:

1. Before Election Day, your identified voters must be highlighted or somehow noted on the lists as supporters. It is best to do this as IDs come in rather than waiting until the end. One thing that has helped speed up data input is that some counties and voter activation networks include bar codes for the voters. The campaign can take advantage of this by renting a bar code scanner, which usually runs around $125 for the entire campaign. As IDs roll in from phone banks and canvassing, your data-input team can simply scan bar codes to link the information into your database of voters.

2. The captain is responsible for recruiting four poll watchers and one standby. These five people need to be certified, trained, and supervised. Poll watchers should meet with their team captain the weekend before the election. Signed certificates for each poll watcher should be provided to the precinct captains at that time.

   > "The important thing in life is not the triumph but the struggle."
   > **PIERRE DE COUBERTIN**

   Your county clerk or county elections office will supply you with all the information and forms you may need.

3. The captain must be present at his or her precinct when it opens at 8 a.m. and supervise the precinct on and off throughout the day.

Poll Watcher Responsibilities

1. Arrive a few minutes early at the polling place.
2. Give your signed certificate to the election judge, who is a member of the polling board.
3. Do not engage in conversation with the election board. You may, of course, answer questions, but do not discuss other topics with the board.
4. As voters arrive and give their names to the board, listen for the name and then cross it out on your list as they are voting or track it on a hand-held device.
5. Two hours before polls close, the final poll watcher should start calling in names to the phone banks.

The Importance of Poll Watchers

In close elections, the work of the poll watchers and the subsequent effort to reach voters can make the difference between a win and a loss. However, because of the amount of organization required and the labor-intensive demands of this activity, few campaigns conduct poll watching anymore. If at all possible, do it.

Regulation of Persons at the Polls

As in all aspects of a campaign, it is important to know the law, but in poll watching, it is imperative. The polling place has special regulations that cover everything from how close individuals may stand to the polls if they are not voting and are not certified poll watchers, to what topics those present may discuss. The campaign should contact the county clerk well beforehand and get the regulatory information to the precinct captains in written form.

> "Democracy is a contact sport."
>
> **RAY MCNALLY** of McNally Temple Associates in Sacramento, California

Authorized poll watchers are allowed in the polling place and must sign a specific section of the front cover of the poll book. Only as many poll watchers are allowed as will not interfere with the work of the election board.

Poll watchers must have written authorization from one of the following:

1. For the purpose of challenging electors at the polling place, either from the county clerk or a political party
2. For the purpose of observing the receiving and counting of votes, from a candidate
3. Poll watchers *may*
   - Take notes
   - Have access to poll books, so long as it does not interfere with the work of the board
   - Challenge persons offering to vote at the poll
   - Challenge entries in the poll book
   - Wear campaign buttons
   - Distribute sample ballots as long as there is no campaigning involved (We did this in Ohio in 2008. As people stood in long lines, they were given sample ballots to familiarize themselves for what lay ahead.)

Poll watchers *may not*

- Campaign in any way
- Circulate any cards, handbills, questionnaires, or petitions
- Fail to follow the instructions of the election board
- Take poll books off tables

All members of the poll-watching effort should familiarize themselves with the specific election law violations.

Plan B

If you're unable to muster the necessary volunteers to conduct a poll watch, you have some options. If it is clear that a precinct has traditionally voted against campaigns such as the one you are working on, don't canvass it, don't call people in that precinct, don't activate them. Forget them for the GOTV effort. Instead, look for precincts that have been split: those that have narrowly supported or narrowly defeated past campaigns similar to yours. These

---

ELECTION DAY PHONE SCRIPT

Hello, this is _____ .

I am a volunteer worker for *(name of the campaign)*.

I am calling to remind you that the polls will remain open until 8 P.M., and also to encourage you to vote. This will be a very close election, and we really need your support for *(name of person or ballot measure)* to win.

Your polling place is located at _____ .

Will you need transportation to the polls?

> ### If transportation is needed, they can call the following numbers:
>
> _____
>
> _____
>
> _____
>
> _____

FIGURE 11.1 Election Day Phone Script

are the precincts in which you should call to ID voters for the GOTV, and on Election Day call only the identified yes voters, even though they may have already voted (figure 11.1).

As for those remaining precincts that have overwhelmingly supported past campaigns similar to yours, don't worry about identifying voter intent because they will tend to vote your way.

On Election Day, while your people are going down the list of supporters in the marginal precincts and calling the identified yes votes, call or canvass all of the voters in the high-priority precincts for an issue-based campaign, and for a candidate race, call or canvass all who are registered in your party; when a volunteer reaches someone who has already voted, cross the voter off the list so he or she will not be called or canvassed again. For those who have not voted, you urge them to get down to the polls.

> "An ounce of action is worth a ton of theory."
>
> ——— **FRIEDRICH ENGELS**

One important note: *Don't duplicate calling lists for phone banks.* Each phone bank caller or phone station needs a separate and unique calling list.

The Absentee Ballot and Early Vote

Voting absentee used to be a service to the voter who was temporarily out of the area or unable to get to the polls. However, many states now allow early voting, and most of those allow no-excuse absentee voting.

For instance, in Ohio 11 percent voted absentee in 2004, versus 17 percent in 2006. By 2008 the percentage of those voting by mail in Ohio nearly doubled again to 30 percent. In California 42 percent of the 13.7 million 2008 general election voters voted by mail; by 2012 this had increased to 52 percent.

Although early voting and absentee voting have become the vote of convenience, there are other factors behind the growing lines for early voting—not the least of which is that a voter, turned away at the polls, still has time to fix whatever problem precipitated the dismissal. In this way, voters are insuring themselves against the debacles that unfolded in battleground states in 2000, when so many voters were turned away at the polls for nefarious reasons.

> "If the only tool you have is a hammer, you tend to see every problem as a nail."
>
> ——— **ABRAHAM MASLOW**

Further, as ballots become longer and more complex, the busy and conscientious voter is choosing to vote absentee so as to have time to vote on the entire ballot in the comfort of his or her home. In a recent California election, it took some voters more than an hour to complete their twelve-card ballot.

With long, complicated ballots, you run the risk of *voter fatigue*. Voter fatigue occurs when voters actually lose interest in voting as they spend more and more time working through their ballot. Once fatigued, they simply turn in their ballot with everything below left blank. This is called *ballot roll-off*. While roll-off is technically an undervote, it happens to everyone and everything at the bottom of the ballot, whereas undervoting on a mail-in or an absentee ballot happens randomly throughout the ballot. Because local elections are at the end of ballots, down-ballot candidates and issues are affected by roll-off. If your candidate or measure is way down on a ballot, encouraging voters to register and vote absentee at home may help minimize the undervote for those races.

There are a number of reasons it is to your advantage to register as many of your supporters as possible to vote absentee or early:

1. Often campaigns don't heat up and get nasty until the final three weeks. As voters become more disillusioned with negative campaigning, their response is to stay home on Election Day rather than voting for or against the candidate slinging mud. If a candidate or party has a huge percentage of the turnout locked in before things get nasty, it's at a decided advantage.
2. If you know who will vote absentee, then your campaign can concentrate on these voters well before Election Day, closer to when they actually will vote.
3. Bad weather can affect voter turnout on Election Day.

Although Oregon has exclusively voted by mail for twenty years, in the last poll-voting election, nearly half of the registered voters requested absentee ballots with 73 percent of those actually voting. Of those who did not request absentee ballots, only 41 percent turned out to vote. The absentee ballot represented over 58 percent of the total voter turnout. Similarly in California, 82 percent of the vote-by-mail registrants turned out to vote in 2012 compared to 60 percent of those voting at the polls.

Although in the 1998 general election Oregon voters approved vote by mail for all elections, they could already register as permanent absentee voters in 1997. The lists of absentee voters were available from the county clerk for a small charge, and about 40 percent of the names also had phone numbers listed. Having lists of those who will

"Vote early and vote often."
AL CAPONE

make up nearly 60 percent of the overall voter turnout is very helpful and means that with a little effort, any campaign can reach a large group of likely votes, ID whom they intend to support in the election, send canvassers to their doors, and make sure that those supporting your efforts return their ballots by Election Day.

In many states the option to register absentee is open to anyone for the asking, up to the day before the election. Those who request absentee ballots within the three weeks before an election are the most likely to actually vote. Some states have a cutoff date for an absentee ballot request; however, for those that allow requests up to Election Day, your county elections office may be able to provide updated lists as requests come in. The campaign should immediately contact these voters as they're added to the list.

Some states have *early vote*. With early vote, the registered voter may go to a designated polling place between certain hours and vote just as though it were Election Day. Depending on the state, it can take place anywhere from four to forty days before an election. As with absentee voting, early vote gives a campaign an opportunity to lock in votes before the election. However, it does require that a campaign peak twice: once for the early vote and absentees and once for Election Day. Voters love the convenience of absentee and early vote, and those who use these options tend to be among the most likely of the likely voters. Whether your state or county has early vote or absentee voting, the following steps can help you reach as many of these voters as possible:

1. Check past elections to determine the number who requested or took advantage of this option. Most election data services, generally available through state parties, keep track of early voters as well as those who always vote on Election Day.
2. See whether a list of those who requested absentee ballots is available to your campaign through the county clerk or election office.
3. Inquire about updated lists of those who actually vote absentee or early as the election draws near. That way, you will not be continually contacting those who have already returned their ballots, burning up campaign money and time.
4. If the lists of absentee voters do not include phone numbers, get them, but remember the most effective way to activate voters is with a knock at the door.[5]
5. If you are in a state that offers early vote, hound your supporters to vote early.

"Poll Watching" for Absentee Ballot Requests

Absentee ballots present some unique challenges to the grassroots campaign. Here is an inexpensive way to deal with absentee ballots if lists are not available from the county elections official.

Assign the task of the absentee voters to an individual who is willing to go to the county clerk's office daily to find out who has requested absentee ballots. This person keeps a running list. The requests must be checked regularly because voters who request absentee ballots will often fill it out and return it very quickly. Once you know which voters

> "You may be disappointed if you fail but you are doomed if you don't try."
> **BEVERLY SILLS**

requested an absentee ballot, you must try to persuade them to vote for your candidate or cause. Forget the precinct analysis for absentee voters. For this group, you are not hoping that those who don't support you will not be voting. You know that nearly all of them will vote. To persuade these voters, you have a number of choices:

1. Use direct mail to persuade—this is most effective if it is a comparison piece rather than an advocacy piece or an attack piece, according to Kathleen Hall Jamieson, in *Everything You Think You Know About Politics . . . and Why You're Wrong* (Basic Books, 2000).
2. Send out volunteers or the candidate to canvass these voters at home.
3. Have the candidate, a friend, or a prominent citizen call; leaving a message is OK.
4. Send a personalized letter from the candidate or from a well-known, well-respected local leader of the same party affiliation as the voter.
5. Do all of the above.

Vote by Mail

A Brief History

The genesis of voting by mail dates back to the 1700s, when landowners, whose homes were vulnerable to attack from Native Americans, were allowed to vote absentee. In 1857 only Oregon made it possible for men away from home to vote. However, it was not until the Civil War that nineteen of the twenty-five Union states and seven of the eleven Confederate states enacted legislation to provide soldiers an opportunity to vote absentee.

> "A low voter turnout is an indication of fewer people going to the polls."
> **GEORGE W. BUSH**

After the Civil War, nearly all states discontinued military absentee voting.

During World War I, when 3 million Americans were inducted, there was renewed pressure to provide military personnel the opportunity to vote absentee. By 1917 most of the forty-eight states provided absentee voting for the military, and twenty-four states had enacted some form of absentee voting laws.

At the close of World War II, work-related reasons were accepted by over twenty states for absentee balloting. Today all states permit absentee voting, with eight states offering voters permanent absentee-ballot status out of the twenty-nine that allow no-excuse absentee balloting.

_____
"Trust in Allah, but tie your camel."

_____ ARAB PROVERB

With vote by mail, all registered voters receive ballots through the mail. Although VBM began as a western-state phenomenon, it is now conducted in some form in fifteen states, from New Jersey to Hawaii. In 1977 California was the first to hold a VBM election.

All states, except for Oregon and Washington state, provide hybrid voting, or poll voting in conjunction with absentee balloting.

Oregon

In 1981 the Oregon legislature approved a test of VBM for local elections. By 1987 VBM was made permanent for local and special elections, and a majority of counties used it. In 1993 and 1995 the first and second statewide special elections were conducted using VBM.

In the summer of 1995, the Republican-controlled legislature passed a bill expanding VBM to primary and general elections. Under pressure from both the Democratic legislator minority, who were concerned that VBM could reduce the power of the state Democratic machine, and Clinton operatives, who were concerned about the president's reelection bid in Oregon, Governor John Kitzhaber vetoed the bill, declaring that more study of the issue was the prudent course. This veto came despite calls from Democratic operatives who tracked local VBM elections and determined it was party-neutral, saved taxpayer dollars, and was easier for campaign organizations than hybrid voting. Both Republican and Democratic leaders believed that VBM would perform like absentee voting, which historically favored candidates who were more conservative.

In 1995, after the resignation of Senator Bob Packwood, Oregon's Democratic secretary of state, Phil Keisling, exercised the option to run the December primary and January general special elections using VBM. After Democrat Ron Wyden defeated Republican Gordon Smith, both caucuses in the legislature reconsidered their previous positions. In the 1997 legislative session Democrats, realizing their error, supported legislation to pass VBM. Although it passed the House, the Republican majority in the Senate allowed the bill to die. The option for statewide VBM never revisited the desk of Governor Kitzhaber, who said that he would have signed the bill into law, given the second chance. When legislation allowing voters to register for permanent absentee status passed, 41 percent took advantage of this option.

In the 1998 primary election, with a record-low turnout, absentee voters accounted for nearly two-thirds of all ballots cast. This election represented the first in the nation where absentee voters, with a 53 percent turnout, cast more ballots than poll voters, who turned out at 22 percent.

In June 1998, Secretary Keisling spearheaded an initiative drive to circumvent the Oregon legislature and, using no paid signature gatherers— only volunteers—successfully garnered the number of signatures required to qualify for the November ballot. Oregon voters approved the initiative to expand VBM to primary and general elections by nearly 70 percent.

Implications of VBM

VBM is credited with increasing voter turnout and saving taxpayer dollars. Indeed, the hybrid voting process (both poll voting and absentee balloting) requires election officials to run two elections: one for absentee voters and one for poll voters. According to the Oregon secretary of state's office, the cost savings of the 2000 VBM primary election over the 1998 primary precinct election was nearly $600,000: "In general, the cost of conducting all-mail elections is one-third to one-half of the amount required for polling place elections."[6]

Michael Hanmer and Michael Traugott conducted a survey of voters in Oregon before and after VBM. They found only modest changes in turnout and composition of the electorate after VBM.[7] Rather than mobilizing new voters, VBM ultimately affected those who generally voted but who might have difficulty participating in any given election. This finding is corroborated in a study by University of Oregon professor Priscilla Southwell, which found that a majority of respondents (two-thirds) indicated no change in their turnout. Of the one-third of the respondents who reported voting more often since the introduction of VBM, the increase came primarily from women, the disabled, homemakers, and twenty-six- to thirty-eight-year-olds.[8]

As with other studies, Hanmer and Traugott and Southwell indicated VBM is party-neutral. Further, the Hanmer and Traugott study showed an absence of ballot roll-off with VBM.

Arguments that VBM hurts the poor and minorities who cannot afford a stamp were dispelled by another Southwell survey after the special state-wide VBM election to replace Senator Packwood. Her study revealed that VBM increased participation of minorities, single parents, younger voters, those who had moved within two years, students, and those registered as nonaffiliated or independent. This same group was also less likely to be retired and more likely to be paid by the hour than traditional voters.[9]

Fraud

Much of the hesitancy to implement full-scale VBM in other states centers on existing voter fraud with absentee balloting. However, election officials consistently cite the difficulty in supervising hybrid elections, in which the volume of absentee-ballot requests and processing competes for time with managing poll sites and poll workers.

Project Vote, a national nonprofit organization focused on mobilizing marginalized and underrepresented voters, associates four forms of ballot fraud with absentee ballots: signature forging or using fictitious names, coercion, vote buying, and siphoning absentee ballots. Despite these problems, Oregon election officials who managed elections both before and after VBM underscore that managing only one type of election, vote by mail, allows closer scrutiny of the integrity of the ballot. Comparison of optically scanned signatures on the ballot and voter-registration form has all but eliminated voter fraud.

> "Voters want fraud they can believe in."
>
> ———— **WILL DURST**

After two decades of VBM, Oregon has had only four cases of fraud resulting in prosecution. One, discussed earlier in this book, occurred when a husband signed his wife's ballot because she was in the hospital.

Real voter fraud, the kind that can have tangible results, is far more effective when placed in the hands of those who know what they're doing; a husband signing a ballot for his hospitalized wife is not in this category. The 2000 general election in Florida, where impediments seemed to have been contrived to prevent voter participation, represents the kind of election that needs attention more than vote by mail.

> Black voters in Florida and around the country turned out in record numbers on November 7 [2000]. Since then, many have complained that Florida election officials removed large numbers of minorities from state voting rolls, wrongly classifying them as convicted felons—and accused Florida officials of using police to intimidate voters in some areas. [Jesse] Jackson cited the reports of students from historically black colleges in Florida, who have said they went to the polls carrying voter identification cards and were told they were not on the voter rolls.
>
> The Florida Supreme Court had ordered a hand recount of all ballots where mechanical counts had registered no vote for president. Many of

those "undervotes" came from majority-black precincts, heavily Democratic, where aging punch-card ballots failed to record votes for president in mechanical counts.[10]

One area of concern remains with VBM: the unregulated collection of ballots by volunteers or party operatives, who then deliver them to election departments for voters. Coincidentally, this was the same concern of Civil War soldiers when they relinquished their ballots to commanding officers, who became responsible for getting the ballots to the soldiers' hometown election authorities.

With little evidence of fraud, opponents now claim that VBM represents one more step in the progression of isolation in American society. Although this view is certainly understandable, and isolation is indeed cause for concern, a better solution might be to ban drive-up windows (as we did in Ashland for the same reason) than to sanction barriers that, once removed, facilitate voter participation. Indeed, establishing universal vote by mail in all fifty states may be the better solution for the Justice Department as opposed to new voter ID laws.

Campaigning with VBM

Campaign managers, party operatives, candidates, and strategists outside of VBM states insist that VBM increases the cost of running a campaign because ballots are mailed to voters about eighteen days before the election. During this period, ballots are returned by voters in two surges: the first week, followed by a lull, and then another surge just prior to Election Day. It is argued that both surges must be met with campaign activities.

The hybrid election, however, requires two separate campaign structures as well: one to communicate with and track absentee voters and another for poll voters. Whether or not a state allows no-fault absentee voting, absentee voters remain the most likely of likely voters; they tend to be Republican, women, and over sixty-five years old. Further, they represent a far greater percentage of the voter turnout. No campaign can afford to ignore them. Communicating with precinct voters requires media, mail, and phoning—paid or volunteer—up to and including Election Day. Tracking identified supporters who vote at the polls is also a massive organizational enterprise for a campaign.

> "Those who cast the votes decide nothing. Those who count the votes decide everything."
> **JOSEF STALIN**

Although VBM has shown only modest improvement in voter participation, there are other advantages. The level of voter enthusiasm, the dramatically reduced administrative costs over hybrid elections, elimination of waiting in line for hours to vote, and a more manageable campaign structure suggest that this simple, low-tech approach should be considered throughout the nation.

The difference between a mail-in and a hybrid campaign isn't money, but rather timing. In a conventional election, canvassing continues up until Election Day, and nearly all of your ads appear in the three weeks before the election. The all-mail-in election must be front-end loaded, so the campaign peaks when the ballots are mailed, not the day they are due back.

This means that all canvassing should be completed by the weekend after the Friday that ballots are mailed. Ads must start to run at least a week before the ballots are mailed, and television should peak the first week voters receive their ballot. Even though many voters will return their ballots immediately, your campaign should maintain a presence in the media until the day before the ballots are due, or until a critical mass of ballots have been returned. In VBM a campaign can actually taper off advertising as Election Day draws closer.

> "The people who win elections are those with the guts to keep on running when nobody else gives them a prayer."
>
> **CHRISTOPHER MATTHEWS,**
> *San Francisco Examiner*

GOTV and Vote by Mail

A GOTV effort for a VBM election is remarkably easy and painless. With VBM, counties and voter activation networks keep track of who has returned ballots as they're received, where they're usually available online. For a GOTV effort, you want to know who has not voted, so if you're only able to get the activity list, then delete those names from the full registration lists.

It's in the Mail

Successfully activating voters by phone has dramatically diminished over the past decade. In fact, I think the last election cycle where I felt it actually helped, even in some small way, was 2006 and the last election where it truly made a difference was in 2000. Still, old habits die hard.

In 2010 many local down-ballot campaigns in Oregon joined forces in the governor's GOTV effort that employed an auto-dialing system in which a computer searched targeted phone numbers of inactive voters from all over the state while volunteers waited at various phone banks. Once an inactive voter picked up the phone, the volunteer sprang into action. Because northern cities were rich with voters the governor's campaign was targeting, those calling from rural regions spent more time rattling the cage of Portland voters than those in their respective outlying areas. While it was helpful for the gubernatorial candidates, turnout numbers in rural areas around the state cratered. Worse yet, this system erased the one thing that down-ballot phone banks had going for them: neighbors calling neighbors. Indeed, the more personal the contact, the more effective a campaign will be on activating a voter.

With turnout of our base vote lagging the opposition by as much as 15 percent, I panicked and immediately gathered people to canvass inactive voters in high-priority precincts, which had dramatic results.

In 2012, with no statewide race competing for our volunteers, we went back to local phone banks with separate banks in separate cities. Still, we reached only 10 percent of those we called. Cell phones and caller ID certainly contribute to the difficulty in reaching voters, but an equally challenging issue is the accuracy of the phone numbers listed in the online voter data systems where better than a third are disconnected or wrong numbers.

Canvassing remains the best way to activate voters and will increase voter turnout by nearly 10 percent. Direct mail increases voter participation by less than a percent and phoning (unless the caller is somewhat familiar to the voter) even less.[11]

If you do not have locals calling locals, I would strongly urge you to drop the notion of activating voters by phone and use the system below to activate votes through canvassing. However, if you're running for office in a small city and have volunteers working phone banks who live and know people in town, here's what you need to know:

Call all voters within your party in targeted precincts and all voters that the campaign identified as supporting their candidate or issue campaign. If you're working on an issue-based campaign, you will call all voters. Each caller can contact fifty voters in a ninety-minute shift. Because you know how many callers you have for each night and how many inactive voters are in each precinct, it is not necessary to print all inactive voters in all precincts—you will need just enough of them to keep your banks busy each night. The next night, you can print out lists for new precincts with that day's active voters already removed. Remember, call only base and identified supporters.

> "The wise don't expect to find life worth living; they make it that way."
> **ANONYMOUS**

In an Oregon House race I worked on in 2000, forty volunteers called 2,000 registered voters each night for seven nights straight. Still, those 14,000 phone calls did not reflect even half of the 35,000 registered voters, and many voters were called two and three times. While a GOTV effort in a state without VBM will focus primarily on support that has been identified, VBM allows your campaign to begin its efforts in precincts where your party historically underperforms and to continue all the way to those precincts of high support and high turnout before going back in to work the high-support and low-to-medium-turnout precincts. By working through precincts, campaign work is really cut to an efficient level.

Organizing the GOTV Phone Banks

Make a spreadsheet listing all volunteers for the GOTV phone bank (figure 11.2). The first column contains their names, and the next, their phone numbers. Then have a smaller column with "CB?" (for "called back?") as the column header; later, a check mark is placed in this column on the printout after a volunteer has been called back and confirmed that he or she will be there for the next day's phone bank. Next are seven columns with dates, one for each night of phone banking. Each phone bank location will have its own spreadsheet, listing only the volunteers who will be calling from that location.

> "Americans know how to find the voting booth when something important is at stake."
>
> **N. DON WYCLIFF**, editorial-page editor, *Chicago Tribune*

Below the dates, list the starting times of the phone banks. For example, the first bank may run from 6:00 to 7:30 p.m., and the second from 7:30 to 9:00 p.m. Or with so many having unlimited minutes on their cell phones, running one big bank from 6:30 or 7:00 to 8:30 is a far better option. So assuming the campaign needs twenty phone bankers for each night of the GOTV and the phone bank location has only five lines, ask fifteen of your volunteers to bring their cell phones and run one ninety-minute shift.

The names on the spreadsheet are kept in alphabetical order. If your lists are short, this detail is less important, but in a phone bank with two shifts of ten for seven nights, the campaign will have 140 volunteers working the GOTV in one location alone. As volunteers let the campaign know whether they can do the early or late shift, the time slot is circled in red so that the lead

NAME	NAME (LAST)	Place lead names here for each night PHONE #	CB?	LEAD NAME Wed. 11/1		Thur. 11/2		Fri. 11/3		Sat. 11/4		Sun. 11/5		Mon. 11/6	
				6:00	7:30	6:00	7:30	6:00	7:30	6:00	7:30	6:00	7:30	6:00	7:30
				6:00	7:30	6:00	7:30	6:00	7:30	6:00	7:30	6:00	7:30	6:00	7:30
				6:00	7:30	6:00	7:30	6:00	7:30	6:00	7:30	6:00	7:30	6:00	7:30

FIGURE 11.2 Example of a GOTV Phone Bank Spreadsheet

or supervisor can easily see it. Each night of calling must have a lead person or a supervisor. The lead's duties are as follows:

1. Arrive a few minutes early and open the phone banks.
2. Have paper cups for water and red pens for marking precinct lists.
3. Bring enough phone bank instructions so that each caller in each shift will have a set.
4. Bring targeted precinct lists with inactive voters—this is provided by the campaign.
5. Have the master copy of all volunteers participating in the GOTV at that location. (I have a satchel with cups, pens, and the GOTV master calling list inside. I secure the precinct calling lists before the phone banks start and either deliver the lists to the leads or have the leads pick them up, at which time the satchel is passed off as well. In outlying phone banks, I have the GOTV coordinator organize everything except the voter lists to call. These are emailed to the coordinator early enough for him or her to print them before the phone banks start.)
6. Welcome the volunteers and give instructions (provided by the campaign).
7. Have callers begin, and then circulate among the callers and answer questions.
8. Fill water cups and distribute one to each volunteer, refilling if necessary.
9. Once questions subside, call *all* volunteers for the next evening's phone banks, using the master lists for the GOTV phone bank and checking off the callback column for each confirmation. Afterward, look over the callback column; any last-minute cancellations must be communicated to the campaign as soon as possible so the spot can be filled.
10. The next shift arrives fifteen minutes early for training. Begin anew, providing instructions to the next team.
11. At exactly 7:30, the next crew pulls the first shift off the phones and takes over at their desk, continuing to call down the sheets provided for the first shift.
12. Again, circulate, answer questions, pick up old water cups and distribute new ones, and be available for as long as necessary.
13. Once questions subside, get on the phone and make GOTV calls until 9 p.m., when the banks close.
14. Clean up all remnants of the work crews: cups, pens, lists, and so on. The pens and the master call list are returned to the satchel along with any unused cups.
15. Lock up and get the satchel to the next lead or back to campaign headquarters.

A couple of years back, I ran a GOTV effort for an issue-based campaign in which the system was set up as outlined above. On the third night of phone banks, my lead called and told me that three callers had not shown up for the first shift, and four for the second. As this had never happened before, I contacted the lead from the previous night's phone banks and found that she had become busy with personal business and never made the calls to remind the next evening's volunteers as instructed. It is important always to call your volunteers and remind them of the location and time; if a lead does not get to the job, he or she must let the campaign know so that someone else can do it in time to ensure a full contingent at the next day's phone banks.

Finally . . . When word gets out that you're running an organized, well-staffed GOTV, every campaign you can imagine will call requesting other names be added to the script. Do not do this. An effective GOTV mentions no more than two names. Remember: GOTV calls are about *activation*, not persuasion. Besides, anyone who thinks a voter can be moved from the dark side by simply mentioning a name on a GOTV call is clueless. It would be better to say no names than to slog through a long list of candidates.

"Out of the strain of the Doing / Into the peace of the Done."

—————— **JULIA LOUISE WOODRUFF**

As noted in the beginning of this chapter, everything done in a campaign is about the GOTV effort. Without your support showing up on Election Day, you will lose, no matter how organized the campaign, worthy the issue, or excellent the candidate. Too often campaigners kill themselves to get everything done and then in the final days run out of steam for the GOTV; reach down and find that last burst of energy to bring your efforts across the finish line, there will be time to rest after the votes are counted.

12

The Campaign Plan

IF YOU'RE RUNNING FOR ANY OFFICE WHERE YOU HOPE TO ATTRACT outside money from special interest groups or the lobby, they will first ask to see your campaign plan before investing in your candidacy. Campaign plans demonstrate organization and forethought, both necessary to pull off a win—especially in a close election—and offer comfort for big-money investors, the campaign team, and the candidate.

Basically a campaign plan lays out exactly what your team intends to accomplish daily from the first day of the race through the day after the election. For a partisan race with both a primary and a general election or one that requires a candidate to receive 50 percent of the votes cast in one election or face a runoff in the general, the campaign will need a plan for both the primary and the general.

Although the process may seem daunting, below you will find a very easy process to complete a campaign plan within a few hours.

Begin with a Flowchart

Although you will be guided through making a flowchart, and should familiarize yourself with the process, there are easy how-to programs for both Word and Excel available online. Just Google: "creating a flowchart."

Meanwhile, know that this process is the first step in creating a campaign plan.

To make a campaign flowchart, start by listing the tasks you need to complete before the election. These might include canvassing, brochure development, media, phone banks, fundraising, and lawn signs. Your choices, of course, are dictated by your resources and the type of campaign you are running. Obviously you will not place anything in the flowchart that you have no intention of doing. For instance, you may not be able to afford direct mail or you may have decided you do not want to do lawn signs or paid media.

> "Simply reacting to the present demand or scrambling because of tensions is the opposite of thoughtful planning. Planning emphasizes conscious, disciplined choice."
>
> VAUGHN KELLER

Once you have the list of campaign tasks, all you need to do is transfer them onto your campaign flowchart in the proper sequence. A mock-up of a campaign flowchart is included in this chapter (figure 12.1).

To construct your flowchart, you will need a long, unbroken wall and the following items:

- Five or more Post-it pads in assorted colors
- A long roll of paper; butcher paper works best
- At least six different-colored marking pens
- A yardstick
- Masking tape
- One or two key campaign people (no more) to help you think

If possible, pull in someone who has worked on other campaigns to help you. Although an experienced campaigner is an invaluable aid in building the flowchart, you can also use the table of contents of this book. That's what I do, and I've done dozens of flowcharts.

To begin your chart, unroll about ten feet of paper and tape it to a wall. On the bottom right-hand of the chart, place the date of the day after the election. On the bottom left-hand corner, place the date of the beginning of your campaign. It may be the date that you start your flowchart or the date of your first "formal" campaign activity, such as your announcement. Draw a single line along the bottom between the two dates (this is your x-axis). Divide the line into fairly equal monthly or weekly parts by drawing in all the dates between the day your campaign begins and the day it will end.

On the y-axis, there will be a list of all the things you intend to do in your campaign: lawn signs, brochure, canvassing, media, fundraising, and so on.

Using different-colored marking pens, draw a horizontal line straight across for each campaign activity the campaign intends to execute. So, for example, clerical may be blue; media, red; lawn signs, green; and so on. You

343

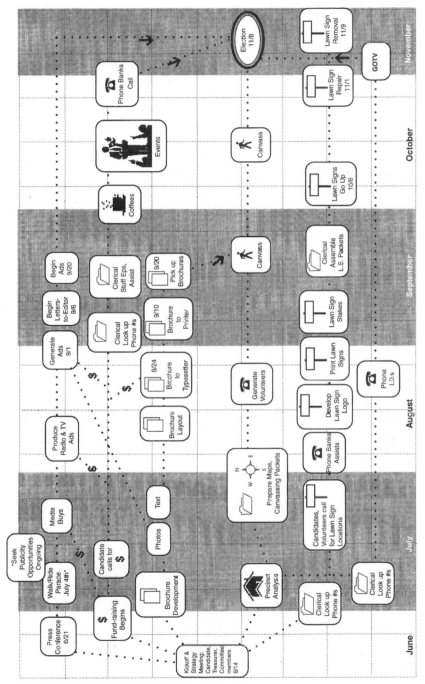

FIGURE 12.1 Example of a Campaign Flowchart

now have on your butcher paper a line across the bottom with dates on it, and parallel to this line are a series of different-colored lines that coordinate with a specific campaign activity listed on the y-axis.

Next, using a Post-it of a different color for each campaign function, begin brainstorming with your helpers. Slap up the appropriately colored Post-it on the corresponding line on the butcher paper. Place the note above the date you want to do that particular campaign function. For example, if lawn signs are represented by green Post-its, put a note that says "Take down lawn signs" on the day after the election, because you know that your crew will have to take down lawn signs on that day.

Work your way backward from the end of the campaign, making decisions as you go. Continuing with the lawn sign example, you know you will need to repair lawn signs the day after Halloween, so place a green Post-it reading "Repair lawn signs" above November 1. Lawn signs usually go up one month before the election, so put that up next: Above the date of October 8 will be a Post-it on your green horizontal line: "Lawn signs go up 10/8."

You'll need a work party to get the signs stapled if you're using poly tag; if you're using corrugated, you'll need a team that will actually attach the sign to the stake. This is a clerical function, so choose a different color Post-it for all clerical work. Write on the Post-it "Assemble lawn signs," and put it up somewhere in the week before the signs will go up.

Before you can attach lawn signs to stakes, you need to buy stakes, so that goes up on a note the week before you assemble your signs. You may also want a Post-it to remind you to secure hardware for corrugated signs (screws, washers, and people who have electric screwdrivers the campaign can borrow for a couple hours), staple guns and staples if you're using poly tag signs, or wickets for plastic sleeve signs.

You also need to get them printed, which takes about ten days, so on a line two weeks before the date your team comes to assemble signs, place a Post-it that says: "Lawn sign design goes to printer."

But before the design can go to the printer, your graphic designer must create the lawn sign. So give him or her a week to get that done. Place another Post-it note saying "Develop lawn sign design" above that date.

Also, before you can put up lawn signs, you need locations. Finding locations is a phone bank activity, so you place a phone-bank-colored Post-it that says "Call for lawn sign locations" on your phone bank line. This may take two weeks, so you are showing this activity on your phone bank line with an arrow to your lawn sign line.

But before your volunteers can call, you need lists of people they can call. So you make a Post-it that says "Secure lists for calling for lawn signs." Also, before you can call, you need to secure a location for the phone banks. That goes on a Post-it that is placed on a line representing the week before the phone bank team begins to call.

Keep working your way back, thinking through each of the campaign activities you have on your list. Review the chapters and headings in this manual. Think in terms of the progression of an activity and all the subactivities needed to support it.

Spread Out the Activities

With this method, time periods with too much campaign activity become immediately apparent. For example, if you find by the concentration of multicolored Post-its that brochure development, two direct-mail pieces, and a phone bank for an event are all happening at the same time, you may consider moving something to another time slot. Brochure development could move up and be done sooner, and the direct-mail pieces may be handled (just this once) by a mailing house, or they may be prepared earlier or later. Your Post-its are mobile for a reason, and you want to take advantage of that during this campaign planning activity. Spread out the activities so that you and the volunteers do not get overworked or burned out. If nothing can move, you will know to line up extra help to organize the work.

By using colored Post-its for every function on the chart, you build a visual representation of the campaign. The process is simple: Just take whatever it is you want to do, give it a color, and work your way back from the date you want to see that function completed to the point where that task must start to be completed on time. Some of the functions will end when others begin. For example, your brochure must be ready in time for canvassing. If canvassing will take you two months, working

"A perfection of means and a confusion of aims seem to be our main problem."
ALBERT EINSTEIN

each day after work plus weekends, then your brochure must be back from the printer by this time. Therefore, the Post-its for "Brochure development" and "Printing" will end on the flowchart before canvassing activities start. Although not all activities are listed in figure 12.1, add or subtract what you intend to do.

Here is a partial list of activities that should be represented on your flowchart:

- Ads—print, radio, and television
- Lawn signs, field signs
- Web page design and social media upkeep
- Coffees, fundraisers, special events
- Letters to the editor

- Direct mail
- Brochure development
- Canvassing and precinct analysis
- Phone banks

Convert the Flowchart to a Campaign Plan

If you're working on a small down-ballot campaign, you may prefer to keep your campaign organized using a permanent flowchart. Since Post-its tend to fall off after a couple days, tape them in place or create a hard copy of your working flowchart. Another option is to convert it to a campaign calendar (figure 12.2) or campaign plan.

The Campaign Calendar

Another option is to transfer the dates and activities of your flowchart to a calendar (figure 12.2). This tool works best for a short campaign with limited activities and can be regularly updated and emailed to your committee or hidden on your Web page for committee members.

> "Time is nature's way of keeping everything from happening at once."
>
> — WOODY ALLEN

Although you can keep a wall-size calendar at campaign headquarters, I generally set one up on Excel with each tab at the bottom of the Excel file marked with the month. So if you're doing a primary election in May, you will have a tab for February, another for March, and one for May within the file. In general, I assign one person to do all scheduling; this is the same person who maintains and emails the calendar to committee members.

The Campaign Plan

Campaign plans used to be stored in three-ring binders with the campaign manager at campaign headquarters. Now we keep them online where the team can see what is to happen on any given day. To create your plan, simply transfer everything from your flowchart to a Word document or calendar with a date at the top of each page and the number of days left till the election. List each activity or job that must be completed on that day.

A campaign plan will organize a team so that each of the necessary tasks may be implemented in an orderly and stress-free manner. Done well and followed religiously, a campaign plan will reduce stress and lighten the load for all involved.

Sunday	Monday	Tuesday	Wednesday	Thursday	Friday	Saturday
15	16 Committee working on Brochure wording → Lawn Sign to Graphic Designer	17	18	19	20 → Lawn Sign to Printer	21
22 8PM Campaign Team Meets	23 Brochure copy to Graphic Designer Call for Volunteers to put up Lawn Signs	24	25 Review Brochure with Committee	26	27 Pick-up Brochure from Graphic Designer	28
29 8PM Campaign Team	30 Brochure to Printer	1 11AM Ground breaking for Senior Center 4PM Opponent on Ken Linbloom Show KCMX Call for $	2 10AM Temple Emek Shalom Ribbon Cutting Golden Class: Meet the Candidates Candidate call for $	3 Pick-up Lawn Signs fromPrinter Organize Lawn Sign Cards	4 Clerical Party to Staple Lawn Signs - Bundle Stakes	5 8-10AM Lawn Signs Go up 12 - firefighters 2 - Carole, Ken 2 - Bill Street Canvass?
6 Canvass 8PM Campaign Team Meets	7 Candidate Calls for $	8 5:30-7PM Chamber of Commerce - Meet the Candidates, AHI	9 12 noon LWV Lunch at the Mark 5-6 Canvass $ Calls	10 Canvass Ashland Mine 6:30-10PM Kathleen Brown Dinner SOWAK, Red Lion	11 12 Noon Welcome Leadership Conference 4-6 Canvass	12 10AM Canvass 3-6PM Make informercial SOU for Cable Access $ Calls
13 Canvass 12-3 3-5 Canvass 8PM Campaign	14 5-6 Canvass $ Calls	15 7AM Lithia Springs Rotary Debate 5 min. + Q&A $ Calls	16 4 PM Office Hours 5-6 Canvass $ Calls	17 10AM Meet the Candidates 1023 Morton St. DEBATE - AAUW/LWV	18 Letter-to-Voters Ad to Graphic Designer 4-6 Canvass Kennedy Roosevelt Dinner	19 10-1 Canvass 4-6 Ribbon Cutting of Environmental Center Design and Write Experience Ad
20 10AM Crop Walk 12-3 Canvass 3-5 Canvass 8PM Campaign	21 Experience Ad to Grahic Designer Camera-ready Letter-to-Voters Ad to paper 4PM Ken Linbloom Radio Show	22 7PM Cable Access Debate	23 5-6 Canvass	24 Camera-ready Experience Ad to paper Run Letter-to-Voters Ad Noon Rotary Debate	25 Run Letter-to-Voters Ad again 4-6 Canvass	26 Bob Miller 2-1001 Welcome Lions Club AHI 10-1 Canvass 3-5:30 Canvass Letter-to-Voters Ad again Call for EndorsementAd
27 12-3 Canvass 3-5 Canvass 8PM Campaign Meeting	28 Run Experience Ad Layout Endorsement Ad Canvass	29 Run Experience Ad Camera-ready Endorsement Ad to paper Canvass	30	31 Run Experience Ad	1 Run Endorsement Ad Lawn Sign Team Clean-up 4-6 Canvass	2 Run Endorsement Ad Canvass 10-1 3-5:30 Canvass
3 12-3 Canvass 3-5 Canvass 8PM Campaign Meeting	4 Run Endorsement Ad	5 - ELECTION DAY -	6 Lawn Signs come down			

FIGURE 12.2 Example of a Campaign Calendar for a Nonpartisan General Election

13

After the Ball

WIN OR LOSE, THERE ARE MANY THINGS YOU MUST DO TO PUT YOUR campaign to bed. However, before taking down your lawn signs, bundling your stakes, paying your bills, finishing reports for the state, closing out bank accounts, and reassembling your house, you must first face election night.

Election Night

On election night, if you are not in a well-known location with other candidates and their volunteer teams, you should let the press know where they can find you. I have held campaign parties in restaurants and at my home. I prefer the latter. In the last days of the campaign, I let my volunteers know that I will be home and throwing a party in honor of them and a great campaign. I live in a small town, so people call and stop by all evening. It is difficult to stay home and watch returns alone if you have been involved in a campaign, especially a winning one. Most people drop by to share the excitement, even if it is just for a few minutes. My home is open.

If your campaign covered an area larger than one city, you need to go to a more central and public location. Again, tell all your volunteers where you will be, and invite them. Spend election day or even the weekend before the election calling and personally thanking volunteers; this is also a good time to remind them of the election-night gathering. Don't wait to thank them until after the election. If you lose, volunteers are anxious to talk and reflect and comfort, and you are anxious to sit alone on the floor of a dark closet with the door closed.

There is no preparing for a loss, and I'm not sure people *ever* get over it. It will change your life, just as winning will. But win or lose, you must be prepared to face the media and do it with class.

In one election on which I worked, I sat with the candidate as the first big returns came in. The shock that went through us as we realized we were losing is indescribable. I remember cameras pointing at our faces. There is something predatory and morose about our society when it comes to watching a leader fall. We had expected a win and were not prepared for what was before us.

The next day, our pictures were in the paper. I looked for shock, disbelief, upset, disappointment. None of it was there. We just sat, stunned, looking at the huge TV screen in the restaurant. In the story that followed, the candidate thanked his volunteers, his campaign team, and his supporters. He thanked everyone for a chance to serve. The end.

Win or lose, that is the speech.

In my second bid for mayor, we won handily, by nearly two to one. On election night, my house was full of friends and volunteers. Well-wishers phoned. Everyone brought something to eat or drink. Then a reporter called and said that one of my opponents was convinced that he had lost because of a damaging letter to the editor that had accused him of criminal wrongdoing twenty

> "When the fall is all there is, it matters."
> **PRINCE RICHARD,** *Lion in Winter* ____

years ago. The reporter said my opponent had suggested that I was responsible for the letter. Although I had nothing to do with the letter and the accusation was without merit, it made me feel as though the campaign wasn't over.

Have you ever watched a game where the coach for the losing team says basically it's no wonder we lost—we made mistakes or didn't play our best—instead of saying our opponents played a great game? While it may make that person feel better, it makes the losers feel guilty and the winning team feel slighted.

I recently had a candidate who believed he would win—100 percent—frankly, we all did. He had everything going for him and was running against a complete idiot. When he lost, he went into hiding and his campaign manager evaporated. The campaign did nothing to retire their debt. In fact, they did the opposite; for example, campaign phones were not canceled

> "Always let losers have their words."
> **FRANCIS BACON** ____

and bills continued to roll in. While it is completely understandable, when a candidate and manager do not follow through on the day-to-day business necessary to exit the stage, it creates validation for those who undervoted or jumped ship and voted for the opposing team. Always take care of your business, always exit with class, and be graceful.

If you lost, say you put together a great effort but that your opponent put together a better one. Give your opponent a little of the limelight if you won and a lot of the limelight if you lost. Don't blame your loss on an insufficient campaign effort. That translates to "My volunteers are responsible for my loss." The most common feeling among volunteers of a losing campaign is, "What a waste of time that was." Say that you had a great campaign team that put in countless hours and that the whole thing was a ball—challenging, instructive, and fun from beginning to end. Take heart in the fact that you have come to know yourself and the democratic process better.

Should you ever run for office again, you will be glad you acted magnanimously.

Retiring a Campaign Debt

I counsel all candidates to spend within their means. Lending money to your own campaign sends the wrong message to the voting public. A campaign that is chronically short of funds is a sure sign of one that is in trouble. Nevertheless, it happens, and when it does, it is up to you, the candidate, with the help of the campaign team and manager, to retire the debt.

Never walk away from debt with businesses that have provided services to your campaign. Graphic designers, print shops, photographers, and even your strategist and campaign manager are trying to make a living, and generally are well-connected with the community in which you live and hope to serve. In politics, nothing is more important than your reputation. But short of taking a second mortgage out on your home, there are a few things you can do to ease your debt. Win or lose, it is tough to retire a campaign debt. However, if you win, you tend to have more options.

> "The two happiest days of my life were the day we moved into the White House and the day we moved out."
>
> **BETTY FORD**

If you ran and won for the state assembly, go through the contributions and expenditures form for all those who gave to your opponent, but not to your campaign. Contact those representing "moderate" interests, and ask them to match the contribution given to your opponent. It should be obvious which among them will double dip, and it should be obvious which ones you do not want listed on your finance form.

Win or lose, you should be able to go to your most faithful donors for help. The simplest and most cost-effective way is to review all individuals who contributed previously and email those you know personally, whether you're the candidate, the campaign manager, or part of the team. Explain that the campaign has a small debt to retire and ask the previous donors whether they are willing to help. Do not send to the contributors as a group but rather individually—it must be a personal ask. Besides being efficient, emailing contributors for an additional contribution adds no further drain to the finances.

As you exit or enter the stage, be graceful and appreciative; thank your family, volunteers, supporters, and the community. If you win, you must be humble, acknowledge the efforts of your opponent, and immediately begin mending fences that might have been broken during the process. If you lose, there is one more call you must make, and that is to your opponent. Congratulate that person, and say you are on board to help make his or her time in office as successful as possible.

> "In everything one must consider the end."
>
> **THE FABLES OF LA FONTAINE**

Afterword

You are now prepared to begin on that time-honored path of a political campaign. Campaigns are enormously fun and exhilarating. If you do everything right, you greatly improve your chances of winning. Just a few reminders before you begin:

1. Know the law.
2. Stay on your campaign theme and message, and you will be in control.
3. Deliver that message to your targeted voters: Aim at the souls that can be saved.
4. Redirect negative campaigning at your opponents, and use it as an opportunity to restate your message.
5. Work hard, and others will work hard for you.
6. Be humble, and listen more than you speak.
7. Know who you are before others find out.
8. Smile. Always look as though you're having a great time.

Win or lose, you will emerge from the process a different person, a leader within your community.

> "Once the game is over, the king and the pawn go back into the same box."
>
> _____ ITALIAN SAYING

Notes

Chapter One

1. Bill Bishop, "You Can't Compete with Voters' Feet," *Washington Post*, May 15, 2005, B2.

2. Alex Lundry, "Microtargeting: Knowing the Voter Intimately," *Winning Campaigns Magazine* 4, no. 1.

3. Rhodes Cook, "Moving On, More Voters Are Steering Away from Party Labels," *Washington Post*, June 27, 2004, B1.

Chapter Three

1. Karl G. Feld, "What Are Push Polls, Anyway?" *Campaigns & Elections,* May 2000, 63.

2. Sam Stein, "Nasty Anti-Obama Push Poll Launched in Ohio," *Huffington Post*, September 11, 2008, available at www.huffingtonpost.com/2008/09/11/nasty-anti-obama -push-pol_n_125607.html.

3. For a general description of the Bradley effect, see "Bradley effect," *Wikipedia*, http://en.wikipedia.org/wiki/Bradley_effect; for the Confederate flag issue, see Sean Wilentz, "How the Confederate Flag Flap Helped the GOP," *Salon,* November 12, 2002, available at http://dir.salon.com/story/politics/feature/2002/11/12/confederate _flag/index.html.

4. John Ritter, "City Council Pays for Lessons in Civility," *USA Today*, October 4, 2007, available at www.usatoday.com/news/nation/2007–10–04-citycouncil-help_N .htm.

Chapter Four

1. See http://blogs.wsj.com/tech-europe/2011/12/22/social-networks-account-for -20-of-time-spent-online/?mod=google_news_blog.

2. See http://blog.bufferapp.com/social-media-stats-studies.

3. Available online at www.pewinternet.org/Reports/2013/Social-media-users.asp.

4. See http://edisonresearch.com/home/archives/2011/03/twitter_awareness_nearly _universal__usage_growth_slows.php.

5. See http://marketingland.com/election-2012-breaks-records-with-31–7-million-political-tweets-26086.

6. See http://marketingland.com/election-2012-breaks-records-with-31–7-million-political-tweets-26086.

7. "The Demographics of Social Media Users—2012," Pew Research Center, February 14, 2013.

8. See http://jeffbullas.com/2012/07/24/72-fascinating-social-media-marketing-facts-and-statistics-for-2012/#lvImQGbW4o6GR2Js.99.

9. See www.theguardian.com/commentisfree/2012/oct/16/twitter-winning-2012-us-election

10. John H. Parmelee and Shannon L. Bichard, *Politics and the Twitter Revolution: How Tweets Influence the Relationship Between Political Leaders and the Public* (Lanham, MD: Lexington Books, 2012).

11. Ibid.

12. Katie Thompson, *All Politics Is Social,* available at http://texasgrizzlette.com/social-media-guide.

13. See http://blog.bitly.com/post/9887686919/you-just-shared-a-link-how-long-will-people-pay.

14. See www.clickz.com/clickz/column/2154074/120-billion-facebook-impressions-tell.

15. See http://pewinternet.org/Commentary/2012/March/Pew-Internet-Social-Networking-full-detail.aspx.

16. "Rethinking Your Digital Spend," *Campaigns & Elections,* July/August 2012, p. 46.

17. See http://blog.bufferapp.com/social-media-stats-studies.

18. See www.clickz.com/clickz/column/2154074/120-billion-facebook-impressions-tell.

19. See www.nytimes.com/2013/08/09/science/internet-study-finds-the-persuasive-power-of-like.html?_r=0.

20. See www.convinceandconvert.com/social-media-research-2/b2c-facebook-results-are-30-above-average-on-sundays.

21. See http://blog.bitly.com/post/9887686919/you-just-shared-a-link-how-long-will-people-pay.

22. See www.newmediacampaigns.com/blog/10-common-mistakes-political-campaigns-make-with-facebook-pages.

23. Colin Delany, TechTrends2012.

24. See www.theatlanticwire.com/politics/2012/11/campaign-reveals-which-obama-spam-guilt-tripped-most-people-donating/59442.

25. Taryn Rosenkranz, "The New Normal Is Digital," *Campaigns & Elections,* November/December 2012.

26. See http://blog.kissmetrics.com/email-marketing-lessons-obama.

27. See www.theblaze.com/stories/2012/10/03/very-creepy-details-of-obama-campaigns-voter-data-mining-effort.

28. Dave Nyczepir, "The Challenge of Analytics," *Campaigns & Elections,* November/December 2012, pp. 33–34.

29. See www.comscore.com/Insights/Presentations_and_Whitepapers/2012/Changing_How_the_World_Sees_Digital_Advertising.

30. See www.theatlantic.com/technology/archive/2012/05/people-click-on-about-one-of-every-2–000-facebook-ads-they-see/257229.

31. "The Next Step in Social Media Monitoring," www.campaignsandelections.com/magazine/us-edition/359207/the-next-step-in-social-media-monitoring.thtml.

32. "Software Will Revolutionize Local Politics," *Campaigns & Elections,* September/October 2012, pp. 50–51.

33. See http://pewinternet.org/Commentary/2012/February/Pew-Internet-Mobile.aspx.

34. Justin Quittschreiber, "What's Next for Mobile," *Campaigns & Elections,* August 15, 2011.

35. "What's New in 2012?" *Campaigns & Elections,* July/August 2012, p. 15.

Chapter Five

1. Center for Responsive Politics, "Money Is the Victor in 2002 Midterm Elections," news advisory, November 7, 2002, www.opensecrets.org.

2. Center for Responsive Politics, "Big Picture: Winning vs. Spending," OpenSecrets.orgWebchart,www.opensecrets.org/bigpicture/bigspenders.php?cycle=2006&Display=A&Sort=D&Memb=H.

3. Center for Responsive Politics, "Blue Team Aided by Small Donors, Big Bundlers; Huge Outside Spending Still Comes Up Short," November 7, 2012, www.opensecrets.org.

4. Blue State Digital, "Case Study: MyBarackObama.com," Blue State Digital website, www.bluestatedigital.com/casestudies/client/obama_for_america_2008.

5. Center for Responsive Politics website, www.opensecrets.org.

6. David Erickson, "Barack Obama's Online Fundraising Machine," January 1, 2009, http://e-strategyblog.com/2009/01/barack-obamas-online-fundraising-machine.

7. Paul Pelletier, "Fundraising Direct Mail: A Success Story," *Campaigns & Elections,* April 1, 2000, 54.

Chapter Seven

1. Alan Gerber, Donald Green, and Ron Shachar, "Voting May Be Habit-Forming," *American Journal of Political Science* 47 (2003): 540–550.

2. Wendy K. Tam Cho, James G. Gimpel, and Joshua J. Dyck, "Residential Concentration, Political Socialization and Voter Turnout," *Journal of Politics* 68 (2006): 156–167.

3. Thomas S. Dee, "Are There Civic Returns to Education?" *Journal of Public Economics* 88 (2004): 1697–1720.

4. Center for Information on Civic Learning and Engagement, Tufts University, www.civicyouth.org.

5. Oregon Secretary of State, www.sos.state.or.us.

6. Mark DiCamillo and Mervin Field, "California's Turnout Increase Coincides with Growing Popularity of Mail Ballot Voting and Permanent Mail Ballot Registration," January 2009, Field Research Corporation, http://field.com/fieldpollonline /subscribers/Rls2296.pdf.

7. US Census Bureau, "Table 400: Voting-Age Population, Percent Reporting Registered, and Voted: 1994 to 2006."

8. Scott Keeter, Juliana Horowitz, and Alec Tyson, "Gen Dems: The Party's Advantage Among Young Voters Widens," Pew Research Center for the People & the Press, April 28, 2008, available at http://pewresearch.org/pubs/813/gen-dems.

9. Scott Keeter, Juliana Horowitz, and Alec Tyson, "Young Voters in the 2008 Election," Pew Research Center Publications, November 12, 2008, available at http:// pewresearch.org/pubs/1031/young-voters-in-the-2008-election.

10. Alan S. Gerber and Donald P. Green, "The Effects of Canvassing, Telephone Calls, and Direct Mail on Voter Turnout: A Field Experiment," *American Political Science Review* 94, no. 3 (September 2000): 653–663.

11. Joe Green, "Software Will Revolutionize Local Politics," *Campaigns & Elections,* September/October 2012, 51.

12. Donald P. Green and Alan S. Gerber, "Getting Out the Youth Vote: Results from Randomized Field Experiments," unpublished report, Yale University, New Haven, Conn., December 29, 2001, available at www.yale.edu/isps/publications/Youthvote .pdf.

13. George Washington University Graduate School of Political Management, *Young Voter Mobilization Tactics* (Washington, DC: George Washington University, 2006), available at www.civicyouth.org/PopUps/Young_Voters_Guide.pdf; and Center for Information and Research on Civic Learning and Engagement (CIRCLE), Tufts University, www.civicyouth.org.

14. Green and Gerber, "Getting Out the Youth Vote," 19.

15. Ibid.

16. Public Opinion Strategies, "Understanding the Election: National Post Election Survey," November 2006, www.scribd.com/doc/7062016/November-2006-Poll.

17. Ronald Brownstein, "The Hidden History of the American Electorate," *National Journal Magazine,* October 18, 2008, www.nationaljournal.com/njmagazine/ cs_20081018_7864.php.

18. "Assignment Desk: Black Turnout and Prop 8," *Stochastic Democracy* blog, November 23, 2008, http://stochasticdemocracy.blogspot.com.

19. Cho, Gimpel, and Dyck, "Residential Concentration."

20. Lake Research Partners, "How to Reach Unmarried Women: Edition II," memo by Lake Research Partners and sponsored by Women's Voices, Women Vote, available at www.wvwv.org/assets/2008/10/23/How_to_Reach_Unmarried_Women_2.pdf; Brownstein, "The Hidden History of the American Electorate."

21. Greenberg Quinlan Rosner Research, "Unmarried Women Play Critical Role in Historic Election," Women's Voices, Women Vote, www.wvwv.org.

22. Voter Participation Center, "Women's Voices; Women Vote," www.wvwv.org.

23. Rose M. Kreider, "Marital Status in the 2004 American Community Survey," December 2006, Working Paper No. 83, US Census Bureau, Population Division, Washington, DC.

24. Women's Voices, Women Vote, Current Population Survey, 2006, www.wvwv.org.

25. Rose M. Kreider, *Living Arrangements of Children: 2004,* Current Population Reports, P70–114 (Washington, DC: US Census Bureau, 2007); and Rose M. Kreider and Jason Fields, *Living Arrangements of Children: 2001,* Current Population Reports, P70–104 (Washington, DC: US Census Bureau, 2005).

26. Jessica Arons and Alexandra Cawthorne, "Fair Pay Is a Better Way," Center for American Progress, April 25, 2008, www.americanprogress.org/issues/2008/04/why_would.html; Page Gardner, "The Impact of a Declining Economy on Unmarried Women," April 6, 2009, Women's Voices, Women Vote, www.wvwv.org/research-items/the-impact-of-a-declining-economy-on-unmarried women.

27. Women's Voices; Women Vote, www.wvwv.org; Priscilla L. Southwell and Justin Burchett, "Survey of Vote-by-Mail Senate Election in the State of Oregon," *PS: Political Science and Politics* 91 (1997): 53–57; Priscilla L. Southwell and Justin Burchett, "The Effect of All-Mail Elections on Voter Turnout," *American Politics Quarterly* 29 (2000): 72–80; Priscilla L. Southwell, "Five Years Later: A Re-assessment of Oregon's Vote by Mail Electoral Process," *PS: Political Science and Politics* (January 2004): 89–93; Adam J. Berinsky, Nancy Burns, and Michael W. Traugott, "Who Votes by Mail? A Dynamic Model of the Individual-Level Consequences of Voting-by-Mail," *Public Opinion Quarterly* 65 (2001): 178–197.

28. Jim Gimpel, "Computer Technology and Getting Out the Vote: New Targeting Tools," *Campaigns & Elections,* August 2003, 40.

29. Gerber and Green, "The Effects of Canvassing, Telephone Calls, and Direct Mail on Voter Turnout."

30. Kathleen Hall Jamieson, *Everything You Think You Know About Politics, and Why You're Wrong* (New York: Basic Books, 2000), 107–110.

31. Dan Romer, Kathleen Hall Jamieson, and Joseph Cappella, "Does Political Advertising Affect Turnout?" in *Everything You Think You Know About Politics, and Why You're Wrong,* by Kathleen Hall Jamieson (New York: Basic Books, 2000), 111–120.

32. Crounse & Malchow Inc., "We've Got Mail! Use of Direct Mail in Political Campaigns," *Campaigns & Elections,* June 1999, 25.

Chapter Eight

1. The Pew Center for the People & the Press, "Key News Audiences Now Blend Online and Traditional Sources," survey report, August 17, 2008, available at http://people-press.org/report/444/news-media.

2. Pew Center for the People & Press, "In Changing News Landscape, Even Television Is Vulnerable: Trends in News Consumption: 1991–2012," September 27, 2012, www.people-press.org.

3. Pew Center for the People & the Press, "Internet Overtakes Newspapers as News Outlet," December 2008, www.people-press.org/2008/12/23/internet-overtakes -newspapers-as-news-outlet.

4. L. Marvin Olverby and Jay Barth, "Radio Advertising in American Political Campaigns; The Persistence, Importance, and Effects of Narrowcasting," *American Politics Research* 34, no. 4 (July 2006): 451–478.

5. Ibid.

6. Ibid.

7. Ibid.

8. Ibid.

9. Jennifer L. Elgin, "Copyrights and Campaigns; Five Tips for the Unwary," *Campaigns & Elections,* May/June 2012, pp. 58–61.

10. Pew Center, "In Changing News Landscape, Even Television Is Vulnerable."

Chapter Nine

1. Michael Lewis, "Obama's Way," *Vanity Fair,* October 2012.

2. David Beiler, "Green, Lean, and Keen," *Campaigns & Elections*, September 1999, 22–27.

3. Owen Abbe, Paul S. Herrnson, David Magleby, and Kelly Patterson, "Going Negative Does Not Always Mean Getting Ahead in Elections," *Campaigns & Elections,* February 2000.

Chapter Ten

1. Phil Keisling, quoted in City Club of Eugene, "Ballot Measure 79," 2005, available at www.cityclubofeugene.org/reports/79.html.

Chapter Eleven

1. Katherine Seelye and Marjorie Connelly, "Signaling Voter Unrest, Schwarzenegger Cut Deep into the Democrats' Base," *New York Times,* October 9, 2003.

2. Donald Green and Alan Gerber, "What Causes Polls to Fluctuate?" Yale University, New Haven, CT, August 2001.

3. This observation comes from data gathered from the political consultants involved in house races for both Democrats and Republicans, and the Oregon secretary of state.

4. Rasmussen Reports, "Most Voters Made Up Their Minds Weeks Ago," November 5, 2008, www.rasmussenreports.com.

5. Alan S. Gerber and Donald P. Green, "The Effects of Canvassing, Telephone Calls, and Direct Mail on Voter Turnout: A Field Experiment," *American Political Science Review* 94, no. 3 (September 2000): 653–663.

6. Priscilla Southwell, "Five Years Later: A Re-Assessment of Oregon's Vote by Mail Electoral Process," report, University of Oregon, Eugene, 2003.

7. Michael Hanmer and Michael Traugott, "The Impact of Voting by Mail on Voter Behavior," *American Politics Research* 32 (2004): 375–405.

8. Southwell, "Five Years Later."

9. Priscilla Southwell, "Final Report: Survey of Vote by Mail Senate Election," report to Vote-by-Mail Citizen Commission, Oregon, April 3, 1996, available at https://scholarsbank.uoregon.edu/xmlui/bitstream/handle/1794/1268/VBM%20Full%20Report.pdf?sequence=5.

10. CNN, "Black Democrats Angered by Supreme Court Ruling," December 13, 2000, available at http://archives.cnn.com/2000/ALLPOLITICS/stories/12/13/african.americans/index.html.

11. Gerber and Green, "The Effects of Canvassing, Telephone Calls, and Direct Mail on Voter Turnout."

Appendix A: Conducting a Precinct Analysis

IN THIS APPENDIX
- Gathering Data
- Assigning the Undervote
- Predicting Voter Turnout
- Alternatives for Finding Swing Voters
- Votes Needed to Win (VNW)

THE 2010 CENSUS AND SUBSEQUENT REDISTRICTING MAY CAUSE SOME additional headaches for a precinct analysis. But unless precincts have dramatically changed, with a little work you should be able to determine how a given constituency within a precinct will perform based on past voting behavior even if those voters have never cast a vote for the particular race you're studying.

Gathering Data

What follows requires some proficiency in Excel. Indeed, other than amassing the data, none of the precinct analysis can be done without a computer. So if you do not have the skills, find someone who does. This is completely worth it.

A precinct analysis can be done on any kind of election, although some analyses are more illuminating than others. In areas of solid homogeneous populations, where races are typically decided in a partisan primary, an analysis reveals the gray tones rather than the black-and-white of mixed rural and urban populations. Typically in these areas, the candidate who works the hardest wins, but a precinct analysis will reveal subtleties that can give one candidate an advantage over another.

In a primary, where candidates of the same party square off, the analysis involves looking at past voting records for candidates of that particular party in that cycle. In nonpartisan primaries, where all candidates run the field, with the two top vote-getters facing each other in the general, the analysis will look a lot like a regular general election analysis. The reason: Nonpartisan primaries typically have a Republican and a Democrat in the race, or one candidate will lean left or right of the other, and voters know which is which. If you're facing opponents in a nonpartisan race in which the winner is determined by the candidate who receives 50 percent of the vote or then faces an opponent in the general election, ways to get 50 percent are covered in Chapter 9.

If the analysis is for a candidate in a general election, compare the past voting trends of all parties in a similar cycle. If it is for an issue-based campaign, compare the voting histories for similar ballot measures or propositions using the same election cycle (presidential general, special election, midterm primary, etc.). Regardless of the type of election, the materials you need to conduct a precinct analysis are the same.

My county keeps election results online for a couple of weeks after the election, but some counties keep them online indefinitely. If your county is of the latter category, download what you need row by row or page by page. Most counties use Excel or an Excel-compatible spreadsheet, but the online data is usually in PDF format. Getting the data online, on a CD, or emailed to you will save time. Online data in PDF format will need to be entered into your Excel spreadsheets by hand unless you have a program to convert the data.

For counties that do not have election results that you can obtain in electronic form or photocopy at the elections office, you will need either to enter the information into a spreadsheet on a laptop computer or to write it down on paper at the election office. If you do not have a laptop, you may want to create an election data form using the spreadsheet categories provided in figures A.1 and A.2 to take with you. Be sure to create at least six blank sheets for each election you want to study. Once you have the data recorded on paper, you must enter them into a spreadsheet. By the way, it saves a lot of time if a friend accompanies you to read off the numbers while you enter them into the laptop or spreadsheet. If you do not have a helpful friend, you might consider just taking a digital camera and shooting each page from which you want to enter data.

If your county does not break down results according to voter registration, you can approximate registration percentages using a primary election where only party registrants can vote to nominate someone within the party. Using the turnout percentage of a party in the primary will allow you to extrapolate an overall party registration to use in the analysis based on percentage of turnout. For example, 100 Republicans in Precinct 2 turned out in the primary and the county says this equals a 50 percent turnout, so you know there are 200 registered Republicans in Precinct 2. Once you have a number of registered Democrats and Republicans, you can calculate what percentage of the total registration they are owed.

Beginning the Analysis

First, you will create one master document that has all the necessary past voting information. In your Excel document, you will have many spreadsheets. Each spreadsheet tab should be labeled according to the election and year of the election. So, one tab may read "2002 General," and included in it will be the following data:

- Precinct number (be sure to put "pct" in front of each precinct number; this is necessary for charting the data later)
- A description of the precinct (e.g., south of Market, east of Van Ness, north county; something to help you identify geographic location)
- Total registration for each precinct
- Registration of parties for each precinct
- Turnout
- Election results of candidates and some pertinent issue-based races, again all by precinct

Note that the precinct number and description can be copied and pasted on subsequent sheets.

The next tab or spreadsheet will have the same information but for another cycle, such as the 2004 primary election. The third might be for the 2006 primary or general, another for 2008, and then another for 2012. Although your election may be a midterm general, having all the years of voter performance and registration will assist in determining voter-registration trends, which is extremely helpful. Typically counties purge deadwood from the voting rolls before an election. For example, if a voter fails to participate in any election in a five-year period in Oregon, he or she will be dumped from the registration lists. Before the 2006 primary in my county, more than 6,000 voters were purged, and 4,000 more were dropped before the same year's general election; charting where people are purged will provide a fascinating glimpse into voter migration.

But for a particular analysis, you are looking for past elections that reflect the one you are about to dive into. So if you're running an election in a general election cycle, you may want to gather only general election data—especially if it needs to be gathered by hand.

Issue-Based Analysis

If you are testing the waters for an issue campaign, again the idea is to look for similarities, especially if your campaign is about raising money. Issue-based campaigns dealing with revenue generally come in two varieties: capital improvements (bricks and mortar), and operation and maintenance. Within these two categories are police, fire, schools, cities, counties, libraries, parks, water systems, special districts, and so on. Issue campaigns that have to do with restricting the power of government, such as term limits, the right to die, abortion, and mandatory sentencing, are covered in Chapter 10. As with candidates, keep in mind that it is best to use identical election cycles, such as a nonpresidential primary, a presidential election year, special election, and so forth, for analyzing issue-based campaigns.

Election Data Form

You begin your analysis by going through the election data and transferring it to your spreadsheet (figure A.1). The election information may include the percentages of registration and turnout, but don't waste your time

| 2008 General | | Total | Total Registration | | | Turnout | | | |
Precinct	Description	Reg	Ds	Rs	Os	Ds	Rs	Os	Total

FIGURE A.1 Sample Spreadsheet Headings for Precinct Analysis

D = Democrat; R = Republican; O = Others (such as independents [NAVs], Green Party, Constitutional, and Libertarian). Eventually, all third-party and NAVs are combined.

| President | | | U.S. Senate | | | | Governor | | | | New Race | | |
Obama	McCain	UV	D	R	O	UV	D	R	O	UV	D	R	UV

FIGURE A.2 Continued Headings for Sample Spreadsheet for Precinct Analysis

D = Democrat; R = Republican; O = Others; UV = Undervote.

entering that, as it is easy to calculate once you have all the information. After the data included in the headings of figure A.1, you will gather data for races you wish to compare (figure A.2).

Although the county printout includes more information than you may think you need, enter as much information as you can about previous elections and outcomes. The additional information can help identify areas where certain issues may be more problematic or helpful than other areas. For example, money issues for public education and libraries can help define a voting area for candidate elections. Blowout elections are less helpful, except in predicting swing voters.

I've found the data from gubernatorial races to be extraordinarily useful in precinct analysis—unless, of course, one of the candidates has attempted to sell a Senate seat or has done something equally damaging. While voters tend to retain congressional incumbents, swinging wildly from party to party to support him or her, this is not true with the governor, for whose elections they stick to party lines.

Create a Master Spreadsheet

Once you have created one complete Excel file of election data, labeled each of the tabs at the bottom by election and year such as general 2002 or primary 2008, then save this entire file and label it: Election Master 2002, 2004, 2006, 2008, or whatever years are included.

After saving your master, create an exact duplicate with which to work for your precinct analysis. Never make any alterations to your master data spreadsheets. Should anything go wrong with any of your spreadsheets while you are doing your analysis, you will need the original spreadsheet to rebuild scrambled information. Believe me, you do not want to go back to the elections office to reenter data halfway through a precinct analysis.

Expanding the Data

Once your master is safely tucked away in your master files, begin the precinct analysis on your duplicate.

First, between each of your headings after the Party Registration column, "insert" columns for the percentages for each registration column (figure A.3). Note that in figure A.3, I have combined nonaffiliated voters (NAVs) and third-party registrants (and labeled them O for "Other") and determined a percentage of that total. If your county does not keep registration breakdown on all the parties, no worries; you really need know the registration

Total Registration			Percent of Registration			Turnout				Percent Turnout			
Ds	Rs	Os	Ds	Rs	Os	Ds	Rs	Os	Total	Ds	Rs	Os	Total

FIGURE A.3 Sample Spreadsheet Headings for Precinct Analysis

D = Democrat; R = Republican; O = Others (such as independents [NAVs], Green Party, Constitutional, and Libertarian). Eventually, all third-party and NAVs are combined.

only of the Democrats and Republicans, because everyone else will be collapsed into their registration percentages.

Next, calculate all the percentages for registration, turnout, and percent candidates received. Don't forget that the formulas remain with cells where they are computed unless you copy a column and then click "values and number formats" within the Paste Special option. Personally, I like to leave formulas in my spreadsheets to help me remember how I came to a number. But should any original number in a column get fiddled with, it will change all subsequent numbers associated with that cell in a formula. This can be a bad thing and a good thing.

For example, what if you transposed a registration number when getting data from the county? This mistake may not be discovered until you go to calculate percentages and notice that the Democrats in some precinct are 150 percent of the registration. Not possible. So, after you call the county and get the correct value for that one item and replace the transposed number with the real number, the percentage will automatically be recalculated because the formula remains in the cell. Sometimes mistakes are not discovered until days after you've begun your analysis and you have multiple formulas stretching across a spreadsheet. One change corrects everything if formulas are left within each of the cells, just as one change can mess up everything that follows. Simply remain aware that for your calculations to work, all the previous components of the formula must be present.

Pressing the Data

Once you've gathered all the information, entered it into Excel spreadsheets, saved a master document, created a duplicate, and calculated percentages, you're ready to press the data—that is, begin the precinct analysis.

The first thing to look at is registration. How a precinct trends in registration can offer great information. Look at registration as many ways as you can. I will typically assign one of my spreadsheets to registration, and line up all the registration by number and percentage of a given year and then compare one year with another. Are the percentages constant, or have they shifted toward or away from your party? If the precinct is even in registration, has it always been even? If it has actually been trending away from your party for years, you will want to take a closer look at that precinct in your swing analysis. Remember that when you move data, like registration percentages, to another spreadsheet, you must copy and Paste Special the "values and number formats," or you will end up with gobbledygook.

Precincts that have flipped registration within a census period can be a gold mine if the flip was toward your party and a warning if it moved away from you. Profoundly shifting registrations always make a statement at the ballot box.

Because precincts can range in size from 400 to 4,000 within the same voting area, it is important to look at registration shifts both by number and by percentage. Once you have compared years, subtracted the growth or fall-off of one party over another, and factored in county purging of inactive voters, you're ready to chart registration.

In the Zone

Unless you're working on a down-ballot race that covers just one small city, you will want to break the area being charted into zones. These are the same zones you will give your pollster should a poll be conducted by your campaign or on its behalf, so think this part through carefully.

Zones should make sense. For example, I break my county into seven zones: One is a city of 20,000 plus surrounding precincts; another is two small adjacent cities and their surrounding precincts. I broke the largest city into two zones, and everything else is grouped into geographic areas. Some of my zones are larger than others, some by population and some by geography.

In another part of the state, I used state House districts for the zones. In another, I combined the small cities of the western part of a rural House district as one zone, treated the unincorporated areas of farmland as another, and worked my way across in similar fashion, going west to east and combining like with like, according to geography or cities.

If your county has organized the precincts in ascending order by geography, you're in luck and you will need to do very little to break your data in and out of zones. This means you can create charts along the way. I like to make charts as soon as I come across interesting data, so that I can study some nuance. However, if the county has a more hodgepodge approach to numbering precincts (often the case, because populations swell and precincts are divided and renumbered), it's best to keep your data together, that is, listed as it comes from the county, until everything is pressed; this will leave all your charts for last. Either way, once precincts are scrambled to make zones for charting purposes, you may need to put them back in the county order for some unforeseen reason. To allow for this, I create a numbered column that is independent of my precinct numbers for quick reorganization.

Chart Your Data

There are many ways to chart your registration data; two examples are shown in figure A.4. The top graph simply charts the net advantage of Republicans within a zone (a group of precincts) and compares year after year of their net advantage by percentage. The bottom chart looks at the net shift of each party between two years comparing growth or loss of registration in number (not percentage). In this example it is between 2004 and 2008, but you can do registration shifts over longer periods of time as well.

Registration trends show where a precinct is headed. Since 1985, when I started tracking registration trends in my county, zones and precincts within those areas of the county have either flipped, gotten to be more of what they were, or stayed relatively constant. Those remaining relatively constant are the ones with the greatest swing.

As indicated above, you can do all sorts of mathematical computations within your Excel spreadsheet. But to chart, you must transpose the data from vertical to horizontal on the page. (Select the area to copy, then click Copy, Paste Special, Transpose, and paste in cells below data, where there are *no* data that might accidentally get erased with your pasted cells.)

For your precinct numbers to remain apart from the bars of the graph, there must be lettering prior to the precinct number. This is why you labeled them "pct 1," "pct 2," and so on. I also include the description of the precinct in my charts because most people don't know one precinct from another. The descriptions can simply be the name of the city the precinct falls in or a description of a portion of your city such as "hospital to university."

After you transpose the data, click on the Chart icon within Excel, and follow the steps—it's easy. Once you have your chart, you can change colors of the bars in the bar graph and change values on the x-axis and y-axis. I make Republicans red, Democrats blue, and undervotes light yellow and light green.

I like to make my charts right below the data and then copy, cut, and paste the charts to another spreadsheet labeled "Charts." *But* if you change anything in your transposed data, remember it is linked to the chart and will change your chart—no matter where it is in your computer. So heads up. Again, this is good and bad. If something is incorrect in the transposed data,

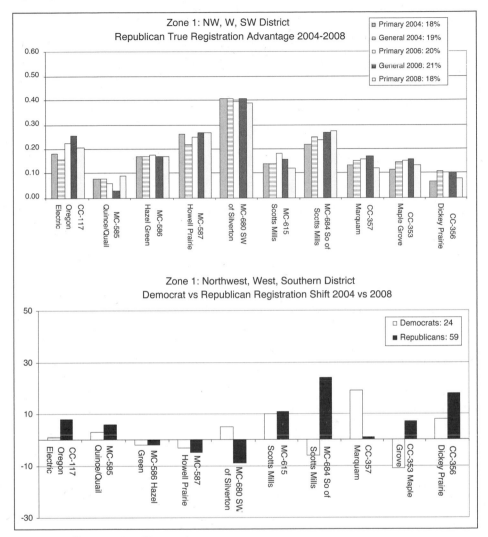

FIGURE A.4 Registration Comparisons

The top graph shows net registration advantage of Republicans, spanning five election cycles; the bottom compares net growth or loss of registration by number by party.

you only need to correct it there for the chart to also get corrected. But if you decide you want a little more room below your spreadsheet and delete the transposed data, the next time you look at the chart, it will be empty.

Excel likes to set the scale for the y-axis but since I want to compare apples with apples, I make everything the same—chart after chart; for example, a scale of 800 to -800 in figures A.7, A.8, and A.9. To change anything within a chart, point and click, and the options become evident. Generally I do all my graphs

Precinct No.	Description	Total Reg	Total Reg Ds	% Reg Ds	Total Reg Rs	% Reg Rs	Total Reg NAVs	% Reg NAVs	TO Total	TO % Total	D + R
2	Ashland	3,613	2,383	66	407	11	823	23	3,325	92	2,790
4	Ashland	3,454	2,237	65	437	13	780	23	3,122	90	2,674

FIGURE A.5A Example of a Spreadsheet with Actual Numbers, Presidential Election 2008

D = Democrat; R = Republican; NAV = nonaffiliated voter; TO = turnout.

Precinct	D + R	% Owed D	% Owed R	Votes Owed Ds	Votes Owed Rs
2	2,790	85	15	2,840	485
4	2,674	84	16	2,612	510
		(D + R) / D reg	(D + R) / R reg	(% owed D) × TO	(% owed R) × TO

FIGURE A.5B Expanded Spreadsheet That Includes Columns for Percentage of Votes Owed and Number of Votes Owed Both Democrats and Republicans, Presidential Election 2008

D = Democrats; R = Republicans; reg = registered; TO = turnout. Formulas for the calculation are shown in the bottom row of the spreadsheet.

Precinct	Votes Owed Ds	Votes Owed Rs	Votes Received Obama	Difference	Votes Received McCain	Difference	UV
2	2840	485	2847	7	384	-101	-94
4	2612	510	2606	-6	398	-112	-118
	(% owed D) × TO	(% owed R) × TO					

FIGURE A.5C Actual Votes Received, Followed by Votes Owed Versus Votes Received, Presidential Election 2008

D = Democrat; R = Republican; UV = undervote; TO = turnout.

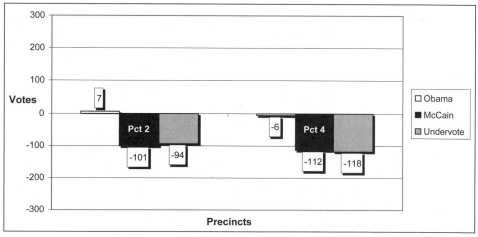

FIGURE A.6 Votes Owed Versus Votes Received, Precincts 2 and 4, Ashland, Oregon, 2008 Presidential Election

and then come back and do the scale on all the graphs at the same time. Some precincts need more room than other precincts and thus end up dictating the high or low points on the scale. Some of my precinct analyses have better than one hundred charts. I make lots of charts, because I'm always looking for patterns and I find this the easiest and quickest way to see things.

Questions? Email me: cathyshaw@mind.net.

Votes Owed

Votes owed is simply a predicted percentage or number of votes that partisan candidates are owed determined only by the Republican and Democratic registration percentages. These percentages are determined apart from NAVs and third-party registrants.

Calculating Votes Owed Versus Received

To calculate votes owed against those received, you will again expand your Excel spreadsheet by adding more columns (figure A.5A). Remember that you're ignoring all third-party and nonaffiliated voters and will determine the percentage only of the Democratic and Republican registration. Therefore, you will need a column labeled "D + R," which represents the registration of the Democrats added to the registration of the Republicans.

What is owed the Democrats is the Democratic registration total divided by the D + R column and, similarly, what is owed the Republicans is the Republican registration divided by the D + R column. In other words, you're finding what percentage the Democrats and Republicans are of their combined total rather than of the total registration (figures A.5A and A.5B).

Next, determine whether the partisan candidates actually received the votes owed. You do this by multiplying the percentage owed for each of the parties by the total voter turnout. This will yield a number of votes owed for each parties. Then subtract this number from the actual votes received by each of the candidates within each party (figure A.5C).

So, for example, in Precinct 2, Barack Obama received 7 more votes than he was owed; John McCain, 101 fewer than he was owed. The undervote is all those who voted for third-party candidates plus the actual undervote. Therefore, in this example, 94 votes were thrown into the undervote for Precinct 2, and 118 for Precinct 4. Votes for third-party candidates can be added to the undervote or subtracted from the voter turnout before subtracting votes owed from votes received.

Next, the data are charted. In figure A.6, the two aforementioned precincts are shown, but typically, all precincts within a zone would be charted.

Nonpartisan Primaries

Within any general election, I have not found an appreciable difference between calculating the percentages of votes owed using total party registration and calculating the same percentages using party turnout totals. But this relationship does not hold when you are calculating the percentages of votes owed for a nonpartisan primary race.

To calculate the percentage of votes owed for a nonpartisan primary, you must use party turnout, because there can be dramatic variations of party performance in a primary, depending upon what is on each side of the ballot. In this case, rather than dividing party registrants by the combined Democratic and Republican registration totals, you will divide party turnout by the Democratic turnout plus the Republican turnout. For example, if the Democratic turnout is 100 votes and the Republican turnout is 75, to calculate votes owed, you would first add 100 and 75, to get 175 votes cast. In this example, the Democrats would be owed 100 out of 175, or 57 percent of the votes cast, and Republicans would be owed 75 out of 175, or 43 percent of the votes cast.

Assigning the Undervote

As mentioned in Chapter 1, in 2004, State Representative Alan Bates (D-Ashland) ran against local businessman Jim Wright (R-Medford). In Precinct 2, Bates was "owed" 80 percent of the ballots cast, and Wright was "owed" 20 percent. However, Bates received only 79 percent and Wright only 17 percent. So where were the other 4 percent of the votes? If there is no third-party candidate—and there wasn't—you will find the missing votes in the undervote. That is, those who voted for neither candidate but who still participated in the election.

The genius of this detail is that you now know who undervoted whom. So, again using our example, for Precinct 2 with a 2004 registration of 3,400 voters, Bates is attributed 1 percent of the undervote, or 34 votes, and Wright is attributed 3 percent of the undervote, or 102 votes. Figure this precinct by precinct for past elections to reveal which party consistently underperforms for the team in which precinct.

Being able to assign the undervote helps diagnose potential problem areas so they may be remedied. For example, in 2006 in another part of the state, I was hired to determine why Democrats, with a 6 percent registration advantage, were consistently losing a state House seat to Republicans. Charting votes owed against those received for previous state House elections revealed that the entire undervote came from the Democratic side of the ticket. This information allowed for a very simple fix. Knowing why past elections were lost provides critical information and opportunities to correct a course to reverse a trend in future elections; undervotes typically reside at the foundation of a loss. In this case, the situation was remedied by tying the incumbent, who voted party lines 98 percent of the time, to the Speaker, who was completely nuts and responsible for the longest back-to-back legislative sessions in Oregon history.

Let me show you two zones in our county (figures A.7, A.8, and A.9). The precincts on the left are one zone, and the precincts on the right are another. Notice how the voters tend to vote like their neighbors in each of the two zones. Because of space limitations on figures A.7, A.8, and A.9, the undervotes (UV) are not marked as attributable to either of the candidates. However, most of the undervote was on the Republican side of the ticket. In the Bates versus Wright race (figure A.7), Bates did have a few undervotes, but the swing from Republicans countered that and then some, giving him 302 more votes than he was owed districtwide. Wright received 3,180 fewer than he was owed—of which 302 went to Bates and 2,878 Republican votes were left on the table. Bates won by 2,462 of 62,664 votes cast. Basically, he won by the undervote.

On figures A.7, A.8, and A.9, anything above the x-axis represents how many more votes a candidate received than he or she was "owed," and anything below represents votes "owed" that were not received by a candidate. The undervote (always below the line) is the smaller bar.

Predicting Voter Turnout

Because turnout can vary dramatically, depending upon the election cycle and the strength of candidates, simply averaging the past three elections will not necessarily give you a clear prediction of voting behavior for your election. To determine the expected voter turnout, find a similar past election in the same season. For example, is your election in a presidential or nonpresidential primary or general election? Is it a special or an off-year election? Whatever it may be, use the same election cycles.

Next, compare what was on the earlier ballot with what will be on yours. If the referenced election had a hotly contested governor's race, this will influence the voter turnout. If you are running in a presidential primary and the Republicans hold the White House and have only the president on the ballot, compared with two candidates in the Democratic field, you can safely assume that Democrats will turn out in larger numbers than Republicans in

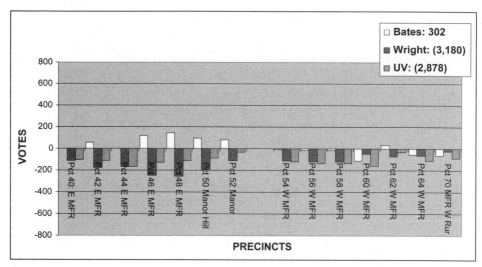

FIGURE A.7 Votes Owed Versus Votes Received, Bates Versus Wright, 2004 Election

In 2004, Democrat Alan Bates and Republican Jim Wright ran for an open state senate seat previously held by a Republican for nearly three decades. This chart includes two of the five zones the senate seat was broken into for study of swing. The final analysis showed that 302 people moved across party lines to vote for Bates, and another 2,878 of Wright's votes were thrown into the undervote (UV). Nearly all campaign efforts focused on the four precincts left of center, which the swing analysis revealed as prime real estate for swing voters. In this 2004 race, the Democrat won by the undervote margin.

the primary. Take such information into consideration, and adjust expected turnout up or down accordingly by averaging three similar cycles.

In the elections you are using for comparison purposes, look at the turnout, precinct by precinct, for each party. Let's say that in Precinct 1, turnout among Republicans was 65 percent, turnout among Democrats was 62 percent, and turnout among NAVs was 35 percent. However, in your election, because of controversial issues on the ballot, you predict that voter turnout will be at least 10 percent higher. So, in Precinct 1, you will multiply the current number of registered Republicans by 75 percent, the current number of Democrats by 72 percent, and the current number of NAVs by 45 percent. Add these numbers together, and you get your predicted turnout for Precinct 1. Do the same for all precincts.

If you are uncomfortable with predicting increases or decreases in voter participation based on ballot issues, you will be close if you simply multiply the percentage of voter turnout of the last identical election by the current number of registered voters. Even if turnout changes substantially in one

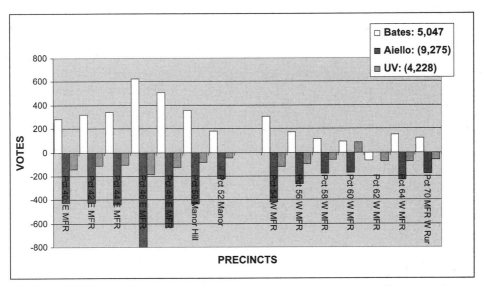

FIGURE A.8 Votes Owed Versus Votes Received, Bates Versus Aiello, 2006 Election

In 2006, Senator Alan Bates was challenged by Republican Lynn Aiello for his state senate seat. Aiello, an unknown and much weaker candidate than Jim Wright in 2004, was owed an additional 9,275 votes that she did not receive. Of those, 5,047 were given to Bates, and 4,228 were thrown in the undervote (UV). Clearly, swing is a function of the candidates; Bates easily overcame the 4 percent registration disadvantage. Again, the chart represents two of the five zones from the senate district.

direction or the other, the parties will track similarly, within a couple of points within any general election. In other words, in a given precinct, all things being equal, you will not see a substantial increase in turnout for one party without seeing a similar spike in the other parties.

The exception to this rule is a primary. Some primaries do not allow NAVs to participate, and some primaries have candidates on one side of the aisle running unopposed while candidates on the other side have heated races. In the 2008 presidential primary in Oregon, where Democrats were slugging it out in both the US Senate and the presidential campaigns, Democrats outperformed Republicans by ten points in the primary. Predicting this sort of turnout can be very useful in a nonpartisan race where the winner of the primary must secure 50 percent of the vote or head off to the general election. For example, if your nonpartisan candidate is running in a primary where all the action is on the Democratic side of the ticket, he or she should lock that party's vote in the primary cycle and then come back and work Republicans in the general.

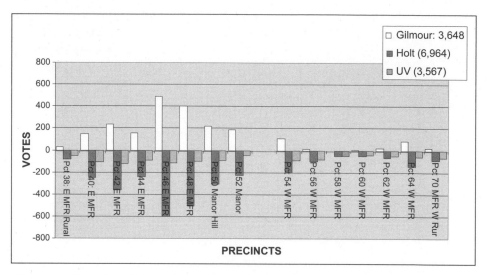

FIGURE A.9 Votes Owed Versus Votes Received, Gilmour Versus Holt, 2002 Election

When Democrat Dave Gilmour challenged incumbent Republican Ric Holt in 2002 for the county commission, Republicans held a countywide 11 percent registration advantage. In this election, Republicans gave Gilmour 3,648 votes owed to Holt and threw another 3,567 into the undervote (UV). Gilmour's win of 2,646 votes out of nearly 73,000 cast can be found entirely in the undervote. Much of the county swing lives in the precincts in the zone on the left side of the chart, where Republicans hold a 22 percent registration advantage.

Base Party Vote

The base party vote is a useful number and is very easy to calculate. It tells you the number of voters in each precinct who will always vote with their party, regardless of how bad the candidate may be. Your base party vote is the number of votes you and your opponent will get, no matter what you do or say (figure A.10).

Here's how to find the base party vote:

1. You need election results in which a candidate in your party was pounded. Since you're going to translate these numbers precinct by precinct, it really doesn't matter if the poor outcome for your party was in the same election cycle. Although it can include more precincts, it must have all the precincts of your campaign area. For example, a heavily lopsided governor's race could be used for a state House or Senate seat.
2. List all the precincts in the area where you are running (column A).

A	B	C	D	E = D x C x B
Precinct Number	Worst Percentage of Votes for Same-Party Candidate	Current Voter Registration (Number)	Percentage Expected Turnout	Number of Voters Who Won't Leave the Party
58	35	655	67	153
59	37	916	73	247
60	38	707	72	193
61	37	676	76	191
62	42	424	66	118
64	45	822	74	274
65	46	693	72	230
66	43	703	67	202
67	37	756	62	173
68	41	740	72	218
69	38	949	70	252
70	36	723	65	169
71	35	1,038	71	258
TOTAL		9,802		2,678

FIGURE A.10 Sample Form for Determining Base Party Support

3. For each of the precincts, list the percentage of votes the candidate in your party received (column B). Remember, this is a race where your party's candidate lost big.
4. List, precinct by precinct, the current voter registration (column C).
5. List the percentage turnout you expect (column D).
6. Finally, multiply the expected percentage turnout by the current number of registered voters, and multiply the result by the percentage of votes the same party candidate got in the previous election (D x C x B). This will give you the number of people who will vote for your party, no matter what.

Repeat these steps with data from an election in which someone in the opposing party lost by huge numbers. The result of this tabulation will be the number of votes your opponent will receive simply because of party affiliation.

Alternatives for Finding Swing Voters

Swing voters are those who are registered in one party but who are willing to vote for someone from another party, and consistently do so. Swing voters are sometimes called "smart voters" because they vote according to issues and

A	B	C	D	E	F	G
Precinct No.	Highest Percent Votes Cast	Lowest Percent Votes Cast	Percent Swing (B - C)	Projected Percent Turnout	Current Voter Registration	Number of Voters Who Could Swing D (E x F)
58	65	35	30	67	655	132

FIGURE A.11 Sample Form for Determining Swing Voters

information rather than party. However, they also include voters who are persuaded solely by emotion and their impressions of the candidates. Your job is to find them and persuade them that they should vote for your candidate.

Although I exclusively calculate swing votes according to the votes-owed model, this is another approach to determine potential swing by precinct. First, calculate the base-party support for both your party and your opponent's (figure A.10). To find swing voters, add columns to your base-party vote spreadsheet and simply subtract the election percentage where your party destroyed the opposition from one where the opposition destroyed the candidate in your party. That will give you a percentage that will potentially swing. Multiply this by the predicted voter turnout, and you will have the predicted number of voters who will potentially swing (figure A.11). An alternative way to compute potential swing is outlined in Chapter 1.

Votes Needed to Win (VNW)

Once you have calculated the predicted turnout, base vote, and swing vote, you're ready to calculate the votes you will need to win. There are a couple of ways to estimate the number of votes you need to win. One is to simply divide the overall predicted voter turnout (number) in half, and add one more vote to your number. A second way, one that will provide a little more insight, is to calculate the predicted voter turnout by party and by precinct, add these up, and divide by two; again, add one more vote to your side.

So, to recap, you know:

1. Your base-party vote—that is, exactly how many people in your party will never stray from you, no matter what you say or do. Add these numbers up.

2. How many will never leave the opposing party—precinct by precinct, so add those up. What's the difference? At a deficit? Look for precincts with the greatest swing. Does the swing consistently go toward or away from your party? By how much? Add these to your column or your opponent's.

3. Generally, one-third of each party sticks with the base; this leaves 40 percent of the remaining voter turnout that's up for grabs. Some of these voters live in left-leaning precincts, and some in right-leaning; you know which is which, because you did a precinct analysis that told you so.

4. Clearly it will be easier to get votes in the right-leaning precincts if you're a Republican and in the left-leaning if you're a Democrat.

5. If registration is skewed—that is, if you're at a fundamental disadvantage because more people are registered in a party other than yours, you need a higher undervote in precincts that will vote for the opposing party to help even the registration numbers. How far down can you drive the opposition support? Your precinct analysis will tell you if there are typically higher undervotes of one party over another, precinct by precinct. If the undervote is greater consistently in your party, then you will go into those precincts and put the fear of God in the voters to activate them to vote. Remember, you cannot activate voters with vacuous mail; it must make sense. And no question, canvassing is the most effective way to activate voters. Think you can do it? Add those underperformers to your list.

6. Look at the consistent undervote of the opposing party. If your registration disparity is great, then you need these voters to remain asleep. Where opposition undervote is consistently high election after election, avoid untargeted activities—like lawn signs. Subtract the number of voters who you think will not participate in this election if you quietly go about your business without pounding the ubiquitous drum. Subtract these from the opposition's abacus.

7. Hopefully, the bottom line has your team ahead. If not, you must change the numbers. For example, send multiple and personal letters to overseas military personnel; register more people in your high-priority precincts; and check the census to see where populations have migrated. For example, the 2010 census revealed that the Hispanic population of a small backwater community in my county increased to 30 percent

of the population from virtually nothing in 2000. With fewer than one-third registered to vote, they were invisible. The 2010 census also revealed that another area had the highest per capita income of any in my county—a complete surprise given that the small community looked like the landed poor from a distance. It was time to have a chat with those people. In other words, if your bottom line is a problem, you must work harder and smarter.

Appendix B: Campaigning on a Shoestring

IN THE FOLLOWING PAGES YOU WILL FIND THE BARE MINIMUM YOU NEED to know to execute a successful campaign in three months while spending less than $3,000.

Getting Started

This section is not for all campaigns; it is designed specifically for city or down-ballot county races and will work only if you live in a homogeneous city or are running in a nonpartisan race. For specific strategy in partisan, legislative, or countywide races, consult the pages of the entire book.

A campaign is a lot of work: Take it seriously and run to win.

In general you will need the following:

- A walking piece/ brochure
- Lawn signs and a strategy for placement, maintenance, and removal
- House parties
- A Web page
- A Facebook page
- Three grand and two to three months

A Committee

Should you decide to get a volunteer committee together (and I advise you do), you want one person to oversee and take responsibility for each of the above activities. Although everyone will help execute the duties of any given category, one individual dogging a job is very helpful.

Campaign Manager

A campaign manager is generally a pretty good friend who will stick with you from beginning to end. But let me caution you here that campaigns eat friendships and marriages alive, so unless you're positive your "pretty good friend" will follow through and truly help, get someone else and consider paying that person a small stipend.

Graphic Designer

I do not pretend to know how to lay out campaign literature or design logos. This is a really inexpensive cost to the campaign, so find someone to do it for you who knows what he or she is doing. This is important: You do not want any campaign materials to look amateurish. It costs very little to class up a campaign, so do it. Similarly, you need some professional photos for your print and online materials.

Treasurer

In Oregon you can spend $3,000 on a campaign and never have to file a contributions and expenditures (C&E) form with the secretary of state. Each state is different, so check with your local election department. Not having to file all that paperwork is liberating. Nevertheless, keep track of all your expenses and contributions. Make copies of checks or maintain a paper trail, and be sure to have a completely separate bank account from your personal account. Never commingle campaign funds with personal funds: Treat a campaign like a business. If you're ever called upon to prove anything, you'll be glad you did.

> "Every election is a sort of advance auction sale of stolen goods."
>
> — H. L. MENCKEN

The Walking Piece

Your walking piece should be no more than 325 words and should include the following:

Occupation. Include years—not "twenty-seven" but rather 1983–2010, that sort of thing.

Occupational background. Include names of companies or jobs held and actual years worked at each. If you have a laundry list, then forgo the years to save on your word count.

Prior government experience. This is where you list the planning commission and such—not Little League coach or pink lady at the hospital.

Educational background. Include degrees starting from the lowest, then work your way up; give the universities or schools and years you attended. If you did not get a degree, just list the school with no actual dates and hopefully voters will think you finished. There's no need to list your high school, as voters will assume you went in order to get into a college; the exception might be if you want to demonstrate longevity in a community.

Military service. If you served in the military, this is important; indicate years and rank. If you never served, omit this category.

Community service. This is where the Little League and chamber of commerce stuff goes; if you received special awards or recognition, list those as bullet points here as well.

Proven leadership. Next you will list things you accomplished that somehow relate to the office you seek. If you're running for reelection you will list what you and the body on which you served accomplished while you were in office. Bullet-point this stuff. People are going to look at your walking piece for exactly ten seconds, so be brief and articulate.

Together We Can Do More. The next section will offer bullet points regarding issues your town or community could do to make the world a better place. For example, dealing with the homeless, upgrading the wastewater treatment plant, placing electric lines underground to prevent future outages, safeguarding the water system by removing dead and dying timber from the watershed, getting sidewalks installed near schools—that sort of thing.

Values We Respect. Depending on word count, this final section will feature two to four quotes from prominent community leaders. They and not you will say just how great you are. They and not the committee will describe the crumbling school or closed library or dilapidated park system that increased taxes will fix. This is also where you provide some reassurance to the voter. For example, if you're a business-person, you will balance that strength with a quote from a credible person who may be considered anti-business. If you're on the left, get a quote from someone on the right. One caution: Do not choose people who are extreme; you want to balance a weakness with someone just slightly over the line in the other camp. Think about your strengths versus the strengths of your opposition, and enhance yours at the opposition's expense.

> "The ax handle and the tree are made of the same wood."
>
> **INDIAN PROVERB**

When I ask people for a quote, I also ask whether I can edit it down for space. No one says no to that. Most will ask that the campaign generate the quote and run it by the endorser. Make the individual sound smart and believable. Also important to note here is that your endorsements can actually say what you highlighted under "proven leadership" above. So if you want to say you worked the floor of a cannery and everyone came to you for advice, have a former coworker say, "He was always there for us with great advice and he set an example by working hard. He's a born leader" (Sally Smith, Borden Foods supervisor).

And Now a Word from our Sponsor. Once you have completed all the above sections and find you still have a few words, this is where you, the candidate, make a special appeal: "It would be an honor to serve our city. I hope I can count on your vote." Then sign it and have your printed signature appear on the walking piece under your appeal.

Off to the Photographer

Every walking piece needs at least one picture of the candidate. If you're working on an issue-based campaign, you may need two or three pictures to evoke emotion to pull voters over to the cause.

Candidates with families should consider a picture of the entire family as well as a solo of the candidate. Your family will be affected by your campaign, so involving them in this small way completely works. But never use a photo that makes any member of your family look bad—especially if your child is a teenager. Be considerate.

Family photos can be of your last vacation together or in your backyard. Indeed, if you already have a great photo that looks spontaneous, it will work better than a studio shot and save you money.

If your family is your dog or cat, then include your pet in the photo; it makes you look genuine and accessible. But if you have dozens of pets and include them all, you will look like a nut, so use some common sense.

Voters' Pamphlet or Voter Guides

If your state or locality has a government-produced voter guide, now is the time to review the requirements and fill out the required information. If a fee goes with it, pay it; getting into a government-sponsored voter guide that goes to each and every home or one that is available online is completely worth the effort and expense. I have won campaigns using a voters' pamphlet entry as the entire campaign.

Graphics

Next you will take the 325-word copy from your completed form above plus a few carefully selected photos to a graphic-design professional.

Create a Logo

Your graphic designer should first create a logo; this will go on your walking piece and also becomes your lawn sign. A logo is your name and the office you seek presented in a memorable way. If you already hold office, be sure to get that "reelect" label in there somewhere. If you do not already hold the office you seek, you cannot place the office name before yours, only after. If you want to include a slogan, you and the committee should mull that over and give it to the designer along with the 325-word copy and the photos. A slogan is unnecessary but lots of people like them. Generally they're along the lines of: "Building a Better Community" or "It's About Community" or something that involves leadership, like "Leadership Matters."

If you're working on an issue-based campaign, there's always the inclination to guilt voters into supporting a tax measure, but in general I think it's best to go with optimism. "A Great Community Deserves a Great Library" works better than "Save our Library." Same goes for schools: "Create Possibilities" works better than "Our Children Deserve Better." Keep it on the "hope and opportunity" side.

The Layout

Your walking piece should be printed on both sides and no bigger than a half sheet of 8½-by-11-inch paper. The first section (occupation, occupational background, education, etc.) should be boxed and to one side; it becomes an easy reference for those who want to know whether you're actually qualified to serve. The second section includes what you've done or will do or both and then the quotes and the pictures get placed where they look best; your designer will get it right. You basically want your piece to breathe. Too much copy, and no one will read any of it; too little, and you will insult the voter. Keep the copy to 325 words and all will be right with the world.

> "In this world there are only two tragedies. One is not getting what one wants, and the other is getting it."
>
> — OSCAR WILDE

An alternative is to create a piece with one black-and-white photo of you at the top and all of the particulars listed on the front of a three-by-eight-inch sheet of paper. Using one-sided printing and converting each sheet of paper to three walking pieces saves on printing and paper stock. It's a little intense to look at (copy-rich) but very affordable.

Spot Color

You can easily afford one "spot color" on your walking piece. It will add a little to the cost of your literature but is completely worth it. So be sure to mention to your graphic designer that you want spot color and keep that color in your logo and lawn signs; consistency in campaign materials declutters the field and provides continuity. With that said, you do not want to use spot color in your photo or lettering but rather on your logo and actual bullet points.

To the Printer!

After you're satisfied with the layout and design of the walking piece, it goes to the printer, usually electronically. Next you will consult with the print shop about the best and most affordable paper to use. Generally speaking, you do not want to use colored paper, anything that's too absorbent, or paper that's high gloss. Use something with just enough finish to allow the copy and photos to pop off the page and enough weight to easily get shoved into doorjambs or screen doors. I really like 80-pound Xerox Digital Color Elite.

Quantities

Your walking piece will go wherever you go: canvassing, house parties, farmers' markets, everywhere. Knowing this, you may be inclined to print "enough," which can easily be too many. Considering how small the difference in cost per piece between 500 and 2,000 is, I suggest you begin with a shorter run. You can always print more, and a short run provides an opportunity to swap out quotes depending upon where you're canvassing.

If you're running for office in a really small city of a few hundred to a few thousand, consider printing your walking piece on your home printer, especially if that printer is of good quality. Otherwise, begin with a few hundred and be prepared to order more.

Paying for Your Walking Piece Without Money

You have now generated two expenses: one with the graphic designer ($100–$200) and another with the printer (up to $200). To get around paying these bills before you have any money, open accounts with the vendors and request that you get billed for their service. You just bought yourself thirty days.

> "Everything should be made as simple as possible, but not simpler."
> **ALBERT EINSTEIN**

When it comes to paying vendors, do so with online bill pay and your bank will issue the check, post an online copy for your records, and pay the postage to get the check to the vendor. The packet of starter checks the bank provides when an account is opened is plenty for a short campaign season.

Name Recognition

If you have never run for or served in office, you need to let the voters know who you are, and there are a number of ways to do that:

- Television, radio, and newspaper advertising
- Direct mail
- Letters to the editor
- Lawn signs, field signs, and billboards
- Canvassing—that is, walking door to door and introducing yourself (or the issue-based proposal) to the voter
- Social media or online advertising

TV, Radio, and Newspaper Advertising

If you're running a campaign in a small market, television may be very affordable to you, but given how fractured the audience is and the number of spots you will need to run to get noticed, your three grand would be gone in less than a week.

Like TV, radio and print media are all outside the budget of a small, down-ballot race. Although social media is cheap, including online advertising, where you pay only if the viewer clicks, for it to be truly effective you need someone who can execute and monitor your presence and knows something about targeting.

Direct Mail

Direct mail is expensive, and all but those making money sending it believe it is of little value.

Still, I would be remiss if I did not tell you there are a couple things you can do to bring the cost of sending direct mail to within your reach—especially for a small city election.

A saturated-mail piece—a piece of mail that goes to every single house within a given postal route—brings down the postage considerably and you don't even need a bulk-mail permit. Clearly you will spend more money to print and mail to homes of residents who are not registered and have no intention of voting, but the cost difference of targeted mail versus saturated mail makes the decision simple. A saturated-mail piece will work best for nonpartisan or homogeneous voting districts—which means you're in luck because most small towns in America are predominantly "like living with like."

If you want to keep this option on the table, here are a few figures for you to use in calculating the cost: Postage for a 5.5 x 8.5 postcard sent by bulk mail runs about 14 cents per piece and the printing will run you another 4 to 5 cents each for full color. So if you live in a city of 10,000 households, you can send one piece of mail for just over two grand—that's $165 for layout, $460 for printing, and $1,440 for postage. But if you live in a city of just 3,000 households, you could send a piece of mail for around $800. Remember: Flip-flip-throw; make it memorable.

Letters to the Editor

While many people will tell you they'll write a supportive letter and send it to the local paper, very few will actually execute the mission. Indeed, so few follow through that your campaign should assign a person to oversee this task; make sure this individual has no other campaign activities to execute. That's how hard this job is.

Once an individual is identified as willing to write a letter to the editor, someone in the campaign must follow up. Early letters get read and have more impact than letters submitted closer to Election Day. Also, shorter letters get read over long letters. Make sure your supporter keeps his or her letter to just eighty words: one thought, three sentences, two paragraphs, and it's done.

Field Signs and Billboards

Printed field signs run hundreds of dollars each and billboards even more. Neither of these offer as good a return for the investment as lawn signs. In a $3,000 campaign, I'd put field signs at the bottom of my list, especially given that many cities will not allow them within city limits.

Lawn Signs and Canvassing

Lawn signs are a great way to get your name before the voters—problem is, you actually need yards in which to place them, and that requires getting permission. One way to get the green light is to simply call people: your friends, business associates, Little League coaches, anyone you know. You can also "cold call" strangers if you want signs on a particular high-traffic street.

> "Nothing will ever be attempted if all possible objections must be first overcome."
> **SAMUEL JOHNSON**

Another way to secure lawn sign locations is to canvass. It's time consuming but if done right it works and serves more than one purpose—always a plus in a cash-strapped, time-limited campaign.

First Things First

The logo designed for your walking piece will now be used for your lawn signs.

To save money, use only one color on your lawn signs. Given that the stock is white, you can create the look of two colors by leaving only the lettering white while printing the rest of the lawn sign with your color. Although it costs about the same to print your logo on stock that's 18"x24"as 11"x24", 9"x24" is considerably cheaper. I've been moving to the smaller sign for a couple reasons. For starters, it will force your design into a bold look—typically just your name and the office you seek—so it has a clean and memorable look. Second, the smaller size, on H-wickets, is more stable in wind and weather. If you intend to use wooden stakes with screws and washers, I'd go with the 18x24 sign. Details on all of this, plus sample signs, can be found in Chapter 6.

As a rule of thumb one-color lawn signs printed on both sides run about $2 each; add another color and you can add 30 cents per sign. Full-color signs run around $5 each, and that's without the H-wickets or lawn sign stakes to hold them in the ground. (H-wickets add about $1/sign.) The fewer signs you print in any given run, the more they cost per sign; so print the right amount or too many. Do not print too few.

Since lawn signs are generally placed five to six weeks before an election, you have enough time to call local printers to compare costs to those on the Web. Lots of shops print lawn signs and some are pretty competitive, so get on this task immediately. Don't forget if you're doing business with a Web printer, you will have shipping on top of the printing costs. And be sure to check the final color before going to print. Indeed, have your graphic de-signer send the actual color number to the printer to make sure that what you get is what you pay for.

Personally, I save H-wickets and lawn sign stakes plus hardware (screws and washers) for reuse. If you have neither in your barn, garage, or basement, call around to other candidates who previously ran for office or to party headquarters to see if they have any you can borrow. If not, you'll have to buy them and can often get the best deal if they're ordered from the place that prints your signs. But check online for deals on metal brackets.

If you intend to use wooden stakes with washers and screws, the lawn sign must be printed so there's room for the stake without blocking the logo, and the interior tubing of the material must run horizontally; otherwise it will fold in the wind and look bad, really bad. For H-wickets, the interior tubing of the material runs vertically. If you have no idea what I'm talking about, go to a shop that prints lawn signs and take a look at them.

Another alternative is to use plastic bags that fit on top of huge croquet wickets. Companies lure you in with very affordable printing quotes on the plastic bag and then you're hit with the cost of the wickets and shipping charges (they weigh a ton). If you have access to the wickets, this can be a pretty cheap way to go but beware: Wickets, like the baggies, come in all sizes, so get the correct-size baggie printed for the wicket you're borrowing. If you have to buy both the baggie and the wickets, this is no cheaper than the H-wicket sign and looks cheesier.

Canvassing for Lawn Sign Locations
So let's say you have every intention of knocking on each and every door in your voting district. Easy to do if you live in a small city and it's effective. But let me suggest that no matter the size of your city or voting district you begin

by canvassing homes on arterial and collector streets. Collectors are sort of large streets that "collect" the traffic of smaller streets, and arterials are the busiest streets running through your town.

A sign placed on an arterial is worth two on a collector and ten on a side street. Plus, when you canvass arterials and collectors, people see you, and voters who see you canvassing others consider themselves canvassed as well. Once you hit all of the arterials and collectors, you can knock on the doors of everyone else.

Anyone who seems even remotely supportive gets asked to host a lawn sign and is told when it will go up and when it will come down. If you're not working with a hand-held GPS system to note voter support, then write everything down including a name and phone number in case those placing the lawn signs cannot find the address during installation. Some cities and counties have regulations that limit size as well as when and how political signs can be placed. Be sure to verify dates. You do not want to start your run for office by breaking the law or appearing to be above it.

Installation of Lawn Signs

If you're running in a small town, chances are you have only fifty to two hundred signs for placement. If that is the case, just get them up as soon as the law allows. Also of note is that when candidates actually install their own signs, people notice and like this humble touch. Normally I would say that a candidate's time would be better spent dialing for dollars, but in a small-town race, you have more options as to how you can make a positive impression.

Show Me the Money

There are a lot of ways to raise money; unfortunately, most of them require money to do so. For example, you can mail a solicitation letter to your family and friends, but each one requires you print the letter as well as the envelope and remittance envelope (remit) that gets stuffed inside. Add to this a first-class stamp and each piece will cost the campaign close to $1. So let's say you mail 200 pieces for a buck each; given that mail solicitation generally has a rate of return of 6 percent, you will get back about 12 envelopes with checks. Just to break even, every one of those must contain a $17 check. Not a tall order. So let's assume all 12 send $25; that means your mailing will generate $100 after expenses. That's a lot of work for $100.

If you hold events, such as an auction or a yard sale, the bookkeeping alone will drive you to drink. Think about it: Someone donates a book and you sell it; the campaign claims as a donation the money received but must list as an "in-kind" the difference between the value of the book and the actual cash received. Likewise, the donor can claim as a political contribution only the difference between the worth of the book and the amount you actually sold it for. Multiply that effort by hundreds of items, and add to this the simple reality that these kinds of events raise very little money while eating up tons of committee and volunteer time, and I say: No way, not in a three-month campaign.

Still, there will be many who tell you that events are "friend raisers" and even in a three-month effort, with the right person overseeing the project, they can be successful with relatively little demand on the committee. (For ideas see "Fundraising Ideas that Take Less than One Month of Preparation" in Chapter 5.)

Online Contributions

The era of texting $10 to a campaign in a room full of people appears to be limited now to nonprofits or huge races, such as for president. Still, money can be raised online with virtually no expense and let's face it, most of us have no idea where a checkbook is anymore. Stay tuned—I will cover this next.

Meanwhile, you need to raise money and given that everything must do double duty in a three-month campaign, so should your fundraising efforts. To that end, house parties or coffees offer a modest financial return for the effort while getting your message out in a personal and believable way. Further, attendees typically give more than money; they will often take a lawn sign, offer to do a coffee for *their* friends, and volunteer time for the campaign.

House Parties

A successful house party begins with the hosts. Your committee volunteer in charge of house parties will call potential or known supporters and ask him or her to sponsor an evening get-together. The host can decide whether to invite neighbors, friends, or both. Generally, tea, coffee, and some sort of dessert, such as cookies or brownies, are served to those attending but I've had people put on house parties that draw hundreds and raise thousands with simple finger food, donated wine, and nonalcoholic beverages. If you can get a big name to a house party, such as the governor or a local celebrity, that will up the attendance as well as the returns.

The committee member overseeing house parties must give some attention to the effort; for example, if not enough people have responded to the invitation, then calls must go out to all the invitees. If too few are willing to attend, put off the event to another date to bring up attendance. Be flexible: Poorly attended coffees or house parties are assumed to be the candidate's fault.

Because the hosts send the invitations and provide the refreshments, the campaign incurs no cost. The best parties are when two or more friends get together to cosponsor one. They then draw from a broader friends list.

Just the facts:
- Typically a house party will last ninety minutes.
- Someone from the campaign must arrive early to help the host set up the event, to lay out materials, and greet people at the door.
- The candidate must arrive early as well, and it is lovely if he or she brings a small gift for the host—such as flowers or a bottle of nice wine.
- Enough time must be allowed for late attendees to arrive and get settled before beginning the evening introductions—usually about thirty to forty-five minutes into the event.
- Once people have gathered, the host welcomes attendees and introduces the candidate (the campaign should provide the copy for the introduction that underscores the candidate's experience and qualifications for the job).
- The candidate thanks the host, then briefly speaks; this is followed by Q&A.
- When the candidate is done and all the questions have been asked and answered, someone with some talent must stand before the group and make the "ask" for money. This individual could be from the committee or another elected official you invite for this purpose alone.
- Walking pieces, a basket for contributions, and remit envelopes are available at a table near the door along with any other materials the campaign may have generated, such as buttons and bumper stickers.
- Be sure to have a sign-up sheet for potential volunteers and lawn sign locations.

Since it is remarkably hard to get people to attend house parties during the summer, when the whole world is numb to politics, they can be delayed until September for a general election or two months before any primary.

Meanwhile, what to do about money?

Candidates can bridge their campaigns to the house parties by spending a couple hours a day calling friends, family, and business associates to contribute. These are well-spent hours because no one wants to turn down the candidate. If you're running for a judicial position and the law does not allow you to solicit directly for money, you will need to have friends and committee members do this task for you.

Web Page and Social Media

Every campaign must have a Web page, if for no other reason than to have a donate button that allows people to contribute to the campaign. Campaigns can spend thousands on a Web page but simply having one is actually enough. Get a professional to put your page together so that everything works, but do not pay a lot of money for it.

The information included in your 325-word walking piece is actually enough for your Web page, but it will be broken up a bit according to buttons on your home page. People love to tell you that you need to generate all kinds of "white papers" on issues of the day, but this is not necessary. Only your opponent will read long narratives you post regarding your position on controversial issues. I'm not saying your Web page should be vacuous, but be brief on all pages.

Everything you place online should be well-written. Typos, grammatical errors, and misspellings will cost you votes. Don't be stupid: If you do not know how to write, get help. Even if you do know how to write, always put more eyes on your words: Run all copy by at least one committee member who is capable of writing and editing. Do not group-edit the copy.

You should have more photos than appear in your walking piece, so dig around for some nice ones. This is where a professional photo shoot can come in handy. Typically this will run you about $500 but believe me, when you are digging daily to find pictures, you'll wish you'd just done it.

Have your graphic designer alter your lawn sign logo to fit comfortably across the top of your Web page.

To be effective you will need to generate at least a little information for those who visit. Typically buttons across the top of a Web page for a political candidate include:

- Home
- Bio
- Experience
- Donate
- Volunteer
- Facebook

When it comes to listing those who support or endorse you or your cause, I strongly suggest you have a method of scrolling the names. If your Web master cannot do this function, you may need to find and pay someone else to set it up. It's worth it and allows names to be added as people jump on board. This is far more effective than a page listing columns of names. Scrolling names are mesmerizing to the visitor. As an aside, this feature should move with the visitor no matter what page she or he visits on your site.

Facebook

Your campaign should have a Facebook page; it's free and easy to set up. However, if you're not the sort of person who lives on social media sites and your Facebook page has no activity, it's a problem. To remedy this, have a volunteer or committee member monitor your site and post your activities as well as pictures of your daily travels as you move through the campaign. If you are willing to update your travels yourself, then set aside some time each night before retiring. It needs to be done on a regular basis.

And We're Out

I've omitted some things from these pages because I consider them common sense; for example:

- Send thank-you notes for contributions, house parties, and volunteerism.
- Maintain your lawn signs so they do not look like litter and quickly remove them after the election.
- Call and knock at reasonable hours.
- Never waste people's time: Keep meetings brief and organized and have materials ready for volunteers, no matter the task they're doing.
- Always dress and act the part of the candidate.

Have fun and remember that additional information on any of the above topics can be found within the pages of this manual.

Index

About the Authors

Catherine Shaw served three terms (twelve years) as mayor of Ashland, Oregon. First elected in 1988, she was the youngest person and the first woman elected to her city's highest post. She also served as a member chief of staff in the Oregon legislature.

For over two decades, she has managed and consulted for scores of political campaigns, successfully passing innovative taxing measures for funding public education, recreation, parks, open-space programs, libraries, and civic buildings.

Outspent in every election, sometimes as much as five to one, Shaw developed and perfected techniques to combat big money and to engineer seemingly impossible wins. She has been a frequent guest speaker and instructor for political science classes and campaign schools.

Shaw currently works as a political consultant. For questions regarding any portion of this book, please contact her by email: cathyshaw@mind.net.

Some of the television ads referenced in this work can be found on You-Tube, www.youtube.com/user/oakstpress.

Sarah Golden works in strategic communications, with years of experience on environmental and political campaigns at the local and state level. She is a multimedia journalist and has managed and maintained social media for campaigns, news sites, politicians, and other public figures. Her expertise is in bipartisan communication and the confluence of media and climate change.

Sarah holds a B.A. in politics and environmental studies from Whitman College and was an Annenberg Dean Scholar at the University of Southern California, where she earned an M.A. in journalism and communication, specializing in radio and social justice issues. She currently is the digital director at Cater Communications in the San Francisco Bay Area.